# INTRODUCTION TO BUSINESS LAW

# INTRODUCTION TO BUSINESS LAW

Third Edition

J G Merritt LLB (Hons) PGCE

*Lecturer in Law*

LAP

Liverpool Academic Press

First published 1994

Second edition 1998

Third edition 2003



First published in Great Britain by Liverpool Academic Press Limited.

A CIP catalogue for this book is available from the British Library

ISBN 1 903499 04 6 (Paperback)
ISBN 1 903499 16 X (Hardback)



Typeset by Bitter & Twisted, bitter@cybase.co.uk

Printed and Bound in Great Britain by
Lightning Source UK Ltd., Milton Keynes.

*To Melinda*

*My wife, my love and my very best friend*

# CONTENTS


Foreword v
Table of Cases vi
Table of Statutes vii
1 Nature and Sources of Law 1
2 The Law of Partnership 13
3 The Law of Companies and Company Borrowing 21
4 Formation of a Contract 51
5 Terms of the Contract 64
6 Invalidating Factors 82
7 Discharge of a Contract 103
8 Arbitration 120
9 The Law of Agency 127
10 The Law relating to the Sale of Goods and Supply of Services 136
11 Transfer of Property in the Goods 148
12 The Common Law Contract of Employment 171
13 Statutory Intervention in the Contract of Employment 179
14 Discrimination 189
15 Trade Union Law 200
16 Consumer Protection and Product Liability 210
17 Consumer Credit Act 1974 218
18 The Data Protection Act 1988 231
19 The Financial Service Act 1986 235
20 Insurance and International Trading 245
21 Intellectual Property 261
22 Negotiable Instruments Generally 278
23 Cheques - In Particular 288
24 Insolvency 308
25 The Concept of a European Union 329
26 The Institutions of the European Community 334
27 Sources and Application of Community Law 345
28 The Foundations of the European Community 353
29 The European Rules relating to Competition 361
30 Conflict of Laws 376
Appendix 1
Appendix 2

# FOREWORD

I am both honoured and delighted to take over the authorship of this pleasingly straightforward and uncluttered text. The work retains its comprehensive coverage of traditional and contemporary aspects of law but with updates in key areas. In particular consideration is given to the following. The Woolf Reforms to Civil Procedure as embodied in the *Access to Justice Act* and numerous pieces of delegated legislation. The impact on privity of contract of the *Contracts (Rights of Third Parties) Act 1999* is also discussed. Sections on the *Data Protection Act 1998* and *Competition Act 1998* are now included. The employment law chapters now contain points on the *Employment Relations Act* of 1996, *National Minimum Wage Act 1998* and *Employment Relations Act 1999*. Numerous other revisions have been made throughout the text to ensure it remains useful, relevant and accessible to students, practitioners and managers in commerce and industry alike.

The chapters have also been re-ordered slightly to guide the reader through the logical sequence of legal issues arising from the formation, growth and successful trading of a business in the 21st Century. Firstly introductory matters concerning the nature and formation of law are considered followed by the key aspects of forming a business as either a partnership or company. All trading requires contracts and the essential elements of contract law are considered followed by some discussion of related matters such as dispute resolution without courts and contracts of agency.

There follow chapters on the law as it protects vulnerable groups like employees and consumers including issues like data protection and financial services regulation. Miscellaneous issues arising from insurance, intellectual property, cheques and insolvency are covered next, followed by a comprehensive discussion of European Union law and international law. It has to be said that European Union law is so all-pervasive now that no book of this type would be complete without commentary on its influence. Where appropriate such discussion is provided throughout this textbook.

Relevant cases and statutes continue to be utilised throughout and study topics provided at the beginning of each chapter. Each chapter also ends with questions to check understanding. Examples of commercial documents continue to be used to illustrate points made and my thanks are extended to those organisations who have allowed such use in the previous edition, retaining, of course, the copyright.

I would also like to thank those who assisted me with certain aspects of the book where they had specialist knowledge. In particular the assistance of Broxtowe College colleagues Rob Bowes and Tim Martin was invaluable on various legal topics and my thanks also to Geoff Hitt for his help on the data protection legislation.

I am grateful also to David Clark for his inside knowledge of the financial services industry which assisted greatly.

I have always contended that law should not just be for the lawyers and my hope is that my work on this latest version of the text will extend the accessibility and continue the clarity of the work done by the original author, Arthur Lewis.

Jonathan Merritt
May 2002

# TABLE OF CASES


| | |
|---|---|
| Ailsa Craig Fishing Co Ltd v Malvern Fishing Co Ltd (1983) | 74, 78 |
| Aitken v Boulen (1908) | 147 |
| Allcard v Skinner (1887) | 92 |
| Aluminium Industrie Vaasen B V v Romalpa Aluminium Ltd (1976) | 41, 154 |
| American Cyanamid v Ethicon (1975) | 115, 261 |
| Anderson v Edie (1795) | 242 |
| Arata Potato Co Ltd v Egyptian Navigation Co (The *El Amria*) (1980) | 121 |
| Aron v Comptoir Wegimont (1921) | 146 |
| Ashley v Ashley (1829) | 242 |
| The Assunzione (1954) | 375 |
| Astro Venecedor Compania Naviera SA of Panama v Mabanaft GmbH (1971) | 124 |
| Atlas Express Limited v Kafco (Importers and Distributors) Ltd (1989) | 91 |
| Attwood v Lamont (1920) | 95, 97 |
| Auchteroni and Co v Midland Bank Ltd (1928) | 292-3 |
| | |
| Baines v National Provincial Bank (1927) | 292 |
| Baldry v Marshall Ltd (1924) | 144 |
| Balfour v Balfour (1919) | 53 |
| Bank of England v Vagliano Brothers (1891) | 289 |
| Barber v Guardian Royal Exchange Assurance Group (262/88) | 194 |
| Beale v Taylor (1967) | 142, 146 |
| Behn v Burness (1863) | 65 |
| Behrend & Co v Produce Brokers Ltd (1920) | 162 |
| Bell v Lever Brothers Ltd (1932) | 83 |
| Bents Brewery v Hogan (1945) | 206 |
| Bettini v Gye (1876) | 108 |
| Bigos v Boosted (1951) | 11 |
| Bisset v Wilkinson (1927) | 87 |
| Boissevain v Weil (1949) | 375 |
| Re Bond Worth Ltd (1980) | 157 |
| Bondina Ltd v Rollaway Shower Blinds Ltd (1986) | 29, 130 |
| Borden (UK) Ltd v Scottish Timber Products Ltd (1981) | 42, 156 |
| Bowes v Shand (1877) | 146 |
| Brace v Calder (1895) | 111 |
| Bradford v Robinson Rentals (1967) | 177 |
| British Eagle International Airlines Ltd v Compagnie Nationale Air France (1975) | 317 |
| Bromley v H & J Quick Ltd (1988) | 195 |
| Broome v DPP (1974) | 208 |

# TABLE OF CASES


| | |
|---|---|
| B S Brown & Sons Ltd v Craiks Ltd (1970) | 146 |
| B T C v Gourley (1956) | 111 |
| Bull v Pitney-Bowes Ltd (1967) | 95 |
| Burnett v Westminster Bank Ltd (1965) | 285 |
| Bute v Barclays Bank Ltd (1954) | 299 |
| Butler Machine Tool Co Ltd v Ex-Cell-O Corpn (England) Ltd (1979) | 69 |
| Byrne v Van Tienhoven (1882) | 56 |
| | |
| Capper Pass Ltd v Lawton (1977) | 194 |
| Car and Universal Finance Co Ltd v Caldwell (1965) | 85, 90, 158 |
| Carlill v Carbolic Smoke Ball Co (1893) | 3, 54 |
| Carmichael v Evans (1904) | 18 |
| Carpenters Co v British Mutual Banking Co (1937) | 300 |
| Cassidy v Ministry of Health (1955) | 173 |
| Cassis de Dijon (1979) | 351, 352 |
| Cehave NV v Handelsgesellshaft mbH (1976) | 66 |
| Cellulose Acetate Silk Co v Widnes Foundry (1933) | 110 |
| Centrafarm B V v Stirling Drug Inc (1974) | 271 |
| Centrafarm v American Home Products (1979) | 272 |
| Centrafarm v Winthrop BV (1974) | 271 |
| Central London Property Trust v High Trees House (1947) | 59 |
| Champanhac & Co Ltd v Waller & Co Ltd (1948) | 147 |
| Chapelton v Barry UDC (1940) | 70 |
| Chaplin v Hicks (1911) | 113 |
| Chapman v Smethurst (1909) | 129 |
| Chappell v Nestle and Co (1959) | 61 |
| Charter v Sullivan (1957) | 11, 112, 168 |
| Clough Mill Ltd v Martin (1985) | 42 |
| Coggs v Bernard (1703) | 134 |
| Collier v Sunday Referee Publishing Co (1940) | 176 |
| Commercial Plastics Ltd v Vincent (1964) | 97 |
| Commission v Ireland (1982) | 352 |
| Consten SA & Grundig v EC Commission (56 & 58/64) | 362 |
| Combe v Combe (1951) | 60 |
| Cowan v Le Tresor Public (186/87) | 353 |
| Cox v Cox and Co (1921) | 288 |
| Crowther v Shannon Motor Co Ltd (1975) | 144 |
| Cuckmere Brick Co Ltd v Mutual Finance Ltd (1971) | 321 |
| Cundy v Lindsay (1878) | 84 |
| Curtice v London City and Midland Bank Ltd (1908) | 287 |
| Curtis v Chemical Cleaning & Dyeing Co (1951) | 67 |
| Cutter v Powell (1795) | 114 |
| Czarnikow Ltd v Koufos (1969) | 110 |

Delbar v Caisse d'allocations familiales (114/88) 353
Demby Hamilton & Co v Barden(1949) 154
Deutsche Grammophon v Metro-SB Grossmarkte (1971) 271
Donoghue v Stevenson (1932) 206-8
Dugdale v Kraft Foods Ltd (1976) 194

Elcock v Thomson (1949) 246
Eley v Positive Assurance Co (1876) 26
Elkington v Amery (1936) 98
Elliot v Bax-Ironside (1925) 129
Equitable Trust Co of New York v Dawson Partners Ltd (1926) 255
Esso Petroleum Co Ltd v Harpers Garage (Stourport) Ltd (1967) 94
Evans v London and Provincial Bank (1917) 288
J Evans & Son (Portsmouth) Ltd v Andrea Merzario Ltd (1976) 68
Express & Echo Publications v Tanton (1999) 173

Re F 132
Fakke v Gray (1859) 166
The Fehmarn (1957) 121
Felthouse v Bindley (1862) 59
Fisher v Bell (1961) 55
Francovich v Italian State (9/90) 347

Garner v Murray (1904) 19
Garnett v McKewan (1872) 285
Gaunt v Taylor (1843) 287
George Mitchell (Chesterhall) Ltd v Finney Lock Seeds Ltd (1983) 78
George Silverman v Silverman (1969) 95
Gilbert & Partners v Knight (1968) 113
Grad v Finanzamt Traunstein (9/70) 344
Grant v Australian Knitting Mills Ltd (1936) 208
Grant v South-West Trains (1998) 192
Re Grays Inn Construction Co Ltd (1980) 317
Great Western Railway Co v London and County Banking Co Ltd (1901) 296
Re Griffith (1986) 314

Hadley v Baxendale (1854) 109
Halford v Kymer (1830) 242
Harbutt's Plasticine v Wayne Tank & Pump Co (1970) 71
Harlingon & Leinster Enterprises Ltd v Christopher Hull Fine Art Ltd (1920) 142
Harris v Nickerson (1873) 55
Harz v Deutsche Tradax GmbH (79/83) 346

| | |
|---|---|
| Hayward v Cammell Laird Shipbuilders Ltd (1988) | 195 |
| Hebdon v West (1863) | 242 |
| Hedley Byrne & Co Ltd v Heller & Partners Ltd (1964) | 87, 176, 208 |
| Henry Lennox (Industrial Engines) Ltd v Grahame Puttick Ltd (1983) | 157 |
| Herbert Clayton & Jack Waller Ltd v Oliver (1930) | 176 |
| Hibernian Bank v Gysin and Hanson (1939) | 287 |
| Hochster v De La Tour (1853) | 107 |
| Hoenig v Isaac (1952) | 105 |
| Holmes v Ashford (1950) | 208 |
| Hong Kong Fir Shipping Co Ltd v Kawaski Kisen Kaisha Ltd (1962) | 66 |
| Horsfall v Thomas (1862) | 87 |
| Household Fire Insurance Co v Grant (1879) | 58 |
| Hudson v Ridge Manufacturing Company (1957) | 177 |
| Hurley v Dyke (1979) | 89 |
| Hurley v Mustoe (1981) | 190 |
| Hyde v Wrench (1840) | 57, 69 |
| | |
| Re Introductions Ltd (1969) | 33 |
| Irish Aerospace (Belgium) NV v European Organisation for the Safety of Air Navigation (1991) | 358 |
| | |
| Re K | 132 |
| Kamann v Land Nordrhein Wesfalen (14/83) | 346 |
| Karlshamns Oljefabriker v Eastport Navigation Corpn (1982) | 151 |
| Keighley, Maxted & Co v Durant (1901) | 130 |
| Kelner v Baxter (1866) | 130 |
| Kemble v Farren (1829) | 111 |
| Kirkham v Attenborough (1897) | 150, 152 |
| Re K M Kushler (1943) | 319 |
| | |
| Ladbroke & Co v Todd (1914) | 296 |
| Lagunas Nitrate Co v Lagunas Syndicate (1899) | 90 |
| L'Estrange v F. Graucob Ltd (1934) | 67 |
| Lewis v Averay (1972) | 85, 158 |
| Litster v Forth Dry Docks Engineering Co Ltd (1989) | 346 |
| Lloyds Bank v Bundy (1975) | 92 |
| London Assurance v Mansel (1879) | 89, 243 |
| London Joint Stock Bank Ltd v Macmillan and Arthur (1918) | 285 |
| London Provincial and South Western Bank Ltd v Buszard (1918) | 287 |
| Lumley v Wagner (1852) | 116 |
| Lumsden & Co v London Trustee Savings Bank (1971) | 297 |

Mackenzie v Coulson (1869) 86
MacWilliams v Sir William Arroll Ltd (1962) 177
Mann v D'Arcy 14
Maple Flock Co Ltd v Universal Furniture Products (Wembley) Ltd (1934) 163
Marfani & Co v Midland Bank Ltd (1967) 297, 298
Marleasing SA v La Comercial Internacional de Alimenticion SA(106/89) 347
Marshall v Southampton & SW Hampshire Area Health
Authority (Teaching) (152/84) 345
Mendelsohn v Normand Ltd (1979) 68
Merck & Co Inc v Stephar BV (1981) 272
MHC Consulting Services Ltd v Tansell (2000) 198
Microbeads A G v Vinhurst Road Markings Ltd (1975) 141
Miller v Karlinski (1945) 93
Re Moore & Company and Landauer & Co (1921) 142
Morris v Saxelby (1916) 95
Munroe & Co Ltd v Mayer (1930) 163
Mutual Life Insurance Co of New York v Ontario Metal Products Co (1925) 243

Nanka Bruce v Commonwealth Trust (1926) 152
Nash v Inman (1908) 99
Nordenfelt v Maxim Nordenfelt Guns & Amm. Co (1894) 94, 97
North East Midlands Co-operative Society v Allen (1977) 190
North and South Wales Bank v Macbeth (1908) 290
Norwich Pharmacal v Customs and Excise (1974) 261
Nova (Jersey) Knit Ltd v Kammgarn Spinnerei GmbH (1977) 121
Nu-Stilo Footwear Ltd v Lloyds Bank Ltd (1956) 299

Officier van Justitie v Kolpinghuis Nijmegen (80/86) 347
Olley v Malborough Court Ltd (1949) 70
Orbit Mining and Trading Co Ltd v Westminster Bank Ltd (1962) 16, 290
Orwell Steel (Erection & Fabrication) Ltd v Asphalt & Tarmac (UK) Ltd (1984) 117

Page v Freight Hire (Tank Haulage)Ltd (1981) 191
Page One Records Ltd v Britton (1967) 116
Pao On v Lau Yiu Long (1979) 91
Paris v Stepney Borough Council (1951) 176
Re Peachdart Ltd (1983) 157
Pearce v Brooks (1866) 93
Pepper v Hart (1993) 11
Pepper v Webb (1969) 177
Peter Symmons & Co v Cook (1981) 75
Pharmaceutical Society of Great Britain v Boots (1958) 54

Philip Head v Showfronts Ltd (1970) 153
Philips v Brooks (1919) 90
Photo Production Ltd v Securicor Transport Ltd (1980) 72, 78
Piddington v Bates (1961) 208
Pignataro v Gilroy (1919) 152
Pioneer Shipping Ltd v BTP Tioxide Ltd (The *Nema*) (1982) 122
Re Pressdee Ltd (1985) 317
Price v Civil Service Commission (1978) 190
Priest v Last (1903) 147
Procureur du Roi v Dassonville (1974) 352
Pubblico Ministero v Ratti (148/78) 345

R v Henn (1981) 338
Raffles v Wichelhaus (1864) 83
Re Rampgill Mill Ltd (1967) 324
Ramsgate Victoria Hotel Company v Montefiore (1866) 56
Reading v Att. Gen. (1951) 132
Ready Mixed Concrete v Minister of Pensions & National Insurance (1968) 173
Regent OHG Aisenstadt und Barig v Francesco of
Jermyn Street Ltd (1981) 162
Rickard (Charles) Ltd v Oppenheim (1950) 108
Roe v R A Naylor Ltd (1971) 67
Rose & Frank Co v Crompton & Brothers Ltd (1923) 52
Ross v London County, Westminster and Parr's Bank Ltd (1919) 298
Rowland v Dival (1923) 141, 146
Royal British Bank v Turquand (1855) 28

Salford Corporation v Lever (1891) 133
Salomon v Salomon & Co (1897) 21
Sanday & Co v Keighley Maxted & Co (1922) 146
Saunders v Anglia Building Society (1970) 85
Savory & Co v Lloyds Bank Ltd (1932) 298
Schloh v Auto Controle Technique Sprl (50/84) 352
Schuler A G v Wickham Machine Tool Sales (1973) 65
Scorer v Seymour Jones (1966) 97
Scott v Coulson (1903) 83
Scriven Brothers and Co v Hindley and Co (1930) 84
Shipton Anderson & Co v Weil Bros (1912) 162
Sika Contracts Ltd v B L Gill and Closeglen Properties Ltd (1978) 129
Simpkins v Pays (1955) 53
Smith v Hughes (1871) 83
Smith v Wilson (1862) 65

# TABLE OF CASES


| | |
|---|---|
| Spencer v Marchington (1988) | 97 |
| Springer v Great Western Railway (1921) | 131 |
| Sterns v Vickers (1923) | 154 |
| Stevenson, Jordan & Harrison Ltd v MacDonald & Evans (1952) | 172 |
| Stilk v Myrick (1809) | 61 |
| Suisse Atlantique v Rotterdamsche Kolen Centrale (1966) | 71 |
| | |
| Tarling v Baxter (1827) | 152 |
| Taylor v Caldwell (1863) | 106 |
| Technograph Printed Circuits Ltd v Mills & Rockley (Electronics) Ltd (1972) | 259 |
| Re Thomas Mortimer Ltd (1925) | 42 |
| W L Thompson Ltd v Robinson Gunmakers Ltd (1955) | 112, 167 |
| Thornton v Shoe Lane Parking Ltd (1971) | 70 |
| Tower Cabinet Co v Ingram (1949) | 17 |
| Re Tramway Buildings and Construction Co Ltd (1988) | 317 |
| Tritonia Shipping Inc v South Nelson Forest Product Corpn (1966) | 124 |
| Turpin v Bilton (1843) | 134 |
| Tynan v Balmer (1967) | 208 |
| Tzortzis v Monark Line A/B (1968) | 375 |
| | |
| Underwood v Burgh Castle Cement Syndicate (1922) | 152 |
| A L Underwood Ltd v Bank of Liverpool & Martins Ltd (1954) | 299 |
| Re Unit 2 Windows Ltd (1985) | 324 |
| Universal Guarantee Property Ltd v National Bank of Australasia (1965) | 286 |
| Universal Steam Navigation Co Ltd v Mckelvie and Co (1923) | 129 |
| | |
| Van Zuylen Freres v Hag A G (1974) | 272 |
| Victoria Laundries v Newman Industries Ltd (1949) | 110 |
| Victors Ltd v Lingard (1972) | 30 |
| Vinden v Hughes (1905) | 290 |
| Von Colson v Land Nordrhein-Westfalen (14/83) | 346 |
| | |
| Warninck v Townsend (1980) | 266 |
| Watteau v Fenwick (1893) | 130, 131 |
| Webster v Cecil (1861) | 115 |
| Wessex Dairies Ltd v Smith (1935) | 97 |
| Westminster Bank Ltd v Hilton (1926) | 287 |
| Westminster Bank v Zang (1965) | 301 |
| White v Bluett (1853) | 61 |
| Re William C Leitch Brothers Ltd (1932) | 29 |
| Wimble v Rosenberg & Sons (1913) | 163 |

With v O'Flanagan (1936) 89

Re Yenidje Tobacco Co Ltd (1916) 308
Re`Yeovil Glove Co Ltd (1965) 42
Yonge v Toynbee (1910) 135
Re Yorkshire Woolcombers Association (1903) 41

# TABLE OF STATUTES


| | |
|---|---|
| Access to Justice Act 1999 | 6 |
| Advertisements (Hire Purchase) Act 1967 | 214 |
| Arbitration Act 1950,1975,1979 | 120 *et seq* |
| Bills of Exchange Act 1882 | 129, 277 *et seq* |
| Business Names Act 1916, 1985 | 15, 25 |
| Cheques Act 1957, 1992 | 286 |
| Civil Liability (Contribution) Act 1978 | 15, 208 |
| Community Patent Convention (CPC) 1975 | 258 |
| Companies Act 1948, 1981, 1985, 1989 | 15, 22 *et seq*, 56, 100, 306 |
| Companies Regulations 1985 | 26 |
| Company Directors Disqualification Act 1986 | 30 |
| Company Securities (Insider Dealings) Act 1985 | 232 |
| Competition Act 1998 | 370 |
| Consumer Arbitration Agreements Act 1988 | 124 |
| Consumer Credit Act 1974 | 214 *et seq* |
| Consumer Protection Act 1987 | 208 *et seq*, 343 |
| Contracts (Applicable Law) Act 1990 | 376 |
| Contracts (Rights of Third Parties) Act 1999 | 104 |
| Copyright Act 1956 | 262 *et seq* |
| Copyright Designs and Patents Act 1988 | 119, 262 *et seq* |
| Courts and Legal Services Act 1990 | 8, 125 |
| Data Protection Act 1984 | 227 *et seq* |
| Deeds of Arrangement Act 1914 | 314 |
| Disability Discrimination Act 1995 | 198-9 |
| Electronic Communications Act 2000 | 63 |
| Employer's Liability (Compulsory) Insurance Act 1969 | 176 |
| Employment Act 1982 | 206 |
| Employment Code of Practice Order 2000 | 209 |
| Employment of Children Act 1973 | 179 |
| Employment Protection Act 1975 | 171, 201 |
| Employment Protection (Consolidation) Act 1978 | 171 *et seq*, 179 |
| Employment Relations Act 1999 | 171, 180, 201 |
| Employment Rights Act 1996 | 171 *et seq*, 179, 181 *et seq* |
| Enduring Powers of Attorney Act 1985 | 132 |

# TABLE OF STATUTES


| | |
|---|---|
| Equal Pay Act 1970 | 189 *et seq* |
| Equal Pay (Amendment) Regulations 1983 | 189 *et seq* |
| Equal Pay Directive 75/117 | 189 |
| Equal Treatment Directive 76/207 | 345 |
| European Communities Act 1972 | 326 |
| | |
| Factors Act 1889 | 254 |
| Financial Services Act 1986 | 231 *et seq* |
| Financial Services and Markets Act 2000 | 242 |
| | |
| Gaming Acts 1835, 1968 | 251 |
| | |
| Health and Safety at Work Act 1974 | 176,183, 186 *et seq* |
| Hire Purchase Act 1964 | 159, 214 |
| Human Rights Act 1998 | 5-6 |
| | |
| Industrial Relations Act 1971 | 182 |
| Infants' Relief Act 1874 | 99 |
| Insolvency Act 1986 | 29, 35, 305 |
| Insolvent Partnerships Order 1986 | 19 |
| | |
| Juries Act 1974 | 181 |
| | |
| Law of Property Act 1925 | 40, 117, 118 |
| Law of Property (Miscellaneous Provisions) Act 1989 | 63, 131 |
| Law Reform (Contributory Negligence) Act 1945 | 177 |
| Law Reform (Frustrated Contracts) | 107 |
| Law Reform (Miscellaneous Provisions) Act 1970 | 53 |
| Legal Services Act 1990 | 8 |
| Life Assurance Act 1774, 1884 | 93, 242 |
| Limited Liability Partnerships Act 2000 | 20 |
| | |
| Marine Insurance Act 1906 | 248 *et seq* |
| Maternity and Parental Leave Regulations 1999 | 180 |
| Matrimonial Homes Act 1983 | 316 |
| Mental Health Act 1983 | 18 |
| Minors' Contracts Act 1987 | 99 |
| Misrepresentation Act 1967 | 88 |
| Moneylenders Act 1900, 1927 | 214 |

# TABLE OF STATUTES


| | |
|---|---|
| National Minimum Wages Act 1998 | 182, 183 |
| | |
| Occupiers' Liability Act 1984 | 75 |
| | |
| Parliament Act 1911, 1949 | 5 |
| Partnership Act 1890 | 13, 17 |
| Patent Cooperation Treaty (PCT) 1978 | 258 |
| Patents Act 1977 | 258 *et seq* |
| Pawnbrokers Act 1872-1960 | 214 |
| Policies of Assurance Act 1867 | 119 |
| Powers of Attorney Act 1971 | 131 |
| Prevention of Corruption Act 1906 | 133 |
| Prevention of Fraud (Investments) Act 1939, 1958 | 231 |
| Public Interest Disclosure Act 1998 | 183 |
| Public Order Act 1986 | 209 |
| | |
| Race Relations Act 1976 | 171, 196 *et seq* |
| Redundancy Payments Act 1965 | 183 |
| Registered Designs Act 1949 | 264 |
| Registration of Business Names Act 1916 | 15 |
| Resale Prices Act 1976 | 93 |
| Restrictive Trade Practices Act 1976, 1977 | 370 |
| Road Traffic Act 1972 | 247 |
| Royal Assent Act 1967 | 5 |
| | |
| Sale and Supply of Goods Act 1994 | 143 *et seq*, 164 |
| Sale of Goods Act 1977, 1979, 1993 | 65, 76 *et seq*, 136 *et seq*, 159 *et seq* |
| Sale of Goods and Services Act 1982 | 138 *et seq* |
| Sale of Goods (Amendment) Act 1995 | 151 *et seq*, 159 |
| Sex Discrimination Act 1975, 1986 | 171, 189 *et seq*, 345 |
| Single European Act 1987 | 327, 335, 339 |
| Social Security Contributions and Benefits Act 1992 | 172 |
| Social Security and Housing Benefits Act 1982 | 180 |
| Stamp Act | 295 |
| Supply of Goods and Services Act 1982 | 138 |
| Supply of Goods (Implied Terms) Act 1973 | 138 |
| Supreme Court Act 1981 | 117, 125 |
| | |
| Third Parties (Rights Against Insurers) Act 1930 | 247 |
| Trademarks Act 1938, 1994 | 265 *et seq* |
| Trade Union Act 1871 | 202 |
| Trade Union and Labour Relations Act 1974 | 102 |

Trade Union and Labour Relations (Consolidation)
Act 1992 171, 200 *et seq*
Trade Union Reform and Employment Rights Act 1993 200
Transfer of Undertakings (Protection of Employment) Regulations 1981 202, 205
Treaty of Amsterdam 1997 329
Treaty on European Union (Maastricht Agreement) 1993 327 *et seq*, 331
Treaty of Paris 1951 325
Treaty of Rome 1957 326 *et seq*, 341 *et seq*, 357
Truck Acts 1831, 1943 181

Unfair Contract Terms Act 1977 73, 74, 79, 139, 164, 211
Unfair Terms in Consumer Contracts Regulations 1999 79 *et seq*
Uniform Law on International Sales Act 1967 378

Wages Act 1986 181
Working Time Regulations 1998 180-1

ONE

# NATURE *and* SOURCES *of* LAW

*Study Topics*

**The important part a right plays in law**
**How a bill becomes a statute**
**The jurisdiction of the civil courts**

"What is law?" Any organisation, be it a club, a college, a trade union or a country, requires some rules and regulations, otherwise the organisation would not be able to function in its most efficient manner; there would be no order or structure in its activities.

The rules and regulations used in any state are called its law. The rules that govern the relations between individuals of the state are called civil law. The law used by the state to preserve order in the state is the criminal law and the law expressly concerned with the institutions of government of the state is its constitution.

It is surely no coincidence that the words for "law" and "right" are the same in most

European languages: in Latin – jus, in German – recht, in Spanish – derecho. The similarity is not surprising because law is concerned with the rights of people. The purpose of law is to delineate and if necessary establish and enforce the rights of people.

A has entered into a contract with B who breaks the agreement. What are A's rights in this matter?
A has his car damaged because B has collided with him. What are A's rights against B?
A has been arrested by the police. What are A's rights?

Thus law is concerned with rights and rights are important – indeed it is true to say that a right is a thing of value. This I believe is a basic concept of law and one that should be appreciated from the start and which will be commented upon from time to time.

A right to a thing is as important as the thing itself, because a right can be enforced in a court of law – and that is the basis of law.

## *Rights and the Law*

There are various kinds of rights but primarily a person may have a right to a thing or a right against a person. In the latter case if A has a right against B, then B will owe A the correlative, i.e. a duty. Right and duty go together.

The law gives people rights or takes rights away from them. In the chapters that follow it must be kept uppermost in one's mind that what the law does is to determine the rights of a person and having determined them it will assist that person to enforce them in a court of law.

If there is a valid contract between A and B, then A has rights against B which A can enforce by suing B, and B owes A duties; conversely B has rights against A, and A owes B the correlative duties.

The subject matter of the right may be an act or goods in the case of a contract and these are decided by the parties to the contract. In torts (which are civil wrongs) it is the law that lays down certain duties on to people generally. For example, one has a duty not to walk on another person's land without permission, or one has a duty to take reasonable care to avoid injuring another. In either case if the duty is broken, then the tort of trespass to land or negligence will have occurred and the injured party can sue the wrongdoer by claiming that the duty was broken and that he, the plaintiff, has a right to expect that it should not have been broken. It can be seen then that liability arising in contract law is assumed voluntarily; in tort law it is not voluntary, such liabilities being imposed by the courts.

## Sources of Law

We must now consider where our law comes from. It is generally agreed that the origin of all law is custom: what people have done habitually or customarily they eventually tend to believe they have right to do. For example, where people are in the habit of walking across another's land, they eventually will acquire a right to walk across the land – a right of way. Sometimes, particularly after the Second World War, homeless people would enter and remain in houses or buildings which had been left uninhabited. After a period of time they acquired squatter's rights which were good against the whole world except against the rightful owner of the property.

The customs which were established were modified from time to time and this body of law became known as the Common Law. It was applied eventually by the courts and this is now our first source of law.

## The Courts

Cases are the result of either a civil action or a criminal prosecution. In a civil action the plaintiff sues the defendant in order to receive compensation or damages.

An example of a civil case is *Carlill v Carbolic Smoke Ball Co Ltd* (1893) 1. Q.B. 256 in which Mrs Carlill (the plaintiff) sued the defendant company because its product did not come up to the manufacturer's claims. In practice the case is read as *Carlill and the Carbolic Smoke Ball Co Ltd*.

A criminal prosecution will arise when it is alleged that the accused has committed a criminal act and so the state must prosecute him in order to punish him with a fine or imprisonment, if guilty. An example is *R v Smith (1959)* 2. Q.B. 35.

R stands for Rex (King) or Regina (Queen) and the fiction is that the Sovereign is prosecuting the defendant on behalf of the state.

The civil cases are heard in the civil courts which are:

House of Lords

Court of Appeal (Civil Division)

High Court

Queen's Bench Division | Chancery Division | Family Division

County Court

## *Precedent*

An important distinguishing feature of English law is the part played by the doctrine of precedent. This merely means that a judge in a lower court has to follow a decision given in a higher court in a similar case. It would be virtually impossible for one case to be exactly repeated in all its details on a later occasion. Consequently only the principle of the higher court's decision will be followed by the court on a later occasion. This principle is called the *ratio decidendi* of the case and will be discussed later. There are ways to avoid following precedent which reduce slightly the apparent rigidity of this system; a previous case can be "distinguished" for example. This means that a judge can decline to follow it on the grounds that its facts were materially different.

Finally the reports of the cases are indexed according to the court which heard the case and this is one source of our law.

## *Parliament*

The other source of law is Parliament and the law from this source is contained in an Act of Parliament or a Statute. Parliament consists of the House of Commons, the House of Lords and, so far as the making of law is concerned, the Queen.

Every Act of Parliament starts with the words "Be it enacted by the Queen's Most Excellent Majesty, by and with the advice and consent of the Lords Spiritual and Temporal and Commons, in this present Parliament assembled, and by the authority of the same as follows".

It would appear therefore that Her Majesty is responsible for a great deal of the law of this country, but that is a fiction. It is sometimes stated that the government makes the law. The truth is that Parliament makes the law in the following way.

The government, whose function it is to govern, notifies the House of Commons of its proposals to introduce a new law or to amend or repeal an existing one. This proposal is contained in a document called a bill and it is introduced to the Commons in what is called a first reading. Nothing of course is read aloud – although at one time that was done: these readings are merely stages of the bill's passage through the Commons.

The second reading is the stage when the general principles of the bill are discussed and after that the bill is discussed in detail by a committee which facilitates the process.

The committee stage is followed by the report stage when the bill comes before the whole House which then considers the bill as reported to it by the committee.

The final stage is the third reading when only formal alterations are allowed and the House votes on the bill.

Having passed through all the stages in the House of Commons the bill is then sent to the House of Lords and follows similar stages in that House.

If the House of Lords wishes to reject or amend a bill then they send it back to the Commons and negotiations take place between the two Houses until agreement is reached. If that cannot be achieved then the bill will fail to become law.

However, by the *Parliament Acts 1911* and *1949* the bill can be represented to the Lords during the following Parliamentary session and then if it fails to pass the Lords again it will automatically receive the Royal Assent and become law, whether the Lords agree or not. The most recent example of the Lords narrowly avoiding the *Parliament Acts* procedure was in late 1999. There had been considerable disquiet about the proposals to reform the disability benefit rules. These proposals were rejected by their Lordships twice but allowed through after the third debate. It can only be conjectured as to whether the Peers' desire to confront the Commons on this issue was muted by the fact that almost the very next business was to vote on their own abolition as an hereditary body!

The House of Lords still has power to delay a bill other than a money bill (one concerned with finance) for a period of one year; a money bill may be delayed for one month only. The Lords have retained their power to completely veto a bill which attempts to extend the duration of Parliament beyond five years.

Finally the bill must receive the Royal Assent. The *Royal Assent Act 1967* provides that an act is passed and becomes law if the Royal Assent is notified to each House of Parliament by the Speaker of that House.

Often an act or statute will not become operational immediately it becomes law, because certain administrative arrangements need to be made. For example the *Human Rights Act 1998* did not come into force in England until October 2000 (see below).

It was said earlier that the government cannot make law, and that is strictly true.

However, it should be remembered that the government is chosen from the party with the majority of seats in the House of Commons. Consequently every proposal made by the government should be passed by the Commons and, ignoring the infrequent revolt by back-benchers, it usually is. The Lords can only delay the passing of a bill and so what the government wants, the government gets. Furthermore, if the Cabinet is controlled by a forceful prime minister there may arise the benevolent democratic dictatorship referred to by a former Lord Chancellor, Lord Hailsham.

This was always one argument in favour of a written constitution and a Bill of Rights similar to that in the USA. The UK is adopting just such a law in the *Human Rights Act 1998* mentioned above. This should provide some redress for individuals whose human rights are not respected by the state. For the first time also courts will be able to refer laws considered to be in breach of this Act back to Parliament for re-consideration.

These then are the two sources of law – the Courts and Parliament, and the law coming from these sources is contained in the Law Reports of decided cases, sometimes called common law, and in acts of Parliament called statutes.

## *Law in the Courts*

Law is practised in the courts by practitioners, namely barristers at law (counsel) and solicitors, whose tools are the decided cases and acts of Parliament or statutes.

There are civil courts, criminal courts and courts of appeal. However, a long time before the court stage is reached a person will probably visit a solicitor to discuss the matter.

## *Solicitors*

There are about 70,000 solicitors in the UK. They often work together with other solicitors in a firm or partnership and they are the lawyers who see the client first. Solicitors have become qualified by passing examinations set by the Law Society and also by being employed by a qualified solicitor for a certain period of time. This used to be known as "articles" but is now described as a training contract.

A member of the public will go to a solicitor and will seek his advice. It may be that he is entitled to Legal Aid and the solicitor can arrange this. Whether or not Legal Aid is awarded will depend on the merits of the case and the financial status of the client.

Initially the solicitor will decide whether or not he can give aid and advice under the Legal Help or Help at Court Schemes (formerly referred to generally as the "Green Form Scheme"). If lengthy representation in court is required then application must be made for a full Legal Aid certificate. Civil Legal Aid has been greatly affected by the recent Civil Justice Reforms culminating in the *Access to Justice Act 1999* and related Court Rules. It is more likely now that a solicitor will take on a civil case on a "no-win-no-fee" basis. The solicitor undertakes not to charge unless he wins but is entitled to a success fee if he does. It should be remembered that the opponent's legal fees remain payable if the case is lost and this event should be insured against. In many instances now Legal Aid will not be available for civil actions.

The vast majority of cases are settled out of court. The reason for this is that there will always be an element of risk in going to court. A person might have taken the very best legal advice available but it is not until the judge finds in his favour that the plaintiff (now known as claimant) knows he has won.

Consequently the process usually starts with a solicitor's letter. This may have the desired effect, but if not then the next stage will be to issue a Claim. The old terminology of summons or writ is no longer used in civil proceedings. This will force the defendant to take some action unless he is content to see the claimant win by default. The defendant's solicitor will be advising him whether or not he considers he has a defence and may advise that a sum is paid into court; less, of course, than the amount claimed by the claimant.

However, before the case reaches this stage each party will, through their solicitors, probably have consulted a barrister, or counsel as he is called. This process is known as "taking counsel's opinion".

## *Barristers*

There are about 6,000 barristers and they are entirely separate from solicitors. Their training requires that they become members of an Inn of Court in London. These are ancient legal universities and are four in number: Inner Temple, Middle Temple, Lincoln's Inn and Gray's Inn. The student who joins an Inn must pursue his legal studies partly in his Inn and partly elsewhere and in addition until recently had to eat a certain number of dinners.

This ancient, and to outsiders, surprising requirement means exactly what it says. The student had to dine with his fellow students, begowned, in the Hall of his Inn on a minimum number of occasions. Indeed, even though the student has passed his examinations he could not be called to the Bar and allowed to act as an advocate in the Courts until he has eaten his dinners as well. The argument for this ancient tradition was that it fosters friendships amongst a small profession since on any one night there will be dining in Hall students, barristers and judges, because nearly all judges have started their legal careers as barristers. There is an argument that this mode of training is somewhat antiquated and merely perpetuates a system where only the wealthy and socially connected may become barristers. It has to be said though that there have been some recent changes to assist those from the ethnic minorities and women to qualify. This includes a recent court decision entitling pupil barristers to minimum wage. They were previously unpaid.

There are also more arguments for fusing the professions into one as in other jurisdictions. There have been moves in this direction with the *Courts and Legal Services Act 1990* granting greater rights of audience to solicitors and others and easing the route for them to become judges.

Barristers may not work in partnership, unlike solicitors; they may not be approached directly by the public but only through a solicitor or in some cases another professional like an accountant. They have no contract with the solicitor and consequently cannot sue for their fees. They can now be sued for professional negligence. A very recent House of Lords decision has extended that to work done as an advocate in civil cases. Previously it was not possible to sue a barrister in such circumstances. Thus a barrister is expected to approach a case without any personal contact with the parties but to look at it with detachment in the same way as the judge will approach it.

Barristers usually work with other barristers in Chambers and have a manager called a barristers' clerk. It is his job to get work for his master and then to get in his fees. Barristers are not supposed to be concerned with money and it may be noticed that a barrister's gown has a small pocket high on the shoulder of the gown so that, at one time, the solicitor could slip in the old golden guinea as a refresher to keep the barrister going.

## *Legal Executives*

Another grade of lawyer which may be mentioned here is the legal executive – the modern equivalent of the old solicitor's clerk. These are assistants to the solicitors. They have their own Institute which prescribes their course of study, lays down entry requirements and sets examinations. Legal executives must acquire a thorough knowledge of law and procedure in the County Court, Magistrates Court, High Court, matrimonial practice and conveyancing. It is much easier now for a Fellow of the Institute of Legal Executives (FILEX) to qualify as a solicitor since the Courts and Legal Services Act 1990 Fellows have acquired greater right of audience in courts.

## *The Civil Courts*

In a civil action the plaintiff must commence his action in what is called a court of first instance – the County Court or the High Court.

### Civil Court Jurisdiction

Lord Woolf, an eminent judge, was asked to report on reforms required in the civil justice system; he did so ultimately in 1996. The changes he proposed were the most far reaching since 1875. Many of them came into force on 1 April 1999. The distinction between County and High Courts is of less importance now and civil actions are allocated to one of three tracks: "Fast Track", "Multi Track" and "Small Claims Track" (dealt with separately below). Fast Track claims are generally less complex and have a financial value of more than £5,000 up to £15,000. Multi Track claims are generally greater than £15,000 and more complex.

The advantage of the new system is that Fast Track claims attract fixed fees enabling the client to budget for litigation. Furthermore there are strict time limits to prevent lawyers or clients unduly delaying cases. These are enforced by the courts who have taken on a case-management function to speed up litigation.

Some courts are designated as "divorce" County Courts. They have jurisdiction in undefended matrimonial matters. Matrimonial cases must be commenced in a divorce County Court and decided there unless directed to be transferred to the High Court.

### Small Claims

A dispute involving a claim for up to £5,000 (£1,000 in personal injury cases) will automatically be referred to arbitration by the district judge. Other cases in the County Court are usually heard by a circuit judge.

## *High Court*

This court is divided into three divisions:

Queen's Bench deals mainly with actions for breach of contract and torts.
Chancery Division deals with property, trusts, the administration of estates, bankruptcy, partnerships, companies and contentious probate matters.
Family Division exercises matrimonial and domestic jurisdiction, wardship, guardianship, adoption and non-contentious probate matters.

When the court is sitting as a division of the High Court it has a single judge who is a knight and addressed as "My Lord". However, each division of the High Court also has a divisional court and then three judges will sit. The Divisional Court of Queen's Bench is the most important of the divisional courts and this court will hear appeals from the Magistrates and Crown Courts on points of law and so it has a criminal as well as a civil jurisdiction.

## *Appeal Courts*

Immediately above the High Court and the Crown Court is the Court of Appeal. It sits in two divisions, the civil division and the criminal division. The civil division is headed by the Master of the Rolls and the criminal division by the Lord Chief Justice of England. Three judges usually sit when it is in session, the other judges are lords justices of appeal.

From the Appeal Court a final appeal will lie to the House of Lords which hears both civil and criminal appeals. When the House of Lords is sitting as a court, as opposed to a debating chamber, it has usually five judges sitting, probably headed by the Lord

Chancellor. These judges all have seats in the Lords and together with others form a panel from which a bench may be formed when required. However, not many appeals reach this rarefied level because there must be an important point of law involved in the case and permission to appeal must be obtained either from the court of appeal or from the Appeals Committee of the House of Lords.

There is a further appeal from the High Court direct to the House of Lords. This is known as a special "leapfrog procedure" and is available where the parties agree and the trial judge certifies that an important point of law is involved concerning either the construction of a statute or more usually a matter upon which the Court of Appeal is bound by a previous ruling and where the House of Lords gives leave.

## *Application of Law*

How the law is applied in the courts depends on the interpretation of the judge. The law will be contained in either reports of cases or statutes, but whichever source is used the judge will be called upon to give his interpretation as to exactly what the law is on a particular point.

## *Case Law*

If case law is to be relied upon each side must put forward one or more cases in which the judgement appears to be in his favour. As was mentioned earlier the decisions given by a higher court in a similar case will have to be followed by a judge in a lower court. The part of the judgement that has to be followed is called the *ratio decidendi* of the case – the reason why the earlier judge came to the decision that he did.

In order to ascertain the *ratio decidendi* of a case, all irrelevant matters must be discarded leaving the bare principle of the decision. Thus in a criminal prosecution, let us say that a young girl with long blonde hair rides a bicycle down a high street and then shoots and kills the clerk behind a counter in a post office. She was convicted of murder because it was proved that she intended to kill the victim. If the definition of murder is that it is committed when a young girl with long blonde hair cycles down a high street and shoots a counter clerk in a post office then it would be unlikely that murder would ever be committed again. However, the irrelevant details are discarded leaving the essential principle or *ratio decidendi* of the case, that murder is committed by a person who kills another with intent to kill or to cause grievous bodily harm.

This principle can be applied in any later case when most of the facts will be quite dissimilar from the earlier case. The judge will have a number of cases cited to him by the advocates of the parties. It is up to him to decide which cases are binding on him, which decisions he is obliged to follow and to interpret the *ratio decidendi* of the case he has to follow. This is sometimes difficult to establish and may lead to legal argument between the barristers on each side and the judge. The part of the judgement which is not the *ratio decidendi* is usually the larger part. This is called the *obiter dicta* or "things said by the way". These statements consider other matters about the case and are not binding on later courts. A skilled lawyer may use these statements to persuade a judge to agree with his argument. *Obiter* statements are therefore termed "persuasive".

## *Citation of Cases*

In order to make it easier to refer to a particular case so that it can be looked up in the Law Reports, each reported case has a reference. The main collections of reports are those published by the Incorporated Council of Law Reporting and called simply the *Law Reports*. Reports of these cases are cited by reference to the court which gave the decision, for example, *Charter v Sullivan (1957)* 2 QB 117. So, a report of this case will be found by consulting the second volume of Queen's Bench reports for the year 1957 at page 117.

Other collections of reports are privately published, such as the *All England Reports* published by Butterworth and Co Ltd (cited, for example, as *Bigos v Bousted (1951)* 1 A E R 92).

The third collection is the TLR or the *Times Law Reports*. The main advantage of these reports is that they appear in the *Times* newspaper often on the day following the decision in court.

## *Statutory Law – Interpretation*

As every writer will appreciate, it is quite a difficult task to transfer thoughts to paper in such a way that the reader can understand what was in the mind of the writer. A similar problem is encountered when reading an Act of Parliament.

It is the task of the judge to interpret the will of Parliament. To assist him there are certain rules. These are not legal rules, but are intended to help him in deciding what was Parliament's intention in writing the Act and to attempt to ensure that the same principles of interpretation will be applied by all judges. In this way some certainty and continuity is imported into the law. The main rules are: the literal rule, the golden rule and the mischief rule. The literal rule means that the words of the Act must be given their normal meaning. However if that results in an absurdity then the golden rule will be applied. This means that a sensible interpretation should be made. Finally, the mischief rule allows a judge to consider what mischief the Act was designed to avoid or prevent.

Since the case of *Pepper v Hart 1993* the old rules have been relaxed and now a judge can consider the reports of debates leading to the passing of an act in order to assist his interpretation of it. These reports are contained in a document called *Hansard* which is an almost word-for-word record of parliamentary debate.

We have now looked at the lawyers who work with the law and use the common law and the statute law and the courts where they practice and put forward the law to the judge, who interprets it and applies it to a particular case.

Appendix I further clarifies how Acts of Parliament are to be interpreted. Appendix II clarifies the interpretation of Case Law.

TWO

# THE LAW *of* PARTNERSHIP

*Study Topics*

**Definition of a partnership**
**The liability of the partners for the contracts of the firm and for the torts committed by the firm or the partners**
**Dissolution of the partnership**

Both partnerships and companies are business associations and if a sole trader decides to give up trading on his own then he can either form a partnership or a company. This would necessitate his joining with other people but that would be a normal step in the progression of a sole trader. Having started on his own he finds that, if his business is prospering, he will soon need more money. He can of course borrow money but there must be a limit to how much can be borrowed. However people may be prepared to supply the money if they, personally, can have some control over how the money is being used and for that situation to arise then a legal bond must be established. Both partnerships and companies are therefore different forms of legal relationships established for the purpose of running a business.

The *Partnership Act 1890* states that a partnership is "the relation which subsists between persons carrying on business in common with a view of profit". The legal term for a partnership is a "firm". Notice that the *Partnership Act* speaks of "a relation which subsists". In other words if some people are carrying on business in common it may be that they are in partnership and do not realise that fact and accordingly the rules relating to such associations are contained in the Act of 1890. From the definition above, three elements must exist before there can be a partnership:

1. there must be a business although this can be for the purposes of a single transaction (*Mann v D'Arcy 1968*);
2. the business must be carried on in common;
3. it must be carried on with a view of profit, even if none is actually made.

The following relationships are therefore not partnerships.

1. Joint or part ownership of property does not of itself create a partnership.
2. Clubs and trade associations.
3. Companies registered under any of the Companies Acts.
4. Barristers are not allowed to enter into partnerships.

No formalities are needed to form a partnership although there must be an agreement between the persons concerned to work in common. It may be that a number of persons are working together in business with a view of profit and they know nothing of partnerships. Nevertheless a court may decide that they are legally in partnership and so the provisions of the *Partnership Act 1980* will apply. In particular Section 24 provides that:

1. all partners will share equally in the profits even though they have contributed different amounts;
2. no partner may receive any remuneration;
3. every general partner may take part in the management of the firm;
4. a partner is entitled to be indemnified by the firm in respect of payments made and liabilities incurred by him
   a. in the ordinary and proper conduct of the business; or
   b. in or about anything necessarily done for the preservation of the business or partnership property.

Section 24 further provides that:

1. no person may be introduced as a partner without the consent of all existing partners;
2. any difference arising as to ordinary matters connected with the partnership may be decided by a majority of the partners;
3. no change may be made in the nature of the partnership business without the consent of all the existing partners;
4. subject to any agreement between the partners, the partnership will be dissolved by the death of any partner.

It will be apparent that if these provisions were to apply then the partners would not always be particularly satisfied. Therefore it is more usual for a partnership agreement called "Articles of Partnership" or, if by deed, a "Deed of Partnership" to be entered into. In such an agreement the partners may agree anything they like and so it is usual, taking some of the previous points, for

1. the partners to agree that if one were to die his share of the partnership would be purchased by the surviving members;
2. the profits to be distributed pro rata to the amount of capital contributed by each of the partners;
3. the partners to receive an annual remuneration like any other employee.

## *The Firm Name*

It sometimes happens that the partners carry on business under a name which is different from the name of the partners. This is known as the firm name. Before the *Companies Act 1981*, it was necessary for the firm name to be registered under the *Registration of Business Names Act 1916*, however that Act was repealed and the provisions relating to business names have been consolidated in the *Business Names Act 1985*. The business name does not now need to be registered, but Section 4 of that Act requires that publicity be given regarding the partners who are trading under the business name. The methods of publicity are as follows.

1. The name of each partner must be disclosed on all business letters, invoices and receipts, unless there are more than 20 individuals, in which case special rules apply.
2. The name and address of each partner must be displayed in any premises where the business is being carried on.
3. There must be disclosed, in relation to each partner, an address within Great Britain at which service of any document would be effective.

Failure to comply with the disclosure requirements is an offence punishable with a fine. Furthermore, if a firm using a business name has failed to comply with the disclosure requirements, and sues for breach of contract, the claim may be dismissed if the defendant can show:

1. that he has a claim against the firm arising out of the contract, which he is unable to pursue because of the plaintiff's non-compliance, or
2. that he, the defendant, has suffered financial loss in connection with the contract, because of the plaintiff's non-compliance.

The court may however in such circumstances permit the proceedings to continue if satisfied that it would be "just and equitable" to do so.

## *Relationship of Partners to Third Parties including Joint and Several Liability*

### Joint and Several Liability

An important feature of a partnership is that each partner is considered, by law, to be the agent of his fellow partner as regards the making of contracts in the course of the partnership business (Section 5). Thus every partner has authority to buy and sell goods commonly used in the partnership business; he can hire and fire staff. If it is trading partnership (which is one which buys and sells goods as opposed to merely giving a service) then each partner has authority to issue negotiable instruments e.g. cheques, to borrow money and pledge goods in the firm's name. Thus if a person is in a partnership (and remember he may not fully appreciate this fact) then he can be made liable for certain contracts made by a fellow partner. As far as the third party who has been dealing with the partnership is concerned it may well be important to have it established that a number of people are in partnership because then the list of defendants is extended and the plaintiff will have a better chance of getting his money.

So much for contracts, but the same reasoning applies as far as wrongful acts committed by a partner are concerned; his fellow partners will be held liable for these, provided of course they are committed in the course of the partnership business. This concept is known as joint and several liability. Under the *Civil Liability (Contribution) Act 1978* a creditor may sue the firm or each of the partners for the wrongdoing of any one or more of them. Furthermore a bank will require joint and several liability because:

1. when a partner is bankrupt or dies the bank may proceed against his estate equally with his personal creditors;
2. if there is a debit balance on the partnership account the bank will obtain a right of combination in respect of a credit balance on the partner's personal account, since the partner is personally liable for the debt.

## *Relationship of Partners Between Themselves*

Between themselves the partners have rights and owe duties and these are set down in the articles of partnership as mentioned earlier, but the contract of partnership is also a contract of good faith in its operation. This means that there need not be the fullest disclosure when the contract is entered into, and so it is up to each partner to satisfy himself that he is doing the right thing by entering into partnership with his fellow partners (rather like marriage). However once the contract is made then there must be the fullest disclosure of all relevant matters concerning the partnership business. A partner may not make a secret profit and must render total account of his dealings. In the same vein a partner must not set himself up in competition with the partnership business. At all times therefore every partner must conduct himself with good faith towards his fellow partners. Section 25 provides that a majority of the partners cannot expel any partner without authority expressed in the Articles of Partnership.

## *Retiring and New Partners' Liability*

In the absence of any contrary agreement, a partner's liability for contracts or debts contracted while he was a partner does not cease upon his retirement. He remains liable for debts incurred whilst he was a member of the firm. The creditors may, however, agree to discharge him from his liabilities and agree to look to the new firm for payment by making a contract of novation which is a "new contract".

A valid contract of novation is usually effected by the introduction of an incoming partner who agrees to be liable together with the remaining partners for the retired partner's share of the debts. Where the surviving partners do not intend to take on a new partner, the retiring partner's release by the creditors must be by deed. An incoming partner is not liable for debts of the firm before he joined unless he is a party to a contract of novation.

### Retiring Partner's Liability for Post-Retirement Debts

Section 36 of the *Partnership Act 1890* provides that a retiring partner may be liable for debts incurred after his retirement. Creditors are divided into two classes:

1. those who had dealt with the partnership before the retirement;
2. those who did not deal with the partnership before the retirement.

The retiring partner is liable for new debts contracted with any creditor in group 1 unless the latter has received individual notice of his retirement. If a creditor is aware of retirement, the retiring partner will not be liable for post-retirement debts even if he has not give notice to the creditor.

With creditors in group 2, notice in the *London Gazette* is sufficient notice of retirement to the creditors. If no *Gazette* notice is given a retiring partner will still not be liable for post-retirement debts to a creditor who did not know that he was a partner. *Tower Cabinet Co v Ingram (1949).*

## *Dissolution of Partnership*

As we have seen, a partnership will usually come into existence because of the agreement of the persons who wish to join in partnership with one another. Thus it is quite logical for such a relationship, which came into being because of an agreement, to be terminated by agreement. On the other hand a partnership may be formed for a particular length of time or to perform some purpose. Obviously when the period of time has expired or the purpose has been achieved the partnership will be at an end. In addition the *Partnership Act* provides that a partnership will automatically be dissolved if one of the partners dies or becomes bankrupt. However the old partnership will not be dissolved if the partnership agreement provides for alternative arrangements to be made (for example the remaining partners to buy the share of the deceased or bankrupt partner). Thus any agreement with A, B and C will continue notwithstanding the death or bankruptcy of A, if this has been agreed.

In the case of the death of a partner the deceased's estate will not normally be liable for debts incurred by the firm after his death and so it is essential that the account with the partnership is broken when the bank is notified of partner's death.

Apart from the above ways in which a partnership may be dissolved, it may be that the partners cannot agree between themselves. In that case an application may be made to the court to issue an order dissolving the partnership. This application must be based on one of the following grounds.

1. The insanity of one of the partners, under the *Mental Health Act 1983*.
2. Where a partner has become permanently incapable of carrying out his share of the partnership business.
3. When a partner wilfully and persistently commits a breach of the partnership agreement.
4. On the ground that the partnership can be carried on only at a loss, and there is no prospect of the firm making a profit.
5. When a partner has committed some act which will prejudicially affect the carrying on of the business. In *Carmichael v Evans (1904)* it was held that a conviction of dishonesty was sufficient reason for the dissolution of a firm of solicitors.
6. In circumstances that the court thinks just and equitable.

**Public Notice of Dissolution**

On dissolution every partner may publish a notice to this effect in the *London Gazette* and may compel the other partners to sign the notice. (S.37). Dissolution rescinds the power of the partners to act as agents for the firm, except in respect of:

1. transactions started but not completed; and
2. acts which are necessary to wind up the partnership affairs, such as employing an accountant to prepare the final accounts. S.38.

## *Partnership Property*

This includes property originally brought into the partnership or later acquired in the course of the partnership business or bought with money belonging to the firm. Naturally, upon the dissolution of the partnership it will be necessary to collect in the partnership property, liquidate it and distribute it. This will be done in the following order:

1. creditors of the firm will be paid;
2. partners will receive their loans to the firm if any;
3. partners will receive their capital contributions;
4. any surplus to be divided amongst the partners in the proportion in which profits are divisible.

If there are insufficient partnership assets to cover items 1, 2 and 3 then each partner must pay towards the deficiency in the proportion in which they shared profits.

If a partner, due to insolvency, is unable to contribute his equal share of the lost capital then the solvent partners are not liable to contribute it for him. In *Garner v Murray (1904)* it was decided that each partner must contribute his share of the deficiency ignoring the share of the insolvent partner. Then the assets are distributed according to the rules mentioned earlier.

## *Bankruptcy of the Partnership*

This must be distinguished from the bankruptcy of a partner which will result in the dissolution of the partnership unless the partners have agreed otherwise. The *Insolvent Partnerships Order 1986* permits partnerships to be wound up as if they were unregistered companies and does not necessarily involve the bankruptcy of the partners. Instead a creditor may present a bankruptcy petition against one or more of the partners; or petition for the winding up of the firm and the bankruptcy of the partners. The *Insolvent Partnerships Order 1986* provides that a creditor has three choices:

1. to wind up the partnership alone as if it were an unregistered company;
2. to make bankrupt the partners alone;
3. to wind up the partnership and make bankrupt all the partners.

A petition for winding up may be presented by a creditor or a partner on the following grounds:

1. the partnership has ceased to carry on its business;
2. the partnership is dissolved;
3. the partnership is unable to pay its debts;
4. it is just and equitable that the partnership be wound up.

A partnership is deemed unable to pay its debts if

1. a creditor who is owed £750 or more has demanded payment in writing and no payment has been made within three weeks or no security has been given;
2. notice of an action for debt has been served against a partner for a partnership debt and he has not paid within three weeks;
3. an execution against the partnership is unsatisfied;
4. the firm's liabilities exceed its assets.

## *Limited Liability Partnerships Act 2000*

This Act creates a new legal identity with a legal personality distinct from its members. Hitherto the only such "corporate bodies" were Limited Companies discussed in the next chapter. The Act provides that by Section 1 (5) the law of partnerships does not apply to such limited liability partnerships and it contains provisions to allow for the determination of the extent to which a member is liable for partnership debts if it is wound up.

**Questions**

What relationships are not partnerships?

What is the importance of Section 24 of the *Partnership Act 1890*?

THREE

# THE LAW *of* COMPANIES *and* COMPANY BORROWING

*Study Topics*

**The importance of *Salomon v Salomon 1897***
**The nature and effect of the memorandum and articles and association**
**The personal liability of the directors**
**Different types of charges**
**Debentures**

In addition to a partnership there is another form of business organisation called the registered company or limited company. It is called by these names because such a company is formed by registering certain documents with the Registrar of Companies and it is a limited company because the liability of its shareholders is limited.

A company is an artificial legal person. In other words it is a person in the eyes of the law and has rights and duties like any human person. It can sue, enter into contracts, employ and dismiss in the same way that real people can. This point was established in the famous case of *Salomon v Salomon and Co (1897)*.

In that case Mr Salomon formed a company to take over his business of manufacturing shoes. The company paid Mr Salomon for his business partly in cash, partly in shares and partly by a charge over the company's assets. The company was wound up and its debts to creditors were in excess of its assets. Therefore the creditors claimed the assets of the company arguing that a person cannot owe money to himself and as Mr Salomon owned the company he and it were the same person. The court held that the company was a separate person from Mr Salomon who owned it.

Being artificial, a company cannot be seen – it exists on paper. One can look at a factory manufacturing soap but one is not looking at Unilever plc or Lever Bros. Plc but at a factory which happens to be owned by a person whose name is Unilever plc. One says one is going to do some shopping Marks and Spencer. The shopping is being done in a shop owned by a single person called Marks and Spencer plc. How does one know that the company exists? As a company exists only on paper, the Certificate of Incorporation is the document that brings a company into existence and this is proof of the company's existence. It is issued by the Registrar of Companies when he has examined the documents filed in his office by the promoters of the company.

The concept that a company exists as a single person on its own is the basis of company law. Together with the principle that the liability of the shareholders is limited to the amount due to be paid (if any) for their shares, it is the main difference between a company and a partnership. As we have seen, the partners contribute money to the assets of the partnership but if this is insufficient to pay the debts of the partnership then the partners must continue to provide more money, even if that means they are bankrupting themselves. In the case of a company the shareholders have contributed to the assets of the company but if this proves to be insufficient to pay the creditors of the company then the shareholders will lose their money in the company, but will not have to provide more money. The other difference is that the company is a person separate from the person (the shareholder) who owns it. A partnership is not a separate person but consists of all the partners. As an illustration, it is often said that if all the partners of a partnership are in a room and a bomb explodes killing them all, that would be the end of the firm. But if all the shareholders of a company were killed in the same circumstances that would not be the end of the company. It would continue its existence, but with different shareholders of course.

The law relating to companies is contained mainly in the *Companies Act 1985*. This, in the main, is a consolidation act.

## *Formation of a Company*

The people who wish to form a company as a vehicle for running their business are called promoters. It is possible to buy a ready-made company or it may be decided to form a company from scratch. The procedure for this is to file with the Registrar of Companies certain documents – the most important being the memorandum of association and the articles of association.

## *The Memorandum of Association*

By Section 2 of the *Companies Act 1985* the memorandum of every company must state

1. the name of the company;
2. whether the registered office of the company is to be situated in England and Wales or Scotland;
3. the objects of the company;
4. in the case of a company having a share capital the memorandum must also state the amount of the share capital which the company proposes to be registered and the division of that capital into shares of a fixed amount;
5. also in the case of a company limited by shares there must be a statement that the liability of its members or shareholders is limited.

This document was of the greatest importance to outsiders dealing with the company because it contained the objects clause which stated the purpose for which the company had been formed and in so doing it established the powers of the company to enter into contracts. The rule was that a company could only enter into a valid and enforceable contract if it had power to do so. If any contract it made was outside its powers (ultra vires) then the contract was null and void. This principle was known as the "ultra vires doctrine" and was intended to protect investors in the company and those who were considering lending money to it. By consulting the objects clause, such people would know the permitted activities of the company.

In practice this was not particularly helpful because the lawyers who drew up a company's documents usually made the object so wide as to cover every possible activity that the company might have wished to enter into in the future. Nevertheless if a company entered into a contract and it was discovered that it lacked the power to enter into that particular contract then the contract would be void and the company could not be sued successfully. Since our entry into the European Economic Community we have had to modify our company law in certain areas to accord with Common Market practices.

The latest position is that the *Companies Act 1989* has amended the *Companies Act 1985*. Sections 108-112 of the 1989 Act have effectively abolished the "ultra vires" rule. These changes came into force on 4 February 1991. Section 35 of the 1985 Act (as amended) abolishes the "ultra vires" rule.

Section 35a of the 1985 Act (as amended) relates to the power of directors to bind the company to acts within the power of the company.

Section 35b of the 1985 Act (as amended) provides that a party to a transaction with a company is not bound to enquire into the terms of the company's memorandum nor as to any limitation in the director's powers.

Section 110 of the *Companies Act 1989* inserts a new section 3a into the 1985 Act which allows a company to state that its objects are "To carry on business as a general commercial company." A company which chooses this option in preference to a traditional objects clause will have power to carry on any trade or business and to do all things incidental or conducive thereto.

The Department of Trade and Industry has issued the following note:

### "Ultra Vires" Reform – Companies Act 1989 (Sections 108-112)

The provisions of the 1985 Act which deal with the ultra vires doctrine and the authority of the board of directors are amended (the ultra vires doctrine is a common law rule which, in the absence of statutory provision, renders void acts by a company which are beyond its stated objects). The main features of the amended provisions are as follows.

1. The validity of a completed act of a company is not to be called into question on the grounds of lack of capacity by reason of anything in the company's memorandum of association.
2. In favour of a person dealing with the company in good faith, the power of the board of directors to bind the company or authorise others to do so is to be free of any limitation in the company's constitution.
3. A third party is to have no duty to enquire as to the capacity of a company or the authority of directors to bind the company.
4. Transactions which are beyond the authority of the board of directors and to which directors or connected persons are a party are to be voidable in certain circumstances at the instance of the company.
5. If a company states that its object is to carry on business as a "general commercial company" it will have the object of carrying on any business or trade whatsoever, and will have the power to do whatever is incidental or condusive to that object.
6. The provisions on capacity and authority are qualified in the case of charitable companies, so as to maintain current controls on charitable companies and to assist in the recovery of misappropriated charitable property. In order to prevent those provisions on charitable companies undermining the provisions affecting companies generally, charitable companies are required to disclose their charitable status in their official documents if the status is not apparent from their name.

### Alteration of the Objects

A company may alter its objects by the passing of a special resolution to that effect. After the resolution has been passed the company must wait for 21 days (before implementing the alteration) to see whether any members who oppose the alteration may apply to the court to have it set aside. An application to cancel the alteration will not be entertained by the court unless it is made by

1. at least 15 per cent of the members; or
2. the holders of at least 15 per cent of any debentures issued by the company.

The court may on such an application make an order confirming the alteration or may provide for the purchase by the company of the shares of any members of the company. If the alteration is confirmed (that is, the dissentients are overruled) the company must deliver to the Registrar a printed copy of the memorandum as altered.

Section 110 of the *Companies Act 1989* inserts a new Section 4 into the *Companies Act 1985*. This allows a company to alter its objects for any reason.

**The Name of the Company**

The name chosen must not be undesirable in the opinion of the Secretary of State for Trade and Industry. A name is undesirable if it is either:

1. too similar to the name of another company, or
2. misleading, for example the name suggests that the company has connections with a government department, a member of the royal family, a district or a country.

Once the Secretary of State has approved a name for the company, it must be painted or affixed on the business premises of the company, engraved on its seal, and mentioned on all business documents and negotiable instruments.

A company limited by guarantee may be allowed to dispense with the word "limited" by the Secretary of State (Section 30) if the following conditions are satisfied:

1. the company is formed for promoting commerce, art, science, religion, charity or any other useful object;
2. its profits are to be devoted to the promotion of those objects; and
3. no part of its profits is to be distributed to the members in the form of dividends.

A company may alter its name provided the following procedure is adopted:

1. the company must pass a special resolution to effect the change, and
2. obtain the written consent of the Secretary of State.

Once the alteration of the name has been made, the Registrar of Companies will issue an altered Certificate of Incorporation.

If a company has a trading name different from its registered name, the *Business Names Act 1985* will apply. The effect of this Act has been noted in the chapter on Partnerships.

## *Articles of Association*

The other important document is the articles of association. This is of importance to the shareholders of the company because it contains their rights as to transfer of shares and payment of dividends. It also contains information regarding the holding of meetings and the appointment of the directors and their powers. Thus the articles are of importance to insiders. If a company does not wish to draw up its own articles then it may adopt the ready-made set of articles known as Table A which is to be found in a statutory instrument called *The Companies (Tables A to F) Regulations 1985*. (S.1 1985 No 805 as amended by Section 1 1985 No 1052). In the case of a company limited by shares, its articles are not registered, Table A automatically applies to it.

The following are some of the matters which are provided for in a company's articles:

1. calls on its shares
2. the company's lien on its shares
3. the transfer of shares
4. the exercise of the borrowing powers of the company
5. the delegation of the management of the company to the board of directors
6. the voting rights of members
7. the payment of dividends
8. variation of the members' rights
9. the conduct of meetings
10. the capitalisation of profits
11. the use of the company's seal.

**Effect of the Articles**

When registered, the articles constitute a contract between the members and the company. This contract binds the members to the company but only in their capacity as members. Hence if the articles confer on a member or any other person a right not shared by all the other members of the company, this cannot be enforced against the company.

In *Eley v Positive Assurance Co (1876)* a member was made a solicitor for life of a company by the articles of the company. When he was dismissed he sued the company but it was held that the contract in the articles should not be enforced by him as the right he sought to enforce was not a "membership right".

The members in their capacity as members are bound to the company. *Companies Act* Section 14.

### Alterations of the Articles

By Section 9 of the *Companies Act 1985* a company may alter its articles of association by a special resolution. Any alteration is as valid as if it was originally contained in the articles.

## *Directors*

Mention has been made of the fact that the company is an artificial person which cannot be seen but only exists on paper. So the question will no doubt occur as to how a company operates. The answer is that it operates through human agents called directors. The directors' powers are contained in the articles and so they operate and decide matters on behalf of the company, provided they have the necessary authority to act. Thus when one says "The company has decided to buy X Co plc" what that really means is that the directors have so decided. However when one considers who appoints the directors, then the answer is the shareholders in general meeting. Thus the shareholders own the company and they appoint the directors to run the company on their behalf. The directors are given certain powers to act without recourse to the shareholders but of course such powers may be curtailed or extended as the shareholders wish. The directors may only act on behalf of the company within the powers of the company and also within their own powers. These powers are set out in the articles of association. Certain matters may need the authority of the shareholders in general meeting, for example the fixing of a dividend, the passing of the accounts or the appointment of the auditors.

As an agent is in a position of trust as regards his principal, so is a director as regards the company. A director must exercise his powers for the purpose for which they are conferred and for the benefit of the company and must not put himself in a position in which his duties to the company and his personal interests may conflict.

Some directors (called non-executive directors) are appointed because of the contacts they can bring to the company. They might have been cabinet ministers, trade union leaders, etc. Other directors perform some particular function within the company, such as financial director, production director, etc. These latter are known as managing directors or executive directors.

Article 70 of Table A states that "Subject to the provisions of the Act, the memorandum and the articles and to any directions given by special resolution, the business of the company shall be managed by the directors and may exercise all the powers of the company."

If a company has as its object "to carry on business as a general commercial company" then it will have the power to do whatever is incidental or conclusive to that object. A person dealing with a company must ensure that

1. the directors have the necessary power to enter into any particular transaction

on behalf of the company;
2. if any particular procedure has to be followed then the transactions must have been made according to that.

If a bank is contemplating lending money to a company it must ascertain the directors' powers to borrow money on behalf of the company by consulting the articles. In some cases the shareholders may desire to restrict the directors' borrowing powers. It can happen that an act is intra vires the company but ultra vires the directors. In that case the unauthorised act of the directors may be ratified by the company.

However it may be that a bank should not consult the Articles because once it does it will have actual notice of any limitation on the powers of the directors. If the bank does not have actual notice then it may be protected by Section 35A of the *Companies Act 1985* (amended).

As regards any particular procedure that needs to be followed, the rule in *Turquand's* case may be of assistance.

**The Rule in Turquand's Case**

This rule reiterates the rule of agency that a person who deals with an agent will be able to bind the agent's principal provided the agent acted within the scope of his actual or apparent authority. The rule merely extends it to the special circumstances of companies when the directors act as its agents.

Every person dealing with a company is deemed to know the contents of its public documents, that is the memorandum, articles and presumably copies of any special or extraordinary resolutions it may have passed. This is because copies of these documents must be filed with the Registrar of Companies and are therefore accessible and open to members of the public to inspect.

An outsider is, however, not entitled to insist on proof by the directors that the rules and procedures for the internal management of the company have been complied with before he contracts with them.

The rule in *Royal British Bank v Turquand* (1855) therefore states that a third party dealing with the agents of the company is entitled to assume that the agents have authority to bind the company with reference to the part of their authority which derives from the "indoor management" of the company. Hence if the directors need an ordinary resolution before they can do a certain act and they do it without the resolution being passed, since the third party cannot know whether it was passed or not, he is entitled to assume that it was passed. The rule is subject to certain limitations such as if the third party knew or should have known of the irregularity.

Now that the ultra vires rule has been abolished then a company will be able to do anything that the directors wish. It will be unnecessary for an outsider to consult the memorandum. However, presumably the powers of the directors may be restricted by the articles but so long as the outsider has no actual notice of the contents of the articles then presumably he will be able to rely on the word of the directors and will be protected if he does so. Although directors are agents of the company, they do have a greater number of restrictions placed upon them.

## *Personal Liability of Directors*

It is the main purpose of forming a company to avoid liability attaching to its members or managers. However there are exceptions to this rule.

1. Guarantee. A loan to a company (usually a small one) may be supported by a guarantee from a director.
2. A director may be liable for breach of warranty of authority.
3. Promoter. A person who contracts on behalf of a company before it is formed is liable on the contract.
4. Bills of exchange. Where a director has failed to disclose that he was acting as agent of the company. He may be personally liable if he signs in his own name unless he uses "for" or "per pro" or "for and on behalf of" or he signs "as agent for the company".
   If he signs a cheque in his own name but the company's name is printed on the cheque and there is an account number this may indicate that liability is attached to the holder of that account, so that if it is the company's account, the company alone is liable. *Bondina Ltd v Rollaway Shower Blinds Ltd (1986).*
5. If the membership of a company falls below two and the company continues in business for more than six months after that, the remaining member is jointly and severally liable with the company for its debts (Section 24 *Companies Act 1985*).
6. Fraudulent and wrongful trading. A feature of the new insolvency legislation has been the attempt to ensure that any liability for fraud or wrongful transactions may be placed upon the directors of a company and that they should not be allowed to shelter behind the corporate facade. Directors may be civilly or criminally liable for fraudulent trading (Section 213 *Insolvency Act 1986*) if it can be shown, in a winding up of a company, that the business of the company was carried on with intent to defraud the creditors of the company.

In Re *William C Leitch Brothers Ltd (1932)* it was held to be fraudulent to continue to trade when the directors must have known there was no reasonable prospect of the company being able to pay its debts.

It is sometimes difficult to prove the necessary "fraudulent intent" on the part of the directors. Therefore Section 214 of the *Insolvency Act 1986* makes a director liable where a company is in insolvent liquidation and the directors should have realised that the company had no prospect of avoiding liquidation. This is known as wrongful trading.

Note that liability for wrongful trading (not fraudulent trading) may attach to "shadow directors". These are persons in accordance with whose directions the company is accustomed to act. A bank therefore could, on occasions, be classified as a shadow director. It must be careful to give advice only and not instructions.

Section 212 of the *Insolvency Act 1986* makes a director liable for misfeasance and breach of duty to the company. Apart from the *Insolvency Act*, eight months earlier the *Company Directors Disqualification Act 1986* was passed. This Act consolidated the law relating to disqualification orders contained in the *Companies Act 1985* and the *Insolvency Act 1985*. Under this Act a director may be disqualified if

1. he has been convicted of an indictable offence in connection with the management or liquidation of a company;
2. he has persistently been in default in delivering any document to the Registrar;
3. he has failed to comply with any provision of the Act and in the five years up to that conviction has been convicted of three or more similar offences.

The director may be disqualified for up to 15 years. A register of disqualified orders will be kept by the Secretary of State.

## *Meetings*

The business of the company is transacted by means of passing resolutions at meetings. The meetings must be properly called and constituted according to the rules contained in the articles of association and according to the general law relating to meetings. For example, all persons who have a right to attend a meeting must be notified that one is to take place. Such persons may have to be given a minimum length of notice to attend. Also there must be a quorum present at the meeting, which means there must be a minimum number present in order for a valid resolution to be passed. Sometimes it is also necessary that the members constituting a quorum must have no personal interest in the matters being discussed or at least must have disclosed any interest they might have.

When a bank lends money to a company and takes security from it, it will require a certified copy of the resolution which authorises the charge. If a quorum was not present or if it was an invalid quorum because one of its number was interested party then it would follow that any resolution passed would itself be invalid. A bank therefore must be on its guard and if it knows that the meeting was invalid then it must reject any resolution made by such a meeting. This situation arose in *Victors Ltd v Lingard (1972)* in which the directors of the company personally guaranteed the company's overdraft with the bank. Later the directors in meeting resolved that the company should issue debentures to the bank as additional security. The articles of the company provided that no director should vote in connection with any matter in which he was personally interested.

In the subsequent case Romer J held that by agreeing to the issue of debentures by the company the directors were thereby relieving themselves of their personal liability for the overdraft and so were interested parties.

To avoid any difficulty which might arise as a result of a similar situation the bank should examine the articles to see how many directors must form a quorum and whether it must be a disinterested quorum. The bank may also rely on the Rule of Turquand's case and Section 35 of the *Companies Act 1985*. If the ultra vires doctrine is abolished in the near future then a bank will be safe so long as it does not have actual notice that a director is exceeding his ostensible authority.

Every company must hold once a year a general meeting of shareholders at which the accounts of the company are presented by the directors, who may have to submit to questioning from the shareholders. At this annual general meeting, of which the shareholders must receive 21 days' notice, they appoint or reappoint the directors and the auditors. They also confirm, or not as the case may be, the dividend proposed by the directors to be distributed. Every company must hold its first general meeting – the statutory meeting – within six weeks of its formation.

Apart from the annual meeting, the directors may, either of their own accord or because they have been so required by members of the company holding not less than one-tenth of the paid-up capital of the company, call an extraordinary general meeting of the shareholders who must be given 14 days' notice. At these meetings proposals are made and if accepted resolutions are passed. If the subject matter of the resolution is not particularly important, then it may be passed by an ordinary majority. However, if the matter is important, for example changing the name of the company or modifying the details of the objects clause of the memorandum, then such a resolution must be a special resolution. Therefore it must be passed by a majority of 75 per cent of those who attend and vote at the meeting. The same majority is required to pass an extraordinary resolution. If it is desired to propose a special resolution then 21 days' notice must be given to those persons entitled to attend.

## *Capital*

The share capital of a company goes under a number of different names. First there is the authorised capital or nominal capital. This is the capital stated in the memorandum of association and which the company is authorised to issue. It may not, at least initially, issue all its authorised capital and so the capital that has been issued is quite reasonably called issued capital or allotted capital. If some shares are issued only partly paid then the amount the shareholders have actually paid for their shares is called the paid-up capital. It is not so common nowadays for a company to issue partly paid shares.

### Preference Shares

The capital is divided usually into two main classes, preference shares and ordinary shares. The preference shares, as their name implies, give the holder of such shares preference over other shareholders in the payment of dividends and also in the repayment of capital in the event of the company being wound up. Preference shareholders receive a fixed dividend from any profits set aside by the directors for distribution. The dividend never varies and so such shares are usually considered solid and dependable and suitable for trustee investments. Preference shareholders are also usually given a preference as to return of capital in a winding up. When the company is a going concern, the following presumptions apply to preference shares.

1. They confer a right to a cumulative dividend. This means that if no dividend is declared in any particular year, the arrears of dividend must be carried forward from year to year until they are all paid, before the ordinary shareholders can receive any dividends.
2. They are non-participating. This means they do not confer any right to participate in the profits of the company after the ordinary shareholders have been paid a dividend.

### Redeemable Preference Shares

A company may, however, issue preference shares which from their inception are redeemable, either at a fixed date or after a certain period of time at the option of the company. Sections 159 and 160 of the *Companies Act 1985* lay down conditions to be fulfilled before a company may redeem redeemable preference shares. Basically these conditions seek to maintain the capital of the company.

For example, the redemption must be made out of profits, and only shares which are fully paid may be redeemed.

### Ordinary Shares

These normally carry the residue of profits available for distribution as dividend after the preference shareholders, if any, have been paid their fixed dividend. Ordinary shares are sometimes called the risk capital. This is because the dividend has been paid then the residue distributed to the ordinary shareholders and of course the amount will depend on the performance of the company.

In a winding up, if preference shares have priority as to return of capital, the ordinary shares will be entitled to the surplus assets, unless there are deferred shares. Hence ordinary shares are sometimes called the equity share capital of the company because they take what is left (the equity). The ordinary shareholders have a vote at the annual general meeting of the company and so the power to control the company rests with them.

These are the two main types of capital, preference or ordinary. There are other types of shares but these are not so common. By issuing shares a company acquires money for its activities. However by issuing shares to the people who contribute money the company is acquiring more shareholders and consequently the control of its existing shareholders is being weakened. An alternative method of acquiring money is for the company to borrow it and in that case it will issue debentures to those people who lend it money. A debenture is a document which is evidence of a debt. The point about debentures is that the holders of these are not members of the company and do not have the same control over the company as do the shareholders. Instead of dividends, debenture holders receive interest on their holdings. However, like shares, debentures may be transferred on the Stock Exchange.

## *Running a Company's Bank Account*

If the bank's customer is a company there are certain matters which must be considered. The bank must see the certificate of incorporation because this document establishes the existence of the company. The bank must examine the company's memorandum of association in order to ascertain the powers of the company. In addition the articles of association must be examined the power of the directors to borrow money for the company. Once the ultra vires rule has been abolished then presumably it will no longer be necessary for a bank to examine the above mentioned documents. A bank will be able to assume that the company has power to do anything it wants so long as it is not aware of any restriction on the company's authority, or on the authority of the directors.

If a company wishes to borrow money the bank must ensure that certain conditions are met.

1. The company has power to borrow. This will be implied in the case of a trading company but is usually stated in the objects clause of the memorandum.
2. The loan is to be used for an intra vires purpose. *Re Introductions Ltd (1969).*
3. The directors have the authority to borrow the money on behalf of the company.
4. The bank will wish to see a resolution of the board of directors appointing the bank as the bankers of the company. At this time the persons with signing powers will be designated in the mandate given to the bank.
5. If the company is a public company the bank will require to see the certificate to commence business.
6. When the account has been opened a bank must take the same care in paying company cheques as it does in the case of an individual. In collecting the proceeds of a cheque the amount must only be credited to the account of the company.

7. In the same way that a loan to a company will be void if it is to be used for an ultra vires purpose a bank may also be in difficulties if it lends money to a company which is to be used for an illegal purpose and this purpose was known or should have been known to the bank. It may be that the bank could be held liable as a constructive trustee if it knowingly pays out money for the purpose of the loan. An example would be when the company proposes to lend money to a director. The rules relating to loans were strengthened following major scandals in the 1970s. Sections 330-342 of the *Companies Act 1985* govern such a transaction and make such a loan illegal if made to a director or to a "connected person" such as
   i. directors' families;
   ii. companies in which the director owns over one-fifth of the equity;
   iii. the trustee of a trust whose beneficiaries include the director or members of the classes referred to above;
   iv. a partner of the director or any person listed above.

In addition to loans purely and simply, other transactions are also caught by the prohibitive section:

i. a quasi loan which includes the provision of credit card facilities as where the company is the cardholder and the card is used by the director;
ii. a credit transaction where goods or services are provided on the undertaking that payment will be made later, for example hire purchase terms;
iii. back-to-back arrangements where company X lends to the directors of company Y on the understanding that company Y will lend to the directors of company X.

Sections 332-338 provide certain exceptions to the above prohibitions. The overall effect is to allow all loans up to £2,500 for each director; to allow credit transactions if they are on normal commercial terms; to exempt loans to cover expenses incurred by a director if the transaction has the approval of the general meeting, subject to a maximum of £10,000 for directors of public companies; to allow quasi loans up to £1,000 if the terms require payment within two months; to allow credit transactions or the making of guarantees up to £5,000.

Money lending companies may make loans or quasi loans to directors on normal commercial terms subject to a maximum of £50,000. The terms may be more favourable if intended for house purchase or improvement. Recognised banks can lend to their directors without limit provided the loans are on normal commercial terms. However the £50,000 limit applies if the loan is for house purchase or improvement.

A public company is not permitted to give financial assistance for the purpose of purchasing shares in the company (Section 151). Exceptions would be if the loan is part of a larger transaction and not merely to purchase shares, for example

i. the distribution of lawful dividends;
ii. the allotment of bonus shares;
iii. reductions of capital confirmed by the court;
iv. provision of money to allow employees to buy shares;
v. lending money is part of the company's business.

The importance to a bank of the points mentioned in 7 and 8 is that the bank may become involved if it lends money to the company for either of these purposes. It may become involved because it may be that the bank will be considered a constructive trustee if it knows or should have known that the company's funds held by the bank were being used for an illegal purpose. If that is so the bank may have to compensate the company for the illegal payments the directors have ordered it to make.

9. Shadow directors. Section 251 of the *Insolvency Act 1986* defines a shadow director as "a person in accordance with those directions or instructions the company is accustomed to act". Thus the definitions could apply to a number of persons such as

   i. an administrative receiver under a bank debenture who continues to trade with the company during the receivership;
   ii. a parent company which exercises control over a subsidiary;
   iii. a bank which is held to have been giving instructions in the liquidation of a company. It will be up to the manager concerned to ensure that he is merely advising and not directing or instructing.

## *Company Borrowing*

As was mentioned earlier, a company may sometimes need to borrow money. A power to borrow money will presumably be implied in the objects clause of every company registered with the "general trading" object. The directors are the persons who will actually arrange the loan on behalf of the company and so they too must have the necessary power to act. Sometimes the shareholders may wish to restrict borrowing powers to a certain maximum amount.

Now that the doctrine of ultra vires has been abolished a company will have implied power to borrow and to give security for the loan but the authority of the directors will still have to be considered. This, no doubt, may continue to be restricted if so desired, but such restrictions will not affect persons dealing with the company unless they are aware of them.

The same principles apply to securities given by companies as to those given by individuals. Some must be by deed, such as a legal mortgage, and in that case the company's seal must be affixed. If the document may merely be signed, the person signing on behalf of the company must be authorised by resolution of the board of directors.

An important requirement as far as charges given by companies are concerned is that Section 398 of the *Companies Act 1985* provides that the prescribed particulars of the charge together with the instrument (if any) by which the charge is created or evidenced must be delivered or received by the Registrar of Companies in Cardiff for registration within 21 days after the date of the charge's creation. Particulars may be delivered by any one interested in the charge. The company no longer receives a certificate. Instead the Registrar sends a copy of the particulars and a note of the date to the company, the chargee and any other interested person. Examples of charges include:

1. a charge securing any issue of debentures;
2. a charge on land;
3. a floating charge on the undertaking or property of the company;
4. a charge on goodwill, patent or trade mark.

A banker who proposes to lend to a limited company should therefore inspect the Register before doing so to see whether any prior charges exist on the company's property.

Even though it is the duty of the company to register the charges, where the company defaults, the creditor himself may register it and recover from the company any fees paid to him. Certain charges are not required to be registered:

1. where a company mortgages shares or assigns a life policy or pledges goods;
2. where a negotiable instrument is given to secure the payment of any book debts of a company;
3. where an unpaid vendor's lien exists.

Section 399 of the *Companies Act 1985*, as amended by Section 95 of the *Companies Act 1989* provides that if particulars are not delivered within 21 days the charge is void as against:

1. an administrator or liquidator; or
2. any person who for value acquires an interest in or right over any property subject to the charge

where the relevant event (for 1, beginning of insolvency proceedings or for 2, the acquisition of the right or interest) occurs after the creation of the charge.

New Section 400 of the *Companies Act 1985* provides that where particulars are delivered more than 21 days after creation the charge is not void where the relevant event occurs after the particulars are delivered. It is therefore no longer necessary to obtain court approval to register out of time.

However the charge will be void as against an administrator/liquidator if at the date of delivery of the particulars the company is unable to pay its debts (as defined by S.123 of the *Insolvency Act 1986*) or becomes unable to do so as a result of the charge and insolvency proceedings begin with the relevant period (beginning with the date particulars are delivered: six months in the case of fixed charges; one year if a floating charge but extended to two years if in favour of a connected person).

Section 401 of the *Companies Act 1985* as amended by Section 96 of the *Companies Act 1989* provides that, where the registered particulars are incomplete or inaccurate, further particulars signed on behalf of the company and chargee may be delivered at any time.

## *Debentures*

Section 744 of the *Companies Act 1985* provides that a debenture includes debenture stock, bonds or any other securities of a company, whether constituting a charge on the assets of the company or not. More usually a debenture is considered to be evidence of a loan and a certificate will be issued to the creditor. A debenture created by a company in favour of a bank will usually give a fixed charge over certain assets of the company and a floating charge over the remainder of the assets.

## *Fixed and Floating Charge*

A fixed charge may be a legal or an equitable mortgage of some fixed or specified assets of the company. The effect of this is that the assets may not be sold or destroyed by the company otherwise the security on which the mortgagee is relying would be affected. If certain assets such as raw materials or finished stock were to be the subject of a fixed charge then they could not be used in the manufacturing process or sold. Consequently a floating charge was devised which would float over certain assets, not fastening on to them until certain events occurred which would have the effect of crystallising the floating charge. The assets which are subject to the floating charge may be used in any way the company desires, even to the extent that they are used up entirely. A floating charge will crystallise or become fixed if the company:

1. defaults in payment of interest or capital or commits some breach of another term of the debenture and the mortgagee takes some step such as the appointment of a receiver;
2. goes into liquidation;

3. ceases to carry on business.

Often a company will borrow money from more than one person and in that case the interests of the creditors are represented by a trustee whose powers are stated in the trust deed. If any breach of covenant occurs then a receiver can be appointed.

Debentures are similar to shares in that they can be transferred on the Stock Exchange. However in the case of a debenture the following applies:

1. the holder is a creditor and not a member of the company;
2. he receives interest and not dividends;
3. he has no voting rights;
4. in a winding-up a debenture holder is treated according to whether the debenture is secured or unsecured;
5. a debenture may be repayable at a future date or may be irredeemable;
6. debentures may be issued at a discount whereas shares may not as a rule be issued at a discount;
7. a company may purchase its own debentures but it may only purchase its own shares in certain circumstances.

Debentures may be registered or issued to bearer. They may be secured or unsecured in which case they are called mortgage debentures or naked debentures. If a bank lends money to a corporate customer it will use its own debenture form and the following are some typical clauses to be found therein.

## *Bank Debenture Form*

The following clauses are usually contained in the bank's debenture form.

The Company hereby covenants to pay to the Bank on demand the sum of One pound (£1) and to pay and discharge on demand all monies obligations and liabilities which may now or at any time hereafter may be or become due owing or incurred by the Company to the Bank on any account (whether solely or jointly with any other person and whether as principal or surety) present or future actual or contingent of the Company to the Bank together with interest and other bank charges so that interest shall be calculated and compounded in accordance with the practice of the Bank from time to time as well as before any demand made or judgement obtained hereunder.

The company agrees to repay all liabilities present, future actual or contingent together with expenses.

The Company as beneficial owner and to the intent that the security created shall rank as a continuing security hereby charges with the payment or discharge of all monies obligations and liabilities hereby covenanted to be paid or discharged (together with all costs and expenses howsoever incurred by the Bank in connection with this Mortgage Debenture on a full indemnity basis):

a. by way of legal mortgage any property referred to in the Schedule hereto (the legally mortgaged property) and/or the proceeds of sale thereof;
b. by way of specific equitable charge all estates or interests in any freehold and leasehold property (except the legally mortgaged property) now at any time during the continuance of this security belonging to or charged to the Company (the equitably charged property) and/or the proceeds of sale thereof;
c. by way of specific charge all stocks shares and/or other securities now and at any time during the continuance of this security to the Company in any of its subsidiary companies or any other company and all dividends and other rights in relation thereto;
d. by way of specific charge all books debts and other debts now and from time to time due or owing to the Company;
e. by way of specific charge its goodwill and the benefit of any licenses.
f. by way of floating security its undertaking and all its property assets and rights whatsoever and wheresoever present and/or future including those for the time being charged by way of specific change pursuant to the foregoing paragraphs if and to the extent that such charges as aforesaid shall fail as specific charges but without prejudice to any such specific charges and shall continue to be effective.

As continuing security the company creates a fixed charge over freehold and leasehold property, plant and machinery, stocks and shares etc. It also creates a floating charge over other property not subject to a fixed charge.

With reference to the property assets and rights subject to the floating charge:

a. The company shall not be at liberty without the consent in writing of the bank to:
   i. create any mortgage or charge ranking in priority to or pari passu with that charge and/or
   ii. sell the whole or except in the ordinary course of business any part of the Company's undertaking.
b. The company agrees to effect and maintain such insurances as are normally maintained by prudent companies carrying on similar businesses.
c. The Bank may by notice to the Company convert the floating charge into a specific charge as regards any assets specified in the notice which the Bank shall consider to be in danger of being seized or sold under any form of distress or execution levied or threatened and may appoint a receiver thereof.

The company agrees not to create any mortgage charge or lien on the property, to rank in priority to the floating charge.

With reference to the legally mortgaged property and the equitably charged property the Company agrees:

a. to keep it in a good state of repair and condition and insured against such risks and in such office and for such amounts as the Bank may require or approve and that failure to do so will entitle the Bank to do so at the expense of the Company and as agent of the Company without hereby becoming a mortgagee in possession;
b. that the statutory power of leasing and/or accepting surrenders of leases conferred on mortgagors shall not be exercised by the Company without the consent in writing of the Bank but the Bank may grant or accept surrenders of leases without restriction;
c. not to part with the possession of it or any part thereof nor confer upon any person firm company or body whatsoever any licence right or interest to occupy it or any part thereof without the consent in writing of the Bank.

To keep insured the property charged.

Immediately upon or at any time after the presentation of a petition applying for an administration order to be made in relation to the Company or at any time after this security shall otherwise have become enforceable the Bank may by writing under the hand of any area director or manager of the Bank appoint any person (or persons) to be an administrative receiver (the Administrative Receiver) of the property hereby charged. Where two or more persons are appointed to be an Administrative Receiver the Bank will in the appointment declare whether any act required or authorised to be done by such Administrative Receivers is to be done by all or any one or more of such Administrative Receivers for the time being holding office. Any Administrative Receiver shall be the agent of the Company and the Company shall be solely responsible for his acts or defaults and for his remuneration and any Administrative Receiver shall have all the powers of an administrative receiver specified in Schedule 1 of the Insolvency Act 1986 or any statutory modification of re-enactment thereof.

The bank may appoint a receiver.

Section 103 of the *Law of Property Act 1925 (the 1925 Act)* shall not apply to this security which shall immediately become enforceable and the power of sale and other powers conferred by section 101 of the 1925 Act as varied or extended by this security shall be immediately exercisable at any time after notice demanding payment of any moneys hereby secured shall have been served by the Bank on the Company.

Section 103 (power of sale) and Section 93 (consolidation) of the *Law of Property Act 1925*, shall not apply.

The Company shall from time to time supply to the Bank such accounts or other information concerning the assets liabilities and affairs of the Company its subsidiary or associated companies as the Bank may require.
The company will send to the bank copies of its trading account and Balance Sheet.

## *Floating Charge*

The characteristics of a floating charge are set out in Re *Yorkshire Woolcombers Association (1903).*

1. It is a charge on a class of assets of a company present and future.
2. The class of assets is constantly changing from time to time.
3. The company may deal with the assets in any way that it wishes, until the holder of the charge takes some step to enforce it.

Useful though a floating charge is it should never be taken without the addition of a fixed charge. The floating charge is only appropriate for certain fluctuating assets. The disadvantages of a floating charge are various.

Because the company may continue to deal with the assets which are subject to a floating charge it may be that when the mortgagee seeks to enforce the charge there will be no assets left. To minimise this risk a bank may ask for statements of assets from the company from time to time.

In the winding up of the company its preferential creditors, such as the Inland Revenue, will have priority over creditors holding a floating charge. Also creditors other than preferential may obtain priority over a creditor holding a floating charge such as a landlord levying distress for rent or the sheriff seizing goods to satisfy a judgement.

On the same point concerning priority of creditors it may be that a supplier has sold goods to the company and has included in the contract of sale a "Romalpa" clause. This is the name given to the clause that was examined by the court in *Aluminium Industrie Vaasen BV v Romalpa Aluminium Ltd (1976).* The case concerned the sale of aluminium foil by a Dutch company to an English company. The seller had inserted a clause to the effect that the ownership of the foil should remain with the seller, that the product of the goods should be stored separately from other stock on the supplier's behalf as "surety" for the remainder of the price. Also that the products might be sold by the buyers as agents for the sellers. When the buyer became insolvent it was held that the seller could assume ownership of the goods in the hands of the buyer thus defeating the receiver.

It seems therefore that if the goods sold remain identifiable then the seller may assert his ownership. However if the goods sold are mixed with other goods so that the original goods lose their identity then problems may arise. In *Borden (UK) Ltd v Scottish Timber Products Ltd (1981)* the original goods became mixed with others and there was no provision in the contract for ownership in the mixed product remaining with the original seller. Consequently the attempt by the seller to retain ownership of the goods he had sold, failed.

In *Clough Mill Ltd v Martin (1985)* the court considered the matter and came to the conclusion that the retention of ownership clause (Romalpa clause) would be effective in relation to unmixed goods. If it had been intended that a charge be created over the goods sold that now form part of the mixed goods then this must have been registered.

It does seem therefore that the retention of ownership clause will be effective, if drawn correctly, in the case of unmixed goods if such a clause provides for separate accountability for the proceeds in the event of a re-sale by the original buyer. There are considerable difficulties in the case of mixed goods.

## *Avoidance of a Floating Charge*

Section 245 of *Insolvency Act 1986* provides that "where a company is being wound up a floating charge on its property created within 12 months of the commencement of the winding up is invalid (unless it is proved that the company, immediately after the creation of the charge, was solvent), except to the amount of any cash paid to the company at the time of or subsequently to the creation of, and in consideration for, the charge, together with interest on that account."

In this connection the rule in *Clayton's* case may operate in favour of the bank, because money paid into a company's account after the charge has been created will be linked with any debt outstanding when the charge was made. Therefore if the amount paid into the account after the charge was created equals the debt the charge was intended to secure, the amount paid in will cancel the debt outstanding when the charge was made and the charge will be valid to secure loans made after the charge was created. *Re Yeovil Glove Co Ltd (1965)* which approved *Re Thomas Mortimer Ltd (1925).*

If the charge was created in favour of a person connected with the company then a floating charge created within two years of the commencement of a winding up will be invalid whether or not the company was solvent.

Any charge made by a company within six months before commencement of a winding up (two years, if a person connected with the company) is void if it is a preference of any of the company's creditors or within two years if it is a transaction at an undervalue.

As a floating charge is an equitable charge, if the company which has given the charge later executes a fixed mortgage or charge over assets comprised in the floating charge then the latter fixed charge may take priority over the floating charge. This situation may be avoided by the bank's inserting a clause into its debenture form to this effect: "The company covenants not to create any mortgage or charge to rank in priority to or pari passu with the floating charge." In order to make this restriction binding on possible later chargees the restrictive clause must be stated in Form 395 when registering the debentures with the Registrar of Companies.

## A Typical Debenture Form

**The Royal Bank**
**of Scotland plc**

**Debenture**

**Date:**

**Branch:**

**Granted by:**

**The Royal Bank of Scotland plc**

**Debenture**
**Secs I (7/95)**

**THIS IS AN IMPORTANT DOCUMENT. YOU SHOULD TAKE INDEPENDENT LEGAL ADVICE BEFORE SIGNING AND SIGN ONLY IF YOU WANT TO BE LEGALLY BOUND. IF YOU SIGN AND THE BANK IS NOT PAID YOU MAY LOSE THE ASSET(S) CHARGED.**

**Date:** 19

**Definitions**

| | |
|---|---|
| **Company:** | |
| **Bank:** | The Royal Bank of Scotland p1c |
| **Interest:** | Interest at the rate(s) charged to thc Company by the Bank from time to time |
| **Property:** | The whole and any part of the undertaking property and assets of the Company charged by Clause I |
| **Registered Land:** | Description of Property Land Registry Title Number |
| **Company's Obligations:** | All the Company's liabilities to the Bank of any kind and in any currency (whether present or future actual or contingent and whether incurred alone or jointly with another) together with the Bank's charges and commission Interest and Expenses |
| **Expenses:** | All expenses (on a full indemnity basis) incurred by tbe Bank or any Receiver at any time in connection with the Property or the Company's Obligations or in taking or perfecting this deed or in preserving defending or enforcing the security created by this deed or in exercising any power under this deed or otherwise with Interest from the date they are incurred |
| **Required Currency:** | The currency or currencies in which the Company's Obligations are expressed from time to time |

**Charge**

I **The** Company covenants to discharge on demand the Company's Obligations and as a continuing security for such discharge and with full title guarantee charges to the Bank:-

1.1 **By** way of legal mortgage all the freehold and leasehold property now vested in or charged to the Company including any Registered Land

1.2 **By** way of fixed charge all estates or interests in any freehold and leasehold property now and in the future vested in or charged to the Company except the property charged by Clause I. I

1.3 **By** way of fixed charge all the plant machinery and fixtures and fittings of the Company present and future

1.4 **By** way of fixed charge all furniture furnishings equipment tools and other chattels of the Company present and future not regularly disposed of in the ordinary course of business

1.5 **By** way of fixed charge all the goodwill and uncalled capital of the Company present and future

1.6 **By** way of fixed charge all stocks shares and other securities of the Company present and future

1.7 **By** way of fixed charge all intellectual property rights choses in action and claims of the Company present and future and the proceeds of any insurance from time to time affecting the Property

1.8 **By** way of fixed charge all book debts and other debts of the Company present and future and the proceeds of payment or realisation of each of them until the receipt of the proceeds from time to time into an account in accordance with Clause 4.2

1.9 **By** way of fixed charge all funds standing to the credit of the Company from time to time on any account with the Bank or any other bank or financial institution or organisation including all receipts from time to time paid into an account in accordance with Clause 4.2

1.10 **By** way of floating charge all the undertaking and all property assets and rights of the Company present and future not subject to a fixed charge under this deed

**Restrictions**

2.1 **The** Company will not without the previous written consent of the Bank:-

2.1. I **Create** or permit to arise any mortgage charge or lien on the Property

2.1.2 **Dispose** of the Property charged by Clauses I . I to 1.9 inclusive

2.1.3 **Deal** with the Company's book debts and other debts otherwise than by collecting them in the ordinary course of the Company's business and in particular the Company will not realise its book debts and other debts by means of block discounting factoring or the like

2.1.4 **Dispose** of the Property charged by Clause 1.10 other than in the ordinary course of business

2.1.5 **Grant** or accept a surrender of any lease or licence of or part with or share possession or occupation of its freehold and leasehold property or any part of it

2.2 **The** Company requests the Chief Land Registrar to enter a restriction on the Register of any Registered Land that except under an order of the Registrar no disposition by the proprietor(s) of the land is to be registered without the consent of the registered proprietor of this deed

**Insurance**

3.1 **The** Company will keep comprehensively insured to the Bank's reasonable satisfaction all of the Property which is of an insurable nature for its full reinstatement cost and in default the Bank may enter and effect such insurance (without becoming liable to account as mortgagee in possession)

3.2 **The** Company will hold in trust for the Bank all money received under any insurance of the Property and at the Bank's option will apply the same in making good the relevant loss or damage or in or towards discharge of the Company's Obligations

**Deeds Securities and Debts**

4.1 **The** Company will from time to time deposit with the Bank all insurance policies (or where the Bank agrees copies of them) deeds and documents of title relating to the Property

4.2 **The** Company will pay into the Company's account with the Bank (or such other account as the Bank may specify from time to time) all money which the Company may receive in respect of the Company's book debts and other debts

**Repair and Alteration**

5. I **The** Company will keep the Property charged by Clauses I. I to 1.4 inclusive in good condition and in default the Bank may enter and effect repairs (without becoming liable to account as mortgagee in possession)

5.2 **The** Company will not without the prior written consent of the Bank make any alteration to the Property charged by Clauses I. I and 1.2 which would requirc Planning Permission or approval under any Building Regulations

**Notice of Crystallisation**

6 **The** Bank may by written notice to the Company convert the floating charge into a fixed charge as regards any of the Property specified in the notice

**Powers of the Bank**

7.1 **The** Bank may without restriction grant or accept surrenders of leases of thc Company's freehold and leasehold property or any part of it

7.2 **Section 103** of the Law of Property Act 1925 shall not apply and tbe Bank may exercise its power of sale and other powers under that or any other Act or this deed at any time after the date of this deed

7.3 **The** Bank may under the hand of any official or manager or by deed appoint or remove a Receiver or Receivers of the Property and may fix and pay the fees of a Receiver but any Receiver shall be deemed to be the agent of the Company and the Company shall be solely responsible for the Receiver's acts defaults and remuneration

7.4 **All** or any of tbe powers conferred on a Receiver by Clause 8 may be exercised by the Bank without first appointing a Receiver or notwithstanding any appointment

7.5 **The** Bank will not be liable to account to the Company as mortgagee in possession for any money not actually received by the Bank

7.6 **Section 93(1)** of the Law of Property Act 1925 shall not apply to this deed

7.7 **In** addition to any lien or right to which the Bank may be entitled by law the Bank may from time to time without notice and both before and after demand set off the whole or any part of the Company's Obligations against any deposit or credit balance on any account of the Company with the Bank (whether or not that deposit or balance is due to the Company)

7.8 **Despite** any term to the contrary in relation to any deposit or credit balance on any account of the Company with the Bank that deposit or balance will not be capable of being assigned dealt with mortgaged or charged and will not be repayable to the Company before all the Company's Obligations have been discharged but the Bank may without prejudice to this deed permit the Company to make withdrawals from time to time

7.9 **The** Bank may exchange or convert to the Required Currency any currency held or received

**Receivers**

8.1 **Any** Receiver appointed by the Bank shall be a - Receiver and Manager and shall (in addition to all powers conferred on him by law) have the following powers which in the case of Joint Receivers may be exercised jointly or severally:-

8.1. 1 **To** take possession of and generally manage the Property and any business of the Company

8.1.2 **To** carry out on any freehold or leasehold property of the Company any new works or complete any unfinished works of building reconstruction maintenance furnishing or equipment

8.1.3 **To** purchase or acquire any land or other property and purchase acquire grant or release any interest in or right over land or the benefit of any covenants (positive or restrictive) affecting land

8.1.4 **To** sell lease surrender or accept surrenders of leases charge or otherwise deal with or dispose of the Property without restriction including (without limitation) power to dispose of any fixtures separately from the land

8.1.5 **To** carry into effect and complete any transaction by executing deeds or documents in the name of or on behalf of the Company

8.1.6 **To** take continue or defend any proceedings and enter into any arrangement or compromise

8.1.7 **To** insure the Property and any works and effect indemnity insurance or other similar insurance and obtain bonds and give indemnities amd security to any bondsmen

8.1.8 **To** call up any uncalled capital of the Company with all the powers conferred by the Articles of Association of the Company in relation to calls

8.1.9 **To** employ advisers consultants managers agents workmen and others

8.1.10 **To** purchase or acquire materials tools equipment goods or supplies

8.1.11 **To** borrow any money and secure the payment of any money in priority to the Company's Obligations for the purpose of the exercise of any of his powers

8.1.12 **To** do any other acts which the Receiver may consider to be incidental or conducive to any of his powers or to the realisation of the Property

8.2 **A** Receiver shall apply all money he receives first in repayment of all money borrowed by him and his expenses and liabilities and in payment of his fees and secondly towards the remaining matters specified in Section 109(8) of the Law of Property Act 1925

**Power of Attorney**

9 **The** Company irrevocably appoints the Bank and any Receiver severally to be the Attorney of the Company (with full power of substitution and delegation) in the Company's name and on the Company's behalf and as the Company's act and deed to sign or execute all deeds instruments and documents or take continue or defend any proceedings which may be required by the Bank or any Receiver pursuant to this deed or the exercise of any of their powers

**Appropriation**

10.1 **Subject** to Clause 10.2 the Bank may appropriate all payments received for the account of the Company in reduction of any part of the Company's Obligations as the Bank decides

10.2 **The** Bank may open a new account or accounts upon the Bank receiving actual or constructive notice of any charge or interest affecting the Property. Whether or not the Bank opens any such account no payment received by the Bank after receiving such notice shall (if followed by any payment out of or debit to the relevant account) be appropriated towards or have the effect of discharging any part of the Company's Obligations outstanding at the time of receiving such notice

**Preservation of other Security and Rights and Further Assurance**

11.1 **This** deed is in addition to any other security present or future held by the Bank for the Company's Obligations and shall not merge with or prejudice such other security or any contractual or legal rights of the Bank

11.2 **The** Company will at its own cost at the Bank's request execute any deed or document and take any action required by the Bank to perfect this security or further to secure on the Property the Company's Obligations

**Memorandum and Articles of Association**

12 **The** Company certifies that this deed does not contravene the Company's Memorandum and Articles of Association

**Notices**

13.1 **Any** notice or demand by the Bank may be served personally on any director or the secretary of the Company or may be sent by post or fax or delivered to the Company at the Company's address last known to the Bank

13.2 **A** notice or demand by the Bank by post shall be deemed served on the day after posting

13.3 **A** notice or demand by the Bank by fax shall be deemed served at the time of sending

**Governing Law**

14 **This** deed shall be governed by and construed in accordance with English law

**Interpretation**

15.1 **The** expressions "Company" and "Bank" where the context admits include their respective successors in title and assigns

15.2 **Interest** will be calculated both before and after demand or judgment on a daily basis and compounded according to agreement or in the absence of agreement monthly on such days as the Bank may select

15.3 **References** to the "Property" include any part of it

15.4 **References** to freehold and leasehold property include all covenants and rights affecting or concerning the same

15.5 **Each** of the provisions of this deed shall be severable and distinct from one another and if one or more of such provisions is invalid or unenforceable the remaining provisions shall not in any way be affected

**In Witness** of which this deed has been duly executed

| | | |
|---|---|---|
| | ) | ______________________ |
| **Signed** and **Delivered** as a deed by | ) | Director |
| the Company acting by a director | ) | ______________________ |
| and its secretary or two directors | ) | Secretary/Director |

For and on behalf of the Bank

______________________

Duly Authorised Official

**Questions**

When will a floating charge become fixed?

Give some examples of the contents of the articles of association.

FOUR

# FORMATION *of a* CONTRACT

*Study Topics*

**The essentials of a contract - agreement, consideration and intention to enter into legal relations**
**The rules of consideration**
**The exception to the rule of acceptance that the offeror must receive the acceptance**

The law is concerned with relationships between parties. In business the most common relationship is the contractual one, because obviously business consists of buying and selling goods and an important contract is that for the sale or purchase of something. Apart from that, organisations employ people and so the contract of employment is an important subject in business law.

In everyday life contracts are important because, in addition to buying and selling goods and land and employment contracts, a person is entering into contract to travel on a train or bus, to purchase insurance cover for his life or his home and its contents, or to enter into a contract of hire in respect of a car or a television set.

A contract may be expressed or implied. An expressed contract will arise when the parties consciously and intentionally enter into an agreement. An implied contract is one which can be assumed to exist because of the surrounding circumstances.

All these situations give rise to contractual relationships and so we must consider some aspects of contracts. It is probably only right that it should be generally agreed that if A promises to do something for B then B should be able to hold him to his promise and to recover compensation from A if A fails to do what he has promised to do. Therefore a contract is usually described as a legally binding agreement. A legally binding agreement is one which can be enforced in a court of law, thus A can sue B if he does not perform his part of the agreement or conversely B can sue A.

Before the claimant can successfully sue the defendant in an action for breach of contract the claimant must be able to prove to the satisfaction of the court that indeed there was a contract. In order to do that reference must be made to some essentials of a contract. The main essentials of a contract are the intention of the parties that their agreement shall be legally binding, the agreement between the parties and consideration, which is usually, but not always, money. This must be provided by the claimant.

## *Essentials of a Contract*

### Intention

It was stated earlier that a contract is described as a legally binding agreement. It follows therefore that there may be agreements that are not legally binding. Whether or not an agreement is legally binding - in other words whether or not a legal action can be brought in respect of it – may depend on:

1. the intention of the parties;
2. an Act of Parliament;
3. whether or not it is a social or domestic agreement.

The parties themselves may agree that an agreement reached between them shall not have any legal repercussions. This is usually effected by inserting an "honour clause" in the agreement. An example would be where a person completes a football pool coupon and signs at the bottom. The printed words at the bottom of the coupon usually contain the words: "This transaction shall be binding in honour only". It follows therefore that if some difficulty arises in regard to the football pool coupon no legal action can be brought in respect of it. In addition large companies can sometimes agree that their agreements shall not have any legal force, so that in the event of a disagreement no legal action will be brought by either party. In *Rose and Frank Company v Crompton and Brothers Ltd (1923)* the Court of Appeal held that the agreement between the parties was not a binding contract because the parties had expressed an intention not to create legal relations. In the contract these words appeared: "This arrangement is not entered into, nor is this memorandum written, as a formal or legal agreement, and shall not be subject to legal jurisdiction in the Law Courts either of the United States or England; that it is only a definite expression and record of the purpose and intention of the three parties concerned, to which they each honourably pledge themselves with the fullest confidence based on past business with each other; that it will be carried through by each of the three parties with mutual loyalty and friendly co-operation".

It is quite common where the parties are in business for them to agree that in the event of dispute this shall be resolved by recourse to arbitration rather than to a court of law.

Some Acts of Parliament decide whether a particular agreement shall be legally binding or not. An example is the *Law Reform (Miscellaneous Provisions) Act 1970* in which Section 1 provides that an agreement between two persons to marry one another shall not under the Law of England and Wales have effect as a contract giving rise to legal rights and no action shall lie in England and Wales of breach of such an agreement, whatever the law applicable to the agreement. Thus it is no longer possible as it was before 1970 for a party who has entered into an agreement to marry and who has been jilted, to sue the other party.

Finally there are a number of social and domestic agreements; these agreements are made by parties who have never given any thought to taking legal action if their agreement should not be complied with. Examples would be a "car pool" agreement between neighbours, an invitation to dinner, meeting a person outside a bingo hall or an agreement between a husband and wife whereby the husband agrees to pay a certain sum of money weekly to the wife for housekeeping. In *Balfour v Balfour (1919)* the House of Lords held that an agreement between a husband and wife "is not a contract because the parties did not intend that it should be attended by legal consequences". Of course that will not preclude a wife from claiming against her husband if she is not adequately maintained by him; nor does it preclude a husband and wife from entering into a binding contract in certain circumstances.

So the first essential requirement of a binding agreement is that the parties must intend their agreement to be carried out and would expect legal consequences if it were not. The second essential is the agreement itself.

### The Agreement

The courts, in practice, are not usually concerned with the manner in which an agreement was entered into by the parties. They are only interested in whether or not the parties were in agreement. However an agreement may be analysed by considering its two constituent parts – the offer and the acceptance of that offer. Sometimes it is not clear who made the offer and who accepted it. In *Simpkins v Pays (1955*) Sellers J held binding an agreement between A, a paying boarder at B's house, B and B's granddaughter C. They entered a fashion competition in a Sunday newspaper each week, each filling in one line, but the entry was sent in B's name. Sellers J found that there was an agreement that, whichever line won, all should share equally and that A was entitled to receive one third of the prize from B.

## *Offer*

The offer itself must be certain, it must be notified to the party to whom it was made (the offeree) although an offer may be made to no one person in particular (as in the reward cases).

### Offer to the World at Large

*Carlill v Carbolic Smoke Ball Co (1893)* QB. The defendants who sold the medical preparation "The Carbolic Smoke Ball" inserted in the *Pall Mall Gazette* an advertisement to the effect that £100 would be paid to anyone contracting influenza after having used the ball three times daily for two weeks. They also stated that £1,000 had been deposited at the Alliance Bank in Regent Street as evidence of their good faith. Mrs Carlill used the ball as directed and then found she had contracted influenza. She sued the manufacturers, claiming the £100. The case is important because it established the following.

1. An offer may be made not to a particular person but to the world at large.
2. The offer was intended to be binding because the defendants had deposited a sum of money at the bank.
3. Mrs Carlill had accepted the offer by complying with its terms.
4. Mrs Carlill had provided consideration by using the smoke ball and this conferred a benefit on the manufacturers because their sales would be increased.

## *Invitation to Treat*

An offer must be distinguished from situations in which it may appear that an offer is being made, for example the display of goods in a shop window or on the shelves of a supermarket are not offers. They are invitations for the public to make offers for them (invitations to treat).

*Pharmaceutical Society of Great Britain v Boots (1958)* QB. A sale of goods occurs when an agreement is made between the seller and the buyer. Therefore if the seller makes the offer the sale is concluded when the buyer accepts or vice versa. This case hinged on whether or not the display of goods on the shelves of a supermarket constituted offers. If they were offers the offer could be said to have been accepted on each occasion when the customer took the article from the shelf and a sale would be made several times within the supermarket. The court decided that the display of goods on the shelves is only an offer to treat or an invitation to the public to make an offer for the goods. Therefore the sale takes place once only, when the customer proffers his money for the goods at the cash desk and the money is accepted.

*Fisher v Bell (1961)* QB decided a similar point in relation to goods on display in a shop window. It is the customer who offers to buy the goods and he may offer whatever he wishes for the goods. It is, of course, up to the shopkeeper whether or not to accept the customer's offer. Thus if there is only one item in stock in a discontinued line, this prevents the shopkeeper from being in breach of contract twice if, say, three customers want to buy it.

The supply of information or a statement of intention, for example to hold an auction sale, is not on offer.

*Harris v Nickerson (1873)* QB. The defendant, an auctioneer, advertised in the London papers that certain articles would be sold by him at Bury St Edmonds on a certain day. Harris went to the sale but the articles he was interested in bidding for were not put up for sale. He sued the auctioneer to recover compensation for two days' loss of time. He failed, because it was held that there was no contract between the parties as Nickerson had merely stated his intention to sell certain articles and there was no offer capable of being accepted.

## *Notification of an Offer*

The offeree must know that the offer has been made, because a person cannot accept an offer if he does not know that it has been made.

1. A has lost his watch and advertises in the local paper: "Anyone finding my watch and returning it to me will receive £10." B reads the advertisement, finds and returns the watch and can now force A to give him the reward.
2. A has lost his watch and advertises in the local paper. B does not read the advertisement but nevertheless finds and returns the watch. Later finding out about the reward offer he asks A, who refuses to give him the £10. B can do nothing - there was no contract.

## *Revocation of an Offer*

An offer can be revoked at any time before it has been accepted. Thus the offeror can change his mind after making his offer but he must notify his cancellation of the offer to the offeree. If the offeror has promised to keep open the offer for a period of time and provided the offeree has given consideration for his promise then the offer cannot be revoked. This is known as buying an option. To post a letter of acceptance is a sufficient act of acceptance, but for revocation of an offer to be effective it must reach the offeree.

> In *Byrne v Van Tienhoven (1882)* T posted a letter in Cardiff on 1 October offering to sell B some tin plate. On 8 October T posted a letter revoking his offer. On 11 October B received a letter containing T's offer and immediately telegraphed his acceptance. On 20 October B received T's letter of revocation. The court held that a contract had not been made when B accepted the offer and the revocation took effect on 20 October which was too late.

As regards notification of revocation of an offer, in some cases the question may arise as to whether or not the offer has in fact been validly revoked. For example, if a notice of revocation has been delivered to the last known address of the offeree that would probably be effective if he had moved without informing the offeror of his new address. When an offer is made by public advertisement, a revocation will probably be sufficient if it is published in such a way that it is likely to come to the attention of those persons who saw the original advertisement.

## *Lapse*

An offer may come to an end by lapse of time. Obviously if the offeror when he made the offer stated that it had to be accepted within a stated period of time, then it follows that if the offer was not accepted within that period then the offer would lapse. If no time was stated by the offeror then the offer will lapse at the end of a reasonable time and what is reasonable will depend on circumstances, in particular probably the general market conditions in which the offer was made. In *Ramsgate VIctoria Hotel Company v Montefiore (1866)* M offered in June to buy shares from the hotel company.

In November, the company allotted shares to M, who refused to take them, contending that his offer had lapsed. It was held that the offer had indeed lapsed through passage of time as acceptance had not been made within a reasonable period of time from the date of the offer. The *Companies Act 1985* now applies.

## *Death of Offeror or Offeree*

On the death of either the offeror or the offeree before acceptance, again the offer will usually lapse. The situation may be different if there is a continuing contract as in the case where A has made a continuing offer to B to guarantee loans to be made by B to C. In that case if A dies unknown to B who makes a further loan to C then B might well be prejudiced if in fact A's death terminated the offer. Note that we are only considering the effect of death on the offer. If the offer has been accepted then a contract would exist between the parties and if either party then died after the contract had come in existence then probably the contract will be unaffected. This of course would not be so if a contract required personal services; for example a person has agreed to sing or to give a concert at a theatre.

## *Rejection*

It should always be remembered that the offeree may of course reject any offer made to him. If he does so then rejection is considered to put an end to the offer and the effect of this is that the offeree cannot subsequently change his mind and accept the offer. In this connection a counter offer is rather similar to a rejection and this will be mentioned when we deal with acceptance.

## *Acceptance*

The basic rule is that an offer must be accepted exactly as it stands and the acceptance must be completely in accordance with the terms of the offer.

## *Counter Offer*

If the person to whom the offer was addressed (offeree) accepts the offer subject to certain conditions, or if the acceptance is not exactly in accordance with the terms of the offer, then there will be no valid acceptance. This is known as a counter offer, and the effect is to destroy the original offer so that it is not possible for the original offeree (who made the counter offer) to change his mind and accept the original offer.

> *Hyde v Wrench (1840).* Wrench offered to sell his farm to Hyde for £1,000. Hyde made a counter offer of £950, which Wrench refused. Hyde then changed his mind and wrote that he would accept the original offer of £1,000 made by Wrench. The court held there was no contract because the counter offer by Hyde had destroyed the offer made by Wrench and it was not possible for Hyde, later, to accept that offer.

## *Notification of Acceptance*

The basic rule is that an acceptance must be brought to the notice of the offeror. If the words of acceptance are drowned by an aircraft flying overhead or if the telephone crackles so that the offeror does not hear or is not aware that the offeree has accepted his offer then there will be no agreement. An exception to the rule that the acceptance must be notified to the offeror occurs in what are called the postal cases.

## *Postal Acceptance*

It is only reasonable that the offeror should be notified by the other party that he has accepted; but if the postal system is used then the offer is deemed to have been accepted when the letter of acceptance is posted. If the letter of acceptance never reaches the offeror there is still a valid contract in existence.

> *Household Fire Insurance Co v Grant (1879).* In a majority verdict the court decided that an offer is accepted when the letter of acceptance is posted even though, as in this case, the letter of acceptance did not reach the offeror. The view was that the Post Office is the common agent of both the offeror and the offeree. The moral of the story is - if you make an offer by post to someone, make sure that he does not intend to accept your offer if you are contemplating making the same offer to another person. The onus is placed upon the offeror. This decision was made purely on the grounds of expediency. Students often wonder how the posting of the letter of acceptance can be proved. There are many ways in which this may be done but quite simply if the posting cannot be proved then there is no point in going to court. Every litigant in any court action must be able to prove his case to the satisfaction of the court. If he thinks he cannot do so then he should be advised to save his money.

A court may rely on the word alone of the witness - if there is some corroborative evidence then he may, more readily, be believed. The burden of proof is that the court must be satisfied "on the balance of probabilities" and not, as in a criminal court, "beyond all reasonable doubt".

Note that although an acceptance will be effective when the letter of acceptance is posted a revocation of an offer will not be made merely by posting it but will only be effective when the offeree receives the notice of revocation.

## *Method of Acceptance by Offeror*

When the offeror makes his offer he may state the manner in which the acceptance must be made, for example by letter or telex. The offeree can then accept only in that way as presumably the offeror has made the requirement for his own protection. An offeror may stipulate acceptance by silence as in *Felthouse v Bindley (1862).* In that case the plaintiff wished to buy a horse belonging to his nephew and wrote to him stating: "I will offer you £X for the horse and if I hear no more from you then I shall consider that the horse is mine." The nephew did not reply to the letter but instead he sold the horse and the action was brought by the plaintiff claiming that he had a contract with the nephew. He was unsuccessful as the court held that there was no valid contract for the sale of the horse. There must be some positive action taken by the offeree in order to make a valid acceptance and it is not possible, or indeed fair, for the offeror to attempt to force an acceptance from the offeree.

Once an offer has been validly made and the offeree has made an effective acceptance there can be said to be an enforceable agreement between the parties. Valid agreement is one which the parties intend should be legally binding. However, there is one other element which is peculiar to systems of law based on the English common law, that is consideration. This has been defined by Pollock as "the price for which a promise is bought". It does not usually cause the courts much difficulty in establishing that consideration is present because it is the element of exchange in a bargain. Only when a person has made a gift to another person will there be no consideration. If there is no consideration and the party who has made the promise breaks it (breach of contract) then the other party will not be able to sue successfully as he gave no consideration in return for the promise of the other. This is known as a bare promise and is not enforceable in English law, but maybe enforced under French law. A says to B, "I will give you my car on Friday." Presumably B will be happy to receive the car, so they are in agreement. However, if A breaks his promise and fails to give B his car, then B can do nothing about it. He, B, has given no consideration in return for A's promise.

There is no good reason why a person who makes a promise to another should not have to pay compensation to the other if he breaks his promise, but that is not the case in English law. However, there is an additional body of rules called Equity which is occasionally brought into use by the judge, purely at his discretion. If it can be shown that to keep strictly according to the letter of the law would result in injustice the judge may diverge slightly from the strict letter of the law. Thus if A makes B a promise and B does some act he would not have done if he had not relied on A's promise then A may be barred (estopped) from going back on his promise notwithstanding that B gave no consideration. This is known as the rule in the *High Trees* case and is an example of a rule of equity being brought into operation.

Sometimes the rule is called "equitable or promissory estoppel", and was first stated in *Central London Property Trust v High Trees House (1947).* In 1937 C let to H a block of flats for 99 years at £2,500 a year. In 1940, owing to war, very few flats were let and C agreed to reduce the rent to £1,250. In 1945, C sued for arrears of rent at the rate of £2,500. It was held that, as the agreement for the reduction of rent had been acted upon, C could not claim the full rent, but that it was only operative during the conditions which had given rise to it. As the flats had been fully let in 1945 the full rent was payable from then. It means that the promisor is estopped or prevented from going back on his word. It is looked upon as a slight inroad into the doctrine of consideration, but it does not in any way do away with that doctrine. In *Combe v Combe* it was called "a shield rather than a sword".

*Combe v Combe (1951)* KB. After divorce proceedings the husband and wife entered into an agreement by which the husband promised to pay to the wife £100 per annum. The husband failed to do this and the wife sued him. In the High Court the wife was successful because although she had given no consideration for the husband's promise the judge followed the principle in the High Trees case. However, on appeal Denning LJ, who was responsible for the principle in the High Trees case when he was in the High Court, stated that it does not do away with the need for consideration in English law. It may only be used to prevent a party from insisting on his strict legal rights, when it would be unjust to allow him to enforce them, having regard to the dealings which had taken place between the parties. The principle may not be used as a basis action but only as a defence.

Apart from these exceptional cases a contract must have consideration and a party will not be able to successfully sue in respect of a broken promise unless he can prove that, in return for the promise, he provided consideration.

### Form of Consideration

Consideration will usually take the form of the payment of a sum of money or the doing of some act. However, as was mentioned earlier, a right is a valuable thing because it can be enforced in a court of law. Consequently if a person has promised to pay a sum of money or to do an act, that will be acceptable as consideration, because the person to whom the promise was made has a right to sue the promisor if he breaks his promise.

Thus if A says to B, "Do you wish to buy my car for £500?" and B says "Yes," there is a valid enforceable contract. Nothing is required to be in writing. A has promised B his car and B has promised to give A £500. That is all that is needed. Of course it would be preferable if there were some witnesses, because A or B might deny what they said. On the other hand, both parties could go to court without witnesses and leave it to the judge to decide which party he chooses to believe. The promise of each of the parties will be consideration.

### Consideration Must be Real but need not be Adequate

Consideration must be real but need not be commensurate to the value of what the other party has done or promised to do. The court will never enquire as to whether any consideration is adequate in relation to the value of the subject matter of the contract. This merely reiterates the principle of freedom of contract. If A wishes to sell his £500 car for £1 that is A's business. Provided B has paid a £1 or has promised to pay him that sum, there will be a valid contract, because B has provided consideration in return for A's promise to sell him his car.

On the other hand the consideration must be real and in the opinion of the court of some value. In *White v Bluett (1853)* a son's promise to stop being a nuisance to his father was held to be not good consideration. However, in *Chappell v Nestle and Company (1959)* some empty chocolate wrappers sent to the chocolate company by the public were held by the court to be valuable consideration.

### It Must be Something more than the Person to whom the Original Promise was made has already Promised to do

*Stilk v Myrick (1809).* The crew of a ship sailing to the Baltic and back to London had entered into an agreement to sail on the round trip and to receive payment at the rate of £5 per month. During the voyage two of the crew deserted and so the captain promised to share the wages of the deserters amongst the crew remaining on board ship. When the voyage was completed the captain failed to pay the extra amount he had promised, and in court it was settled that he was not liable on his promise because no consideration had been given in return for it. The crew who remained on board ship had done nothing more than they were already bound to do by the terms of their contract. If they could have proved that they had done extra work (which they could not do in this case) that would have been consideration for the promise of the captain.

### Payment of a Smaller Sum

Payment of a smaller sum will not discharge liability to pay a larger unless the smaller sum was paid earlier than the agreement required or in a different form of place from that originally intended. This point arises where A has lent B £100 and B repays £75. A then says to B, "I will release you from payment of the balance." A therefore has made a promise to B but cannot be held to that promise because B has not given any consideration. However if the loan of £100 was for a period of three weeks and B repays £75 in two weeks then he would be providing consideration because he would be conferring a benefit on A by letting him have some of the debt earlier than was necessary. Now A will not be able to go back on his promise. Also the High Trees principle could apply here if B can show that, in reliance on A's promise not to sue him for the balance of the £100, he, B, did something he would not have done if A had not made to him that promise.

**Consideration Must not be Past**

Past consideration occurs when it has been given or executed before the promise is made. Thus if X gives Y £500 and Y promises to go to London to transact some business for X this is executed consideration since the promise to go to London is given at the time the £500 is handed over.

If Y without any arrangement with X goes to London and transacts some business for X, and when he returns X promises to pay Y £500 for what he has accomplished in London, this is past consideration because Y has provided his services (consideration) before X has agreed to accept and pay for them.

In this chapter we have been looking at the main essentials of a contract. It must be remembered that a contract is an agreement and that an agreement takes place in the minds of the parties. It may be necessary to have some evidence that an agreement has been reached, but in most cases written evidence is not needed. Also the agreement may take place without the contract being performed. Of course it will have to be performed but that may be some time after the agreement (or contract) has been made. We have seen that a legally binding contract will only exist if:

1. the parties intend their agreement to have legal effect;
2. the parties are in agreement;
3. there is consideration present provided by the party who seeks to enforce the contract (plaintiff).

## *Formation of a Contract*

A number of people believe, quite wrongly, that a contract must be made in writing and be signed by the party making it. This is an understandable mistake because a very large number of contracts are in writing. But the reason is rather that it is sometimes more convenient to have a written record of the terms of the contract than that the law requires it so. In fact a contract may be made by word of mouth or even by implication, as when a passenger steps on to a bus and thus enters into a contract with the bus company.

The law only requires a contract to be in writing in a small number of cases, for example, a share transfer, a hire purchase agreement, a bill of exchange (i.e. a cheque) or a contract for the purchase or sale of land. As regards the last example the law has recently been changed by the *Law of Property (Miscellaneous Provisions) Act 1989*. It provides that

1. a deed may be written on any substance, not only paper or parchment;
2. if an individual is executing the deed there is no need for a seal to be used although the document itself must state that it is a deed. Companies will presumably still have to use their seals;
3. two witnesses are required to attest the parties' signatures;
4. the contract for the sale of land must incorporate all the terms agreed by the parties together with all the signatures of the parties.

It is worth noting here that Section 7 of the *Electronic Communications Act 2000* gives electronic signatures explicit recognition. With the amount of business being conducted electronically via web pages and e-mail, such a move is intended to reduce the need for signatures on paper in these circumstances.

## *Invalidating Factors*

It can be said that a contract (a legally binding agreement) cannot exist unless all three requirements are present. However the converse does not hold good: sometimes even though the three essentials are present there may still not be a legally binding contract because some other invalidating factor might prevent a contract coming into existence. For example, force might be used to get one of the parties to agree; the parties might be in mistake; one party might deceive the other; the contract might be for an illegal purpose. In all these cases even though the three essentials might be present, the contract would be either void or voidable because of these additional invalidating factors.

**Questions**

What are the exceptions to the rules of acceptance?

What is a deed?

What is a counter offer and what is its effect?

FIVE

# TERMS *of the* CONTRACT

*Study Topics*

**Difference between a condition and a warranty**
**The effect of the *Unfair Contract Terms Act***
**Fundamental breach**

Every contract contains terms or stipulations. Usually these are expressly stated in the contract. However, sometimes terms are implied into a contract. Such terms may be implied by fact, by law or by custom.

## *Terms Implied by Fact*

These are terms which the court decides that partners must have intended to include. At one time the test was: "would an officious bystander have assumed that the parties would have intended to include some term". Now the courts seem to insist that the implication must be obvious to both parties.

## *Terms Implied by Law*

The best example of terms implied by law is the preparation of the *Sale of Goods Act 1979*. That Act implies terms into every contract for the sale of goods, primarily that the goods should not be defective.

## *Terms Implied by Custom*

When parties have traded in a particular market for a period of time they will be assumed to go along with any custom of the market. Thus in *Smith v Wilson (1862)* it was proved that by local custom when a sale of 1000 rabbits took place this meant 1200 rabbits. Everyone surely has heard of "a baker's dozen", that is 13.

## *Express Terms*

These may be a condition or a warranty. A condition is a fundamental term, breach of which allows the plaintiff to rescind the contract (that is, to bring it to an end and recover his or her money). A warranty is a less important term, breach of which does not give rise to rescission but only to an action for damages. Whether a term is a condition or warranty depends upon the intention of the parties, which is ascertained by examining their statements and the surrounding circumstances.

*Behn v Burness (1863).* A ship, the *Martaban*, was chartered to transport coal from Newport to Hong Kong. The charter party described the ship as "now in the port of Amsterdam" whereas in fact the ship was at Niewdiep, about 62 miles from Amsterdam. The ship was late in arriving at Newport, and the charterers refused to load it. It was held that the charterers were justified in their refusal. In a charter party, the situation of the ship when the charter was made was a term of great commercial importance, and had to be treated as a condition.

*Schuler AG v Wickham Machine Tool Sales (1973).* A concluded a four year contract with B giving sole rights to sell panel presses in England. One of the contractual provisions stated that it was a condition that B's sales representative should visit six named firms weekly, seeking orders. On a few occasions, B's sales reps did not do so. A sought to repudiate the contract on the ground that even a single failure was a breach of condition. The House of Lords held that such minor breaches did not entitle A to repudiate the contract; the clause was considered to be so unreasonable that the parties could not have intended it to be a condition giving a right to repudiate for breach, as opposed to a warranty giving a right to sue for damages.

## *Complex or Intermediate Terms*

Terms found in certain contracts may be neither conditions nor warranties, but what are known as complex, intermediate or "innominate" terms. These can best be described by reference to the following important case.

> *Hong Kong Fir Shipping Co Ltd v Kawaski Kisen Kaisha Ltd* (1962). In that case, a time charter party provided that the vessel was to be "in every way fitted for ordinary cargo service". The ship kept breaking down because its engine room staff were incompetent and inadequate, and accordingly it was unseaworthy. It was held by the Court of Appeal that this did not entitle the charterers to repudiate the contract since the clause as to the ship's fitness did not, in the circumstances, amount to a condition. The Court stated that there are many contractual undertakings of a complex character which cannot be characterised as being conditions or warranties, such as the shipowner's promise to provide a seaworthy ship. These terms will combine the nature of a condition and warranty insofar as in some events the breach of such an obligation may entitle the innocent party to rescind the contract and in other events the breach only entitles the innocent party to claim damages and not rescission of the contract.

> *Cehave NV v Bremer Handelsgesellschaft mbH (1976).* A purchased from B citrus pulp pellets for making cattle food. A contract term provided for "shipment to be made in good condition". The cargo was to be delivered by several consignments. One such consignment arrived at Rotterdam when the market price had fallen and 1260 out of 3293 tons were found to be damaged. A rejected the whole cargo and claimed the price of £100,000. However, C purchased the goods from B at £33,720 and resold them to A at that price. The Court of Appeal held that the term was not a condition within the meaning of the Sale of Goods Act; it was an "intermediate term". Lord Denning MR observed: "If a small portion of the whole cargo was not in good condition and arrived a little unsound, it should be met by a price allowance. The buyer should not have the right to reject the whole cargo unless it was serious or substantial."

The court will seek to determine the quality of the contractual term by weighing the seriousness of the act or event by which the term has been in fact broken. A ship, for example, may be technically unseaworthy because it is short of one able seaman; but that does not entitle the other party to repudiate the contract.

## *Standard Form Contracts and Exclusion Clauses*

It is now common practice in some areas for one party to present to the other certain terms, usually set out in printed form. The advantages of this system are obvious, as it avoids the necessity of establishing the terms of the contract each time an agreement is reached. In this way a standard pattern of dealing is set up. Such standard terms are to be found on railway tickets, insurance contracts, and contracts between suppliers of goods and services and the purchasers of these. When there is a business document given by one party and received by the other as the document containing the terms of the contract, the offeror is under no obligation to call the offeree's attention to all the terms of the document, unless the terms are printed in such a manner or are in such position as to mislead a reasonably careful business person.

*Roe v R A Naylor Ltd (1971).* R ordered four lots of timber from N's traveller. The traveller left a sold note setting out the sale and containing a clause "Goods are sold subject to their being on hand and at liberty when the order reaches the head office." N did not deliver the timber, and, on being sued by R, pleaded the clause set out above. R did not know of the clause and had not read it. It was held that, R was bound by the clause, unless it was so printed that from its position in the document and the size of the type an ordinary careful business person, reading the document with reasonable care, might miss it.

When the offeree has signified his or her acceptance by signing a document presented by the offeror, the offeree cannot plead ignorance of the terms of the offer, in the absence of fraud or misrepresentation, even if he or she is in fact ignorant of them.

*L'Estrange v F Graucob Ltd (1934).* The proprietress of a cafe bought an automatic cigarette vending machine from the defendants. She signed a document which contained a number of clauses in small print, amongst them a clause excluding "any express or implied condition statement or warranty, statutory or otherwise, not stated therein". She refused to pay the price on the ground that the machine did not work and contended inter alia that she was not bound by the exclusion clause as she had not read it. It was held that the clause was binding on her.

If the contractual document is signed as a result of the offeree's oral misrepresentation of one of its terms, the offeree will not be able to rely on that term.

*Curtis v Chemical Cleaning & Dyeing Co (1951).* C took a dress to D to be cleaned and was asked to sign a receipt which contained, among other terms, a clause: "This article is accepted on condition that the company is not liable for any damage howsoever arising." C asked why she had to sign and was told that D would not accept liability for damage to beads or sequins. She then signed. The dress was returned stained. It was held that D could not rely on the clause, because C's signature was obtained by misrepresentation of the effect of the document.

Similarly, if at the time when the contract is made a person gives an oral promise which cannot be reconciled with a term in the printed contract, the oral promise takes priority over the printed clause.

> *Mendelsohn v Normand Ltd (1979).* M left his car in N's garage. Contrary to the rules of the garage, the car attendant who took the car over told M he must not lock the car. M informed the attendant that there was valuable property in the car and the attendant promised to lock the car after he had moved it. By the terms of the ticket which the attendant gave M, N excluded responsibility for the loss of contents of the car. A suitcase containing valuables was stolen from the car. It was held that N was liable. Though the attendant had no actual authority to promise to lock the car, he had ostensible authority to make a statement concerning the safety of the car and its contents. The printed exclusion clause was repugnant to the express oral promise and could not be relied upon by N.

Where printed conditions in a contract are repugnant to a binding oral promise they do not provide exemption from liability for breach of that promise.

> *J Evans & Son (Portsmouth) Ltd v Andrea Merzario Ltd (1976).* The plaintiffs were importers of machines. For some years they had employed the defendants, who were forwarding agents, to make the transport arrangements for the carriage of the machines to England. Until 1967, the machines were packed in crates and always shipped under deck to prevent rusting. In that year it was decided to use containers in future instead of crates, and the defendant's manager gave the plaintiffs an oral assurance that if containers were used the goods would, as before, be shipped under deck. On that basis the plaintiffs agreed to the changeover and dealings continued. In 1968, due to the defendants' fault, the plaintiffs' machines, in a container, were shipped on deck. The goods, worth nearly £3000, were lost overboard. The plaintiffs sued for breach of contract. The defendants claimed inter alia that there was no contractual promise that the goods would be carried under deck. It was held by the Court of Appeal that the oral assurance amounted to an enforceable contractual promise.

### Battle of Forms

In business transactions a contract may be entered into by each party exchanging a printed form of contract with the other party. It should never be forgotten that if one receives a printed form and there is a clause with which one does not agree then this may be altered or deleted. It is only what actually appears on the form which is eventually signed that is binding on the parties. The situation where each party sends the other a printed form of a contract containing standard clauses is sometimes referred to as the "battle of forms". The leading case on this point is *Butler Machine Tool Co Ltd v Ex-Cell-o Corporation (England) Ltd (1979)*.

> In *Butler Machine Tool Co Ltd v Ex-Cell-o Corporation (England) Ltd* (1979), the plaintiffs quoted to the defendants a price for a machine tool and their quotation was stated to be subject to the seller's standard terms which included a price variation clause. In addition the quotation made it clear that their standard terms and conditions should prevail over any terms contained in the buyers' order. The buyers ordered the product and their printed order was on the buyers' standard terms which did not include a price variation clause. The buyers' order form stated on a tear-off slip: "We accept your order on the Terms and Conditions stated thereon". This was intended to be signed by the sellers and this was duly signed and returned to the buyers; a covering letter stated that this order was accepted in accordance with the original quotation.
>
> When the sellers delivered the product they relied on the price variation clause in their standard terms and asked for a price increase of nearly £3,000. The buyers argued that their terms applied and these made no provision for a price increase. When the case came before the Court of Appeal that court held that the plaintiff sellers' quotation was an offer. Ex-Cell-O's order was a counter offer and the return of the acknowledgement slip by Butler amounted to an acceptance of the counter offer. Therefore the contract was made on the terms put forward to Ex-Cell-O. It could be argued that by accepting the offer from Butler, Ex-Cell-O had agreed to the terms of the offer. However it could also be argued that EX-Cell-O had not accepted the offer on the same terms as the offer and so had in fact rejected the offer.

What is certain is that this situation is fraught with difficulties and maybe the courts will have no choice but to adopt the established solution, *Hyde v Wrench (1840)*.

In order to avoid such difficulties the party must ensure that, when exchanging forms containing standard terms, each party must study closely the other party's form to make sure that new terms to the agreements have not been introduced.

## Exclusion or Exemption Clauses

Amongst these standard terms is often to be found a clause which seeks to exempt or restrict the liability of the party who inserted the clause. For such exemption clauses to be valid and enforceable at common law the courts have laid down certain principles, including the following.

1. The existence of such a clause must be brought to the attention of the other

party. It matters not whether he or she has read it, but at least he or she must know that the clause exists. Thus the holder of a ticket should be notified on the ticket that "the conditions of contract are obtainable on request".

2. Such exemption clause or references to them must be contained in "a contractual document and not in a mere voucher or receipt".

*Chapelton v Barry UDC (1940).* C hired a chair from the council, paid for it and was given a ticket which he put in his pocket unread. The chair collapsed and C was injured. The ticket had a clause that the council were not be liable for accidents or damage. It was held that this was not binding on C.

*Thornton v Shoe Lane Parking Ltd (1971).* Mr Thornton wished to park his car in a multi-storey automatic car park belonging to the defendants. A traffic light at the entrance of the car park showed red. A ticket was extruded from a machine. When Mr Thornton took the ticket the light turned green and the car was taken up. When Mr Thornton collected the car, an accident occurred and he was injured. The defendants pleaded that the ticket contained a notice in small print that it was issued "subject to the conditions of issue as displayed on the premises", and that these conditions, displayed inside the garage, contained a clause exempting the defendant from liability for personal injury. Mr Thorton had not read the small print. It was held that the exempting clause on the conditions did not protect the defendants. First, Lord Denning MR held that the contract was concluded when Mr Thornton positioned his car at the appointed place and the light turned green, and the ticket was only a receipt which could not alter the terms of the contract. Second, all three judges of the Court of Appeal agreed that the defendants had failed sufficiently to bring to the notice of Mr Thornton the limitation of liability.

3. Finally, the clause must be notified to the other party either before or at the time the contract is made. When the guest at a hotel read the notice, which was affixed to his bedroom door, after he had booked in to the hotel, the court held it was ineffective.

*Olley v Marlborough Court Ltd (1949.)* The plaintiff and her husband took a room in a residential hotel owned by the defendants. At the reception desk they were asked to pay a week in advance. They did so and went to their bedroom, in which a notice was displayed stating that the proprietors did not hold themselves responsible for the loss or theft of articles unless handed to the manageress for safe keeping. Owing to the negligence of the defendants' personnel, a stranger gained entrance into the hotel and stole articles from the plaintiff's room when she was absent. Held, the defendants were liable. The contract was concluded at the reception desk and the terms of the notice in the bedroom were not incorporated in it.

## *Doctrine of Fundamental Breach*

This doctrine, as developed by the courts, had provided that a party who committed a fundamental breach of contract (in other words, who had done something fundamentally different from what he or she had contracted to do) could rely on an exemption clause to exclude or limit his or her liability for resulting loss. Attempts were made in the cases to distinguish a fundamental breach of condition so that an exemption clause protecting only the latter would be ineffective to exclude liability for the former.

The consequences flowing from a fundamental breach of contract had given rise to judicial controversy. On the one hand it was considered that such a breach brought the contract to an end and thereby defeated the exemption clause. On the other hand it was thought that the question was one of construction of the contract, which would enable a court to uphold an exemption clause in a proper case. In 1966, the House of Lords (casting doubt on earlier cases) accepted the latter view in the following case.

*Suisse Atlantique v Rotterdamsche Kolen Centrale (1966).* The defendants chartered a ship from the plaintiff shipowners for "two years' continuous voyages". The contract provided for demurrage of $1000 a day to be paid by the charterers if the vessel was detained in port longer than the loading time allowed under its terms. Delays were considerable. Although demurrage was paid, the shipowners sustained a loss of freight beyond the sums received. They claimed damages, arguing that the delay was deliberate, enabling them to treat the contract as repudiated, that therefore the demurrage terms did not apply, and that they could sue for their full loss. They also contended that in the light of previous decisions on fundamental breach and exemption clauses, the demurrage clause could not extend to the serious breach in this case. It was held, first, that a fundamental breach of contract does not automatically defeat an exemption clause, and that the issue involves construction of the contract; second, that the demurrage term was not essentially an exemption clause but rather a provision for liquidation damages, though it was sufficient to cover the breaches here; and, third, that even if the breaches had given rise to an entitlement to treat the contract as repudiated, this had not been done by the shipowners. The contract, including the demurrage clause, consequently remained in force.

In 1970 the case of *Harbutt's Plasticine v Wayne Tank Pump Co* was decided by the

Court of Appeal. The Court of Appeal purported to apply the judgement of the House of Lords in the Suisse Atlantique, by which of course it was bound; though the effect of the two cases appeared to be as follows.

1. There is no breach of contract more fundamental than a breach of condition.
2. A breach will usually be fundamental where it renders performance completely different from that contemplated by the contract.
3. If the innocent party chooses to repudiate the contract, or the breach ends it automatically, any exemption clause falls with it.
4. If the innocent party elects to continue with the contract the exemption clause may survive:
   i. if it is clear and unambiguous;
   ii. if it neither creates absurdity nor defeats the object of the contract; and
   iii. if the party relying on it has not deviated from the contract.

The Court of Appeal seemed in effect to be reverting to the law before the 1966 House of Lords decision. However, in the House of Lords judgement in *Photo Production Ltd v Securicor Transport Ltd (1980)* the Court of Appeal decision in Harbutt's Plasticine was over ruled as being inconsistent with the Suisse Atlantique authority.

> *Photo Production Ltd v Securicor Transport Ltd (1980).* The contract between Photo Production Ltd and Securicor provided for a night patrol of a factory, the principal hazards being fire and theft. During his patrol an employee of the security company deliberately started a fire which destroyed the factory and its contents, causing a loss of over £600,000. Securicor was sued on the ground that it was vicariously liable for the act of its employee; and in turn it pleaded an exemption clause in the contract which provided:
>
> > Under no circumstances shall the company be responsible for any injurious act or default by any employee of the company unless such act or default could have been foreseen and avoided by the exercise of due diligence on the part of the company as his employer; nor in any event shall the company be responsible for any loss suffered by the customer through . . . fire . . . except insofar as such is solely attributable to the negligence of the company's employees acting within the course of their employment.
>
> The Court of Appeal had held that there had been a fundamental breach of the contract which prevented Securicor from relying on the exemption clause. The House of Lords reversed that decision and held:

1. there is no "rule of law" by which exemption clauses are eliminated, or deprived of effect, regardless of their terms, where there has been a "fundamental" breach of contract;
2. the question whether and to what extent an exemption clause is to be applied to any breach of contract is a matter of construction of the contract.

The House of Lords confirmed existence of the notion of fundamental breach of contract, which it recognised had served a useful purpose. It referred to the *Unfair Contract Terms Act 1977* (see below) as having dealt with the problem of exemption clauses in relation to contracts with consumers and contracts of adherence, pointing out the contrast where commercial parties "were not of unequal bargaining power, and when risks were normally borne by insurance" where "the case for judicial intervention" was "undemonstrated" and where the parties' freedom to apportion the risks should be respected.

The House of Lords further held that, although there had been a breach of duty to have due and proper regard for the safety and security of the factory, the exemption clause applied. Such clauses had to be construed strictly. In this case, the exemption clause was clear. The risk more appropriately fell on the factory owners, who were more aware of its value and the fire precautions, and in a better position to insure economically. The clause was capable of being construed to cover the deliberate act of the employee, and Securicor's liability was successfully excluded.

Certain principles of contract law were enunciated in the *Photo Production* case, as follows.

1. Contracts are comprised of primary and secondary obligations (which may be express or implied).
2. Primary obligations are those duties owed by the parties to the contract.
3. Secondary obligations come into being when a primary obligation is broken by a party to the contract, for example to pay damages (though the parties may beforehand modify such obligations by limiting such sums).
4. Every failure to perform a primary obligation is a breach of contract, but the unfulfilled obligations of each party remain unchanged, save for two exceptions:
   i. fundamental breach: where the result of a breach of primary obligation is to deprive the innocent party of the substantial benefit of the contract which he or she was intended to have, so that such party may elect to put an end to the primary obligations of both parties;
   ii. breach of condition: where the breach of the primary obligation does not go to the root of the contract, but the parties have agreed beforehand that such breach will enable the innocent party to elect as under "fundamental breach" above.

All primary obligations thus remain alive unless the innocent party elects to end them.

5. Where there is such election as in the preceding point, then:
   i. for the unperformed primary obligations of the party in default is substituted (by implication of law) an obligation to pay damages to the innocent party;
   ii. the unperformed primary obligations of the innocent party are discharged.

Provided it is clear, precise and relevant, an exemption clause may be applicable in the two exceptional cases so as to exclude a secondary obligation to pay damages for an unperformed primary obligation.

*Ailsa Craig Fishing Co Ltd v Malvern Fishing Co Ltd (1983).* Due to the negligence of a security company, which had contracted to supervise vessels in a Scottish harbour, two vessels sank. The owners of the vessels sued the security company for negligence. The defendant sought to rely on a clause which limited to £1,000 its liability whether arising under the contract or at common law or in any other way for any loss or damage to the owners. It was held by the House of Lords that, whilst a limitation clause would be interpreted contra proferentem, the specially exacting standards which applied to exclusion and indemnity clauses did not apply. It was sufficient if the clause was clear and unambiguous. The clause in question was such and its meaning was unaffected by the existence of an unclear exclusion clause in the contract. Moreover the expression "at common law or in any other way" was wide enough to cover liability for negligence; consequently, the security company's liability was limited to £1,000.

## *Unfair Contract Terms Act 1977*

If there is liability in contract (or tort), consideration of an alleged exemption term apart, and if in fact the term is a part of the contract, and if on its true construction the term applies to the liability in question, the question arises whether the term is affected by the *Unfair Contract Terms Act 1977*.

That Act is a landmark in the field of contract law. It has the effect of imposing further limits on the extent to which civil liability for breach of contract or for negligence or other breach of duty can be avoided by means of contract terms and otherwise. The Act came into force on 1 February 1978. The following are the main provisions of the legislation.

## *Business Liability*

For the most part, the Act is concerned with terms that restrict or exclude business liability, that is liability for breach of obligations or duties arising:

1. from things done or to be done by a person in the course of a business; or
2. from the occupation or premises used for business purposes of the occupier.

The liability of an occupier of premises towards a person obtaining access to the premises for recreational or educational purposes (being liability for loss or damage suffered because of the dangerous state of the premises) is not a business liability of the occupier unless the granting of such access falls within the business purposes of the premises: Section 1(3) of the 1977 Act as amended by the *Occupiers' Liability Act 1984*. "Business" includes a profession and the activities of any government department or local or public authority.

## *Dealing as Consumer*

The Act is primarily concerned to afford protection to persons who deal as consumers. A party to a contract "deals as consumer" in relation to another party if:

1. he or she does not make the contract in the course of business;
2. the other party does make the contract in the course of business;
3. in the case of a contract governed by the law of sale of goods or hire purchase, the goods passing under or in pursuance of the contract are of a type ordinarily supplied for private use or consumption.

On a sale by auction or by competitive tender, the buyer is not in any circumstances to be regarded as dealing as consumer. In *Peter Symmons & Co v Cook (1981)* a partnership bought a Rolls-Royce from a car dealer. It was held that the firm had dealt as consumer when it made the purchase, and that to be in the course of business, the transaction "must form at the very least an integral part of the buyer's business or be necessarily incidental thereto".

## *Negligence Liability*

A person cannot be reference to any contract terms or to a notice given to persons generally or to particular persons exclude or restrict his or her liability for death or personal injury resulting from negligence. Section 2(1). "Personal injury" includes any disease and any impairment of physical or mental condition.

In the case of other loss or damage, a person cannot exclude or restrict his or her liability for negligence except insofar as the term or notice satisfies the test of reasonableness (see below). Section 2(2). Where a contract term or notice purports to exclude or restrict liability for negligence, a person's agreement to or awareness of it is not of itself to be taken as indicating his or her voluntary acceptance of any risk. Section 2(3).

## *Liability Arising in Contract*

As between contracting parties where one of them deals as consumer (as defined in the Act) or on the other's written standard terms of business then, as against that party, the other cannot by reference to any contract term:

1. when himself or herself is in breach of contract, exclude or restrict any liability of his or hers in respect of the breach; or
2. claim to be entitled:
   i. to render a contractual performance substantially different from that which was reasonably expected of him or her; or
   ii. in respect of the whole or any part of his or her contractual obligations, to render no performance at all, except insofar as the contract term satisfies the requirement of reasonableness.

## *Unreasonable Indemnity Clauses*

A person dealing as consumer cannot by reference to any contract term be made to indemnify another person (whether a party to the contract or not) in respect of liability that may be incurred by the other for negligence or breach of contract, except insofar as the contract term satisfies the requirement of reasonableness.

## *Guarantees*

In the case of goods of a type ordinarily supplied for private use or consumption, where loss or damage arises from the goods proving defective while in consumer use and results from the negligence of the person concerned in the manufacture or distribution of the goods, then liability for the loss or damage cannot be excluded or restricted by reference to any contract term or notice contained in it or operating by reference to a guarantee of the goods.

This provision does not apply as between the parties to a contract under or in pursuance of which possession or ownership of the goods passed.

## *Sale of Goods*

Although the 1977 Act makes provision also in relation to contracts for hire purchase and other supply of goods, we note here its provisions only in relation to the sale of goods.

Liability for breach of the obligations arising from Section 12 of the *Sale of Goods Act 1979* (seller's implied undertaking as to title, etc.) cannot be excluded or restricted by reference to any contract term.

As against a person dealing as consumer, liability for breach of the obligations arising from Sections 13, 14 or 15 of the 1979 Act (seller's implied undertakings as to conformity of goods with description or sample, or as to their quality or fitness for a particular purpose) cannot be excluded or restricted by reference to any contract term. But as against a person dealing otherwise as consumer, such liability can be excluded or restricted, but only insofar as the term satisfies the requirement of reasonableness. The liabilities referred to are not only the "business liabilities" referred to earlier, but include those arising under any contract of sale of goods.

## *Requirement of Reasonableness*

In relation to a contract term, this requirement is that the term must have been a fair and reasonable one to be included, having regard to the circumstances which were, or ought reasonably to have been, known to or in the contemplation of the parties when the contract was made.

In relation to a notice (not being a notice having contractual effect), the requirement of reasonableness is that it should be fair and reasonable to allow reliance on it, having regard to all the circumstances obtaining when the liability arose or (but for the notice) would have arisen.

These provisions are made in Section 11, which also provide that where a contract term or notice seeks to restrict liability to a specified sum of money, and the question arises whether the requirement of reasonableness is satisfied, particular regard is to be had to:

1. the resources which the person relying on such term or notice could expect to be available to him or her for the purpose of meeting the liability should it arise;
2. how far it was open to him or her to cover himself or herself by insurance.

The Act lays down certain "guidelines" for the application of the reasonableness test in relation to liability arising from the sale or supply of goods. They include:

1. the strength of the bargaining position of the parties relative to each other;
2. whether the customer received an inducement to agree to the exemption clause;
3. whether the customer knew or ought reasonably to have known of the existence and extent of the clause;
4. where the term excludes or restricts any relevant liability if some condition is not complied with, whether it was reasonable at the time of the contract to expect that compliance with that condition would be practicable;
5. customs of the trade and previous dealings between the parties;
6. whether goods were manufactured, processed or adapted to the special order of the customer (in other words, the availability of supplies).

Section 9 provides that, where for reliance upon it a contract term has to satisfy the test of reasonableness, it may be found to do so and be given effect to accordingly despite the contract having been repudiated. Where on a breach the contract is nevertheless affirmed by a party entitled to treat it as repudiated, this does not of itself exclude the requirement of reasonableness in relation to any contract term.

## *Exclusions from the 1977 Act*

Schedule 1 lists a number of contracts to which the Act does not extend, in whole or part. Amongst others, the Act does not extend to any contract of insurance or to any contract for the transfer of an interest in land.

Section 2(1) extends to contracts of marine salvage or towage, charter parties of a ship or hovercraft, and contracts for the carriage of goods by such means; but, subject to that, Sections 2 to 4 and 7 do not extend to any such contract except in favour of a person dealing as consumer.

Broadly, the Act does not apply to the international supply of goods: Section 26. Sections 2(1) and (2) do not extend to a contract of employment except in favour of the employee. Where the proper law of a contract is English law by choice of the parties, and the contract otherwise has no connection with such law, Sections 2 to 7 do not apply: Section 27.

The Act extends to and prevents the imposition of restrictions on the making of claims, the rights and remedies available and the rules of evidence or procedure. But a written agreement to submit disputes to arbitration is not regarded as restricting or excluding liability.

*George Mitchell (Chesterhall) Ltd v Finney Lock Seeds Ltd (1983).* Seed merchants negligently supplied the plaintiffs with defective cabbage seeds resulting in a crop of useless foliage. When sued for the loss, the defendants sought reliance on the standard term in the contract which excluded all liability for any loss or damage from use of the seed and which limited their liability to the price of the seed. It was held by the House of Lords:

1. Applying the *Photo Production* and *Ailsa Craig* decisions, although a limitation clause was to be construed *contra proferentem* and had to be clearly expressed, it was not subject to the very strict rules of construction applicable to total exclusion clauses

2. On its true construction, the clause was effective at common law since it was concerned with "seed", albeit the wrong seed had been delivered: it was unambiguous and could not be construed as limiting liability only in the absence of negligence.

3. Applying the provisions of section 55 of the *Sale of Goods Act 1979* (now

superseded by Sections 6 and 11 and Schedule 2 of the *Unfair Contract Terms Act 1977).*

## *The Unfair Terms in Consumer Contracts Regulations 1999*

These regulations implement Council Directive 93/13/ECC on unfair terms in consumer contracts. They revoke and replace the Unfair Terms in Consumer Contracts Regulations 1994. Particularly Regulations 3 to 9 re-enact Regulations 2 to 7 of the 1994 Regulations reflecting a closer relationship to the wording of the EU Directive.

The Regulations apply to unfair terms in most contracts between seller or supplier and consumer. An unfair term is one which has not been individually negotiated and which, contrary to the requirement of good faith, causes a significant imbalance in the parties' rights and obligations under the contract to the detriment of the consumer. Schedule 2 (reproduced below) provides assistance as to the type of term which may be regarded as unfair. Unfair terms are not binding on the consumer.

The 1999 Regulations retain the obligation on the Director General of Fair Trading (DGFT) to consider complaints on such terms. A new power is added to enable the DGFT to force production of traders' standard contracts and other information to facilitate investigation.

The Regulations provide for the first time that a qualifying body named in Schedule 1 (reproduced below) may also apply for an injunction to prevent the continued use of an unfair term provided it has notified the DGFT. The DGFT retains the power to arrange for the dissemination of information and advice concerning the operation of the Regulations.

## *Schedule 1*

### QUALIFYING BODIES

### PART ONE

1. The Data Protection Registrar
2. The Director General of Electricity Supply
3. The Director General of Gas Supply
4. The Director General of Electricity Supply for Northern Ireland
5. The Director General of Gas for Northern Ireland
6. The Director General of Telecommunications
7. The Director General of Water Services

8. The Rail Regulator

9. Every weights and measures authority in Great Britain

10. The Department of Economic Development in Northern Ireland.

**PART TWO**

11. Consumers' Association.

## *Schedule 2*

**INDICATIVE AND NON-EXHAUSTIVE LIST OF TERMS WHICH MAY BE REGARDED AS UNFAIR**

1. Terms which have the object or effect of-

(a) excluding or limiting the legal liability of a seller or supplier in the event of the death of a consumer or personal injury to the latter resulting from an act or omission of that seller or supplier;

(b) inappropriately excluding or limiting the legal rights of the consumer vis-à-vis the seller or supplier or another party in the event of total or partial non-performance or inadequate performance by the seller or supplier of any of the contractual obligations, including the option of offsetting a debt owed to the seller or supplier against any claim which the consumer may have against him;

(c) making an agreement binding on the consumer whereas provision of services by the seller or supplier is subject to a condition whose realisation depends on his own will alone;

(d) permitting the seller or supplier to retain sums paid by the consumer where the latter decides not to conclude or perform the contract, without providing for the consumer to receive compensation of an equivalent amount from the seller or supplier where the latter is the party cancelling the contract;

(e) requiring any consumer who fails to fulfil his obligation to pay a disproportionately high sum in compensation;

(f) authorising the seller or supplier to dissolve the contract on a discretionary basis where the same facility is not granted to the consumer, or permitting the seller or supplier to retain the sums paid for services not yet supplied by him where it is the seller or supplier himself who dissolves the contract;

(g) enabling the seller or supplier to terminate a contract of indeterminate duration without reasonable notice except where there are serious grounds for doing so;

(h) automatically extending a contract of fixed duration where the consumer does not indicate otherwise, when the deadline fixed for the consumer to express his desire not to extend the contract is unreasonably early;

(i) irrevocably binding the consumer to terms with which he had no real opportunity of becoming acquainted before the conclusion of the contract;

(j) enabling the seller or supplier to alter the terms of the contract unilaterally without a valid reason which is specified in the contract;

(k) enabling the seller or supplier to alter unilaterally without a valid reason any characteristics of the product or service to be provided;

(l) providing for the price of goods to be determined at the time of delivery or allowing a seller of goods or supplier of services to increase their price without in both cases giving the consumer the corresponding right to cancel the contract if the final price is too high in relation to the price agreed when the contract was concluded;

(m) giving the seller or supplier the right to determine whether the goods or services supplied are in conformity with the contract, or giving him the exclusive right to interpret any term of the contract;

(n) limiting the seller's or supplier's obligation to respect commitments undertaken by his agents or making his commitments subject to compliance with a particular formality;

(o) obliging the consumer to fulfil all his obligations where the seller or supplier does not perform his;

(p) giving the seller or supplier the possibility of transferring his rights and obligations under the contract, where this may serve to reduce the guarantees for the consumer, without the latter's agreement;

(q) excluding or hindering the consumer's right to take legal action or exercise any other legal remedy, particularly by requiring the consumer to take disputes exclusively to arbitration not covered by legal provisions, unduly restricting the evidence available to him or imposing on him a burden of proof which, according to the applicable law, should lie with another party to the contract.



**Questions**

1. What is meant by the Battle of Forms?

2. What is the effect of the *Unfair Terms in Consumer Contracts Regulations 1999*?

SIX

# INVALIDATING FACTORS *in the* FORMATION *of the* CONTRACT

*Study Topics*

**The various types of mistake**
**Misrepresentation and its effects**
**Restraint of trade**

The first of these invalidating factors is mistake. In this case the effect of mistake will be to destroy the basis of the agreement. A mistake which does not do that will of course have no effect on the contract.

When buying goods a person may buy the wrong size or colour or later find that he could have bought the same article at a cheaper price. He could say that he has made a mistake, but legally he can do nothing about it. However, if the existence of certain mistakes means that there never was a true agreement because the minds of the parties were not together, then the contract will be void. Agreement takes place in the minds of the parties and so if one party is thinking of one thing and the other is thinking of something quite different then their minds are not at one - there is no agreement (consensus).

If the mistake is of a fundamental nature it is called an operative mistake and its effect will be to render a contract void. A void contract is one which is without legal effect. It is a complete nullity in law and confers no rights on either party. The following are examples of operative mistakes.

**Mistake as to the Identity of the Subject Matter of the Contract**

The parties may be mistaken as to the identity of the subject matter of the contract or even as to whether it exists or not.

> *Raffles v Wichelhaus (1864)* (Exchequer). It so happened there were two ships both named *Peerless*. What caused the difficulty was that both of them were leaving Bombay at around the same time. The defendant entered into an agreement to buy cotton "ex *Peerless*" and he was thinking of the ship that left Bombay in October. The plaintiff agreed to sell cotton "ex *Peerless*" and he had in mind the ship that left Bombay in December. The court held there was no binding contract because of the operative mistake. The parties were not thinking of the same thing.

If both parties believe the subject matter of the contract to be in existence, but in fact at the time when the contract is made it is non existent, there is no contract. In *Scott v Coulson (1903)* G agreed to assign to H a policy of assurance upon the life of L. Unknown to either L had died before the agreement was made. It was held that there was no contract.

> *Bell v Lever Brothers Ltd (1932)*. B and S were employed by L under agreements for a fixed time. Later L paid B and S £50,000 to be discharged from these agreements. B and S had been making secret profits, which would have entitled L to dismiss them without notice, but this was unknown to L at the time the £50,000 was paid. There was no evidence of fraud on the part of B and S. The court held L could not recover the £50,000. There was no mistake on either side as to the contracts which were being released. The fact that L could have obtained the release on much cheaper terms did not, in the absence of fraud or breach of warranty, render the contract void.

The general rule is that if a person makes a mistake as to the offer of the other party to the contract, the contract is nevertheless binding upon him. In *Smith v Hughes (1871)* Blackburn J stated: "If, whatever a man's intentions may be, he so conducts himself that a reasonable man may believe that he was assenting to the terms proposed by the other party, and that other party upon that belief enters into the contract with him, the man thus conducting himself would be equally bound as if he had intended to agree to the other parties' terms".

In *Smith v Hughes*, S sold H a quantity of oats, a sample of which S had shown H. The oats were new oats but H who had inspected the sample erroneously thought that he was buying old ones. The price was high for new oats but oats were very scarce at that season. It was held that H's mistake was irrelevant unless S positively knew that H wanted to buy old oats only.

If, in *Smith v Hughes*, S had known that H had made a mistake in accepting his offer, there would have been no contract. In *Scriven Brothers and Company v Hindley and Company (1930)* an auctioneer was selling tow and hemp. A lot of tow was put up for sale and M was under the impression that it was hemp and made a bid for it. The bid was extravagant for tow, but reasonable for hemp. From the price bid the auctioneer knew that the bidder was under a mistake. The court held that there was no contract.

### Mistake as to Identity of the Other Party Contracted With

A party may be mistaken as to the identity of the other party to the agreement. This mistake can only arise if the parties are apart and are in correspondence. If the parties are contracting face to face then they cannot be mistaken as to the person with whom they intend to make the contract. In other words, the identity of the other contracting party is irrelevant.

*Cundy v Lindsay (1878)* AC. In this case the rogue wrote to Messrs Lindsays in Belfast and acquired some handkerchiefs by means of forging the name of a reputable merchant with whom Lindsays had previously done business. The rogue disposed of the handkerchiefs to Cundy and Lindsays tried to recover them. The case hinged on the point as to whether the right of ownership of the goods had passed to the rogue. If he had acquired the right of ownership or title to the handkerchiefs then he would have been able to pass this on to Cundy, who would then have been able to retain possession of the goods because he would have been the owner. However, the court held that the contract between the rogue and Lindsays was void on the grounds of mistake and so the right of ownership never left Lindsays. Consequently they were able to recover possession of the handkerchiefs from Cundy because they had remained owners of the goods.

We shall consider the sale of goods later. It should be remembered that when a person "buys goods" he is in fact in law wishing to acquire the title or right of ownership in the goods. If the seller has the right of ownership and the contract between him and the buyer is valid, then the seller's title will pass to the buyer and he will become the owner of the goods. In *Cundy v Lindsay* the contract of sale between the rogue and Lindsays was void and so the rogue did not acquire title to the handkerchiefs. Consequently the rogue did not become the owner of the handkerchiefs and when he sold them to Cundy he could not pass right of ownership on to Cundy. Therefore Lindsay was entitled to have the goods returned to him.

In *Cundy v Lindsay* the parties were in correspondence and some distance apart. Consequently Lindsays only had the signature on the letter to help to identify the person with whom they intended to make the contract. In *Lewis v Averay (1971)* AC the parties were face to face.

Again Lewis was mistaken as to the identity of the other party. Lewis thought he was dealing with a film star called Richard Greene, and gave possession of the car to the rogue, who disposed of it to Averay. If Lewis was to be successful in recovering possession of his car then, as in *Cundy v Lindsay*, he would have to prove that his title to the car had never left him. However the court held that the contract between Lewis and the rogue was not void for mistake because Lewis had made no mistake "as to the person with whom he intended to make the contract of sale". The identity of the rogue was not material. Consequently the rogue acquired a title to the car; but because of the deception the contract between the rogue and Lewis was voidable. This meant that Lewis could escape liability under the contract, provided he took steps to avoid the contract before a third party became involved. To avoid a contract which is voidable the other party should be notified of the intention to avoid liability under the contract, and if that is impossible then the police, or the Automobile Association, in the case of a car, should be notified. *Car and Universal Finance Co Ltd v Caldwell (1965).* If such steps are taken before the goods are transferred to the third party then the contract will have been voided. However, in this case the rogue acquired a voidable title to the car and he passed this to a third person, Averay, before Lewis took steps to avoid the contract. Lewis therefore could not recover his car.

### Mistake as to the Type of Written Contract Signed

If a person has made a mistake as to the contents of the contract then, if he has signed it, he cannot escape liability under it. That is the basic rule regarding signing contracts. The well known advice is to make sure you read the small print before you sign a contract and indeed that is very good advice. Whether you have read the contents of the contract or not or whether you have not fully understood the contract matters not. Quite simply if you have signed it you are bound by it. However, a written contract may be voided after a person has signed it if he can prove that he was mistaken as to the type of contract that he was signing and that when he signed he was not negligent.

*Saunders v Anglia Building Society (1970)* is the leading case on this point. It provides that a person who has made a mistake as to the type of contract he has signed may be able to have it set aside if he was not negligent when he signed it. In practice, it would seem that the person who signs a contract different in nature from the one he thought he was signing, must have been deceived by the other party. It would not be possible for that to happen unless there had been fraud present. In the *Saunders* case an old lady, Mrs Gallie, wished to transfer her house to her nephew. A friend of the nephew called Lee persuaded her to sign a document to transfer in his (Lee's) favour. The court held that Mrs Gallie had not signed a contract radically different from the one she thought she was signing and also she had been negligent. Although she did not succeed, the case is important for the guide-lines it sets out.

## *Rectification*

If the parties were in agreement on all important terms but by mistake wrote them down wrongly, rectification of the written document may be ordered. To obtain rectification it must be proved:

1. there was complete agreement between the parties on all the important terms;
2. the agreement continued unchanged until it was reduced into writing; and
3. the writing did not express what the parties had already agreed.

It will be noticed that here there has been a mistake not as to the contract itself but a mistake as to what was written down and so a document will normally only be rectified if both parties have made a mistake as to its contents. For example, if an oral agreement were made for the sale of peas and a written document recorded a sale of beans, the written document could be rectified by the substitution of "peas" for "beans". If the written document does accurately record the previous agreement then it cannot be rectified on the grounds that the previous agreement was itself made under some mistake. Equity does not rectify contracts but only documents. *Mackenzie v Coulson (1869).*

## *Misrepresentation*

When parties are considering entering into a contract with each other then invariably statements will be made by each of them. These statements are called representations. For example, if A is attempting to sell a motor car to B then A will probably say "It's an excellent vehicle" or "It's a good runner" or "It has only done 10,000 miles". All these statements are representations and are perfectly in order unless a representation happens to be a false statement. In that case it is called a misrepresentation.

A misrepresentation is defined as "a false statement of material fact made by a party to the contract or his agent which induces the other party to enter into the contract". The important points of this definition are:

### The False Statement Must be a Fact not Opinion

A fact is usually said to be capable of proof. An opinion on the other hand is usually so vague as to have no legal effect at all. These are constantly used in advertising. In *Bisset v Wilkinson (1927)* Bisset said the land he was selling was large enough to support 2,000 sheep. The court held this was merely his opinion. Or again "This car is a good runner" or "This car will last you a life time" are statements of opinion. On the other hand "This car has travelled 10,000 miles" is a statement of fact.

### The False Statement Must have been Made by a Party to the Contract

This means that only if the statement was made by a person who intended to be a party to the contract can any false statement be called a misrepresentation. If the false statement was made by a person who is not a party to the contract then it would not be misrepresentation. The person who made the false statement may never the less be liable in law. In *Hedley Byrne and Company Ltd v Heller and Partners Ltd (1964)* A was induced to enter into a contract with B because he relied on a statement made by C. This was not misrepresentation but never the less the court held that it would be possible for C to be liable for the false statement he had made. This is known as a negligent miss-statement. This principle was established in the *Henley Byrne* case and in that case it was held that it may be possible for C to be made liable for his false statement if it can be shown that C made the statement negligently and knew that the person to whom he was making the statement was going to rely upon it.

### The False Statement Must have been Relied upon by the Other Party

If A makes a false statement intending to deceive B but B takes no notice of the statement and makes his own investigations before deciding to enter into the contract then B cannot later claim that he has been deceived by the false statement of A.

In *Horsfall v Thomas (1862)* the seller of a gun filled in a crack in the barrel with the intention of deceiving the purchaser into thinking that the gun was in good condition. However the purchaser agreed to buy the gun without examining it. The court held that he could not claim to have been deceived. This then is the definition of a misrepresentation. It will be apparent that a misrepresentation may be made by a person intending to deceive, or it may be made by a person innocently, who does not know that the statement he is making is false. Nevertheless the other party will still have been deceived. The distinction between the various types of misrepresentation is of some importance. There are three types of misrepresentation:

1. Innocent misrepresentation. This arises where the person making the statement does not know that it is untrue.
2. Innocent but negligent misrepresentation. In this case the person who makes the statement does not know that the statement is untrue but should have checked up before making the statement. In this sense he may be said to have been negligent.

3. Fraudulent misrepresentation. In this case the person making the statement knows that he is making a false statement and intends to deceive the other party.

In all these cases the person hearing or receiving the false statement has been deceived but the importance of the distinction between the various types of misrepresentation hinges on whether damages may be awarded. At one time damages could only be awarded for fraudulent misrepresentation. In the case of fraudulent misrepresentation it has always been possible for the person who has been deceived to bring a civil action based on fraud. Such an action is available without reference to any contract.

As regards negligent misrepresentation it had also been possible since *Hedley Byrne and Company Limited v Heller and Partners Limited* for an action to be brought based upon the wrongful act, again irrespective of contract. However, the *Misrepresentation Act 1967* Section 2(1) provides that damages are payable "where a person has entered into a contract after a misrepresentation has been made to him by another party". Thus an action since 1967 may be brought for negligent misrepresentation based on contract. It is always true to say that if a choice exists as to whether to sue in contract or in tort it will usually be easier to bring an action based on contract. In the case of negligent misrepresentation all that the plaintiff has to show is the existence of a contract after the misrepresentation has been made. The other party, the defendant, is assumed to have been negligent unless he can prove to the contrary.

In the case of a wholly innocent misrepresentation the party misled has no right to damages but the judge has a discretion to award them.

## *Disclosure of Material Facts*

The general rule is that mere silence is not a misrepresentation. A party is not usually obliged to disclose all material facts to the other party, even if he knows that the other party is ignorant of some important fact.

In contracts for the sale of goods this rule is called "caveat emptor", which means "let the buyer beware". However as we shall see when we consider the law relating to the sale of goods the caveat emptor principle has been modified. In the following cases a party is under a duty to disclose all material facts unasked.

1. When, in the course of negotiations, a party has made a representation of fact which was true when made but before the contract has been made becomes untrue to his knowledge, then the person who made the statement is under a duty to correct the statement he originally made. In negotiating the sale of a medical practice in January, X represented the takings to be at the rate of £2,000 a year. In May, when the contract was signed, the takings had, due to the illness of X, fallen to £5 a week. The court held that the contract could be rescinded

owing to X's failure to disclose the fall in the takings. *With v O'Flanagan (1936).*

2. If part only of a series of facts is disclosed, and the undisclosed part so modifies the part disclosed as to render it, by itself substantially untrue, there is a duty to disclose the full facts.
3. A latent defect may not merely affect the value of the subject matter of the contract but also cause further loss or injury to the buyer. In this case the seller may be liable in negligence for failing to warn the buyer of the existence of the defect if he knows that it does exist. In *Hurley v Dyke (1979)* the defendant was a garage owner who sold a three-wheeler car by auction on terms that it was sold "as seen and with all its faults and without warranty". The vehicle was resold by the purchaser to a person named Clay and eight days later it crashed because of corrosion in the chassis, injuring the plaintiff passenger. The plaintiff's claim failed because the defendant had given warning to the purchaser and had no knowledge of the specific defect.
   The point was not taken but it would appear that if the defendant had known of the defect he might have been in breach of duty.
4. Contracts of utmost good faith, sometimes referred to as "contracts uberrimae fidei", are the main exception to the rule that silence does not amount to misrepresentation. In these contracts, one party has full knowledge of all material facts and so a duty is imposed on him to make full disclosure to the other party. Examples are:
   a. contracts of insurance
   b. contracts of family arrangement
   c. certain contracts for the sale of land
   d. contracts of suretyship and partnership in their operation.

Contracts of insurance are the most important contracts in this category and in *London Assurance v Mansel (1879)* M, in reply to questions which asked whether any previous proposals had been turned down by any other insurance company, answered negatively. In fact several other offices had declined his proposals. It was held that there had been a material failure to disclose, and the policy could be set aside.

## Recission

Rescission means the cancellation of a contract. It enables an innocent party to recover any property transferred under a contract or any payment made in advance, whilst at the same time he must restore any property he obtained under the contract. Rescission may be obtained by application to the court or by giving notice to the other party.

Rescission is known as an equitable remedy. This means that it is within the discretion of the court whether or not to grant the remedy. Some factors which will be taken into account by the court in deciding whether or not to rescind the contract are as follows:

1. The judge may declare the contract to continue to exist and award damages in lieu of recission.
2. If the deceived party, with knowledge of the misrepresentation, takes a benefit under the contract or in some other way affirms it, then the contract may not be rescinded.
3. the parties cannot be restored to their original positions. In *Lagunas Nitrate Company v Lagunas Syndicate (1899)*, L Syndicate sold Nitrate Works to the Lagunas Nitrate Company under a contract which contained misleading particulars. The company sued for rescission of the contract. It was held that, owing to alteration of the property consequent on its being worked by the company, the position of the parties had been so changed that they could not be restored to their original positions, and therefore the contract could not be rescinded.
4. A third party has acquired, for value, rights under the contract. If A obtains goods from B by fraud and pawns them with C, B will not normally be able to rescind the contract on learning of the fraud so as to be able to recover the goods from *C. Phillips v Brooks (1919).*
5. The fact that the contract has been performed does not deprive the deceived party of his right to rescind.

As was stated above, a contract may be rescinded either by the deceived party applying to the court for rescission or by his notifying the other party that he intends to rescind the contract. It is in fact sufficient if the deceived party does all that he can in the circumstances to rescind the contract even though he has been unable to get in touch with the person who made the false statement.

In *Car and Universal Finance Company Limited v Caldwell (1965)* the facts were that on 12 January 1960 C, the owner of a Jaguar car was persuaded to sell and deliver the car to a rogue who gave C a car of much lower value than the Jaguar. The next morning C ascertained that the cheque was worthless and at once asked the police and the Automobile Association to recover his car. The rogue sold the car to a person who did not acquire it in good faith and only on 15 January was the car acquired by a purchaser in good faith. It passed through several hands and eventually was acquired by the Car and Universal Finance Company Limited which acted in good faith. The court held that while normally the rescission of a voidable contract must be communicated to the other contracting party, that was not necessary if, as in the present case, the other party deliberately absconding put it out of the power of the rescinding party to communicate. Consequently C had rescinded the contract when he notified the police and the Automobile Association.

## *Duress*

The essence of any agreement is the valid consent of each of the parties and so it follows that if consent has been obtained by improper use of pressure then there will be no valid agreement. If consent is obtained by actual or threatened violence which puts the other party in fear for his life or physical well being then the contract may be set aside. Such a situation rarely happens in practice. However, in recent years the notion of economic duress has gradually become accepted by the English courts. In *Pao On v Lau Yiu Long (1979)* Lord Scarman stated: "There is nothing contrary to principle in recognising economic duress as a factor which may render the contract voidable, provided always that the basis of such recognition is that it must always amount to a coercion of will, which vitiates consent."

In *Atlas Express Limited v Kafco (Importers and Distributors) (1989)*, K were basketware importers and had a contract to supply 800 Woolworth's Stores. Needing a carrier to transport their products K entered into a contract with A whereby A agreed to carry the cartons at £1.10 each; the contract was to run from 15 October 1986 to 31 May 1987. Some weeks later A realised it had under priced the job and realised that, if K failed to deliver as agreed with Woolworth's, K would lose its business and be sued. A took advantage of the situation by getting one of its drivers to deliver to K an updated agreement and informed K that he would not carry away any goods unless K signed the agreement. Unable to arrange alternative transport K signed the agreement under protest. K now refused to pay A's invoices and when sued by A one of its defences was economic duress. This defence succeeded on the grounds that K's apparent consent to the new agreement was vitiated by A's threat to withdraw transport facilities, so that the new agreement had been secured unlawfully.

## *Undue Influence*

This is another form of unlawful pressure and falls outside the originally narrow common law definition of duress. In this case the act of coercion need not be unlawful but there must be present some form of exploitation by one party over a weaker party. In addition there is a presumption that in certain relationships undue influence does exist. Such relationships are those between parent and child, doctor and patient, solicitor and client, trustee and beneficiary; but not between husband and wife, nor between banker and customer. The mere existence of such a relationship is not, on its own, a ground for relief. The party seeking to set the transaction aside on the ground of undue influence must show that it was unfair and that he, the innocent party, was put at a disadvantage. The other party for his part may protect himself by showing that there was independent and professional advice given before the transaction was entered into. At one time it was always the practice of a bank which is entering into a contact with a young lady to get her to agree that she had taken independent legal advice before signing the agreement. However since the sex discrimination legislation this matter has to be treated very carefully.

There may be a presumption of undue influence even though the relationship between the parties is not within the above mentioned categories.

> *Lloyds Bank v Bundy (1975).* Mr Bundy had been a customer of Lloyds Bank for many years, and relied exclusively on his local bank manager for financial advice. Mr Bundy owned a farm and lived in the farmhouse, which was effectively his only significant asset. His son, who was an optimistic but unsuccessful businessman, borrowed from the bank and his father gave guarantees of his son's overdraft. By a series of successive transactions, the father was persuaded to increase the amount of the guarantee and to give mortgages over the farm to underwrite the guarantee. The final transaction involved a guarantee and mortgage equivalent to the whole worth of the farm. The documents relating to this transaction were signed by Mr Bundy in his house, the manager having brought them to him to sign. The manager did not point out, as any independent financial adviser would have been bound to do, that the transaction was a very foolish one for Mr Bundy to enter into, since there was a significant risk that he would loose all his assets and be turned out of his home.
>
> In due course, the son's business failed and the bank attempted to call in the guarantee and the mortgage. It was held that this was a classic example of undue influence because the bank manager was in a situation of conflict of interest. He had an interest on behalf of the bank to secure that the loans to young Bundy were recovered. He also had a duty as Mr Bundy's financial adviser. He should have realised that he could not perform this duty in this situation, since he could not hope to take a dispassionate view of whether the transaction was sensible from the point of view of the bank itself.

An action for rescission to set aside a contract on the ground of undue influence is subject to the same limitations considered earlier. In particular, the action must be commenced promptly after the removal of the influence under which the transaction was made, for "Delay defeats equities."

> *Allcard v Skinner (1887).* A young woman, on entering a convent, made over her property to the convent. After a year, she left the convent but delayed for five years before applying to the court to rescind her gift. It was held that she was defeated because of the unreasonable delay. Once she had left the convent, any undue influence had ceased and she should have taken prompt action in the matter.

# *Illegality*

A contract may be illegal by statute or at common law. A statute may expressly prohibit a certain act such as traders agreeing between themselves the price at which goods may be resold. Such an agreement would be contrary to the *Resale Prices Act 1976*. Another example is the *Life Assurance Act 1774* which provides that "No insurance shall be made by a person on the life of another in which he has no insurable interest". Contracts which contravene this prohibition have been held to be illegal. Obviously a contact for the deliberate commission of a crime would be illegal; also if a contract is capable of being performed in an unlawful way then again it would be unenforceable.

**Contracts Contrary to PublicPolicy**

In addition to the above contracts certain contracts have been declared by the courts over the years to be contrary to public policy. In such cases the judges have refused to enforce certain contracts on the grounds that to do so would be harmful to society. Examples would be as follows.

1. A contract damaging the administration of justice (for example stifling a prosecution). In a somewhat similar vein, if any person interferes with the course of justice by giving aid to a litigant without good reason or by agreeing to share the proceeds with one of the parties, then such an agreement shall be void. This has given rise to some debate about certain types of "no win no fee" schemes since their introduction in 1995. It seems clear, however, that Conditional Fee Arrangements (CFAs) at least are lawful.
2. A contract to defraud the Revenue. In *Miller v Karlinski (1945)* a contract was considered which provided that one of the parties could include in his expenses account the amount of the income tax he was due to pay. It was decided that this was a fraud upon the Revenue and so was declared illegal.
3. A contract tending to promote sexual immorality. In the well known case of *Pearce v Brooks (1866)* the defendant was a prostitute and she had hired a carriage in which to ply her trade. The court held that the supplier of the carriage could not succeed in an action against her for the money he was owed as he knew of the use to which the carriage was to be put and that it was an illegal contract.
4. A contract damaging to the institution of marriage. Contracts which could damage the institution of marriage would be a marriage brokerage contract (marriage bureau), or a contract for possible separation of husband and wife in the future.
5. A contract to oust the jurisdiction of the courts.

All these contracts have been held by the courts to be contrary to public policy and therefore harmful to society.

## *Contracts in Restraint of Trade*

Originally, these were always declared void, but in the nineteenth century it was realised that not all such restraints were bad. The following are types of restraint which are recognised as possibly valid.

1. The vendor-purchaser of a business type. It is natural that the purchaser of a business should wish to protect himself or herself by contract from the vendor's competition.
2. The employer-employee type. It is natural that an employer should want to safeguard himself or herself against disclosure by an employee (or an ex-employee) of trade secrets and other confidential information.
3. The tied business type, such as the solus agreement with an oil company to sell only its petrol and oil. See *Esso Petroleum Co Ltd v Harper's Garage (Stourport) Ltd (1967)*.
4. Restrictive trade agreements, which are subject to competition legislation.

The first three types, which are most important from the legal point of view, are dealt with on ordinary common law rules.

## *Test to be Applied*

How far can the purchaser go in restraining the vendor's competition? How far can the employer go in restraining his employee? What conditions can an oil company lawfully impose on the owner of a filling station? The answer to these questions depends upon the results of two tests.

1. Is the restraint reasonable as between the parties?
2. Is it harmful to the public interest?

These tests were laid down by the House of Lords in the following case.

> *Nordenfelt v Maxim Nordenfelt Guns and Amm. Co (1894).* Nordenfelt sold his armament manufacturing business to a company which subsequently amalgamated with another company. Nordenfelt became managing director of the new company, and in his contract of employment he made two promises:
>
> 1. not to carry on an armaments business in competition anywhere in the world for 25 years;
> 2. not to carry on any other business in competition with a business carried on by the company for the time being.
>
> It was held that the first promise was valid and enforceable because it was

> reasonable in the circumstances. Nordenfelt's business was worldwide when he sold it and any restraint on him would also have had to be worldwide to be effective. Nor was the restraint harmful to the public interest because it secured for England the inventions and business of a foreigner. But the second promise was unreasonable and void. The purchaser of a business cannot protect all his or her businesses from the vendor's competition; only that which he or she has just purchased from the vendor.

Note that in *Morris v Saxelby (1916)* the House of Lords ruled that to satisfy test (1) the restraint must be no wider than necessary to safeguard the convenantee's interests.

### Points to Note about the Tests

The first test is more important than the second. It is very rare for a restraint to fail solely on the ground that it is harmful to the public interest. One example is the following case.

> *Bull v Pitney-Bowes Ltd (1967).* The plaintiff worked as a sales director for the defendants, and he joined their pension scheme. One rule said that his rights and benefits would be cancelled if, on retirement, he competed with or did anything detrimental to the defendant's interests. In 1964 the plaintiff retired and began work for a rival company. The defendants purported to stop his pension and the plaintiff sued for a declaration that the rule in the pension scheme was an enforceable restraint of trade and void. It was held that it was void because it was against public policy to restrain an experienced salesman, who could possibly aid the export drive, in this way.

In considering what is "reasonable" the court takes into account:

1. The type of restraint: what does it seek to do?
2. The area of restraint: how far does it extend?
3. The duration of restraint: how long is it to last?

The court generally interprets the employer-employee type of restraint more stringently than the other types because of the unequal bargaining power of the parties. But see *George Silverman v Silverman (1969).*

If the restraint is void it is not binding, even though a person may have agreed voluntarily to the restraint. Each case depends on its own particular facts. There are many decided cases on restraint.

> *Attwood v Lamont (1920).* The plaintiff owned a shop in Kidderminster which was organised into several departments. The defendant was manager of the tailoring

department, and he had nothing to do with the other departments. On leaving the plaintiff's employment, the defendant promised that he would not at any time engage in the trades of tailor, dressmaker, general draper, milliner, hatter, haberdasher, gentlemen's, ladies' or children's outfitter at any place within ten miles of Kidderminster. It was held that the restraint was unreasonable and void. The employer was trying to prevent the employee from getting another job, and he was attempting to protect all the departments of this shop and not merely the one in which the employee had been employed. The employer could do neither of these things.

*Commercial Plastics Ltd v Vincent (1964).* The plaintiffs were manufacturers of thin PVC calendered plastic sheeting. The defendant was employed by them to research into and develop the production of a thin PVC calendered plastic sheeting for sticky tape. In his contract of employment the defendant promised not to seek employment with any other of the plaintiff's competitors in the PVC field for at least one year after leaving their employment. Later the defendant resigned and immediately proposed to work for one of the plaintiff's competitors. The plaintiff sued for an injunction. It was held that the restraint was unreasonable and void because, first, it prevented work in any PVC field, not merely the one in which the defendant had been engaged (sticky tape); and, second, no area was mentioned, which could not be justified. The Court of Appeal issued a warning to amateurs who draft restraints: "It would seem that a good deal of 'know-how' is required for the successful drafting of a restrictive convenant."

*Wessex Dairies Ltd v Smith (1935).* A milk roundsman solicited his employer's customers in his employer's time with a view to setting up a milk delivery business of his own. It was held that the employer was entitled to damages because the employee had broken his contract of employment. It would have made no difference if the milkman had approached the customers in his own time. In a case like this the employer need not rely on an express restraint clause but can rely on an implied term in the employee's contract that he or she will observe good faith.

It does not matter whether the breach of good faith is initiated by the employee (as in the *Wessex Dairies* case) or by the customer.

*Spencer v Marchington (1988).* P was employed under a one-year fixed-term contract by D to manage two employment agencies, one in Banbury and one in Leamington Spa. Her contract contained a restrictive covenant which prohibited her from being involved in the same business within 25 miles of Banbury and ten miles of Leamington Spa. P was informed after approximately ten months that her contract would not be renewed and, in view of her reaction to this, she was asked to stop work immediately. P subsequently set up her own employment agency in Banbury. P made a claim for payments due to her under the contract and D counter-claimed for damages for breach of the restrictive convenant.

It was held that D's request that P stop work immediately after ten months of the fixed-term contract had expired did not amount to a repudiatory breach so as to render the restrictive covenant unenforceable. However, on public policy grounds, the covenant purporting to prevent P from being involved in a competing business within twenty-five miles was too wide to be enforceable. The purpose of the public policy rule was to promote competition and to protect customers in the market.

## *Severance*

When a contract contains some terms which are legal and others which are illegal, the court will enforce the legal terms if they can be severed from the illegal terms. But severance is only possible if the illegal term can be removed, so as to leave the contract substantially the same. The court will not use severance to make a new contract for the parties. For example, the court will not cut down an unreasonable restraint of trade to what it considers reasonable. Severance was possible in the *Nordenfelt* case because there were two distinct, unrelated promises. But severance was refused in *Attwood v Lamont* because the restraint was so wide that severance would have produced an entirely new contract. Severance was also possible in the following case.

*Scorer v Seymour Jones (1966).* The plaintiff was an estate agent in Dartmouth, Devon. He opened a new branch in Kingsbridge and employed the defendant to run it. The defendant promised in his contract that during his employment, and for three years after it ended, he would not engage in the business of estate agent within a radius of five miles of the plaintiff's premises at Kingsbridge or Dartmouth. After eight months the defendant was dismissed as unsatisfactory and he immediately set up as an estate agent at his home in Salcombe (which is within a radius of five miles from Kingsbridge), where he did business with some of the plaintiff's clients. It was held that the plaintiff was entitled to an injunction to restrain the defendant in relation to Kingsbridge but not in relation to Dartmouth because the defendant had never been employed at the Dartmouth branch. But the restraint was severable. Note that although this restraint prevented competition, the plaintiff was genuinely trying to protect his confidential information.

## *Effect of Illegality*

The effects of illegality are as follows.

1. If the contract is in itself illegal, it is void and neither party can enforce it.
2. If the contract is in itself legal, but one party tends to use if for an illegal or immoral purpose, the guilty party cannot enforce it but the innocent party can.
3. If the contract is in itself illegal, collateral transactions are likewise illegal and void.
4. Money paid or properly transferred under an illegal contract cannot be recovered. There are two exceptions to this rule:
   i. where the parties are not equally guilty, the one less at fault can recover any money or property he or she has paid or transferred;
   ii. where the illegal purpose of the contract has not been substantially performed, a party who has a change of heart and repudiates the contract can recover his or her money or property, provided he or she has truly repented. Repentance must be the only explanation for the change of heart.

## *Capacity to Contract*

Most adults have full capacity to enter into contracts but certain persons have limitations on this.

### Minors

These are persons under the age of 18 years. Such persons can enter into a valid contract for the purpose of goods called "necessaries" or services which are for the benefit of the minor. A necessary can include food, clothing, lodging and educational books provided they are "suitable to the condition in life of the infant and to his actual requirements at the time of sale and delivery".

> *Elkington v Amery (1936)*. The minor son of an eminent politician had bought on credit from the plaintiffs an engagement ring, an eternity ring and a gold vanity bag. The Court of Appeal held that both rings were necessaries (in the case of the eternity ring, by treating it as a wedding ring); but the bag was classed as a thing of pure luxury incapable of ranking as such. It followed that the contract was valid as respects the rings, and the son had therefore to pay for them, but void as respects the bag, so that he could not be ordered to pay for that.

As regards actual requirements, the proposition is simply that goods cannot be classed as necessaries if the minor is already well stocked with them. Thus, by way of illustration in the following case.

> *Nash v Inman (1908).* A minor who was an undergraduate at Cambridge was supplied by a Savile Row tailor with clothes to the value of £145. The clothes, which included 11 fancy waistcoats, where held to be suitable to his station in life (his father was a wealthy architect), but to be non-necessaries because the evidence showed that his wardrobe was already sufficiently extensive. The contract was therefore void.

Although agreements for necessaries are placed under the heading "valid contracts", they are not quite true contracts. This is so in two respects.

1. They bind the minor only if they have been "executed", that is only if, say, the plaintiff has delivered the goods or rendered the services in question. No action lies against the minor for simple "non-acceptance".
2. Even if the contract is executed, if the goods or services are necessaries, the minor can be made to pay only a "reasonable price" for them. This will not necessarily be the same as the agreed contract price.

In contracts for the minor's benefit by education, all kinds of education are covered, but the contract must benefit the minor and be connected with his or her education. "Education" is construed widely and will include contracts of apprenticeship and of services as well as vocational training. If the contract as a whole is burdensome to the minor, it will not be binding on him or her.

The *Infants Relief Act 1874* made absolutely void the following contracts with a minor:

1. all contracts for the repayment of money lent or to be lent;
2. all contracts for goods supplied or to be supplied, other than "necessaries";
3. all accounts stated (an "account stated" is an acknowledgement by one person that he or she owes a specific amount of money to another person).

However, the *Minors' Contracts Act 1987* repealed the 1874 Act, and so the position now is that the above contracts are voidable by the minor but unenforceable against him or her. The minor can enforce them but he cannot be sued on them. The 1987 Act empowers the court to order restitution of goods obtained by a minor under such a contract.

A voidable contract is one by which a minor acquires an interest in property of a permanent nature to which obligations are attached. The minor may avoid such contracts as:

1. taking a lease of land;
2. taking shares in a company;

3. becoming a partner in a firm.

**Mentally Disordered and Drunken Persons**

A person who makes a contract and is incapable of understanding what he is doing will not be bound by such a contract if he can prove:

1. he did not understand the nature of the contract;
2. the other party knew of this situation.

## *Corporations*

The law recognises two classes of person: "natural persons" (that is to say, human beings) and "artificial persons" (that is to say, corporations). A corporation is a notional "being" upon which the law confers a personality which is quite distinct from that of the person or persons of whom it from time to time consists. There are two types of corporation: corporations sole, and corporations aggregate.

A corporation sole is, as its name suggests, a corporation which consists at any given time of one member only. It is an office which enjoys corporate status either by virtue of the common law or by Act of Parliament and its member is the holder of that office for the time being. Examples are the Crown, archbishops and bishops, and (statutory) the public trustee.

Corporations aggregate (with which we are primarily concerned here), by contrast, consist of two or more members. Corporations may be bodies:

1. incorporated by Royal Charter;
2. incorporated by statute (for example, nationalised industries); or
3. incorporated by registration as a company (under the *Companies Acts*).

Corporate bodies possess what is called legal personality and can make contracts, but their contractual capacity is limited by the following.

1. Natural impossibility: since it is not a natural person it can only contract through its agents;
2. Its powers: a corporation can only act within its powers, that is, intra vires. If a corporation acts outside its powers or exceeds its powers it will be said to have acted ultra vires and the contract will be void.

As far as companies formed by registration under the *Companies Acts* are concerned, the ultra vires doctrine is not of particular importance nowadays.

Section 35 of the *Companies Act 1985* had modified the ultra vires doctrine in favour of persons dealing with a company in good faith in a transaction decided upon by the directors, so that it will be no longer necessary for such persons to enquire into any limitation on the capacity of the company or the directors' powers to enter into a contact.

Of course if there are any rules as to the form the contract must take, then such rules will apply to a company as well as to a human person. If a certain statute requires a particular contract to be made under seal, or in writing, then a company must comply with that requirement. Otherwise the servant of a company can make a verbal contract which will be binding on his or her employer so long as he or she has the necessary authority to make such a contract.

## *Unincorporated Associations*

### General

An unincorporated association consists of two or more persons who are associated together for the purposes of some common enterprise, but have not obtained incorporation for those purposes. It is therefore, a "body" which is not a legal person in its own right.

Some unincorporated associations (partnerships) exist for business purposes, others (trade unions and trade associations) for the purpose of promoting the interests of different groups (of workers and employers), and others (historical societies, parent-teacher associations, amateur dramatic societies, sports clubs, and working men's clubs) for the widest possible variety of educational, recreational and social purposes. Partnerships and trade unions are subject to legislation by virtue of which their legal position differs in some respects from that of other unincorporated associations.

Four basic propositions may be put forward about unincorporated associations, all of them based on the fact that they do not in law "exist".

1. An unincorporated association cannot own property. Its premises, equipment and funds must be held by trustees, on behalf of its members for the time being.
2. An unincorporated association cannot itself contract. A member or members of the association may enter into a contract on its behalf but any liability arising under the contract will be the responsibility of the member or members concerned, together with any other member who either authorised the making of the contract or subsequently ratified it.
3. An unincorporated association cannot itself incur liability in tort. For acts done on its behalf by members, responsibility rests purely with the members concerned. For an act done by one of its servants in the course of his or her employment, vicarious liability can fall only upon the member or members who employed him or her. For damage caused by the condition of the premises used by the association, liability will normally be that of the members as a whole, they being treated for the purpose as the occupiers of the premises.

4. An unincorporated association cannot sue or be sued in its own name. Where, however, the number of plaintiffs or defendants in an action would otherwise be unduly large, it is open to the court to make a "representative order" whereby the action is brought by or against a limited number of members as representing the total numbers actually involved.

## *Trade Unions*

Notwithstanding that it is an unincorporated association, a trade union can, like a partnership, sue and be sued in its own name; but as in the case of partnership this is a matter of procedural convenience only. A trade union is no more a person than any other unincorporated association. Its property is vested in trustees, and liability under contracts entered into on its behalf rests personally upon the member or members concerned, as determined in accordance with the principles we have already discussed. See Section 2 of the *Trade Union and Labour Relations Act 1974*.

**Questions**

What is an operative mistake?

What is the definition of misrepresentation?

When may a court rescind an agreement?

SEVEN

# DISCHARGE *of a* CONTRACT

*Study Topics*

**Methods of discharge**
**Remedies for breach of contract**
**Injunction**

One does not refer to a contract as merely being performed but of its being discharged. This is because when the contract was originally made by the parties then the rights and duties already referred to were set up. Consequently when those rights and duties have been extinguished then the contract can be said to have been discharged. Performance is merely one, albeit the most obvious, method of discharge.

If A and B have entered into a contract then rights and duties have been created between them. A has rights against B and B owes duties to A and vice versa; B has rights against A and A owes duties to B. If both A and B do what they have promised to do under the contract then the contract is at an end. Of course if only A performs his duties then B no longer will be able to enforce his rights against A but naturally A will still retain his rights against B and may enforce them in a court of law if he wishes. The methods of discharge are performance, agreement, frustration and breach.

The rights discussed above could, until recently, only be enforced by those who are parties to the contract; those who actually made it. Third parties could not normally seek to enforce any right under the contract. This was always known as the "Doctrine of Privity of Contract". This position has been significantly undermined by the *Contracts (Rights of Third Parties) Act 1999*. The main impact of this Act is that third parties can now enforce rights under a contract. This is however subject to the following important points:

1. The contract must expressly provide that the third party may enforce the right (subsection1(1)a).
2. The term must purport to confer a benefit on the third party (subsection1(1)b).
3. The third party must be expressly identified by name, as a member of a class or as answering a particular description (subsection 1(3)).

Obviously this is a recent statute and in time a body of case law will develop illustrating how this law is to be applied.

## *Performance*

A contract may be said to have been discharged when each party has completely performed his duties under the contract. The operative word is "completely" and so it follows that if a party has only partially performed his part of the contract then he will not have discharged his duties under it and so the other party will likewise be relieved of his obligations.

If each party has performed his part of the contract then the contract is discharged, but the performance of each party must be complete and exactly in accordance with the terms of the contract. If the contract is an entire contract and the party only performs half of it then he is not entitled to any payment at all. If A has two large lawns and he agrees to pay a jobbing gardener £10 if he mows the two lawns then he does not have pay anything at all if the gardener only mows one lawn and then leaves the job. On the other hand sometimes it is agreed between the parties that the contract should be split up into sections and then the situation is that as each instalment is completed the other party is obliged to pay for that instalment. Building contracts are often arranged in this way, otherwise the builder would have to await payment until the job was completed and this might entail a large outlay of capital by the builder unless the work was split up into instalments. This is known as a severable or divisible contract. In addition, it may be agreed between the parties that the payment shall be made in stages so as to encourage the completion of the contract. The supplier of goods may receive payment in advance of completion provided the work is being done according to schedule.

Sometimes it is difficult to be certain when a contract has been completely performed. This may be the case in contracts of service. So in order to avoid the possibility of one party evading his liabilities by claiming that the contract has not been completely performed, the doctrine of substantial performance has been created. Thus if the contract is performed as well as a reasonable man would expect then the court will state that the contract has been performed, with possibly some adjustment to the actual price paid.

*Hoenig v Isaac (1952)* CA. Plaintiff agreed to redecorate the defendant's flat for £750. The defendant paid £400 but complained that the contract had not been carried out to his satisfaction. The Court of Appeal held that the plaintiff had substantially performed his part of the contract and that he was entitled to his price less an amount to cover the defects.

Performance very often calls for the payment of money and when this is the case then the following will apply.

1. The exact money must be tendered and the party making payment has no right to any change if he tenders a sum larger than is called for by the agreement. In practice it would be unthinkable that a shopkeeper who wanted to stay in business would refuse to give change to a customer. However, the legal position is that he is not required to do so. In fact it is on that particular point that certain transport operators are enabled to run their services and state that "no change will be given".
2. Payment by cheque is at the discretion of the payee and in any case is only a conditional payment. This means that if the cheque turns out to be worthless then the payer still has an obligation to pay the amount agreed. The statement "No cheques accepted here, not even good ones" says it all. It is up to the payee to decide whether or not he wishes to be paid by cheque.
3. If cash is paid the rules of legal tender will apply. This means that only cash in the following denominations may be tendered in payment of a debt:
   Notes of any amount
   Gold coins of any amount
   50p coins up to £10
   Silver/cupro-nickel coins of 20p or less up to £5
   Bronze coins up to 20p
   Legal tender is intended to avoid the situation where A owes B money but is reluctant to pay. Eventually he agrees to pay (say £5) and A goes along to B and hands over 500 pennies and says "Here is the money I owe you". Legally there has been no payment because it was not in legal tender and B can sue A for non-payment. In practice, a creditor would probably be so pleased to receive payment in any form, that he would not insist on legal tender.

## *Agreement*

A contract comes into existence because of an agreement between the parties so it must follow that it can also be discharged by agreement. Thus A and B enter into some agreement. A wants to change his mind and not carry out his terms of the contract. Of course if he does this unilaterally then he will be in breach of contract to B. However, if A approaches B and states that he would like to be released from his liabilities under the contract then B might agree. In that case the contract is discharged. In effect B has promised not to sue A if he does not perform his part of the contract and the consideration for this promise is A's promise not to sue B.

Of course if A has actually performed his part of the agreement but wants to release B from his obligations then, to make such an agreement legally binding, B would have to provide some fresh consideration in return for A's promise not to sue him. This is technically known as "accord and satisfaction", which is the equivalent of "agreement and consideration". Note that in the case of discharge by agreement, the contract is at an end but neither party has performed what he has promised to do under the contract.

After an agreement is reached between A and B, A then agrees with B not to carry on with the contract. In effect A is saying "I promise not to enforce the agreement against you if you promise not to enforce the agreement against me". This amounts to mutual promises which is good consideration.

If A has performed his part of the contract and then promises to release B from his obligations then B must supply fresh consideration to support A's promise not to sue him. Either that or a deed of release signed by A, because an agreement contained in a deed does not require consideration.

## *Frustration*

Sometimes, after a contract has been made, something occurs to make the contract impossible to perform. What effect does this situation have on the parties? As always it will depend on the particular facts of the case. If one party has given his absolute undertaking that something will be done by a certain time then probably he will be liable for breach if he is unable to do what he has promised to do. However, if whatever happens to prevent the contract from being performed

1. has not been caused by either party;
2. could not have been foreseen; and
3. its effect is to destroy the basis of the contract

then the courts will probably state that the contract has been frustrated. If that happens then the contract will have been discharged and neither party will have any liability under it.

*Taylor v Caldwell (1863)*. Caldwell had agreed that Taylor could use "The Surrey Gardens and Music Hall" on four named days for the purpose of holding concerts there. Just before the time for the performance of the contract, the Music Hall was destroyed by fire. Taylor wanted compensation from somebody so he sued Caldwell. But the fire was not due to the negligence of Caldwell. The court held that as the Hall had ceased to exist, without fault of either party, both parties must be excused from performance of their contract.

The courts will not readily say that a contract has been frustrated because by doing so they are taking away the rights of each party to sue the other and to get compensation. A frustrating event will arise without any warning and it may be that each party loses his right to sue the other. What happens if one party has incurred some expenses before the frustrating event occurred, or has promised to pay sum to the other? Until 1943 the position was unsatisfactory but in that year the *Law Reform (Frustrated Contracts) Act* was passed and since then the position is that

1. money due but not in fact paid ceases to be payable;
2. a party who has incurred expenses may be awarded compensation;
3. a party who has gained a benefit may be requested to pay a just sum for that.

In practice, and to avoid the necessity of having to go to court for a decision on the liability of the parties to a contract which has become impossible to perform, an appropriate clause may be inserted in the contract. This is called a "force majeure" clause and its purpose is to deal with the situation where a contract becomes impossible to perform because of the happening of some event outside the control of the parties. Events such as strikes, accidents to machinery, delays in delivery and changes in government policy are often included in such clauses, and a party is asked to suspend or cancel the operation of that contract if one of these events has occurred.

## *Breach*

A breach of contract will occur if one party

1. fails to perform his part of the contract by the agreed date;
2. makes it impossible for himself to perform the contract;
3. repudiates his liabilities under the contract.

It will be seen that the second and third of these may occur before the date fixed for performance of the contract. In that case an action may be brought immediately and there is no need to wait until the date fixed for performance. This is known as "anticipatory breach".

*Hochster v De La Tour* (1853) is a case usually remembered as it concerns a travel agency who decided to employ a person as a courier in the summer, the appointment having been made earlier in the year. Soon after the appointment the travel agency wrote saying it would no longer require the services of the courier in the summer. The question was whether the courier had to wait until the date fixed for performance of the contract before he could sue, or whether he could sue immediately he knew the other party had repudiated his liabilities. The answer, said the court, was that he could sue immediately.

It is up to the party concerned whether he wishes to look upon a breach as a breach of a fundamental term or condition and thus treat the contract as discharged and in addition claim damages, or whether he is happy to look upon the breach as a minor matter and is willing to sue for damages for breach of a warranty rather than to treat the contract as discharged. The difference between a condition and a warranty is illustrated in the following case.

*Bettini v Gye (1876).* An Italian opera singer had agreed to undertake a tour in this country on certain dates and also to arrive in this country six days before the start of the tour. He did turn up for the tour but not the required number of days prior to the commencement. The organiser tried to escape liability under the contract claiming that the singer had broken the contract. He was not successful as the court held that the singer had broken a minor term of the contract (a warranty) and was liable in damages in respect of that. He had not broken a condition which is a major term of the contract and one on which the contract hinges.

As regards the time when a contract must be performed, this is often not agreed between the parties. It is usually said that "time is not of the essence of the contract". On the other hand there is no reason why it should not be so. If the time of performance is not agreed when the contract is made then the contract must be performed within a reasonable time. Either party may make the time of performance important and if so the contract must contain an appropriate clause to ensure that it is performed by a certain time or during a specific period. If the contract is not performed by that agreed time then the defaulting party will be in breach of contract.

If a time of performance is agreed between the parties then normally a party who fails to perform on the due date will be in breach of contract, because the time of performance will then be a condition of the contract. Sometimes a party may make time of the essence by giving notice to the party who has delayed performance that he must complete his part of the agreement within a reasonable specified time, otherwise he will treat the contract as broken.

*Rickard (Charles) Ltd v Oppenheim (1950).* Oppenheim purchased a Rolls Royce chassis with a body built on it from Rickards. The delivery date was to be by 20 March. The delivery date passed and Oppenheim pressed for delivery. Eventually Oppenheim notified Rickards in June that he would not accept delivery after 25 July. The car was still not delivered so Oppenheim bought another one.

Rickards offered to deliver the car in October but Oppenheim refused. Rickards sued for the price. The court held that Oppenheim had waived the original time for delivery but was entitled, by giving reasonable notice, again to make time the essence of the contract.

## *Remedies*

When two parties have entered into a contract and one of them has broken his part of the bargain then it is only natural that the other should seek compensation. This is called damages in law and takes the form of a money payment. It is a common law remedy which means that it is the usual remedy which will be awarded by the courts and the successful party in any action has a right to damages.

When one considers the losses for which compensation might be claimed one is immediately involved with the topic of remoteness. In other words the law seeks to restrict the losses for which damages are awarded to those losses which arise naturally as a result of the breach of contract. Other losses which are too far removed from the breach cannot be eligible for compensation. The rule relating to this matter is the rule stated in the following case.

*Hadley v Baxendale (1854).* In that case a miller delivered the broken shaft of his mill to a carrier with instructions to take it to a manufacturer to be repaired. The carrier took an unreasonable length of time to transport the shaft and so the mill was out of use for longer than it should have been. The court held the carrier was liable for negligent performance of his contract; but when it came to the assessment of damages it held the carrier was not liable for loss of profits during the delay. The carrier, in the opinion of the court could not have known, and was not informed, that the miller had only one shaft.

The problem of remoteness also arises in areas other than that of the damages for breach of contract. It arises in tort: "for what harm will the defendant be liable?" Basically only those injuries for those damages which he should reasonably have foreseen would be likely to result from his acts. Also in criminal law where it is spoken of as causation. If one person stabs another and then the friends of the victim carry him to the medical aid centre and drop him twice on the way, were they responsible for the victim's death or was the person who stabbed him in the first place?

In contract the matter of remoteness is only concerned with establishing the harm for which the defendant may have to compensate the plaintiff. Basically the rule is that the plaintiff in a breach of contract action will be awarded compensation for any loss which the defendant knew or should have known was likely to result from his breach of contract.

The rule has been confirmed notably in *Czarnikow Ltd v Koufos (1969)* also called The *Heron II.* In this case in which a ship is concerned, the report of the case is often referred to by the name of the ship. In that case the ship was the *Heron II* and its owner had agreed to transport a cargo of sugar from Constanza to Basrah. The sugar reached the destination later than it should have done owing to the fault of the shipowner. The owners of the sugar sustained a loss because the price of the sugar had dropped. The court held that the shipowner must pay the loss of profit to the charterer because he must have known that the sugar was to be sold.

In *Victoria Laundries v Newman Industries Ltd (1949)* a manufacturer of boilers was late in delivering a boiler to the laundry. Consequently he was sued for loss of profits that the laundry would have earned if they had received the boiler on time. The plaintiff was not able to recover damages in respect of another contract to dye materials, made by the laundry with a government department, and of which the boiler makers had no knowledge.

Damages may be either liquidated or unliquidated. A liquidated sum is a fixed or ascertainable sum. One speaks of the liquidation of a company when its assets are sold and converted into cash. In bankruptcy proceedings a liquidated sum may be claimed or proved but not if it still has to become fixed, in which case it is a contingent liability. Liquidated damages are those damages which the parties have agreed, when they made their contract, should be paid by the defaulting party to the other in the event of the contract being broken. Liquidated damages are frequently encountered in building contracts or in contracts for the charter of a ship. In these contracts the parties agree that in the event of, say, the builder failing to complete the building by the agreed date, he will pay to the other party £X for each week or part of a week he is late in finishing the building. If the other party's actual loss is more that the amount agreed to be paid then he can only recover the liquidated sum and not the actual loss.

In *Cellulose Acetate Silk Co v Widnes Foundry (1933)* Widnes Foundry agreed to erect a plant for Cellulose Acetate Silk by a certain date and also agreed to pay £20 for every week they took beyond that date. They were 30 weeks late, and Cellulose Acetate Silk claimed £5,850, their actual loss from the delay. It was held that Widnes Foundry had only agreed to pay £20 a week for delay and was not liable for more.

On the other hand if the sum agreed to be paid is held by the court to be excessive by reference to the actual loss, then the agreed amount may be classified as a penalty and not liquidated damages and will not be payable. The courts will not enforce payment of an agreed sum if they consider that the payment of this money has been held over the head of the other party (*in terrorem*). This was the case where an actor agreed to pay a large sum of money if he broke any of the rules of the theatre where he was appearing. Those rules contained some minor matters such as smoking in dressing rooms and so the court considered the amount to be paid was in the nature of a penalty and not true liquidated damages.

*Kemble v Farren (1829).* Farren agreed to act at Kemble's theatre and to conform to all the regulations of the theatre. Each agreed to pay £1,000 as liquidated damages. Farren broke the contract and damages were assessed at £750. It was held that the sum of £1,000 was a penalty because it was payable even if Farren had broken any of the most minor regulations of the theatre.

Unliquidated damages on the other hand are to be assessed by the court and the plaintiff must plead special damages which are those losses he can quantify himself such as loss of earnings, damage to his car, etc. He should also claim general damages which are awarded in the discretion of the court. There are other principles which the courts will apply when deciding the question of damages, and these include mitigation and the question of compensation.

## *Mitigation*

The injured party must do what he reasonably can in order to reduce the amount of loss he is suffering. He must "not sit around in the sun".

*Brace v Calder (1895).* Brace had a contract of employment with a partnership for a period of two years. After six months the partnership was dissolved and although Brace was offered employment by two of the remaining partners, he declined. The court held that Brace was wrongfully dismissed but should have attempted to find alternative employment.

## *Compensation not Punishment*

Damages are not of course subject to the income tax laws but nevertheless the effect of these laws should be taken into account when assessing the damages to be awarded.

In *BTC v Gourley* (1956) the plaintiff's estimated future earnings amounted to £37,000. However, it was pointed out that such earnings, if actually paid, would have had tax deducted from them. The House of Lords decided that the damages should also be reduced because of the tax element and Mr Gourley received £6,000. In this context taxation is intended to refer to income tax.

In another context it should be remembered that taxation was until recently the name given to the procedure where the party to litigation has its costs examined by a judge to see which costs may be allowed and which may be disregarded. This process is now known as "assessment of costs". This was a tort case but the same principles apply as in contract. This point also illustrates the fact that a claimant must not be allowed to make a profit. The purpose of awarding damages is to attempt to put the claimant back into the same position as he would have been in had the contract been performed. Damages are intended as compensation and not as punishment. This is in contrast to the position in the USA where juries are still used in many civil cases. These juries sometimes award huge sums often with a punitive element. In the UK damages mostly equate to the sum actually lost or a forecast of loss and are much more modest.

Incidentally the party who benefited from this decision was BTC because the damages they had to pay were considerably reduced.

This point also arises when there is a contract for the sale of goods and the contract goes off. If there is a market for the goods then if the seller is in default the buyer can go and buy similar goods and can only claim damages for the difference between the contract price and the market price. Likewise if the buyer is in default then the amount of damages depends on whether or not the seller can easily sell the goods. If he can, then he may not deserve compensation. If there is no market for the goods then the seller will have lost a sale and will be able to recover the profit he would have made if the sale had gone through.

*W L Thompson Ltd v Robinson Gunmakers Ltd (1955).* The defendants bought a Standard "Vanguard" motor car from the plaintiffs and then refused to accept it. The seller's profit would have been £61. As the supply of this particular vehicle exceeded the demand the sellers could not re-sell it and so lost their profit. They succeeded in recovering the whole loss of profit.

*Charter v Sullivan (1957).* The defendant bought a Hillman Minx motor car from the plaintiff. The latter's profit would have been £97.15s. When sued for non-acceptance the defendant was only ordered to pay nominal damages because it was proved that the seller could sell as many Hillman Minx cars as he could obtain. Therefore he had not incurred any appreciable loss.

## *Difficulty of Assessing Damages*

Sometimes it may be difficult for the judge to estimate the amount of damages he should award; however, this should not deter him.

> In *Chaplin v Hicks* (1911) Hicks advertised a beauty competition, by which readers of some newspapers were to select fifty girls, and from them Hicks would select twelve for whom he would provide theatrical bookings. Chaplin was one of the fifty but, owing to Hicks's breach of contract, she was not present when the final selection was made. Held, although it was problematic whether she would have been one of the twelve selected and although it was difficult to assess damages, Chaplin was entitled to have damages assessed. Also it is permissible for a sum to be awarded respect of nervous shock suffered or the effect of loss of status following demotion in employment or loss of enjoyment of a holiday.

The common law remedy for breach of contract, is, then, damages. Other remedies are said to be equitable, and they are as follows.

## *Quantum Meruit*

*Quantum meruit* means literally "as much as it is worth". A claim on a *quantum meruit* can be used to recover a reasonable price or a fee where a contract has been made for the supply of goods or the performance of services in circumstances where a promise to pay can be implied, but no precise sum has been fixed.

It is available as an alternative to claiming damages in cases where damages would not be appropriate. For example, when one party breaks the contract the other can sue on a *quantum meruit* for a reasonable sum for work already completed before the breach.

It is available to enable a reasonable sum to be claimed for work done under a void contract. The remedy is available also where there never was a contract. However, where A agrees to pay B an agreed fee for certain work and B subsequently agrees to do further work without mentioning a further fee, B cannot seek a *quantum meruit* for that further work while the initial contract exists and has not been discharged. *Gilbert and Partners v Knight (1968).*

A claim on a *quantum meruit* cannot be made in respect of a "lump sum contract", that is, a contract in which one party promises to complete the whole task before being paid anything. *Quantum meruit* is not available here because an express promise to accept a lump sum at the end and nothing in the meantime takes precedence over an implied promise to pay a reasonable sum for whatever is completed. This is illustrated by following the 200-year-old case.

*Cutter v Powell (1795).* P agreed to pay C 30 guineas for acting as second mate aboard a vessel sailing from Jamaica to Liverpool. After 49 days, and only 19 days short of Liverpool, C died. It was held that this was a lump sum contract and his executors could recover nothing for the work he had done before he died; completion of the voyage was a condition precedent to payment.

Obviously injustice is caused by a case like *Cutter v Powell*, which has been severely criticised. To reduce the harshness the courts have developed the doctrine of substantial performance. If the plaintiff substantially performs the task, he or she can recover the whole lump sum less a deduction to compensate the defendant for the minor omissions or defects. *Hoenig v Isaacs (1952).*

The ordinary contract between an employer and an employee is not of the lump sum type as the employee is paid weekly or monthly and not by a lump sum, and therefore *quantum meruit* is available.

## *Specific Performance*

A decree of specific performance is an order of the court expressly instructing the defendant to perform the contract. It is an equitable remedy devised to remedy a defect in the common law which would only award damages for breach of contract. Like all equitable remedies, specific performance is discretionary. The court is not bound to decree it simply because the usual conditions for it exist. But over the centuries the discretion has become exercisable in accordance with certain rules. The discretion will not be exercised and specific performance will be refused in the following cases.

1. Where the plaintiff's loss would be adequately remedied by damages. Specific performance is a superior remedy and will not be wasted when an ordinary remedy would be adequate. For example, specific performance will not be ordered of a contract for the sale of ordinary commercial goods. Only damages will be awarded because such goods are readily available elsewhere. But specific performance may be ordered where the goods are rare and not easily obtainable.
2. Where constant supervision by the court would be necessary, for example a building contract.
3. Where the contract is for personal work or services, for example a contract of employment. The court is not a slave-driver and will not compel a person to work against his or her will. Also the court is not in a position to supervise the performance of the contract.
4. Where the contract is voidable at the option of one of the parties, specific performance will not be granted because there is a lack of mutuality. For example, certain contracts made by minors are voidable at their option, so that they cannot be enforced by specific performance against minors by adults. Equity will not grant specific performance of the same contracts by minors

against adults.

5. Where the plaintiff is guilty of dishonesty or sharp practice. "He who comes to equity must come with clean hands." See the case of *Webster v Cecil (1861)*.
6. Where consideration does not exist, for "equity will not assist a volunteer".
7. Where specific performance would cause hardship to the defendant. For example, A contracts to buy a house from B and pays his deposit before completing his mortgage arrangements. The building society turns down his mortgage application and A breaks the contract by refusing to complete the transaction. A will lose his deposit but will not have specific performance awarded against him.

Defiance of a decree of specific performance is contempt of court for which the defendant can be imprisoned or fined.

## *Injunction*

This is an order of the court to prevent the doing, continuance or repetition of some wrongful act (such as breach of contract, or a tort such as nuisance). The injunction is an equitable remedy and therefore discretionary. It will not be awarded if damages would adequately compensate the plaintiff, or where the court cannot make sure that the order is obeyed. Note also the following points concerning injunctions.

1. An injunction can be either interlocutory (temporary) or perpetual (permanent). An interlocutory injunction is granted before the trial of the action basically in order to preserve the status quo. If it is granted, the plaintiff normally undertakes to pay damages to the defendant if it transpires that the plaintiff loses his or her action at the trial. Before 1975, an applicant for an interlocutory injunction needed to show that he or she had a prima facie case. In *American Cynanamid v Ethicon (1975)*, the House of Lords held that the applicant need only show that there was a serious issue to be tried. Subject to that, and unless there was no material to indicate that the applicant had any real prospect of success at the full trial of the action, the court should consider the balance of convenience. In that connection, the court would consider whether, if the plaintiff succeeded at the trial after initial refusal of an injunction, an award of damages would be sufficient compensation for any interim loss suffered; and whether, if an interlocutory injunction were granted and the plaintiff lost at the trial, the plaintiff's undertaking as to damages would adequately compensate the defendant for any loss he or she had sustained until the trial. A *quia timet* injunction is a special kind of interlocutory injunction which is granted (rarely) where the applicant can show that he or she will suffer imminent and substantial loss as a result of a threatened

act. Literally translated, *quia timet* means "because he or she fears". A perpetual injunction is granted after the trial when the dispute has been resolved by the court. It may last forever.

2. An injunction can also be prohibitory or mandatory. A prohibitory injunction orders that the wrongful act shall not be done: this is the usual type. A mandatory injunction orders the doing of a certain positive act is not applicable in contract law because specific performance is available, but it could be used, for example, to order the demolition of a wall which had been constructed in breach of a restrictive covenant.
3. Specific performance and a mandatory injunction must be distinguished. The former is used to compel the performance of a contract which has not been performed; the latter is used to order the undoing of something already done in breach of contract.
4. The injunction is particularly useful in contract law to restrain the breach of a negative term, that is, where a party promises not to do something. The court may grant an injunction in such cases even where damages would be adequate and the contract is one for personal work or services.

*Lumley v Wagner (1852).* Miss W agreed to sing in L's theatre for a specific period during which she agreed to sing nowhere else. She was induced into singing elsewhere by a third party. L sued Miss W for specific performance and an injunction. It was held that he could have an injunction but not specific performance. The contract was one of employment and the court refused to order Miss W to sing in L's theatre by an order of specific performance. But the contractual term she had broken was in negative language ("not to sing elsewhere"), and she could be restrained by injunction from singing anywhere but in L's theatre while the contract was in force.
Note that in no circumstances must the non-availability of specific performance be circumvented by the award of an injunction (against Miss W). In other words, if the grant of an injunction against Miss W would have resulted in driving her back to L's theatre to sing, L would have been refused an injunction because its effect would have been the same as if specific performance had been decreed. *Page One Records Ltd v Britton* (1967). Older students may remember the pop group "The Troggs". This case involved the group being sued by their manager.

## *"Mareva" Injunction*

This type of injunction is an exception to the general rule that a court will not prevent a person from disposing of his or her assets (for example, a debtor) in order to aid a plaintiff (for example, a creditor). The remedy, which has evolved substantially in recent years, is designed principally to prevent a foreign defendant from removing asserts outside the jurisdiction of the court so that they are not available when the plaintiff (as must appear likely) obtains judgement for damages or other sum. Section 37(3) of the *Supreme Court Act 1981* recognises the extended powers of the High Court to grant a Mareva injunction by providing:

> The powers of the High Court ... to grant an interlocutory injunction restraining a party to any proceedings from removing from the jurisdiction of the High Court, or otherwise dealing with, assets located within the jurisdiction shall be exercisable in all cases where that party is, as well as in cases where he is not, domiciled, resident or present within that jurisdiction.

A Mareva injunction can be a useful remedy to a person suing for breach of contract in the relevant circumstances, particularly bearing in mind the frequent international nature of business transactions.

In *Orwell Steel (Erection and Fabrication) Ltd v Asphalt Tarmac (UK) Ltd (1984)* it was held that the High Court had power to grant a Mareva injunction, after judgement but before execution, to restrain a judgement debtor from disposing of assets pending execution.

## Assignment of Contractual Rights

This is a process by which rights under a contract are transferred to a person not party to the original contract. Contractual rights are a form of personal property known as "choses in action" (that is, things in action). Another example is the right to receive payment of a debt. Assignment can be either by act of the parties or by operation of law, or according to special rules.

## Assignment by Act of Parties

An assignment by act of the parties can be legal or equitable.

## Legal Assignment

This is governed by Section 136 of the *Law of Property Act 1925*, which provides as follows.

1. The assignment must be in writing.
2. It must be signed by the assignor.
3. It must be absolute (that is, it must transfer the whole chose in action and not

merely part of it).

4. Express notice in writing must be given to the other party to the contract.
5. In addition, by common law, the assignment is "subject to equities", that is, the debtor can raise against the assignee any defence or counter-claim he or she would have had if sued by the assignor.

For example, B owes A £100 and A owes B £50. A can assign the right to receive payment of the £100 to C, but C will take it subject to equities and will obtain no better title to the debt than A had. If C sues B for the £100, B can set off the £50 that A owes him because this defence would have been available to B if he had been sued by A.

If Section 136 of the *Law of Property Act 1925* is complied with, the effect of the assignment is to transfer to the assignee the legal right to the debt or other chose in action. In other words, the assignee becomes the new owner. But Section 136 can only be used to assign a legal chose in action and cannot be used to assign an equitable chose in action. Legal chooses include debts and other contractual rights. Equitable chooses include rights under a trust, a share in a partnership, and a share in an intestacy.

## *Equitable Assignment*

This is appropriate in two cases.

1. An attempted legal assignment which does not completely satisfy Section 136 of the *Law of Property Act 1925* may still be a valid equitable assignment. The maxim "equity looks to the intention rather than the form" applies here. Unlike legal assignment, an equitable assignment need not be in writing and no other formalities are required provided the intention of the parties is clear.
2. An equitable chose in action must be assigned by means of an equitable assignment.

The drawback of an equitable assignment of a legal chose is that the assignee cannot sue the debtor in his or her own name. After a legal assignment under the *Law of Property Act 1925*, the assignee becomes the new legal owner of the chose in action and can personally sue the debtor.

But after an equitable assignment of a legal chose the assignee becomes equitable owner of the chose only; the assignor remains legal owner. The equitable assignee must joint the assignor as a co-plaintiff in order to sue the debtor. If the assignor refused to join the equitable assignee, the assignor must be used as a co-defendant.

An equitable assignment of either type is also "subject to equities", as explained above.

## *Special Methods of Assignment*

Some choses in action are not assigned under Section 136 of the *Law of Property Act 1925*, but in a special manner peculiar to themselves. These choses are:

1. shares in a company registered under the Companies Acts, by share transfer forms;
2. patents: legal assignments must be by deed and must be registered at the Patents Office;
3. copyrights, which must be assigned in writing signed by or on behalf of the owner of the copyright: *Copyright, Designs and Patents Act 1988*;
4. life assurance policies, which can be assigned either by endorsement on the policy or by a separate document of transfer. Written notice to the insurers must be given to complete the assignment: *Policies of Assurance Act 1867*;
5. negotiable instruments (such as bills of exchange, which are not assigned; they are negotiated. This means they are transferred by mere delivery, sometimes with an endorsement.

## *Assignment by Operation of Law*

The death of a person passes all his or her rights and liabilities under a contract to his or her personal representatives, except in the case of contracts for personal work or services. (These are discharged on death). The bankruptcy of a person transfers all his or her rights and liabilities to his or her trustee in bankruptcy.

**Questions**

In what circumstances may a court declare a contract to have been frustrated?

In what ways may a breach of contract occur?

How are damages assessed?

EIGHT

# ARBITRATION

*Study Topics*

**How commercial disputes can be resolved through arbitration**
**The advantages of arbitration**
**Alternative dispute resolution**

Where a contract is made between two parties in the course of a business, it is becoming increasingly more common for the parties to agree that any dispute shall be resolved by arbitration. This is because using the courts is often slow and expensive compared to proceedings before an arbitrator.

> All disputes, differences or questions between the parties to the Contract with respect to any matter or thing arising out of or relating to the Contract shall be referred to the arbitration of two persons, one to be appointed by X and one by the Contractor or their Umpire.

Such contracts, providing as they do that any disputes shall be solved extra-judicially, are perfectly valid. Indeed if one party disregards such a clause the court may stop the action and in effect will compel the party to go to arbitration. (*Arbitration Act 1950* S4 (1)).

In this connection a distinction must be made between a domestic arbitration agreement and a non-domestic arbitration agreement. A domestic agreement is one in which the parties are UK citizens or UK companies. In this case a stay of proceedings may only be granted if the matter in question is within the scope of the arbitration agreement and the applicant has taken no steps in the court proceedings (S4(1)). Also he must have been ready to do everything necessary for the proper conduct of the arbitration and there must be no good reason why the dispute should not be referred to arbitration. The same principles will apply when the parties have agreed on an exclusive jurisdiction clause and not an arbitration clause.

*The Fehmarn (1957).* A cargo of turpentine was loaded at a Russian port into a German vessel. The bills of lading were held by an English company which claimed that the turpentine was contaminated in transit and bought an action against the German vessel in the English courts. The owners of the German vessel applied for a stay on the grounds that the bills of lading provided that all the disputes should be judged in the USSR. It was held that the stay should be refused because the dispute had little connection with the USSR. None of the parties had Soviet nationality and virtually all the witnesses and other evidence were to be found in England.

*Arata Potato Co Ltd v Egyptian Navigation Co (The El Amria) (1980).* Egyptian Spring potatoes were carried in the *El Amria*, a ship owned by an Egyptian shipping company, from Alexandria to Liverpool. The bill of lading provided that any disputes should be decided in the country where the carrier had his principal place of business, i.e. in Egypt. The plaintiffs, who were the cargo owners, alleged that the cargo was found to be in a deteriorated condition when unloaded. They brought an action in the English courts against the defendant shipowners, claimed damages for breach of contract, and for negligence. The defendants alleged that the deterioration of the cargo had occurred as the result of the unreasonably slow discharge and applied for a stay of proceedings in the English courts on the grounds that the parties had agreed that the dispute was to be decided by the Egyptian courts. It was held the application for a stay of proceedings should be refused and the case should be allowed to proceed in the English courts. The issues raised between the parties relating to the alleged slow discharge solely concerned events which occurred in England and since the plaintiffs had issued a writ against the Mersey Docks and Harbour Co it would be a matter of great convenience if that action could be tried at the same time as this action. Further, the most important evidence was in England. There were therefore strong reasons for refusing a stay of the English proceedings.

In the case of a non-domestic arbitration the court must order a stay of proceedings unless it is satisfied that the arbitration agreement is null and void or incapable of being performed or that there is not in fact any dispute between the parties with regard to the matters agreed to be referred to arbitration. *Arbitration Act 1975* S1 (1).

*Nova (Jersey) Knit Ltd v Kammgarn Spinnerei GmbH (1977).* In 1970 the plaintiffs Nova, an English company, entered into a partnership agreement with the defendants

Kammgarn, a German company, whereby the plaintiffs were to supply the defendants with knitting machines. The contract contained an arbitration clause and there was also a separate arbitration agreement. In 1972 the plaintiffs sold 12 machines to the defendants and received 24 bills of exchange for a total of £173,558. The first six of these bills of exchange were honoured by the defendants but the others were not paid on the ground, as the defendants alleged, of fraud. The defendants commenced arbitration proceedings in Germany and the plaintiffs issued a writ in the English courts for service out of jurisdiction claiming payment of the outstanding bills of exchange. The defendants applied for a stay of the court proceedings. One of the issues was whether the arbitration agreement extended to the claims of the plaintiffs for payment of the outstanding bills of exchange. If this question had to be answered in the affirmative, the court was bound by section 1 (1) of the *Arbitration Act 1975* to grant a stay of court proceedings. It was held, however, the arbitration agreement did not extend to claims made under the bills of exchange and the application for a stay of court proceedings on the bills of exchange should be dismissed.

## *Judicial Review*

The court may still retain some control over the resolution of the dispute and may grant leave to appeal from a decision of an arbitrator on a point of law. However this leave will only be given sparingly and in particular a party to the dispute must have informed the arbitrator before the award was made that a reasoned award was requested or that there was some special reason why the arbitrator was not notified.

The appeal may be brought to the High Court if the parties consent or by leave of the Court. The Court will only give leave if it considers that the determination of the question of law could substantially affect the right of one or more of the parties to the arbitration agreement. *Arbitration Act 1979* S(3) and (4). Usually leave will only be granted in a "one-off" contract. This is a contract of a single occurrence and not made on standard contract forms.

*Pioneer Shipping Ltd v BTP Tioxide Ltd* (The *Nema) (1982)*. The owners of the *Nema* chartered her for seven consecutive voyages to Sorel in Canada. Sorel was at the St Lawrence River and was icebound for many months of the year. After one round voyage the Nema arrived back at Sorel but was unable to load owing to a strike. The owners, who were permitted by the terms of the charter party to take the Nema on one transatlantic voyage, took her to Spain. The main issue between the parties was whether, as the charterers claimed, the *Nema* was bound to proceed from Spain to Sorel and wait there until either the strike ended and she could load or the open water season ended and loading was made impossible. Or whether, as the owners contended, their obligations to make the *Nema* available for the outstanding voyages had ended by frustration. The parties agreed on arbitration by a single arbitrator who decided that the whole charter party, as far as not performed, was frustrated. On appeal to the Court, Robert Goff J gave leave for judicial review of the arbitration award and held that the charter party was not frustrated, but his decision was reversed by the Court of Appeal. The charterers then appealed to the House of Lords. It was held, (i) Robert Goff J should not have granted leave to appeal from the decision of the arbitrator nor should leave have been given to appeal to the Court of Appeal; and (ii) the arbitrator rightly decided that the whole charter-party, as far as not performed, was frustrated.

Appeals may also lie to the Court of Appeal with leave of the High Court or Court of Appeal.

## *Exclusion Agreement*

The parties may sometimes exclude a judicial review, and so the effect will be that there will be no appeal to the High Court on a point of law. In domestic arbitrations the parties may exclude a judicial review by an exclusion agreement if the agreement was made after the commencement of the arbitration proceedings. S3(6). In non-domestic arbitrations the parties may enter into an exclusion before or after the commencement of the arbitration proceedings. S4(1).

Where the dispute is concerned with a claim falling within the Admiralty jurisdiction of the High Court (i.e. concerning shipping), a dispute arising out of a contract of insurance or out of a commodity contract, then the exclusion clause will be admitted after the commencement of the arbitration or if the contact is governed other than by the law of England and Wales.

## *The Arbitration Agreement*

The main reasons why the parties may insist on an arbitration clause in their agreement are:

1. the procedure is quicker than going to an established court of law;
2. consequently the dispute can be resolved more cheaply;
3. the arbitration proceedings can be conducted out of the glare of publicity;
4. the arbitrator will usually be someone who is qualified in the technical aspects of the matter in dispute.

Every agreement is assumed to include the following provisions unless a contrary consideration is expressed.

1. reference is to a single arbitrator;
2. if there is reference to two arbitrators they may appoint an umpire at any time after they themselves have been appointed;

3. if the arbitrators have informed the umpire in writing that they cannot agree, he may act;
4. the parties to the arbitration proceedings must allow themselves to be examined under oath and must produce all relevant documents;
5. witnesses must also be examined on oath;
6. the award when made by the arbitrator will be final and binding on the parties;
7. the arbitrator can order specific performance of any contract, except one relating to land;
8. an interim award may be made;
9. costs are in the discretion of the arbitrator and he can award costs to be paid by either party;
10. where the reference is to a single arbitrator or an umpire, and the parties do not agree or the arbitrator or umpire dies or refuses to act, any party may serve notice on the other to make an appointment and if not made within seven days the court will appoint.

*Tritonia Shipping Inc v South Nelson Forest Product Corpn (1966).* The *mv Tanais* was under charter for a voyage between Canada and Italy. The charter party provided, *inter alia*, for "arbitration to be settled in London". A dispute arose between the shipowners and the charterers and the shipowners requested that the charterers agree on the arbitrator, but the latter refused to cooperate. It was held that the dispute should be settled by arbitration and an arbitrator be appointed by the court.

11. a similar situation will arise when a third party, for example a chamber commerce or the president of a professional association fails or declines to appoint an arbitrator. After seven days the court may appoint.

## *The Award*

1. must be certain and follow the agreement.
2. if a contract contains an arbitration clause and a claim is made in negligence (a tort) then provided it is connected with the contract, it is within the jurisdiction of the arbitrator.

*Astro Venecedor Compania Naviera SA of Panama v Mabanaft GmbH* (The *Damianos*)*(1971)*. Charterers thought that they had a claim for damages against the shipowners who had stopped the discharge of goods from the ship. In pursuance of their claim, the charterers arrested the ship. The shipowners claimed that the arrest was wrongful and demanded damages. The charter party contained an arbitration clause and the arbitrators decided the claim for damages for wrongful arrest in favour of the shipowners. It was held that the claims for damages for wrongful arrest of the ship was found in tort, the arbitrators had jurisdiction to dispose of the claim as the arrest of the ship was only the sequel to the claim of the charterers and so closely connected with the alleged breach of charter party that it was within the scope of the arbitration.

3. the award must be final, legal, reasonable and possible;
4. it must be reasoned if so requested by a party.

References on arbitration in this chapter have been to the *Arbitration Acts 1950, 1975* and *1979*. These Acts were superseded by the *Arbitration Act l996*. This Act received Royal Assent on June 17 1996. The new Act replaced the *Arbitration Acts 1950*, *1975* and *1979* and the *Consumer Arbitration Agreements Act 1988*. The purpose of the new Act was to improve and refine current arbitration law so there would be easier access to a speedier and fair system of resolving disputes. The Act combines a restatement of current statute law, modified to strengthen the arbitral process, with codification of the more important principles of arbitration law developed through the courts. Nevertheless the actual content of the existing law was altered very little. Some important provisions are set out below. The principles of the Act are set out in *Section 1*. These are, in essence: to obtain fair and impartial resolution without undue expense and delay, to allow parties to agree how to resolve their disputes, subject to the public interest and to limit interference of the court. This interference is now limited to four situations only. For example *S67* allows intervention if the arbitrator has acted outside his jurisdiction. *S68* sets out the criteria for intervention if there has been an "irregularity" in proceedings. The court will, however, have greater powers to intervene in domestic rather than international arbitration.

Arbitration as described above has existed for a very long time. It was devised to to avoid the expense and slow pace of a court action, and principally because arbitration proceedings are held in private. This last point is important if the parties are companies in the public eye or partners in dispute. However arbitration is very similiar to litigation. In each case the solution is imposed by an arbitrator or judge and is binding on the parties.

Arbitration has now overspilled into the legal arena and there is provision for arbitrators in the courts. The *Courts and Legal Services Act 1990* and the *Supreme Court Act 1981* provide for judges of the Commercial Court and the Official Referees to act as arbitrators. Also the rules of evidence will apply in such proceedings and the parties must state their case in writing, similar to a pleading in the High Court. In these cases, of course, it is up to the parties whether they wish to use the arbitration procedure. There is no compulsion. However in a small claim (under £5,000) heard in the County Court the District judge will act as an arbitrator instead of as a judge.

## Alternative Dispute Resolution

A different form of arbitration is Alternative Dispute Resolution known as ADR. This, like arbitration, can only take place by agreement between the parties. The main feature of this system of solving disputes is that a decision will not be imposed by a judge or an arbitrator but will be reached by the parties themselves. ADR was initiated in the USA over ten years ago and is intended to overcome some of the disadvantages of going to court.

There is nothing new in the idea because it has been realised by lawyers that it is usually preferable to settle out of court. The risks of allowing a dispute to be decided by a judge are obvious and the expenses can sometimes be considerable. Also if a dispute can be resolved by agreement between the parties then each part will consider that he has won whereas if the case is decided by a judge then there will be a loser and a victor.

The parties who have been in dispute can resolve their differences and then carry on business in the future on a friendly basis. ADR consists of mediation or conciliation and this may take the form of oral hearings in the presence of both parties or maybe documents only are submitted. Usually the mediator will see one side in one room and after listening to their grievances will see the other side in another room. Eventually some common ground may be reached which will form the basis of a compromise. In this way a great deal of money may be saved compared with the costs of going to court.

A more formal type of mediation is the Structured Settlement Procedure which is organised on the lines of a trial. In this case management representatives of each party are given the facts as viewed by both sides. Then, with the assistance of a neutral adviser, they enter into negotiations to solve the dispute.

If each party is intent on sticking to his strict legal rights then ADR will probably not be a success. What is essential is that both sides should be prepared to discuss the question of compromise.

If ADR is not successful then litigation may follow. This will not be prejudiced by the use of ADR because any evidence arising from the ADR procedure will be confidential and without prejudice and may not be disclosed in later litigation. Sometimes ADR may be used after litigation has commenced. In that case the court action will be suspended to permit the mediation method to be given a chance to solve the dispute. At the end of the day the question is whether the parties want a solution imposed by a court with its attendant expense and publicity or do they want to try to solve the dispute themselves, with the help of a mediator. Another factor is that since the changes introduced by Lord Woolf's Report into Civil Justice discussed in Chapter 1, failing to use mediation when it is a reasonable alternative may count against the parties. Lord Woolf also recommended that mediation be extended to such areas as medical negligence to achieve a less adversarial process of settlement.

**Questions**

What is the difference between a domestic and a non-domestic arbitration?

What are the advantages of ADR?

NINE

# THE LAW *of* AGENCY

*Study Topics*

**Nature of agency and how it may arise**
**Rights and duties of an agent**
**Liability of an agent to third parties**

The examples of agencies that exist are commonplace and everyone probably appreciates their purpose. An estate agent is someone who acts on behalf of another to sell or buy his house or land. Theatrical artistes have agents who negotiate terms with producers of theatrical or TV shows. The agents are people who bring their principals into contractual relationship with third parties. In other words they make contracts with people; but these contracts will be binding not on themselves but on the people they are representing. In a typical agency relationship the agent makes the contract and then disappears, leaving the contract proper between the principal and the third party.

Of course there may probably be a contract between the principal and the agent but this is not the main contract – the important one is that between the principal and the third party.

The purpose of the law of agency is to establish whether or not the agency relationship exists. Depending on the answer to that question the rights and duties of the parties can be determined. As always the law seeks to determine the rights and liabilities of the parties: is the agent himself to be liable, may the third party sue the principal or may the principal sue the third party?

## *Liability of the Agent*

From a practical point of view one should consider the matter from the point of view of the third party. Does he know that he is dealing with an agent? That depends on whether or not he is informed on this point. Quite obviously an agent does not go round wearing a cap bearing the word "Agent". So only if the agent notifies the person he is dealing with that he is an agent will the third party know this fact.

The normal agency situation is when the agent informs the third party that he is an agent acting for a certain principal. In that case the third party knows the position and the contract will be between the principal and the third party.

Looking at the agency relationship from the point of view of the principal, as a general rule it all depends on whether or not he has authorised the agent as to whether he will be liable or not. Thus if the agent is authorised to enter into a contract and the third party knows that he is dealing with an agent and maybe knows the identity of the principal then the contract when made will lie between the principal and the third party. The agent will have neither rights nor duties under the contract.

If the third party does not know he is dealing with an agent, because the agent has not informed him of the fact, then the third party will naturally conclude that he is dealing with the person who is the agent in his own right. Consequently the third party may only sue the agent, if the need arises. However if he later does discover the existence of the principal and his identity then he may sue him. He cannot of course sue both agent and principal. This is sometimes referred to as the doctrine of the undisclosed principal.

Another situation may arise when the agent informs the third party that he is an agent but does not identify his principal. This may occur when a large important company is wishing to buy certain property and if it became known that such a wealthy client had an interest in acquiring the property the price might become inflated. In this case the third party knows he is dealing with an agent and so it is up to him whether he continues to deal with a principal whose identity he does not know. At any rate the agent will have no liability in the matter.

## *Signatures*

An agent may be liable if he signs a document, but it depends on the manner in which he signs it.

1. The agent may sign in his own name. In that case it is probably true to say that the agent has accepted liability unless of course he makes it clear that he is signing as agent. However he must be careful to make sure that he is not

merely describing his relationship to his principal (for example, A signs in his name and adds "Chartered Civil Engineer"). In Sika Contacts Ltd v B L Gill and Closeglen Properties Ltd (1978) it was held that A was liable as he had merely described his occupation. However in Universal Steam Navigation Co Ltd v Mckelvie and Co (1923) A was not liable when he signed in his own name "as agents". Section 26 of the Bills of Exchange Act 1882 provides:

a. Where a person signs a bill as a drawer, indorser or acceptor, and adds the words to his signature, indicating that he signs for or on behalf of a principal or in a representative character, he is not personally liable thereon; but the mere addition to his signature of words describing him as an agent, or as filling a representative character, does not exempt him from personal liability.
b. In determining whether a signature on a bill is that of the principal or that of an agent by whose hand it is written, the construction most favourable to the validity of the instrument shall be adopted.

The effect of this is that where an agent signs, in his own name, a deed or a bill of exchange then he will be liable on these documents. P will not be liable if his name does not appear on these documents. An exception would be if A signed a deed and was authorised by a power of attorney.

2. If a person signs "per procurationem" then it indicates that he has only a limited authority. Often a person will sign in this way on behalf of a company. The principal therefore will only be liable if the agent is acting within his actual authority.

3. The principal may of course authorise the agent to sign using his (the principal's) name. This is in order.

4. No-one has a proprietary right to any name, unless it is subject to the trade mark rules. Therefore a person may use any name that he wishes so long as there is no dishonest intent.

5. In Chapman v Smethurst (1909) a promissory note was signed by the managing director who signed it "S Ltd – S.M.D." The court held that this showed that the company S Ltd was to be bound and not S.

In *Elliot v Bax-Ironside* (1925) two directors signed a cheque as "I and M directors F Ltd" and on the back they indorsed it by signing "F Ltd" "I and M – directors". The two directors were held liable for the second signatures because they had merely indicated their occupations and the company was already liable because of the signatures on the front.

In *Bondina Ltd v Rollaway Shower Blinds Ltd* (1986) the printed cheque form of a company contained its name, the branch of the bank and the number of the cheque. It was signed by two directors who added their names (W,M). It was held that the directors had adopted all the printing on the cheque including the name of the company and so the directors were not liable.

## *Liability of Principal*

From the principal's point of view he will usually only be liable if he has authorised the agent to enter into his contract. This is known as the express appointment of an agent. However an agency relationship may arise in other ways.

1. The principal holds out the agent as having his authority. That means the principal gives the third party the impression that the agent has the authority of the principal to make the contract he is making with the third party. A case in point here is *Watteau v Fenwick (1893)* where a firm of brewers forbade the manager of a public house to buy cigars for the business. The manager did in fact buy cigars in disobedience of this order and the court held that the brewers were nevertheless still liable. They had held out the manager as having the normal authority of a manager of a public house which was to buy cigars for the business and had not communicated their restriction on his authority to the seller of the cigars.

2. The agent may have exceeded his authority but nevertheless the principal decides to adopt his contract. This is called "ratification" and is only possible if the agent notified the third party that he was an agent. In *Keighly, Maxsted and Co v Durant (1901)* no ratification was possible because the agent had contracted in his own name. Also in order for the principal to ratify an unauthorised contract of his agent, he must have had contractual capacity both at the time the contract was made and when it was ratified. Finally if the principal was a company then it must have been in existence when the contract was made. Thus a pre-incorporation contract will not bind a company when it is later incorporated. *Kelner v Baxter (1866)*.

3. The agent is a carrier and is carrying perishable goods belonging to the principal. Something occurs to prevent their delivery and so the carrier must do something immediately otherwise the goods are going to become worthless. He sells the goods in order to minimise the principal's loss. On the face of it he will be liable to the principal, however if he can show that he tried to get in touch with him and failed and it was an emergency then he will be declared to be an "agent of necessity".

In *Springer v Great Western Railway* (1921) the delivery of a consignment of tomatoes was delayed and so the carrier sold the perishable goods and the question arose: was he liable for interfering with the goods of another and did the purchasers get a good title to the goods which they bought? The court held that an agency of necessity had arisen and so the carrier was not liable to the owner, and the purchasers of the goods acquired good title to them.

Thus it can sometimes be said that an agent has been appointed expressly. In other cases the agency relationship merely arises because of circumstances: a relationship (for example, husband and wife); a situation (for example, perishable goods prevented from being delivered and the carrier sells them); or the holding out of a person as having the authority of another as in *Watteau v Fenwick (1893)*.

Where a man and a woman are living together (not necessarily as man and wife) then the woman has the right to pledge the man's credit for the purchase of necessaries such as food and certain articles for the home. This is the common law position and it is interesting to consider how this position may be affected by the modern approach to sexual equality.

There is one case when an agent must be appointed by a deed and that is when his principal expects him to execute a deed. The deed appointing the agent is called a power of attorney and often old people incapable of acting for themselves appoint some other person to deal with their affairs.

## *Power of Attorney*

A power of attorney is required by the agent if it may become necessary for him to make a transaction by deed. In this case the attorney or agent must himself be appointed by deed. The law has always treated a transaction by deed in a special way. A deed was quite simply a document to which had been affixed a seal. At one time a seal was a large piece of wax on which a person's coat of arms would be impressed when the wax was in molten state. It was necessary for the person executing the deed to state, with his finger on the seal, "I deliver this as my act and deed". Since the *Law of Property (Miscellaneous Provisions) Act 1989* a seal is not necessary but it must be made clear in the document that it is intended to be a deed. Certain transactions will have no legal effect unless contained in a deed, for example conveyance of the legal estate in land, or a legal mortgage of property.

### *Powers of Attorney Act 1971*

Signature and sealing may be by a person other than the donor if in his presence and by his direction; in this case two witnesses are necessary. The power of attorney must be stamped within 30 days of its execution.

The advantage of taking a power of attorney from the point of view of a bank is that the power can be made irrevocable and, if it is given to secure a proprietary interest of the donee or the performance of an obligation owed to him, then so long as the obligation of interest continues the power will not be revoked by death, bankruptcy or mental incapacity of the donor. Such a situation could arise when a bank takes an equitable mortgage of a legal estate by receiving the title deeds. The deposit will be accompanied by a memorandum authorising the bank to sell the property in certain circumstances. Here the bank will have a proprietary interest in the land and so the power cannot be revoked.

Powers which have not been given by way of security will be revoked by the death or mental incapacity of the donor. The situation has been improved by the *Enduring Powers of Attorney (Prescribed Forms) Regulations 1986* which specifies the form that must be completed by the donor and the attorney.

If the attorney believes that the donor is becoming incapable he must apply for registration of the instrument creating the power to the Court of Protection. Before applying for registration he must give notice to certain relatives of the donor. If the donor does eventually become incapable, the attorney may only act in accordance with the directions of the court until the instrument has been registered as mentioned above.

The timing of the creation of the enduring powers is of the greatest importance because a sane person may not be willing to execute the document and once he has become insane it is too late as the instrument could then be declared invalid.

In two cases, *Re K* and *Re F,* the court decided that it was sufficient if the donor understood the nature and effect of the power of attorney he or she was signing. It will not be necessary for the donor of the power to be able to manage his own affairs.

## *Duties of an Agent*

The relationship between the principal and the agent, no matter how the relationship arose, is essentially one of trust (a fiduciary relationship).

1. The agent must obey the instructions given to him by his principal even if he thinks the instructions are wrong. Sometimes of course the principal may expect the agent to advise him and indeed this may be the reason he is employing an agent, viz. to use his skill and care. The agent must not delegate his duty to another person unless such delegation has been agreed with the principal, is the custom of the trade or the delegation merely takes place in relation to purely administrative matters.
2. An agent must not allow his personal interests to come into conflict with those of the principal.
3. The agent must not make a secret profit or take a bribe from a third party. In *Reading v Att. Gen. (1951)* it was held that a sergeant in the British Army had misused his position by sitting on a lorry thereby giving the impression

that it was a military convoy and so it was not inspected. He was ordered to repay the money he had received to the State.

4. If the agent accepts a secret commission or a bribe the following consequences may ensue.

*Salford Corporation v Lever (1891)* Lever agreed to pay the Corporation's agent 1 shilling per ton if his tender for the supply of coal was accepted. When the bribe was discovered it was held that both the giver and the taker of the bribe could be sued and prosecuted under the *Prevention of Corruption Act 1906.* Also the agent could be dismissed without receiving his commission and the contract with the third party could be set aside. In that case it was held:

i. The principal may dismiss him.
ii. He can recover the secret commission from the agent. If the commission has not been paid over to the agent, the principal may recover it from the person who promised the agent.
iii. Whether he has recovered the secret commission or not, the principal may still bring an action for damages against the person who gave the agent the bribe.
iv. He may refuse to pay the agent any commission or remuneration. If he has already paid it, he may recover it from the agent.
v. The principal may repudiate the whole contract entered into by the agent whether the offer of a bribe did influence the agent's course of action or not.

5. The agent must not disclose any confidential information he has obtained through acting as agent. He must inform the principal of all matters relating to the agent. He must inform the principal of all matters relating to the agency when they come to his notice.
6. There must be no delegation. This duty is often expressed by the Latin maxim "delegatus non potest delegare". This is because the relationship between a principal and agent is a personal one. Where the agent's authority is coupled with a discretion (for example, to inspect a picture, and if it is genuine, to buy it), delegation of such authority will be a breach of the confidence reposed in the agent. Delegation is permissible in the following cases.

   a. Where delegation was in the contemplation of the parties at the commencement of the agency.
   b. Where the appointment of a sub-agent is necessary for the proper execution of his work.
   c. If delegation becomes necessary as a result of a sudden emergency.

d. Where delegation is sanctioned by trade, custom or usage.
e. Where the work will not call for the exercise of any discretion by the sub-agent.
f. Where part of the work requires special skill (for example a solicitor to draft a conveyance of a house) and the agent does not have that skill.

## *Care and Skill*

A paid agent is liable to the principal if he fails to do the work and as a result the principal suffers damage, as held in *Turpin v Bilton (1843)*. A gratuitous agent is not liable for non-feasance. However, once he commences the work he will be liable if he does not exercise appropriate care and skill. *Coggs v Bernard (1703)*. A gratuitous agent must use the care and skill he will give to his own affairs. This means he must use such skill as he possesses. A paid agent must use the skill he claims to possess, or may be implied from his profession.

## *Rights of the Principal*

The duties of the agent give corresponding rights to the principal. He may sue the agent for damages if he commits a breach of any of these duties.

## *Rights of the Agent*

1. Right of re-imbursement. Any reasonable expenses necessarily incurred by the agent in performing his duties must be repaid to him by his principal. This obligation may be enforced even where no amount has been fixed, by a quantum meruit.
2. Set-off. If the principal brings an action against the agent for breach of duty, the agent may exercise his right of set-off for any sums due to him either as commission or as indemnity for expenses incurred.
3. Lien. If the principal has failed to pay the agreed commission or an indemnity to the agent and the agent has any goods of the principal in his possession, then, subject to certain conditions, the agent may exercise a lien on such goods and retain possession until the principal has honoured his obligation.
4. Action for the agreed commission or remuneration. The agent is entitled to his commission after he as performed his agency.

## *Duties of the Principal*

The rights of the agent impose corresponding duties on the principal, for example a duty to pay the agent the agreed commission and to indemnify the agent for any expenses incurred by him.

## *Termination of the Agency*

As the agency relationship is usually based upon agreement between the principal and agent then it follows that it may be terminated by mutual agreement. Apart from that however the principal may withdraw or revoke the authority of his agent; but if he does that he must remember to notify any third party with whom the agent may have had dealings, otherwise the principal might be liable if the agent contracts with them. Where the agent's authority is coupled with an interest then revocation is not possible, for example where the principal owes a debt to a person and authorises him to collect rents from houses he owns.

Furthermore the agency relationship may be terminated by operation of law. This means if a certain event occurs, such as the death or insanity of either principal or agent, or the bankruptcy of the principal, then the agent's authority will be terminated. The point about this means of terminating the agency contract that should be borne in mind by the agent is that any of these events will take away the agent's authority whether or not he knows that the event has occurred. Consequently if the event occurs unknown to the agent he may be acting without authority and this will result in his being made liable for any contract he makes after the event has occurred.

In *Yonge v Toynbee (1910)* the principal became insane, unknown to his solicitors, who were acting for him in litigation. Because the solicitors took steps which resulted in the other party incurring expenses the court held that they were liable to reimburse the other party. The solicitors had acted without authority, although innocently, and thus were liable for breach of implied warranty of authority. This action is interesting because it means that when an agent notifies a party that he is an agent then the other party is entitled to assume that he has the authority he professes to have. If that turns out not to be so then the agent will be liable for breach of his warranty of authority

**Questions**

In what circumstances may a principal ratify an unauthorised act of his agent?

What are the rights and duties of an agent in respect of his principal?

# TEN

# THE LAW RELATING *to the* SALE OF GOODS *and* SUPPLY OF SERVICES

*Study Topics*

**The terms implied into every contract for the sale of goods**
**The difference between ownership and possession**

In recent years "consumerism" has become very prominent. Most shoppers know that if goods are defective they probably have a right to their money back. Most shopkeepers also appreciate this fact. However, there is nothing new in this situation. It has certainly existed, in statute form, since the *Sale of Goods Act 1893*. It was one thing to have the law on your side, but it was another thing, and a more expensive thing, to put it into motion. Consequently it was only when the small claims procedure in the County Court became available that people began to consider the possibility of taking legal action. The Small Claims Court is already the busiest court in terms of volume. With the upper limit for claims being raised to £5,000, it is likely that this expansion of small consumer claims is likely to continue.

It may now be quite widely appreciated that purchasers have their rights and consequently that sellers owe them duties, but we shall have to look at the current Act, *Sale of Goods Act 1979*, to fully appreciate the extent of these rights and duties. This is one of the statutes referred to when shop goods are labelled with the terms "your statutory rights are not affected" when restricting the refund or exchange terms in the event of dissatisfaction.

First of all one must understand that a sale is a contract and, if we remember what has been already written about a contract, we will understand that it is merely an agreement between two parties, in this case an agreement between the seller and the buyer. An agreement takes place in the minds of both parties and so if A says to B "Do you want my car for £2,500?" and B says "Yes", that is a contract of sale. There is an agreement between seller and purchaser. They both intend their agreement to be legally binding and B's consideration for A's promise to let him have his car is his promise to pay £2,500. On the other hand A's consideration to support B's promise to pay him £2,500 is his promise to give B his car. There is no need for anything in writing but of course both A and B might be in a happier position if they had witnesses to back them up if a contract had in fact been made.

It is perfectly possible for one party to sue another without the help of witnesses but that means that it is up to the court in decide which party to believe. This is within the power of the court, and judges are usually quite adept in deciding which party is telling the truth. In the case of business contracts very often one party or the other wishes to put certain terms of his own into the contract. Therefore it is more convenient for a contract which may be quite complicated to be in writing, even though legally this may not be necessary.

Once the contract has been made, what do the parties have to do as far as performing their side of the bargain is concerned? Obviously, B must pay A £2,500. Equally obviously A must hand the car to B. However, the physical fact of A handing the car to B tends to confuse the situation because although, more often than not, that is in fact what will happen, the important thing to remember is that what A is selling and what B is buying is A's ownership in the car. Sometimes ownership is called property or title.

The *Sale of Goods Act 1979* Section 2(1) states: "a contract of sale is a contract whereby the seller transfers, or agrees to transfer, the property in goods to the buyer for a money consideration called the price." Thus if goods are given in exchange for goods, that is not a sale - it is barter or exchange. However, part exchange where a person hands over his car to a dealer together with a sum of money in exchange for a car that the dealer is selling, is a contract of sale.

## *Ownership and Possession*

At this point a distinction must be made between ownership and possession. Possession is said to be a matter of fact, ownership a matter of law. The fact that I have certain goods (such as a book, a car or some golf clubs) in my possession does not mean that I am the owner of them. I may be, but if called upon to prove my ownership I might be in difficulties. In that case I would be thrown back upon the phrase "possession is nine-tenths of the law". In other words if I have some personal property in my possession there is a presumption that I own it unless the true owner can prove his ownership of the thing. But I might have borrowed the book from the library; I might have hired the car; I might have stolen the golf clubs. In all these cases I would have the things in my possession but in all cases I would be the owner of none of them.

## *Property in the Goods*

To return to the example of B buying A's car, in legal terms B is buying A's right of ownership in the car. If he acquires ownership then this will give him a right to possession of the car also. But it may be that B merely wants to own the car so that he can resell it and does not necessarily want possession of it. Again, only the owner of a thing can sell it because what the buyer is buying is the right of ownership and if a person has not got ownership in a thing, he cannot sell it. There is a Latin phrase which describes this situation and it is "Nemo dat quod non habet"; this means that no-one can give what he has not got. There are some exceptions to this rule and we will consider these later.

If B wanted to resell the car he would have to have ownership himself first, but he would not necessarily want possession of it. Indeed, say B was a wholesaler and, instead of one car, was buying 100 cars, he might immediately resell them to dealers and probably would arrange for the cars to go directly from the manufacturer to the dealers and would not, himself, wish to acquire possession of them. Thus we can say that a contract of sale is an agreement to transfer the ownership in goods to the buyer. If one were to say "I am going to buy the right of ownership in a pair of shoes on Saturday," it would seem rather strange, but that is legally what would be happening. One would probably, but not necessarily, acquire possession as well.

## *Goods*

So much for the meaning of "sale" in the phrase "Sale of Goods". The meaning of goods is defined in the Act as "including all personal chattels other than things in action and money". In other words goods includes anything that is not land.

## *Supply of Goods and Services Act 1982 and the Supply of Goods (Implied Terms) Act 1973*

A distinction must be made between a contract for the sale of goods and one for the sale of services. Sometimes there may be a mixed contract. For example, when a lady buys a hair dye from a chemist, she is buying goods; when she goes to a hairdresser just for hair-styling that is a contract for services. However if she has her hair dyed at the hairdressers that would be a mixture of sale of goods and services.

Whether or not a person has any complaint about the service he has paid for is another matter. In fact the *Supply of Goods and Services Act 1982* covers the situation where there is exchange or barter and also when a person is carrying out some repairs or is painting a house. In the latter case the contract is predominantly one for the provision of services but there may be the sale of the paint also.

Sometimes the goods part of the contract is so insignificant that it is swamped by the services or skill element, as when one's portrait is painted by a well known artist. The finished work is on canvas and consists of paint and may have a frame but predominantly one is paying for the skill of the artist. However, a reproduction painting from a shop is a contract for the sale of goods. The purpose of the *Sale of Goods Act 1979* is to:

1. protect the purchaser of goods;
2 to set out rules for determining when the ownership of the goods passes from the seller to the buyer;
3. to lay down some remedies available to the seller if he does not get his money and to the buyer if he does not get the goods.

The 1982 Act also covers agreements for hire and implies similar terms into these agreements as those discussed here in relation to sales of goods together with a term relating to quiet possession of the item.

Hire purchase agreements are dealt with by the *Supply of Goods (Implied Terms) Act 1973* which also implies virtually identical terms into these contracts as those discussed above.

## *Protection of the Purchaser*

The basic principles of the law of contract were settled many years ago when laissez-faire was the prevailing philosophy. Consequently it followed that parties to a contract were permitted to enter into any type of agreement they wished, provided it was legal. Nobody was going to interfere with them and likewise they had to stand on their own feet. Thus if the contract turned out to be disadvantageous to them they had only themselves to blame. This was called "freedom of contract".

Over the years the picture has changed as the courts and Parliament have slowly attempted to protect the weaker party; to ensure that no party should profit from his own wrongdoing or bad faith; and to bring the concept of reasonableness into consideration as affecting exclusion clauses. *Unfair Contract Terms Act 1977.*

This new approach has also been evident in the contract for the sale of goods. The principle used to be exclusively caveat emptor, "let the buyer beware". This meant and sometimes still does, that the buyer does not have to enter into a contract to buy goods; nobody is forcing him, and if he has any doubts he should not agree to buy. However, once he has agreed to buy, if it turns out that he regrets his decision, there is nothing he can do about it.

This principle still applies in many contracts and also to the contract for the sale of goods except that some protection has been given to the consumer in certain circumstances. So if a person buys goods from another, not in the course of trade, and the goods prove to the defective there is nothing that can be done. However, if the seller sold the goods in the course of a business then the buyer will have his remedies against him.

It can be seen therefore that this protection only applies when a seller is selling the goods in the course of a business. The carrying-on of a profession or the activities of a government department or a local authority are all regarded as businesses. At one time the seller had to be in the business of selling the goods; now it is sufficient if he is in a business and sells the goods.

## *Terms of a Contract*

Every contract will contain some terms which are normally put in by the parties themselves. One obvious term is the price. These terms will be binding as long as both parties agree to them and anything can be put into a contract so long as it is legal. The terms or stipulations in a contract may be either conditions or warranties.

## *Conditions*

A condition is a representation of fact which is vital to the existence of the contract, a representation on the truth of which the existence of the contract may depend. Conditions go to the root of the contract and it is reasonable to suppose that if the buyer had known it to be untrue he would not have contracted at all.

## *Warranties*

The other type of term or stipulation in a contract is called a warranty. This is an agreement with reference to the goods forming the subject matter of the contract of sale but collateral to the main purpose of such a contract. It relates to a matter of subsidiary importance and does not go to the root of the contract.

It is important to distinguish between a condition and a warranty because the remedies available are different in each case. As a condition is fundamental to the contract then it follows that the party breaking it is in effect attempting to substitute something different in kind from the performance which the contract contemplated. To compel him to take the goods and merely to attempt to compensate him by damages would be, in substance, to force on him a different contract from that which he actually made. So the law gives to a party injured by a breach of condition a right to rescind the contract altogether. Rescission, however, is not the only remedy open to him. He may if he wishes waive the condition, or he may treat its breach as a breach of warranty giving rise to an action for damages and not as a ground for repudiating the contract. *Sale of Goods Act*

*1979.* Section 11 (3).

On the other hand a warranty is not so serious as a condition and since a warranty does not affect the foundation of the contract but is collateral to its main purpose, then a breach of warranty gives rise to a claim for damages but not to a right to reject the goods and treat the contract as repudiated. Section 11 (3).

Some terms or stipulations are implied into a contract. These terms may not be known to the parties who probably know nothing about the law. One term, which happens to be a condition, is that the goods shall be of merchantable quality, that is, reasonably fit for the purposes for which they are normally used. So the contract would read, if it were to be written down: "I, A, agree to sell you, B, my car for £2,500 and it is a condition of this contract that the car shall be of merchantable quality". Of course this is not written down and is not expressed by A who may know nothing of the *Sale of Goods Act.* Nevertheless, if the car proves not to be of merchantable quality then A the seller will be in breach of a condition and B the purchaser will have his rights against A. One other point is that A must have sold the car in the course of a business, so this provision would not apply to a private sale.

## *Implied Conditions*

**Condition No. 1**

Section 12 of the Act provides that there is "an implied condition on the part of the seller that in the case of a sale he has a right to sell the goods, and in the case of an agreement to sell he will have such a right at the time when the property is to pass."

It should be noticed that since the implied stipulation that the seller has a right to sell the goods is a condition, the breach of it entitles the buyer to recover the whole of the price he has paid for the goods, as upon a total failure of the consideration. In *Rowland v Divall (1923)* R bought a motor car from D and used it for four months. D was not the owner of the car and so R in due course had to return the car to the rightful owner. R now sued D for the total purchase price he had paid to D. The court held that R was to recover in full not withstanding the fact that he had the use of the car for four months.

Section 12 also includes two warranties: that the goods are free from encumbrance (such as a mortgage) and that the buyer will enjoy quiet possession of the goods. These warranties sometimes overlap with the condition in Section 12 but sometimes they are important as in *Microbeads AG v Vinhurst Road Markings Ltd (1975).* In that case, after the sale a third party obtained a patent which interfered with the buyer's right to use the machines (that is, with his quiet possession). There had been no breach of the condition in Section 12 because the seller had had the right to sell. However the buyer was entitled to recover damages for breach of the warranty in Section 12.

**Condition No. 2**

Section 13 provides that "where there is a contract for the sale of goods by description there is an implied condition that the goods shall correspond with the description". This condition will apply where goods are ordered through a catalogue or where some article is ordered from manufacturers through a dealer. In these cases the goods will always be sold by description. Even if the purchaser sees the goods and chooses them they can still be sold by description and a customer is entitled to expect that the goods he chooses from the shelf of a supermarket will correspond to the description on the tin or packet.

The word description can of course apply to a variety of matters concerning the goods. Descriptions can refer to the quantity, to the weight, to the ingredients, and even packaging has been held to be part of the description.

In *Re Moore and Company and Landauer and Company (1921)* the buyer described in the contract how he wished a consignment of canned fruit to be packed. He specified that he wanted 2,100 cases of Australian canned fruits, the cases to contain 30 tins each. When the goods were delivered, the total quantity was delivered but about half the cases contained 24 tins and the remainder 30 tins. There was no difference in market value between the goods packed 24 tins and the goods packed 30 tins to the case. The court held that as the goods delivered did not correspond with the description with those ordered then the buyer could reject the whole.

As stated above goods will be sold by description if the buyer does not see them; but they may also be sold by description if he does see them.

In *Beale v Taylor (1967)* a buyer inspected a car described in an advertisement as "a 1961 model". After buying it he discovered that the car had been cannibalised and consisted of half a 1961 model and half of an earlier car. It was held that the seller was liable under Section 13 because the buyer had relied to some extent on the description.

In *Harlington and Leinster Enterprises Ltd v Christopher Hull Fine Art Ltd (1990)* the purchaser bought a painting which the seller said was by a German expressionist painter called Munter. However, the purchaser did not rely on the description because he relied on his own inspection instead. This situation was known to the seller and the purchaser. The Court of Appeal decided therefore that the purchaser could not complain when it turned out that the painting was not by Munter since he, the purchaser, did not rely upon the statement by the seller but used his own judgement and assessment. The court decided that as there had been no connection between the description and the sale, in other words the buyer had not relied upon the description given by the seller, then there could be no sale by description.

## *Implied Terms about Quality or Fitness*

Section 14 used to refer to the merchantable quality condition. This changed on 3 January 1995. On that date the *Sale and Supply of Goods Act 1994* came into force. Section 14(2) now states:

> When the seller sells goods in the course of a business, there is an implied term that the goods supplied under the contract are of satisfactory quality.

The new term is "satisfactory quality" not "merchantable quality" and also note that in the 1979 Act merchantable quality was a "condition" but that satisfactory quality is a "term". The definition of satisfactory quality is important. It is wider than merchantable quality.

The Act states that:

> goods are of satisfactory quality if they meet the standard that a reasonable person would regard as satisfactory, taking account of any description of the goods, the price (if relevant) and all other relevant circumstances.

For the purposes of this Act, the quality of goods includes their state and condition and the following (among others) are in appropriate cases aspects of the quality of goods:

1. fitness for all the purposes for which goods of the kind in question are commonly supplied;
2. appearance and finish;
3. freedom from minor defects;
4. safety; and
5. durability.

Of course, as in the case of the old Section, the term "satisfactory quality" does not extend to any matter making the quality of goods unsatisfactory:

1. which is specifically drawn to the buyer's attention before the contract is made;
2. where the buyer examines the goods before the contract is made, which that examination ought to reveal;
3. in the case of a contract for sale by sample, which would have been apparent on a reasonable examination of the sample.

This is the emerging section, but we shall have to await an extensive body of judicial decisions on it before we will know exactly what it means.

The "fitness for purpose" condition is contained in Section 14(3). This section states that:

> Where the seller sells goods in the course of a business and the buyer, expressly or by implication, makes known:
> (a) to the seller, or
> (b) where the purchase price or part of it is payable by instalments and the goods were previously sold by a credit broker to the seller, to that credit broker, any particular purpose for which the goods are being bought, there is an implied condition that the goods supplied under the contract are reasonably fit for that purpose, whether or not that is a purpose for which such goods are commonly supplied, except where the circumstances show that the buyer does not rely, or that it is unreasonable for him to rely, on the skill or judgement of the seller or credit broker.

Note that in each case of these implied conditions as to quality or fitness, the seller must have been selling the goods in the course of a business. In other words the conditions are not implied in the case of a private sale. Also there may be an overlap between the "satisfactory quality" and "fitness for purpose" sections, but sometimes there will be no overlap. An article may be of satisfactory quality yet still not be fit for the purpose stated by the buyer. Equally if the buyer states the purpose for which he or she wants the goods then, notwithstanding that they are of satisfactory quality, if they are still not fit for the purpose stated, again the seller will be in breach of the fitness for purpose condition.

*Baldry v Marshall Ltd (1924).* B told M, who were dealers in motor cars, that he wanted a car which "was comfortable and suitable for the ordinary purpose of a touring car". M sold B a Bugatti car for £1,050. B found the car unsatisfactory for touring, and as he had relied on the seller's skill and judgement M was in breach of the condition that the goods should be reasonably fit for the purpose specified.

*Crowther v Shannon Motor Co Ltd (1975).* The plaintiff paid £390 for a 1964 Jaguar car in 1972, with 82,000 miles on the clock. He drove 2,000 miles within three weeks of buying it and the engine seized up. It was held that when the car was sold the engine must have been near the point of failure and so the seller was in breach of the condition that the car should be reasonably fit for the purpose of being driven on the road.

## *Sale by Sample*

The final condition in Section 15, implied into every contract for the sale of goods, is that if the sale is by sample then there is an implied condition:

1. that the bulk will correspond with the sample in quality;
2. that the buyer will have a reasonable opportunity of comparing the bulk with the sample;
3. that the goods will be free from any defect, making their quality unsatisfactory, which would not be apparent on reasonable examination of the sample.

## *Modification of Remedies for Breach of Condition in Non-Consumer Cases*

Section 15A of the *Sale and Supply of Goods Act 1994* has modified the remedies available in non-consumer cases. It reads as follows.

1. Where in the case of a contract of sale:
   a. the buyer would, apart from this subsection, have the right to reject goods by reason of a breach on the part of the seller of a term implied by Section 13, 14 or 15 above, but
   b. the breach is so slight that it would be unreasonable for him to reject them then, if the buyer does not deal as consumer, the breach is not to be treated as a breach of condition but may be treated as a breach of warranty
2. This section applies unless a contrary intention appears in, or is to be implied from, the contract.
3. It is for the seller to show that a breach fell within subsection (1)(b) above.
4. This section does not apply to Scotland.

## *Stipulations about Time*

Section 10 states:

1. Unless a different intention appears from the terms of the contract, stipulations as to time of payment are not of the essence of a contract of sale.
2. Whether any other stipulation as to time is or is not of the essence of the contract depends on the terms of the contract.
3. In a contract of sale "month" prima facie means calendar month.

*Notes:*

i. Stipulations as to time of payment: in deciding whether time is of the essence, the court will have regard to the nature of the goods and the intention of the parties.
ii. Other stipulations as to time: time is of the essence of the contract in most commercial transactions and in some non-commercial transactions: see *Aron v Comptoir Wegimont (1921).*
iii. A stipulation as to time being of the essence may be waived by the party in whose favour it would otherwise operate.

## *Illustrative Cases*

**Section 10: Stipulations about time**

*Sanday and Co v Keighley, Maxted Co (1922).* There was a contract for the sale of grain to be shipped from the River Plate on a vessel "expected to be ready to load late September". The vessel was not ready to load until the middle of November. The seller had no reasonable ground for stating that it would be ready in September. It was held that the buyer might refuse to accept the goods.

*Bowes v Shand (1877).* It was agreed by the sellers to ship a quantity of Madras rice during the months of March and/or April. It turned out that the greater part of the rice was shipped at the end of February and only about one-eighth was actually shipped during March. It was held that the buyers were entitled to reject the goods even though it was conceded that there was no difference between the rice actually shipped and the rice which might have been shipped in March.

**Section 12: Condition as to title**

See *Rowland v Divall (1923).*

**Section 13: Sale by description**

See *Beale v Taylor (1967).*

**Section 14: Undertaking as to quality and fitness**

*BS Brown and Sons Ltd v Craiks Ltd (1970).* B ordered cloth from the manufacturers, C. B wanted the cloth for dresses but did not inform C of their intentions. C thought the cloth was wanted for industrial purposes. The price was 36.25p per yard (higher than the normal price for industrial cloth, but not significantly so). The cloth was unsuitable for dressmaking. B and C were left with large amounts of material, some of which C sold at 30p per yard. Having failed in a claim under Section 14(3), B claimed damages under Section 14(2). It was held by the House of Lords that the action failed: the cloth was still saleable, albeit at a slightly reduced price; it was not a necessary requirement of merchantability that no difference should exist between purchase and resale price. It was not the case here, but if that difference was substantial, it might well be inferred that the goods were not of merchantable quality. B did not make known to C the purpose for which he wanted the cloth. Therefore he did not succeed with Section 14(3). However, he claimed under Section 14(2): the "merchantability" clause. The same reasoning could apply today now that it is known as the "satisfactory quality" clause.

*Priest v Last (1903).* The plaintiff asked the defendant shopkeeper for a hot-water bottle. The plaintiff inquired whether the one produced would stand boiling water. The defendant sold him an American rubber bottle, stating that it would withstand hot but not boiling water. When in use the bottle burst and injured the plaintiff's wife. It was held that the bottle was not fit for use as a hot-water bottle. There was a breach of condition and the seller was liable in damages.

## Section 15: Sale by sample

*Aitken v Boulen (1908).* There was a contract for the sale by sample of a quantity of maroon twill. It was found that part of the twill actually supplied was inferior to the sample. It was held that the buyer could reject the entire consignment of twill, or he could retain the whole batch, claiming damages for that part inferior to the sample. However, the buyer could not keep the part equal to the sample and reject the other part.

*Champanhac and Co Ltd v Waller and Co Ltd (1948).* There was a contract for the sale of government surplus balloons. The contract provided that the goods were to be "as sample taken away" and to be sold "with all faults and imperfections". It was held that the sellers were still bound to deliver a bulk which corresponded with the sample. However, since the buyers had not rejected the balloons, the condition had become a warranty and the defendants were liable in damages only.

## Questions

What are the purposes of the *Sale of Goods Act*?

When is time of the essence of the contract?

# ELEVEN

# TRANSFER *of* PROPERTY *in the* GOODS

*Study Topics*

**The passing of property in the goods from the seller to the buyer**
**The "Romalpa" clause**
**Transfer of title**
**Remedies of the buyer and the seller**

In this section we shall deal with the transfer of property and in the following section with the transfer of title. There is a confusion sometimes between these two phrases. Property signifies total control over an object: "the sum of all the ways in which a movable or immovable thing can be lawfully used and enjoyed, together with the right to the possession of the same." Property is said to be a right, or a sum of rights. However preceding such a right there is a title and title is a fact which vests the right of property in the person who enjoys it. Thus property may be transferred from the seller to the buyer and that means that, at that moment in time, the buyer assumes the risk of loss or damage to the goods because property has been transferred to him. However a title may be valid or defective and it does not necessarily follow that because the property in the goods has passed from the seller to the buyer that the buyer will be able to keep the goods as his own. For example, some third person may claim the goods from the buyer on the grounds that he has a better title to them.

Some authors write of the transfer of property as a transfer of risk to the buyer. This is quite acceptable because once the property has been transferred to the buyer then he becomes responsible for any loss or damage to the goods.

Note that the transfer of property is a matter of law and does not refer to the physical transfer of the goods. So it is important to remember that the property in goods may be transferred from the seller to the buyer notwithstanding the fact that the goods physically remain in the possession of the seller. Thus even though the goods remain in the possession of the seller, if property in those goods has passed to the buyer, then he, the buyer, will be liable for any loss or damage to them.

## *Time when the Property Passes*

The question of the time when the property in the goods passes from the seller to the buyer may often be of considerable importance. If the goods are being transported some distance then it may be that the buyer, who may be the owner of them at that time, will wish to insure against loss or damage to them. If the buyer were to be made bankrupt then only the goods he owns may be taken over by the trustee in bankruptcy for liquidation and distribution of the proceeds to creditors.

Thus the rules for determining the precise moment when the property in goods is transferred to the buyer are of considerable importance.

## *Specific Goods*

Section 16 provides that no property in the goods may be transferred to the buyer unless and until the goods are ascertained. However some goods are called specific goods and that means that they are goods which both parties have agreed upon at the time of the sale. Thus if A is selling to B the Vauxhall Astra motor car, registration number A123 BCD, this is an example of specific goods, because the thing to be sold has been identified and agreed upon when a contract of sale was made. When the goods are specific goods then the rules for the transfer of property are as follows.

### Rule 1

Where the goods are in a deliverable state the property passes to the buyer when the contract is made and it is immaterial whether the time of payment or the time of delivery or both be postponed. This reinforces a point made earlier that property in goods may pass from the seller to the buyer even though the buyer has not paid for them and even though the goods themselves physically remain in the possession of the seller. The point is that when the property in the goods has passed to the buyer then he of course will from that moment be responsible for any loss or damage to them, irrespective of where they may be located.

**Rule 2**

This provides that where there is a contract for the sale of specific goods and the seller is bound to do something to put them into a deliverable state then the property does not pass until the thing is done and the buyer has notice that it has been done. This means that if the seller has agreed, for example, to put four new tyres on a car then he must put these new tyres on the car before the car is in a deliverable state, and must inform the buyer.

**Rule 3**

This provides that if the seller is bound to weigh, measure or to do something to the goods for the purpose of ascertaining the price, again the property does not pass to the buyer until what needs to be done has been done and the buyer has been notified that it has been done. For example, where a person goes to a fishmonger who is selling a whole salmon which is priced at £2.50 per pound. The buyer agrees to buy the salmon but of course the salmon then has to be weighed, in order to find out what the total price is going to be.

**Rule 4**

This concerns goods which are delivered to the buyer on approval, or on sale or return. In such a case the property in the goods passes to the buyer either when he signifies his approval or acceptance to the seller or does any act adopting the transaction. If he does not signify his approval or acceptance to the seller but keeps the goods without giving notice of rejection then the property will pass when the time has been fixed for the return of the goods has passed or, if no time has been fixed, when a reasonable time has passed.

> In *Kirkham v Attenborough* (1897) jewellery was delivered "on sale or return" and the person to whom it was so delivered pledged it with a pawnbroker who took it in good faith. It was held that the original seller could not recover it from the pawnbroker because by pledging it the original purchaser had done an act "adopting the transaction" and the property in the goods had passed to him and so therefore he could give the property to the pawnbroker. The original owner of the jewellery of course had his remedy in an action on the contract for the price.

These are four rules which indicate the moment in time when the property in specific goods will pass from the seller to the buyer. However it is important to keep in mind the fundamental principle, which is that the property in the goods will be transferred to the buyer at such time as the parties to the contract intend it to be transferred. The above rules will only apply unless a contrary intention appears.

## *Unascertained Goods*

If the goods cannot be identified when the contract of sale is made then they are called unascertained goods. This situation will arise when the goods being sold form part of a bulk or of a large number of identical things and the precise things being sold are not immediately identifiable.

If A is selling to B 10 tonnes of coal and A has 500 tonnes in his stock yard then the exact 10 tonnes of coal B is to receive will not have been identified when the contract of sale was made. They are then said to be unascertained.

Rule 5 of Section 18 concerns the moment when the property in unascertained goods passes from the seller to the buyer. This rule provides that the unascertained goods will become ascertained when the seller takes the goods out of bulk and is said to appropriate them to the contract.

Property will pass at this moment because the goods have then, by being taken out of bulk, become specified goods.

The method of appropriation to the contract will usually be where the seller delivers the goods to the buyer or to a carrier and does not reserve the right of disposal.

## *The Sale of Goods (Amendment) Act 1995*

For some time the rule in the *Sale of Goods Act 1979* regarding the point in time when ownership in unascertained goods passes to the buyer has caused some problems. Rule 5 of Section 18 of the *Sale of Goods Act 1979* requires that the goods must be appropriated to the contract either by the buyer or the seller. Usually unascertained goods are appropriated to the contract by the seller delivering the goods to a carrier or other bailee for the purpose of transmission to the buyer. However in *Karlshamns Oljefabriker v Eastport Navigation Corpn (The Elafi) (1982)*, the court decided that goods could be ascertained by exhaustion. The *Sale of Goods (Amendment) Act 1995* has given this statutory recognition. In that case Swedish buyers bought 6,000 tons of copra. The goods were carried in the *Elafi* together with another 16,000 tons of copra making a bulk of 22,000 tons. The 16,000 tons were unloaded at intermediate ports. The buyers sued the shipowners in negligence. Their defence was that the buyers had no title to the copra. They were unsuccessful as the court held that property in the goods passed to the buyers when the goods were ascertained and this had occurred when the 16,000 tons of copra had been offloaded leaving 6,000 tons on board. The buyers could then say that all the copra on board was destined for them.

An additional provision of the Act concerns undivided shares in goods which are part of a bulk. If the goods in question have been identified in the contract of a sale or by the parties and the buyer has paid the price for the goods, then the property in an undivided share in the bulk will be transferred to the buyer who becomes an owner in common of the bulk. The undivided share of the bulk owned by the buyer will be in the proportion that the amount paid bears to the quantity of goods in bulk at the time.

## *Illustrative Cases*

### Rule 1

*Tarling v Baxter (1827).* There was a contract for the sale of a stack of hay. The contract was made on 6 January. The price was to be paid on 4 February. The hay was not to be removed until 1 May. On 20 January, the stack was destroyed by fire. It was held that the property and risk passed when the contract was made and the loss therefore fell on the buyer.

### Rule 2

*Underwood v Burgh Castle Cement Syndicate (1922).* There was a contract for the sale of a condensing engine. It was to be severed from the floor of the building and delivered free on rail at a specified price. The engine was destroyed in transit before it reached the railway. It was held that the property in the goods did not pass because when it arrived at the railway it was not in a deliverable state.

### Rule 3

*Nanka Bruce v Commonwealth Trust (1926).* A sold 160 bags of cocoa at 59s per load of 601b. A knew that B intended to resell the cocoa to C and that the weights would be tested at C's place of business. It was held that the check-weighing was neither suspensive of the contract of sale, nor a condition precedent to the property in the cocoa passing to B.

### Rule 4

See *Kirkham v Attenborough (1897).*

### Rule 5

*Pignataro v Gilroy (1919).* B ordered 140 bags of rice from A. B paid for the rice and requested delivery. A sent B a delivery order for 125 bags and asked B for the other 15 bags at A's place of business. B delayed one month before sending for the rice. In the meantime the 15 remaining bags had been stolen. It was held that the property in the 15 bags of rice had passed to B and therefore he had to bear the loss.

*Philip Head v Showfronts Ltd (1970).* A ordered carpets from B. B was to lay the carpets at A's premises. B delivered the carpets to A's premises. Before they were laid, however, the carpets were stolen. It was held that the carpets were not in a deliverable state and consequently the property in the carpets had not passed to A.

## *Reservation of Right of Disposal*

Section 19 provides the following.

1 Where there is a contract for the sale of specific goods or where goods are subsequently appropriated to the contract, the seller may, by the terms of the contract or appropriation, reserve the right of disposal of the goods until certain conditions are fulfilled; and in such case, notwithstanding the delivery of the goods to the buyer, or to a carrier or other bailee or custodier for the purpose of transmission to the buyer, the property in the goods does not pass to the buyer until the conditions imposed by the seller are fulfilled.

2 Where goods are shipped and by the bill of lading the goods are deliverable to the order of the seller or his agent, the seller is prima facie to be taken to reserve the right of disposal.

3 Where the seller of goods draws on the buyer for the price, and transmits the bill of exchange and bill of lading to the buyer together to secure acceptance of payment of the bill of exchange, the buyer is bound to return the bill of lading if he does not honour the bill of exchange, and if he wrongfully retains the bill of lading the property the goods does not pass to him.

The effect of this section is that notwithstanding the physical delivery of the goods to the buyer, the property in the goods will not pass to the buyer until the conditions imposed by the seller have been fulfilled. Section 20 provides that risk prima facie passes with property.

1. Unless otherwise agreed, the goods remain at the seller's risk until the property in them is transferred to the buyer, but when the property in them is transferred to the buyer the goods are the buyer's risk whether delivery has been made or not.
2. But where delivery has been delayed through the fault of either buyer or seller the goods are at the risk of the party at fault as regards any loss which might not have occurred but for such fault.
3. Nothing in this section affects the duties or liabilities of either seller or buyer as a bailee or custodier of the goods of the other party.

Note that prima facie the risk passes with the property. The maxim is *res perit domlno* ("the loss of a thing falls on its owner") although the rule can be varied (for example so that the risk passes to the buyer before the property in the goods passes) by the parties expressly or impliedly agreeing, or by trade usage.

*Demby Hamilton and Co v Barden (1949).* There was a contract for the sale of 30 tons of apple juice to be delivered weekly on the buyer's instructions. The seller put the final 10 tons into casks ready for delivery, but the buyer failed to give any instructions. As a result, the juice went bad. It was held that, although the property remained in the seller, the loss was the fault of the buyer and was at his risk.

*Sterns v Vickers (1923).* There was a sale of 120,000 gallons of white spirit out of 200,000 gallons held in a tank on wharf. There was no appropriation to the contract. However, a delivery warrant was issued to the buyer and the wharfingers attorned to the buyer. The warrant was not acted upon for some months and the white spirit deteriorated in the meantime. It was held that the loss fell on the buyer.

## *The "Romalpa" Clause*

The principle of reservation of right of disposal, or retention of title as it is sometimes referred to, has been enforced by the courts.

In several European countries it is common practice for a seller of goods to reserve his or her title in the goods supplied to the buyer until payment for them is received. This practice affords the seller real advantages. If the buyer subsequently falls into liquidation or receivership, the seller who has had a "retention of title" clause inserted in the contract of sale will be able to claim the unpaid price for the goods supplied ahead of any unsecured creditor who may only receive a small percentage of that due to him or her. If there has been a subsale of the goods by the buyer, where they have remained in an unaltered state, the seller can claim the proceeds of sale. Even if the buyer had admixed the goods in a manufacturing process, the seller will be in a better position with a "retention of title" clause than otherwise. That is because he or she can claim a lien or charge over the goods.

It was not until 1976 that the Court of Appeal decided that such a clause would be given effect to by the law of this country following the *Romalpa* case.

*Aluminium Industrie Vaassen BV v Romalpa Aluminium Ltd (1976).* Aluminium foil was sold by the plaintiff to the defendant for manufacture and resale. The contract of sale contained the condition that title to the goods would not be transferred to the buyer until the price was paid. Additionally, the contract stated that if the foil was made into other objects, the plaintiff would retain ownership and the defendants be the "fiduciary owners", although they were specifically permitted to sell such objects. Nothing was provided in the contract regarding the subsale of un made-up foil. The defendants fell into financial problems, and a receiver was appointed. The unpaid plaintiffs sought a declaration that they were entitled to invoke the equitable doctrine of tracing to recover from the receiver £35,000, being the proceeds of aluminium foil resold by the defendants to third parties (who obtained good title under section 25(2) of the Sale of Goods Act 1893; and a claim for £35,000. The relevant clause in the contract of sale provided:

"The ownership of the material to be delivered by AIV will only be transferred to purchaser when he has met all that is owing to AIV no matter on what grounds. Until the date of payment, purchaser, if AIV so desires, is required to store this material in such a way that it is clearly the property of AIV. AIV and purchaser agree that, if purchaser should make (a) new object(s) from the material, mix the material with (an) other object(s) or if the material in any way whatsoever becomes a constituent of(an) other object(s) AIV will be given the ownership of this (these) new object(s) as surety of the full payment of what purchaser owes AIV. To this end AIV and purchaser now agree that the ownership of the article(s) in question, whether finished or not, is to be transferred to AIV and that this transfer of ownership will be considered to have taken place through and at the moment of the single operation or event by which the material is converted into (a) new object(s), or is mixed with or becomes a constituent of (an) other object(s). Until the moment of full payment of what the purchaser owes AIV purchaser shall keep the object(s) in question for AIV in his capacity of fiduciary owner and, if required, shall store this (these) object(s) in such a way that it (they) can be recognised as such. Nevertheless, purchaser will be entitled to sell these objects to a third party within the framework of the normal carrying on of his business and to deliver them on condition that - if AIV so requires - purchaser, as long as he has not fully discharged his debt to AIV, shall hand over to AIV the claims he has against his buyer emanating from this transaction".

The Court of Appeal held:

1. that the obvious purpose of the clause, in the context of the general conditions, was to secure the plaintiffs, as far as possible in the event of insolvency, against the risk of non-payment after they had parted with possession but not the legal title to the goods delivered, whether or not they retained their identity before payment was received;
2. that, in order to give effect to that purpose, there had to be implied into the first part of the clause, in addition to the undoubted power to sell the material to subpurchasers, an obligation on the defendants to account in accordance with the normal fiduciary relationship of principal and agent, bailor and bailee, as expressly contemplated in the second part of the clause;
3. and that accordingly, the plaintiffs were entitled to trace the proceeds of the subsale into the hands of the receiver, and to recover them, thereby gaining

priority over the defendants' general creditors.

The *Romalpa* clause or "retention of title" clause was reconsidered by the Court of Appeal in the flowing case.

> *Borden (UK) Ltd v Scottish Timber Products Ltd (1981).* In this case the plaintiffs supplied resin to the defendants for use in the manufacture of chipboard. This was pursuant to a contract under which property in the resin was to pass when all goods had been paid for in full, it being clearly contemplated that the resin would be used in the manufacturing process before being paid for. Once admixed in that process the resin could not be recovered. Following appointment of a receiver and manager of the defendants, the plaintiffs brought an action for the sum outstanding claiming inter alia that any chipboard manufactured with such resin or any money or property representing the proceeds of sale of such chipboard was charged with the outstanding sum. The relevant clause in the contract of sale provided the following.
>
> Risk and Property. Goods supplied by the company shall be at the purchaser's risk immediately on delivery to the purchaser or into custody on the purchaser's behalf (whichever is the sooner) and the purchaser should therefore be insured accordingly. Property in the goods supplied hereunder will pass to the customer when:
>
> a. the goods the subject of this contract; and
> b. all other goods subject of any other contract between the company and the customer which, at the time of payment of the full price of the goods sold under the contract, have been delivered to the customer but not paid for in full, have been paid for in full.

The Court of Appeal held, distinguishing the *Romalpa* case:

1. that once used in the manufacture of the chipboard, pursuant to the intention to the parties, the resin as such ceased to exist and with it the plaintiff's title to it;
2. that, as the resin had lost its identity in the manufacturing process, the chipboard being a wholly new product, it could not be traced into the chipboard;
3. that no interest or charge on the chipboard in favour of the plaintiffs could be implied from the contract; and that, accordingly, the plaintiffs acquired no interest of any kind in the chipboard.

The *Romalpa* case was distinguished under four heads.

1. In that case it was conceded that the defendants were bailees of the foil for the plaintiffs; but not so in *Borden.*
2 In *Romalpa* there had been no admixture of the foil; in *Borden* there had been.
3. *Romalpa* turned on construction of the clause and the basis on which the

defendants could sell the foil; *Borden* was not concerned with any sale of the resin.

4. In *Romalpa* the defendants were selling the foil as agents for AIV; this was not at all the case in *Borden*.

Two cases have further considered the application of the *Romalpa* decision.

> *Re Peachdart Ltd (1983).* In the contract of sale of leather, the seller reserved legal ownership, until fully paid, in the leather and products made from it and a right to trade any proceeds of their sale in equity. It was held that, on a true construction of the contract, it must have been intended by the parties that, as soon as the process of making handbags from the leather had begun, the seller should have only a charge on it by way of security; similarly with completed handbags.

> *Henry Lennox (Industrial Engines) Ltd v Grahame Puttick Ltd (1983).* In a contract for the supply of engines (to be incorporated into diesel generator sets for resale to sub-buyer) the seller reserved, until full payment was made, legal title to the engines only. The defendants went into receivership, owing over £700,000 to a bank which held a charge on their assets. It was held that the sellers did not have a direct claim for the proceeds of sale. The contract did not contain a term that the proceeds of resale would be kept separate and belong to the sellers; the express terms were only concerned with the property in the goods, which countered any argument that the buyers were implicitly in a fiduciary position as regards the proceeds of sale.

In the case of *Re Bond Worth Ltd (1980)* it has been held that the reservation of a mere equitable title in goods merely creates a charge registrable under the *Companies Act 1948* Section 95.

## *Transfer of Title*

The general rule is that only a person who is the owner of goods can pass the ownership of these goods on to the purchaser. This is expressed by the Latin phrase "Nemo dat quod non habet" ("No one can give what he or she has not got"). Thus if a person has stolen goods and then sells these to an innocent purchaser, a purchaser who knows nothing about the fact that he or she is buying stolen goods, the fact remains that he or she cannot become the rightful owner of the goods. The reason of course is that the seller of the goods, the thief, had no title to them. However, there are exceptions to this rule, and these are contained in the Act as follows.

## *Sale by a Seller under a Voidable Title*

When a person acquires goods and the right of ownership in those goods by deception, he is said to have a voidable title because he acquired ownership by means of a voidable contract. In this case whoever acquires the goods will get a good title to them provided he does so before the rightful (and deceived) owner has taken steps to escape liability under the contract.

*Car and Universal Finance Co Ltd v Caldwell (1965).* In this case, which was mentioned earlier, on 12 January 1960 C, the owner of a Jaguar car, was persuaded to sell and deliver the car to a rogue who gave C a car of much lower value and a cheque. On the next morning C ascertained that the cheque was worthless and at once asked the police and Automobile Association to recover his car. The rogue sold the car to a person who did not acquire it in good faith and only on 15 January was the car acquired by a purchaser in good faith. It passed through several hands and eventually was acquired by the Car and Universal Finance Company Ltd, which acted in good faith. The court held that, while normally the rescission of a voidable contract must be communicated to the other contracting party, that was not necessary if, as in the present case, the other party, by deliberately absconding, put it out of the power of the rescinding party to communicate. Consequently, C had rescinded the contract on 13 January when he notified the police and the Automobile Association, and the finance company had not acquired the title to the car.

*Lewis v Averay (1972).* In this case, the rogue deceived Lewis into letting him take his (Lewis') car. The rogue then sold it to Averay. The rogue did not have a good title to the car, merely a voidable title, which meant that Lewis could avoid the contract if he did so before a third party became involved. Unfortunately for Lewis, Averay acquired the car before Lewis had taken sufficient steps to avoid his contract with the rogue and so Averay got a good title to the car.

## *Seller in Possession of Goods after Sale*

When a person having sold goods continues to be in possession of them or of the documents of title to them, and then resells the goods to another person who takes delivery of them, the third person will get legal ownership or a title to the goods. The moral of the story seems to be that once you have bought goods you should take possession of them as soon as you can. Of course the original buyer will have his or her remedies against the seller, but that is not always a satisfactory solution.

## *Sale by Buyer in Possession*

Section 25 provides:

> Where a person having bought or agreed to buy goods obtains, with the consent of the seller, possession of the goods or the documents of title to the goods, the delivery or transfer by that person, or by a mercantile agent acting for him, of the goods or documents of title, under any sale, pledge or other disposition thereof, to any person receiving the same in good faith and without notice of any lien or other right of the original seller in respect of the goods, has the same effect as if the person making the delivery or transfer were a mercantile agent in possession of the goods or documents of title with the consent of the owner.

The importance of Section 25 is that if a buyer obtains possession of the goods with the consent of the seller, then notwithstanding that the buyer may not have become the owner of them, if he or she then sells to a third person, the third person gets a good title to the goods. This provision is particularly important in recent years because of the widespread use of the *Romalpa* clause which was mentioned earlier. Thus if a buyer obtains goods from a seller and in the contract of sale there was a *Romalpa* clause by which the seller retained ownership of the goods until such time as the buyer paid for them, then if the buyer now resells to a third person that person will get a good title to the goods.

This provision will only apply in a sale contract. A person who possesses goods subject to a hire purchase contract cannot pass a good title under Section 25. The same applies to a person who obtained possession under a conditional sale agreement.

The above examples of circumstances in which a person who is not the owner may nevertheless still sell the goods to a third party, so that the third party can become the owner, are contained in the *Sale of Goods Act 1979*. Additional examples follow.

## *Sale by Agent*

If an agent has the authority of his or her principal to sell the goods then obviously anyone buying from the agent will obtain ownership of the goods.

## *Sale of Motor Vehicle Under Hire Purchase Agreement*

A general rule is that a person who is buying goods under a hire purchase agreement cannot sell those goods so as to pass a good title to any purchaser because the person who is buying the goods under the hire purchase agreement is merely hiring them and the ownership lies with the finance company. However, the *Hire Purchase Act 1964* provided that in the case of the sale of a motor vehicle which is subject to a hire purchase agreement then any private purchaser can claim protection. In other words a private purchaser will get a good title to a motor vehicle; whereas a car dealer or a car finance house will be unable to do so. The reason for this is that Parliament decided that as a most important purchase of ordinary private persons is the buying of a motor vehicle then such people should be protected. Car dealers of course have access to a register of hire purchase agreements and so they can, and will, before purchasing a vehicle check whether it is subject to an HP agreement.

## *Market Overt*

Until 3 January 1995 there was an additional situation in which a buyer could obtain a good title to goods from a seller who had no title. This occurred when goods were sold in an "open market". However, the *Sale of Goods (Amendment) Act 1994* abolished this ancient provision.

## *Performance of the Contract*

It is the duty of the seller to deliver the goods and of the buyer to accept and pay for them in accordance with the contract of sale. Delivery means the voluntary transfer of possession from the seller to the buyer, and Section 28 provides that delivery of the goods and payment of the price are concurrent conditions. In other words the seller must be ready and willing to give possession of the goods to the buyer and the buyer must be ready and willing to pay the price for the possession of the goods.

## *Rules of Delivery*

The rules of delivery are as follows.

1. Delivery will take place at the seller's place of business or his or her residence. However, as in a number of other cases, this provision of law may be varied by agreement between the parties. Obviously if a person is buying a large quantity of products from the seller then it probably will be in the agreement that the seller will undertake to transport the goods to the buyer's place of business.
2. Where the seller is bound to send the goods to the buyer and no time for sending them has been fixed, then the seller is bound to send them within a reasonable time.
3. Where the goods, at the time of sale, are in the possession of a third person, then there is no delivery by the seller to the buyer until the third person has acknowledged to the buyer that he or she holds the goods on the buyer's behalf.
4. Delivery in the sense of transporting the goods to the buyer must be made at a reasonable hour.
5. Finally, unless otherwise agreed the expenses of putting the goods into a deliverable state must be borne by the seller.

## *Delivery of Wrong Quantity*

Section 30 of the *Sale of Goods Act 1979* states the following.

1. Where the seller delivers to the buyer a quantity of goods less than he or she contracted to sell, the buyer may reject them. If the buyer accepts the goods as delivered, he or she must pay for them at the contract rate.
2. Where the seller delivers to the buyer a quantity of goods larger than he or she contracted to sell, the buyer may accept the goods he or she has agreed to buy, and reject the rest, or he or she may reject the whole. In practice it will usually be the case that the parties will agree in their contract of sale that a certain variation from the strict contract quantity will be permitted.

Note that Section 30, as amended by the 1994 Act, states:

(2A)A buyer who does not deal as consumer may not

- (a) where the seller delivers a quantity of goods less than he contracted to sell, reject the goods under subsection (1) above, or
- (b) where the seller delivers a quantity of goods larger than he contracted to sell, reject the whole under subsection (2) above,

if the shortfall, or, as the case may be, excess is so slight that it would be unreasonable for him to do so.

(2B) It is for the seller to show that a shortfall or excess fell within subsection (2A) above.

(2C)Subsections (2A) and (2B) above do not apply to Scotland.

3. Where the seller delivers a quantity of goods larger than he or she contracted to sell and the buyer accepts the whole of the goods so delivered, then he or she must pay for them at the contract rate.
4. Where the seller delivers to the buyer the goods he or she contracted to sell mixed with other goods of different descriptions, then the buyer may accept the goods which are in accordance with the agreement and reject the rest, or he or she may reject the whole.
5. These particular provisions are as always subject to any usage of trade or any special agreement or course of dealing between parties.

## *Illustrative Cases*

*Behrend and Co v Produce Brokers Ltd (1920).* There was a contract for the sale of two lots of cotton seed (200 and 500 tons) at different prices. Part of each lot was delivered. The contract price was paid in full. The ship then continued to another port. Two weeks later it returned and delivered the remainder of the cotton seed. It was held (in this case under Section 30(1)) that the buyer may retain what has been delivered initially but may reject the rest and recover the amount paid in respect of the rejected part of the goods subject to the subsequent delivery.

*Shipton Anderson and Co v Weil Bros (1912).* This case concerned a contract for the sale of a cargo of wheat which would amount to 4,950 tons under a limit of variation clause in the contract. The actual amount rendered was 4,950 tons and 55lb. The seller did not insist on payment for the additional 55lb. It was held (in this case under Section 30(2)) that this amounted to a good tender and the buyer could not reject it.

## *Instalment Deliveries*

Unless otherwise agreed the buyer of goods is not bound to accept delivery of them by instalments. Where there is a contract for the sale of goods to be delivered by stated instalments which are to be paid for separately, and the seller makes a defective delivery in respect of one or more instalments, or the buyer neglects or refuses to take delivery or to pay for one or more instalments, then it is a question in each case depending on the terms of the contract whether the breach in respect of one instalment is a repudiation of the whole contract, or whether it is a severable breach giving rise to a claim for compensation but not to a right to treat the whole contract as repudiated.

The tests to be applied are, first, the ratio quantitatively which the breach bears to the contract and, second, the degree of probability that such a breach will be repeated. For example, if the buyer fails to pay for one instalment under such circumstances as to suggest that the or she will not pay for future instalments, or the seller fails to deliver goods of the contract description under similar circumstances, then the contract can be repudiated. In *Regent OHG Aisenstadt und Barig v Francesco of Jermyn Street Ltd (1981)* a clothing manufacturer contracted to sell 62 suits to a retailer, delivery to be by instalments over an agreed period, the number and size of each delivery to be at the seller's discretion. The buyer informed the seller that the buyer wished to cancel the order. The seller insisted on making deliveries because the seller was already in production. Each of the attempted deliveries (five in all) was rejected by the buyer. In defence to the seller's claim for damages for non-acceptance, the buyer claimed that as the attempted deliveries had been one suit short of the total contract quantity of 62, the buyer was entitled to reject all the goods under Section 30(1). Judgement was given for the seller. Section 30(1), which provides that in the case of a short delivery the buyer can reject all the goods, does not apply in the case of a severable contract. Section 30(1) was inconsistent with and had to yield to Section 31. Applying Section 31, the short delivery was not sufficiently serious to amount to a repudiation of the whole contract.

## *Illustrative Cases*

*Maple Flock Co Ltd v Universal Furniture Products (Wembley) Ltd (1934).* A agreed to buy from B 100 tons of flock at £15 per ton, to be delivered three loads weekly, 1½ tons per load, as required. The 16th delivery was defective. A repudiated the contract and refused to accept further deliveries. B sued for breach of contract. It was found by the court that the first 15 deliveries were as per contract; and that there was unlikely to be a recurrence of the defect. It was held that the matter was covered by Section 31(2) of the *Sale of Goods Act* and that the principal tests applicable are:

1. the ratio quantitatively which the breach bears to the contract as a whole; and
2. the degree of probability that such a breach will be repeated.

Since in this case only 1½ out of 100 tons were defective and there was unlikely to be a repetition, A did not have a right to treat the whole contract as repudiated and was in breach of contract. A could have sued for damages in respect of the 1½ tons if the defect had been discovered before he used that flock in his manufacturing process.

*Munroe & Co Ltd v Mayer (1930).* X agreed to buy from Y 15,000 tons of meat and bone meal. Under the contract of sale, Y agreed to deliver the goods in equal weekly instalments. When delivery had been made of 611 tons it was found that all the meal delivered was unsatisfactory. In these circumstances it was held, applying the earlier equivalent of Section 31(2), that X was entitled to treat Y's breach as a repudiation of the entire contract.

Note Section 32 on delivery to a carrier. If authorised to send the goods to the buyer, delivery of goods to a carrier is prima facie deemed to be delivery to the buyer. The seller should take reasonable precautions, however.

*Wimble v Rosenberg and Sons (1913).* Some goods were sold FOB (free on board) to Antwerp to be shipped as required, payment to be by cash against the bill of lading. The buyer directed the seller to ship goods to Odessa, leaving the seller to select the ship. The ship sailed on 25 August and was lost on 26 August. The buyer received no notice of the shipment until 9 August. It was held that the buyer must pay for the goods, even though he had not insured, because he had sufficient information for him to insure before the goods were shipped.

## *Acceptance*

The buyer for his part has a duty to accept the goods, and Section 35 provides that acceptance is deemed to take place when the buyer:

1. intimates to the seller that he has accepted the goods; or
2. does any act to the goods which is inconsistent with the ownership of the seller, or
3. retains the goods, after the lapse of a reasonable time without intimating to the seller that he has rejected them.

Section 34 provides that a buyer has a right to examine the goods for the purpose of ascertaining whether they are in conformity with the contract. The seller on his part must give the buyer a reasonable opportunity to examine the goods for that purpose.

Once the buyer, as stated above, either tells the seller that he has accepted the goods or does any act inconsistent with the ownership of the seller, such as reselling the goods or pledging them, or if the buyer keeps the goods after a reasonable time has elapsed then, then all these cases he will be held to have accepted the goods. It is often made a term of the contract that if 14 days have elapsed after delivery of the goods to the buyer then the buyer will be deemed to have accepted the goods. The purpose of this is naturally to clear up any confusion which might arise as to whether or not the buyer has accepted them.

If the seller attempted to remove the right of the buyer to reject for breach of contract, then such a clause would be subject to the *Unfair Contract Terms Act 1977*. If the relationship is business to business the clause must be fair and reasonable.

Sections 34 and 35 have been altered by the *Sale and Supply of Goods Act 1994*. That Act provides that the rights of examination cannot be removed from a buyer in a consumer contract. Furthermore, by Section 2(6) of the 1994 Act, the buyer is not by virtue of this section deemed to have accepted the goods merely because

1. he asks for, or agrees to, their repair by or under an arrangement with the seller, or
2. the goods are delivered to another under a sub-sale or other disposition.

## *Right of Partial Rejection*

Under the 1979 Act, if the buyer accepted part of a consignment and then discovered that the remainder did not comply with the terms of purchase, he was unable to reject the latter. However, the 1994 Act Section 35A provides as follows in respect of the right of partial rejection.

1. If the buyer:
   (a) has the right to reject the goods by reason of a breach on the part of the seller that affects some or all of them, but
   (b) accepts some of the goods, including, where there are any goods unaffected by the breach, all such goods,

   he does not by accepting them lose his right to reject the rest.
2. In the case of a buyer having the right to reject an instalment of goods, subsection (1) above applies as if references to the goods were references to the goods comprised in the instalment.
3. For the purposes of subsection (1) above, goods are affected by a breach if by reason of the breach they are not in conformity with the contract.
4. This section applies unless a contrary intention appears in, or is to be implied from, the contract.

Note that, as with so many of these provisions, they may be excluded by the parties to the contract.

## *Remedies of Buyer and Seller*

### Buyer's Action against the Seller

Whether the property in the goods has passed or not, the buyer is entitled under the contract of sale to delivery in accordance with the rules. If the seller wrongfully neglects or refuses to deliver the goods to him, the buyer may bring an action for damages for non-delivery. Section 51(2) provides that the measure of damages is the estimated loss directly or naturally resulting, in the ordinary course of events, from the seller's breach of contract.

That provision is merely a restatement, in statutory form, of the general rule with regard to damages for breach of contract. However the Act gives a particular application of it where it provides in Section 51(3) that "where there is an available market for the goods in question a measure of damages in prima facie to be ascertained by the difference between the contract price and the market or current price of the goods at the time or times when they ought to have been delivered, or (if no time was fixed) at the time of the refusal to deliver."

However a buyer will often be buying goods in order to resell these goods to a third party and the seller's failure to deliver may render the buyer unable to fulfil his obligations under the subcontract. The question then arises whether the buyer can claim as damages the profit which he would have made on the subcontract, had he been able to fulfil it, and also any liability incurred to the other party to the subcontract by reason of its non-fulfilment. Normally such damages cannot be recovered as they cannot be said to be "a loss directly and naturally resulting, in the ordinary course of events from the seller's breach of contract." However Section 54 of the Act expressly provides that nothing in the Act will affect the right of the buyer or the seller to recover special damages in any case where by law special damages are recoverable. It is well settled that a party suing for breach of contract may recover as special damages loss which, although it does not arise naturally from the breach, may be recoverable provided it should have been in contemplation of both parties at the time they made the contract.

Finally, the buyer may sue the seller for damages where there has been a breach of warranty by the seller or where the buyer chooses to treat any breach of condition by the seller as a breach of warranty. Remember that the breach of condition entitles the buyer to reject the contract completely, whereas a breach of warranty will only entitle him to sue for damages.

**Specific Performance**

The buyer's remedies are not confined to an action for damages but he may in special cases obtain from the court an order for a specific performance of the contract. The *Sale of Goods Act* provides in Section 52 that "in any action for breach of contract to deliver specific or ascertained goods a court may, if it thinks fit, on the application of the plaintiff direct that the contract shall be performed specifically". This Section merely gives a statutory statement to an equitable jurisdiction which the court would already possess apart from the *Sale of Goods Act*.

Specific performance is an extraordinary remedy which will only be granted in extraordinary cases. It will only be ordered where the court can effectively superintend and enforce the carrying out of its order. It would seem to follow that specific performance would not be decreed of a contract for the delivery of goods by instalments, for it might require the constant supervision of the court to see that each instalment was delivered. In the same way the Section confines the remedy to cases where the goods in question are specific or ascertained. If the court were to order specific performance of a contract for the sale of unascertained goods, the court itself might have to ascertain the goods which were to be delivered.

However even if the goods are ascertained the court may still not grant specific performance. It will never do so, for example, in a case where damages would afford adequate compensation to the injured party, and this rule precludes specific performance of most contracts for the sale of goods. "If a contract is for the purchase of a certain quantity of coals this court will not decree a specific performance because a person can go in to the market and buy similar articles and get damages for the difference in the price of the articles in a court of law". *Fakke v Gray (1859).*

Thus it is only in exceptional cases such as where the article in question is unique, such as an heirloom, or where it possesses some peculiar value to the buyer over and above the ordinary market value of similar goods that the order of specific performance will be made. The normal remedy of the buyer is an action for damages for non-delivery.

It should always be remembered that over and above an action for damages for non delivery and an action for specific performance a buyer always has a right to reject the goods and to end the contract when the term broken by the seller is a condition (not a mere warranty). Most of the terms implied by Sections 12-15 are conditions. Also the courts have held that late delivery by a seller is a breach of condition which entitles a buyer to reject the goods and to end the contract. Section 11(4) provides that where the contract of sale is non-severable, the rights to reject the goods and treat the contract as repudiated are lost as soon as the buyer has accepted the goods, or part thereof. A buyer is deemed to have accepted the goods when he does any act outlined in Section 35.

**Seller's Action Against the Buyer**

The seller has corresponding rights of action against the buyer if he, the buyer, neglects or refuses to perform his side of the contract. Section 49(1) provides that "where under a contract of sale the property in the goods has passed to the buyer, and the buyer wrongfully neglects or refuses to pay for the goods according to the terms of the contract, the seller may maintain an action against him for the price of the goods." Usually delivery of the goods and payment of the price are concurrent conditions; but the contract may provide for the payment irrespective of delivery. Section 49 provides that "where under a contract of sale price is payable on a day certain irrespective of delivery, and the buyer wrongfully neglects or refuses to pay such price, the seller may maintain an action for the price, although the property in the goods has not passed and the goods have not been appropriated to the contract".

In addition if the buyer breaks a contract by not accepting the goods then the seller may maintain an action against him for damages for non-acceptance. Again the measure of damages, as in the case where the seller is at fault, is the estimated loss naturally resulting from the buyer's breach of contract. The measure of damages is to be ascertained by reference to the contract price and the market price.

Note that in the references to an action by the seller for the price of the goods and an action by the seller for damages, a distinction must be made between each of these. Remember that if the seller has a right to recover the price that is quite straight forward. If he can merely sue for damages then the amount he will be awarded will depend on the amount of compensation he deserves, which in some cases may amount to little or nothing.

*WL Thompson Ltd v Robinson (Gunmakers) Ltd (1955).* The defendants bought a Standard "Vanguard" motor car from the plaintiffs and then refused to accept it. The seller's profit would have been £61. As the supply of this particular vehicle exceeded the demand the sellers could not re-sell it and so lost their profit. They succeeded in recovering the whole loss of profit.

*Charter v Sullivan (1957).* The defendant bought a Hillman Minx motor car from the plaintiff. The latter's profit would have been £97.15s. When sued for non-acceptance the defendant was only ordered to pay nominal damages because it was proved that the seller could sell as many Hillman Minx cars as he could obtain. Therefore he had not incurred any appreciable loss.

Also because the rights of seller against the buyer will usually only be enforced because the buyer has not paid for the goods then it may be of no help to the seller to allow him to bring an action against the buyer because the buyer will not be able to pay damages. It will be preferable if the seller can exercise rights against the goods themselves.

### Rights of the Unpaid Seller Against the Goods

In addition to the remedies by way of action, the Act gives to the seller, in certain circumstances, rights against the goods themselves. To be able to claim these rights he must be an unpaid seller, that is one to whom the whole of the price has not been paid or tendered, or who has received a condition payment, a bill of exchange or other negotiable instrument which has been subsequently dishonoured (Section 38). To such an unpaid seller the Act gives, in certain circumstances, three rights against the goods themselves, namely lien, stoppage and resale.

## *A Lien*

A lien is a right to retain the goods of another. In this case it is the right of a creditor who is in possession of the goods belonging to his debtor to retain possession of them until payment is made. A lien is a right over the property of another. For a seller to exercise his lien merely because he has not been paid is not sufficient. One at least of the following conditions must be satisfied.

1. The goods must have been sold without any stipulation as to credit.
2. Where the goods have been sold on credit the term of credit has expired.
3. The buyer must have become insolvent. The meaning of insolvent is to be found in Section 61(4). This provides that a person is deemed to be insolvent if he has either ceased to pay his debts or he cannot pay his debts as they become due.

Lien is founded on possession, and so it follows that once possession is lost the lien, as a rule, is lost also. The unpaid seller of goods will lose his lien or right of retention:

1. when he delivers the goods to a carrier for the purpose of transmission to the buyer without reserving the right of disposal of the goods;
2. when the buyer or his agent lawfully obtains possession of the goods;
3. by waiver of the lien or right of retention.

Merely because an unpaid seller has made part delivery of the goods does not of itself deprive him of his right of lien on the remainder, unless the circumstances under which the part delivery was made show an agreement to waive the lien. In other words a lien is only lost in such cases if it appears that both parties intended the part delivery to be regarded as constructive delivery of the whole.

## *Stoppage in Transit*

When the unpaid seller has delivered the goods to a carrier it may be that he has lost his lien. Therefore this second remedy of the unpaid seller is that in certain circumstances he can stop the goods in transit.

This means that he can order the carrier to redeliver the goods to him. Section 44 provides that when the buyer of the goods becomes insolvent the unpaid seller who has parted with the possession of the goods has the right of stopping them in transit. In other words he may resume possession of the goods as long as they are in the course of transit and may retain them until payment or tender of the price. It is therefore important to determine whether or not the goods are in the course of transit. They are deemed to be in the course of transit from the time when they are delivered to a carrier for the purpose of transmission to the buyer until the buyer or his agent takes delivery of them. If the buyer or his agent obtains delivery before their arrival at the appointed destination the transit is at an end. The essence of stoppage in transit, it has been said, is that the goods should be "in the possession of a middle man". It is not necessary that the goods should actually be in motion for if the goods are deposited with a person who holds them merely as an agent to forward them, then they are as much in transit as if they were actually moving.

Sometimes it is agreed that the goods shall be sent to some intermediate place, and the question then arises whether the delivery of them at that place terminates transit or transit continues until the goods reach their ultimate destination. Thus A in India may order goods from B in Manchester to be sent to London whence they are to be forwarded to India. Does transit terminate when the goods reach London or not until they reach India? The answer to that question depends on whether the intermediate place is merely a place of rest in the course of one journey or whether, having reached the intermediate place, the goods cannot again be set in motion without fresh orders from the purchaser. In the latter case transit ends at the intermediate place, but in the former transit continues until the goods arrive at their ultimate destination.

If goods are delivered to a ship chartered by the buyer then a difficulty may arise. The

Act provides in Section 45(5) that it is a question depending on the circumstances of the particular case whether the goods are in the possession of the master as a carrier or as an agent for the buyer. Of course if the ship is owned by the buyer, transit is usually at an end as soon as the goods are put on board.

In order to stop the goods in transit it is not necessary for the seller to recover actual physical possession of them. He may exercise his right of stoppage in transit either by taking actual possession of the goods or by giving notice of his claim to the carrier in whose possession the goods are. Such notice may be given either to the person in actual possession of the goods or to his principal. In the latter case the notice must be given at such time and under such circumstances that the principal may communicate it to his servant or agent in time to prevent delivery to the buyer. Section 46(3).

Where the carrier in possession of the goods receives notice of stoppage in transit from the seller, it is his duty to re-deliver the goods to the seller and seller must bear the expense of such re-delivery. Section 46(4).

## Right of Resale

Merely because the seller has retained possession of the goods or has had them stopped in transit and now possesses them does not give him automatically a right of resale. However Section 48 of the Act gives the unpaid seller a right to resell the goods in following circumstances:

1. where a right of resale is expressly reserved by the terms of the contract;
2. where the goods are of a perishable nature; or
3. where the unpaid seller gives notice to the buyer of his intention to resell and the buyer does not within a reasonable time pay or tender the price.

Where the resale is at a profit, so that the seller gets more than the original contract price, the seller can keep the profit. If an unpaid seller resells wrongfully, for example without giving reasonable notice, the new buyer gets a good title but in this event the seller must account to the old buyer for any profit as compared with the original contract price. In the above cases the unpaid seller may resell and he also has, against the buyer, a claim for damages for breach of contract.

**Questions**

At what point in time does the property in unascertained goods pass from the seller to the buyer?
What is the importance of the *Romalpa* clause?
What are the exceptions to the *nemo dat* rule?

TWELVE

# *The* COMMON LAW CONTRACT *of* EMPLOYMENT

*Study Topics*

**How the law distinguishes between employees and independent contractors**
**The terms implied in a contract of employment by common law**
**The duties of employer and employee at common law**

Employment law is concerned with the contract of employment. Like any other contract this sets up rights and duties between the parties. In this case the parties are the employer and the employee. The contract of employment is affected by various Acts of Parliament. In particular there is the *Employment Protection Act 1975* and the *Employment Protection (Consolidation) Act 1978*, now consolidated in the *Employment Rights Act 1996*. In addition there are the *Race Relations Act 1976* and the *Sex Discrimination Act 1975 1986*, the *Trade Union and Labour Relations (Consolidation) Act 1992* and the *Employment Relations Act 1999*. All affect the implementation of the contract of employment. There are also a host of Regulations relating to the maximum working week and minimum wage for example which must be taken into account. See the next chapter for a fuller discussion.

One has to take into account that a person may be employed by another in one of two ways. The basic division is between those who are employed persons (employees) and those who are self-employed (independent contractors). It is sometimes said that an employed person works under a contract of service, where as the self- employed person works under a contract for services. The distinction may be illustrated as follows: a person may be transported by a chauffeur or by a taxi driver. In both cases it is obvious that the chauffeur and the taxi driver are working, or are employed by the person in the back of the car. It is equally obvious that the relationship between the person in the back of the car and the chauffeur is different from that between the taxi driver and his fare. It is important to make this distinction because the employment statutes only affect the parties who have entered into a contract of service.

The *Social Security Contributions and Benefits Act 1992* requires an employer to pay secondary class I contributions in respect of employed earners. An employee is entitled to receive details of his terms of employment under the *Employment Rights Act 1996* and to receive certain minimum periods of notice of his dismissal. In addition he has protection against unfair dismissal and can claim redundancy payments in appropriate circumstances. None of these benefits applies if a person is a self-employed independent contractor.

Furthermore an employer will not normally be vicariously liable for the tortious acts committed by an independent contractor. However he would be liable if a tort were committed by his employees in the course of their employment which caused injury or damage to third parties.

Thus it can be seen that it is important to make the distinction between an employee under a contract of service and an independent contractor employed under a contract of services.

## *Making the Distinction*

Originally the main test to be used was "what degree of control may the employer exercise over the employee?" If the employer could tell the employee not only what to do but how to do it thus exercising a substantial degree of control then the relationship would probably be that of master and servant. This was the old phraseology to describe a contract of service.

### The Organisational or Integration Test

In *Stevenson, Jordan and Harrison Ltd v MacDonald and Evans (1952)*, Denning LJ suggested that a more up-to-date test would be: "under a contract of service a man is employed as part of the business and his work is done as an integral part of the business". This test includes skilled employees who are "integrated" into an enterprise. It applies to a specialist operating in a hospital who could hardly be said to be controlled by the hospital committee but at least he could be said to be integrated into the hospital service.

The *Stevenson* case followed *Cassidy v Ministry of Health (1955)* in which the court held that the defendants were liable for negligent treatment in the operating theatre in spite of the fact that there was an absence of control over the work done by the doctors employed by them.

### The Multiple Test

In recent years it has been accepted that the problem of deciding the relationship between an employee and an employer is too complex to be capable of being resolved by the application of any single simple test.

Nowadays the court will look at surrounding features and apply a multiple test. The contractual provisions should be examined, the degree of control exercised by the employer, the obligation of the employer to provide work and the obligation on the employee to do that work, the duty of personal service, provision of tools, equipment and instruments, arrangements made for tax, national insurance, VAT and statutory sick pay and other contractual provisions including holiday pay, sick pay, notice, fees and expenses. Finally the degree of financial risk and responsibility for investment and management should be considered, also whether the relationship of being self-employed is a genuine one or whether there is an attempt to avoid modern protective legislation. The best example of the Multiple or "Economic Reality" test in use was in *Ready Mixed Concrete v Minister of Pensions and National Insurance (1968)*. Here the court had to look at a multitude of factors surrounding the use of owner-drivers for delivering concrete. It found them to be sub-contractors based on the fact that they bought, painted and maintained their own lorries and had to engage substitute drivers to cover absence for example. This was despite restrictions on who they could work for and other contractual terms which one might expect to find in an employment contract.

The position was considered again recently in *Express and Echo Publications v Tanton (1999)*. It was re-stated that a contract which required a worker to provide an alternative person to perform his duties if he was ill could not be a contract of employment. A key element then of a contract of employment is that services are required personally.

## *Formation of a Contract of Employment*

A contract of employment may be entered into either formally or informally. It may be a verbal contract or it may be in writing by means of an exchange of letters. Apprenticeship deeds and articles for merchant seamen of course must be written. Some people are surprised that a contract of employment legally is not required to be in writing and this surprise originates because the *Employment Rights Act 1996* provides that no later than two months after the commencement of employment the employer shall give the employee a written statement containing the following information.

i. The names of the employer and the employee.
ii. The date when the employment began.
ii. The date on which the employee's period of continuous employment began, taking into account any employment with a previous employer which counts towards continuity.

As at a specified date, not more than seven days before the statement is given.
i. The scale of rate of remuneration or the method of calculating remuneration.
ii. The intervals in which remuneration is paid.
iii. Any terms and conditions relating to hours of work.
iv. Any terms and conditions relating to
   a. entitlement to holidays including public holidays and holiday pay (being sufficient to calculate the entitlement, including accrued holiday pay, on the termination of employment;
   b. incapacity for work due to sickness or injury, including any provision for sick pay;
   c. pensions and pension schemes.
v. The length of notice the employee is obliged to give and entitled to receive to determine the employment.
vi. The title of the employee's job.
vii. If the employment is not intended to be permanent, the period for which it is expected to continue; if it is for a fixed term, the date when it is to end.
viii. Either the place of work or where the employee is required or permitted to work at various places, an indication of that and the address of the employer.
ix. Any collective agreement which directly affects the terms and conditions of employment; where the employer is not a party to the agreement, the persons by whom they are made.
x. Where the employee is required to work outside the United Kingdom for more than one month:
   a. the period for which he is to work outside the United Kingdom;
   b. the currency in which remuneration is to be paid whilst so working;
   c. any additional remuneration payable to him and any benefits to be provided by reason of his working abroad;
   d. any terms and conditions relating to his return to the United Kingdom.

Instead of stating all the above terms the employee may be referred to some other document which he has a reasonable opportunity of reading in the course of the employment and which is readily accessible to him. This is particularly appropriate in respect of sick pay and pension schemes.

In addition to the above matters the written statement shall include a note specifying any disciplinary rules which apply to the employee and must specify by description or otherwise a person to whom the employee can apply if he is dissatisfied with any disciplinary decision relating to him.

It is not necessary to give written particulars to an employee if his employment continues for less than one month or if his contract normally involves working for less than eight hours weekly.

## *Collective Agreements*

A collective agreement is an agreement made between an employers' association or a single employer on the one hand and a trade union on the other. Such an agreement will govern the relationship between the signatories and will also provide for the terms and conditions of employment of those covered by the agreement.

The basic terms of a collective agreement may be incorporated into the individual contract of employment by an express provision to this effect. Employment for example may be undertaken on the basis of "union rates of pay" or "union conditions". As has already been mentioned it is quite common for the terms of a collective agreement to be incorporated into an individual contract by means of the statement given to the employee under the *Employment Rights Act 1996*.

## *Implied Terms*

As in the case of any other contract it may be that certain terms are implied into the contract of employment by the courts. Such implied terms are based on the theory that in the court's view it was "obvious" where the contract was silent and that any particular implied term would be so obvious that the parties did not see the need to state it expressly.

There is an implied term that an employer will treat the employee with respect and trust and not treat him in an arbitrary or vindictive manner. There is an implied term that the employer will not prevent the employee from performing his contract of employment or delay or hinder him so as to prevent him from earning his full remuneration.

On the other hand there is no implied term that an employer will look after the employee's property, clothes or car, etc. which are left on the employer's premises. Also there is no implied term that the employer will provide personal accident insurance for the benefit of an employee who is required to work abroad.

## *Duties and Rights of the Parties to a Contract of Employment*

As in any contract the parties have rights and owe duties to the other party. Sometimes these are called common law rights and duties which means that they are implied into the contract by the courts. Sometimes Acts of Parliament place duties upon the parties.

In the case of a Contract of Employment the intervention of Parliament is especially noticeable.

## *Common Law Duties of the Employer*

1. Duty to provide work. As a general rule employer is not obliged to provide work for his employee so long as he pays him the agreed remuneration. In *Collier v Sunday Referee Publishing Company (1940)* Asquith J said "Provided I pay my cook her wages regularly, she cannot complain if I choose to take any or all of my meals out". However if failure to provide work leads to a reduction in the employee's actual or potential earnings or if failure to provide work can lead to a loss of reputation or publicity then it may be that the employer will find himself in breach of contract if he fails to provide a reasonable amount of work. *Herbert Clayton and Jack Waller Ltd v Oliver (1930).*
2. Obligation to pay the agreed remuneration. A problem may arise if there is no work for the employee to do and the basic rule is that the employer is still obliged to pay the employee. However this may be varied by an express or implied term to the contrary such as might arise during a lay-off or in respect of short-time working.
3. Duty of confidentiality. As there is a duty placed on employees not to disclose confidential information about the employer's business there is a similar duty on an employer not to disclose confidential information about the employee.
4. Duty to indemnify. Any expenses incurred by the employee in the performance of his contract should be met by the employer.
5. Duty to insure. In respect of work activities taking place within the United Kingdom an employer is obliged to take out compulsory employer's liability insurance for the benefits of his employees. *Employer's Liability (Compulsory) Insurance Act (1969).*
6. References. An employer is under no legal duty to provide an employee with a reference. If the employer gives a derogatory reference then he may be exposed to an action for defamation. If he gives a reference which untruly praises the employee then he may be subject to an action by the prospective employer for deceit or negligent misstatement. *Hedley Byrne and Company Ltd v Heller and Partners Ltd (1964).*
7. Duty to ensure employees' safety. This is the most important aspect of the employer's duty implied by law. This duty of course is in addition to any duties which may be placed upon the employer by the *Health and Safety at Work Act 1974.*
8. The employer may find himself liable under the law of negligence. In *Paris v Stepney Borough Council (1951)* the court stated that "care which an ordinary prudent employer would take in all the circumstances is the standard of care which the employer must observe".

In his defence the employer may deny negligence or may attempt to show that the injury was as a result of the fault of the employee either in whole or in part. The *Law Reform (Contributory Negligence) Act 1945* provides that if a person is injured partly through his own fault and partly to the fault of another then damages shall be reduced to the extent that the court thinks the claimant is to blame for the damage.

The duty of care of the employer is usually covered in three areas:

1. Safe plant and appliances. This means that the equipment and machinery used by the employee shall be reasonably safe for use. In *Bradford v Robinson Rentals (1967)* a driver was required to drive an unheated van on a 400-mile journey during a bitterly cold spell of weather. The court held that the employer was liable when the driver suffered frostbite as a consequence.
2. Safe system of work. This covers the systems laid down, the training and supervision of the employee. If the employer can show that even though he had provided safety precautions the employee would not have used them, he may still escape liability. In *MacWilliams v Sir William Arroll Ltd (1962)* a steel erector fell from a scaffolding and was killed. The employer had provided safety belts in the past, but these had not been used and they had been taken away to be used on another site. It was held that even though the employer was negligent in not providing the safety belts it was unlikely that the employee would have used them had they been available. The court held that the employer's negligence was not the cause of death.
3. Reasonably competent fellow employees. If an employer engages an incompetent person by whose actions another employee may be injured then the employer may be liable for failing to take reasonable care. In *Hudson v Ridge Manufacturing Company (1957)* an employee was known to be in the habit of committing practical jokes. On one occasion he put out his leg while the plaintiff was passing and this caused an injury. It was held that the employer was liable.

## *Common Law Duties of the Employee*

1. To render faithful service. The employer is entitled to expect that the employee will serve his employer faithfully and will perform his duties carefully and competently.
2. To obey lawful and reasonable orders. The employer can expect his employee to obey all lawful and reasonable orders given to him. In the well-known case of *Pepper v Webb (1969)* the employer ordered his gardener to do certain lawful acts and in return the gardener used agricultural language to tell the employer what he could do with his job. The court held that the refusal to

obey lawful orders was a breach of contract.

3. Duty to use skill and care.
4. Receiving secret bribes and commissions. The employee must not accept secret bribes or commissions from third parties.
5. Confidentiality. The employee must not disclose any confidential information about the employer's business.

## *Termination of the Contract of Employment*

A contract of employment may be terminated in the same way as any other contract. It can be terminated in the following ways.

1 By mutual consent of the parties.
2. By frustration, such as where the employee falls sick for a long period and is unable to continue with his work. Obviously the length of time an employee is likely to be away from work is a material factor.
3. By performance. This will occur where a contract is for a fixed term or where the employee is required to perform a particular task.
4. By the death of either party. The compulsory winding up of the company or the appointment of a receiver on the employer's cessation of business.

All these events will automatically terminate the contract of employment. However, if an employer transfers his business to another owner then the Transfer of Undertakings (Protection of Employment) Regulations 1981 provide that the contracts of the employees are automatically transferred to the transferee of the business.

5. Termination by one of the parties. If the contract is terminated by the employee it is termed a resignation. If the employer brings the contract to an end it is known as a dismissal. Dismissal will occur when a contract of employment is terminated by the employer, with or without notice. However where the employee terminates the contract with or without notice, but he does so by reason of the employer's conduct, then this may be known as "constructive dismissal".

**Questions**

What tests are available to the courts for distinguishing between employees and independent contractors?

What are some of the common law duties owed by an employee to his employer?

THIRTEEN

# STATUTORY INTERVENTION *in the* CONTRACT *of* EMPLOYMENT

*Study Topics*

**The Employment Rights Act 1996 and other acts involved in employment legislation**
**Dismissal**
**The duties of the employer and the employee under the Health and Safety at Work Act 1974**
**The impact of the Social Chapter of the Maastricht Treaty**

Probably more than any other contract, a contract of employment is affected by legislation, especially if the employee is a minor (under the age of 18). Certain statutes seek to protect such persons. Children aged 13 or over may engage in part-time work, provided this does not amount to more than two hours per day on school days or on Sunday. They may not work during school hours, or before 7am or after 7pm on school days. Local authorities have certain supervisory powers over the employment of children under the *Employment of Children Act 1973*.

Apart from the common-law obligations which are implied into every contract of employment by the courts and by custom, there are additional obligations set out in legislation. In particular, the *Employment Rights Act 1996* consolidates many key provisions particularly from the *Employment Protection (Consolidation) Act 1978*. The

*Employment Relations Act 1999* deals with, for example, dismissal and trade union recognition so is discussed both here and in the chapter on trade union law.

It was not until a change of government in 1997 that the UK was bound by the "Social Chapter" of the *Maastricht Treaty*. This produced further UK law to comply with these provisions. The resultant leave, minimum wage and maximum working week stipulations are also discussed below.

## Sick Pay

Since April 1983 employers have been under a statutory obligation under the *Social Security and Housing Benefits Act 1982* to pay statutory sick pay to their employees for up to eight weeks sickness absence in any single tax year, or a single period of sickness spanning two tax years.

## Maternity Pay and Leave

An employee who is absent from work due to pregnancy or confinement is entitled to receive maternity pay from her employer. Furthermore there is an independent right to return to work following confinement and a right not to be dismissed on grounds of pregnancy.

A woman has a right to a maternity leave period of 14 weeks irrespective of the length of her period of continuous employment. She must notify her employer of the date her maternity leave is to commence not less than 21 days before the commencement or as soon as is reasonably practicable.

A woman has a right to return to work any time up to 29 weeks from the end of her maternity leave period. To qualify for this right she must have been continuously employed for not less than two years or five years if she works between 8-60 hours per week. At any time after three weeks before the end of the maternity leave period her employer may request her to give a written confirmation that she intends to exercise her right to return to work.

The adoption of the "Social Chapter" meant that the Parental Leave Directive had to be complied with. This introduced two new rights for employees: Dependant Leave and Parental Leave. Dependant leave is available by virtue of the *Employment Rights Act 1996*, S57A and S57B. Employees are entitled to take time off for urgent family reasons. There is no qualifying period for this.

The right to (unpaid) Parental Leave after a one year qualifying period is given by the *Maternity and Parental Leave etc. Regulations 1999*. The leave is to be taken only by a person having responsibility for a child and is to look after a child or make arrangements for the good of a child.

Minimum periods of paid annual leave are now governed by the *Working Time*

*Regulations 1998* (as amended by the 1999 Regulations). This is the legislation which limits a worker's maximum week to 48 hours unless both parties agree to exclude this provision. Certain workers such as emergency services personnel are also exempt. In any leave year beginning after 23 November 1999, a worker is entitled to four weeks paid leave. There does not seem to be much public awareness of this provision. Nationally, voluntary advice centres have recently reported an increase in enquiries from workers not receiving sufficient paid holidays.

## Other Time off Work

An employee who is dismissed for reason of redundancy shall be entitled to be given reasonable time off during his working hours to look for new employment or to make arrangements for retraining (Section 31).

An employee who is pregnant and on the advice of a doctor has made an appointment to attend a place for the purpose of receiving antenatal care shall have the right not to be unreasonably refused time off during her working hours to keep the appointment.

An employee who is summoned for jury service must be given time off work for that purpose. *Juries Act 1974*.

An employee also has a right to have time off work for trade union duties and activities and also is entitled to time off for the purpose of performing duties as a magistrate, a member of a local authority, a member of a statutory tribunal or a regional health authority, a member of the managing or governing body of an educational establishment, or a member of a board of visitors for prisons.

## Wages

Until 1986 it was a requirement of the *Truck Acts 1831-1940* that manual workers be paid in the coin of the realm. That Act was repealed by the *Wages Act 1986* and it is now perfectly lawful for all employees to be paid in any manner other than cash. The actual method of payment of wages is still a matter for agreement between the employer and the employee.

Wages is defined as any sums payable to the worker by his employer in connection with his employment including any fee, bonus, commission, holiday pay or other emoluments referable to his employment whether payable under his contract or otherwise.

Note that expenses and redundancy payments are not included in this definition, although statutory sick pay, statutory maternity pay and certain payments due to an employee on the employer's insolvency are included.

*The Employment Rights Act 1996* has largely replaced the *Wages Act*. S 13 to 22 of the *ERA 1996* cover protection of wages from most deductions. Deductions are possible however in the following circumstances:

1. the deduction is required to be made by a statutory provision, for example PAYE or National Insurance;
2. the deduction is authorised by a provision in the worker's contract such as a contribution to an occupational pension scheme; or
3. the worker has signified his agreement to the deduction in writing in advance such as the repayment of a loan made to purchase a season travel ticket.

## *Pay Statements*

Every employee has the right to an itemised pay statement, by virtue of S8 the *ERA 1996,* giving particulars of:

1. the gross amount of pay
2. the amount of variable deductions and their purpose
3. the amount of any fixed deductions
4. the net amount of pay.

If the employer has provided a standing statement of fixed deductions then he does not need to provide an itemised list of fixed deductions.

In the event of non-payment of wages then the ordinary courts have a jurisdiction concurrent with the industrial tribunals. However if an employee is wrongfully dismissed and is not given pay in lieu of notice then his claim must be taken to a County Court as it is for damages for breach of contract. Likewise the following disputes must be taken to a County Court and not to an industrial tribunal:

1. any dispute concerning a deduction by the employer for overpayment of wages;
2. deduction made in consequence of disciplinary proceedings under a statutory provision;
3. deduction authorised by statute such as an attachment of earnings order;
4. payment made to a third party on behalf of the worker in accordance with a provision within his contract to which he has signified his consent in writing;
5. deduction made because the worker has taken part in a strike or other industrial action.

*The National Minimum Wages Act 1998*, discussed above, is also the product of European legislation. Its purpose is fairly obvious and it has had the effect of ensuring that there is a minimum level of income that a worker can expect to earn.

## *Dismissal*

Since the *Industrial Relations Act 1971* an employee has had a right not to be unfairly dismissed. This right has been continued in later legislation and is now to be found in the *Employment Rights Act 1996*.

A dismissal may be summary; this will occur when an employer dismisses an employee because of gross misconduct, wilful refusal to obey a lawful and reasonable order, gross neglect or dishonesty. A summary dismissal takes effect immediately and any rights an employee may have such as for pay in lieu of notice may be claimed in an action for damages for breach of contract in the courts.

## *Lawful Dismissal*

In this case the employee will be entitled to a period of notice specified or implied into his contract of employment. If the contract does not specify the period of notice then the *Employment Rights Act 1996* states that an employee is entitled to one week's notice and this will apply until he has been employed for up to two years. After two years' employment he will be entitled to one week's notice in respect of each year's employment until a maximum of 12 weeks' notice in respect of employment which has continued for 12 years or more.

## *Unfair Dismissal*

Under the *Employment Rights Act 1996,* an employee who complains that he has been unfairly dismissed has a right of action in the industrial tribunal. If he wants to bring an action in respect of wrongful dismissal because he has been sacked without the necessary period of notice or payment in lieu, he must bring his action in the ordinary courts.

The qualifying period for some employment rights is still two years but an action for unfair dismissal will now be possible for those who have been in employment for one year or more. This qualifying period is waived however if the complaint relates to dismissal connected with pregnancy or childbirth, the *Public Interest Disclosure Act 1998* (designed to protect "whistleblowers" who do so in the public interest), the *National Minimum Wage Act 1998*, trade union membership or assertion of rights under the *Health and Safety at Work Act 1974*. The employment must have taken place inside Great Britain and so does not apply to employees outside Great Britain or to those employed as master or member of a crew of a fishing vessel where they are remunerated by a share of the profits.

When a dismissal has taken place it must then be determined whether or not it was unfair. The *Employment Rights Act 1996*, S98, lays down five grounds on which a dismissal is capable of being fair.

1. A reason relating to the capability or qualifications of the employee for performing the work of the kind which he was employed by the employer to do.

2. A reason which relates to the conduct of the employee.
3. The redundancy of the employee.
4. Because the employee could not continue to work in the position which he held without contravention of a restriction or a duty imposed by or under a statute.
5. Some other substantial reason such as to justify the dismissal of employee holding the position which he held.

## Redundancy

The law relating to redundancy has now been consolidated in the *Employment Rights Act 1996.*

The stated purpose of the Redundancy Payments Scheme is

1. to compensate for loss of security and
2. to encourage workers to accept redundancy without damaging industrial relations.

A redundancy payment is compensation for loss of a right which a long-term employee has in his job. It is to compensate him for loss of security, possible loss of earnings and fringe benefits.

## Persons Covered by the Act

The *Employment Rights Act 1996* applies to "employees". These are defined as persons who have entered into a contract of service or apprenticeship and who have had at least two years continuous employment with that employer.

## Redundancy Payments and Dismissal

An employee may apply for a redundancy payment if he can establish that he has been "dismissed" and the employer cannot rebut the presumption of redundancy which arises. A dismissal takes place if:

1. the employer terminates the contract (with or without notice);
2. a fixed-term contract expires without being renewed;
3. the employee terminates the contract with or without notice in circumstances which are such that he is entitled to do so by reason of the employer's conduct;
4. the employment is terminated by the death, dissolution, liquidation of the employer or the appointment of a receiver.

In order to succeed in his claim the employee must be dismissed for reason of redundancy. There is a statutory presumption that if an employee is dismissed it is presumed to have been for reason of redundancy. It will be up to the employer to show, if he can, that the dismissal was for a reason other than redundancy. A dismissal shall be for reason of redundancy, if it can be attributed to

1. the fact that the employer has ceased or intends to cease to carry on that business for the purposes for which the employee was employed;
2. the employer has ceased or intends to cease to carry on that business in the place where the employee was employed or
3. the fact that the requirements of that business for employees to carry out work of a particular kind or for them to carry out that work in the place where they are so employed, have ceased or diminished or are expected to cease or diminish.

## *Alternative Employment*

An employer may make an offer to the employee to renew the contract of employment or to re-engage him under a new contract which is to take effect on the expiry of the old contract or within four weeks thereafter. The employee who has been dismissed will lose his right to a payment if he unreasonably refuses such an offer. But, of course, the offer must be one of "suitable employment", and regard must be had to the employee's status, the nature of the work to be done, the remuneration and other terms and conditions. The employee is then entitled to have a trial period of four weeks or such longer period as may be agreed for the purpose of retraining under the new contract.

## *Lay-off and Short-time*

An employer may, instead of dismissing his employees, decide to lay them off temporarily or to put them on short-time. A lay-off is where there is no work for the employees and no remuneration provided. Short-time working is defined as being where less than half the normal week's pay is earned. If the lay-off or short-time has lasted for more than four consecutive weeks or more than six weeks in any 13 then the employee may give written notice that he intends to claim a redundancy payment.

The employer can either make the payment or, within seven days of the employee's notice of intent to claim, issue a written counter notice contesting the claim stating that there is a reasonable chance that within 4 weeks of the date of the counter notice, the employee will commence a period of 13 weeks consecutive full employment. If the counter notice is withdrawn by the employer, or the 13 weeks continuous employment fails to materialise, the employee is entitled to be paid redundancy money.

## Claims

An employee who considers he has been dismissed for redundancy must make a claim on his employer in writing. If the employer still refuses to make such a payment the matter must be referred to an industrial tribunal. This must normally be done within six months of the termination of the contract.

The amount of redundancy payment is determined by the age of the employee. For each year's employment between the ages of 18 to 21 he is entitled to one half of a week's pay, between the ages of 22 and 40 he is entitled to one week's pay and between the ages of 41 and 64 he is entitled to one and a half week's pay. In respect of employees over the age of 64, there is a reduction of one-twelfth in the total entitlement in respect of each month over the age of 65. All this is subject to a maximum of 20 years reckonable employment and a maximum week's pay of £205. The maximum payment therefore possible for an employee over the age of 60 with 20 years' continuous employment is 20 x 11/2 x £205, i.e. £6,150.

## Health and Safety at Work

As has been mentioned the common law has always imposed obligations upon the employer to protect and take care of the safety of his employees. Thus an employer under common law is obliged to provide competent employees, with a proper system of working, safe working premises and equipment and to provide safety and protective equipment. The *Health and Safety at Work Act 1974* replaced a number of statutory measures and imposed general duties on a number of different categories of persons.

### Duties of Employers

It is the duty of every employer to ensure, so far as is reasonably practicable, the health, safety and welfare at work of his employees. He must have regard to:

1. the provision and maintenance of plant and systems of work;
2. the use, handling, storage and transport of articles and substances;
3. the provision of information, instruction, training and supervision;
4. the maintenance of the place of work and the provision of maintenance of means of access and to egress from such places;
5. provision and maintenance of a healthy and safe working environment and adequate welfare facilities and arrangements.

### Duties of Employees

Every employee at work has a duty:

1. to take reasonable care of his own and other persons' health and safety and
2. to co-operate with his employer and any other person to enable them to perform their statutory duties.

### Safety Policy

Section 2(3) requires an employer who employs five or more employees to prepare and revise a written statement of his general policy with respect to the health and safety at work of all his employees. An employer has a duty to consult with safety representatives over a wide range of issues. A trade union which is recognised by an employer may appoint safety representatives from among the employees. The employer shall establish a safety committee when at least two safety representatives make such a request.

## *Health and Safety Regulations*

Section 15 Schedule 3 of the Act gives the Secretary of State power to make regulations on a wide range of matters. The most important of these are:

1. repeal or modification of existing statutory provisions;
2. the exclusion or modification of the general duties in relation to a specific class of case;
3. making a specified authority responsible for the enforcement of any statutory provision;
4. imposing requirements by reference to the approval of the Commission or other specified body or person;
5. provision that any reference of a regulation to a specific document shall include a reference to a revised version of that document;
6. provision for specified defences either generally or in specified circumstances.

The number of these regulations has increased as the years go by and in particular the European Commission has issued a number of directives which have to be taken account of. The most recent regulations are six regulations which came into force on 1 January 1993 as a result of directives issued by the European Commission.

## *Codes of Practice*

Section 16 of the Act provides that codes of practice may be issued for the purpose of providing practical guidance with respect to the general duties imposed by the Act or by any regulation or any existing statutory provision. Breach of a provision of a code does not of itself render a person liable to criminal or civil proceedings but, in criminal proceedings, the provisions of a code of practice are admissible in evidence to show that an offence has been committed.

## *Enforcement*

The enforcement of the Act will generally be the responsibility of the Health and Safety Executive. However the Secretary of State may require local authorities to enforce certain provisions. The enforcing authorities will appoint inspectors who will have the following powers for the purpose of giving effect to the statutory provisions. They may enter at any reasonable time premises where they suspect there is a dangerous situation. They may take samples of any articles or substances found in any premises, may take photographs and measures and such recordings as are considered necessary. They also may require information to be given by any person whom they believe to be able to give such information.

### Improvement Notices

Section 21 empowers an inspector, who is of the opinion that a person is contravening a statutory provision or has done so, to serve on such a person an improvement notice giving reason why he is of that opinion. He may require the person to remedy the contravention within a certain period of time but not less than 21 days.

### Prohibition Notices

Section 22 empowers an inspector to serve a prohibition notice. This will state his opinion when certain activities are contravening the provisions of the Act and may require the person on whom the notice is served to cease until the matter is remedied.

An appeal from the imposition of an improvement notice or a prohibition notice may be made to the industrial tribunal. It can then cancel it or affirm it with modifications.

Where a person is convicted of an offence under any provision in the Act the court may, in addition to imposing any punishment, order him to take such steps to remedy the matters specified. After the expiry of the time given to him to remedy the matters, if then he continues with the contravention he can be sentenced to six months' imprisonment and/or fined up to £20,000 in the Magistrates' Courts or up to two years' imprisonment and/or an unlimited fine in the Crown Court.

### Questions

When is a dismissal deemed to be fair?

What is the purpose of a redundancy payment and who is entitled to it?

FOURTEEN

# DISCRIMINATION

*Study Topics*

**The three types of discrimination under the Sex Discrimination Act 1975**
**Genuine occupational qualifications under the Race Relations Act 1976**
**New Rights for disabled people under the Disability Discrimination Act 1995**

In recent years the most important body of legislation is contained in the statutes which seek to do away with discrimination as regards sex, race or disability. It is worth bearing in mind that many of these provisions also relate to situations outside the employer/employee relationship. It is possible to suffer discrimination and have a remedy as a customer or even a tenant for example. This chapter is mainly concerned with discrminiation in employment however.

## Sex Discrimination

The *Sex Discrimination Act 1975* is concerned with the elimination of discrimination in recruitment, training, promotion and other aspects of the employment relationship. The *Equal Pay Act 1970* as amended by the *Sex Discrimination Act* and by *Equal Pay (Amendment) Regulations 1983* is concerned with the establishment, where necessary, of equal terms and conditions of employment. Over and above these United Kingdom statutes is European Law as applied by the European Court of Justice. This is contained in Article 119 of the Treaty of Rome and the Equal Pay Directive.

## *Sex Discrimination Act 1975*

In determining whether or not discrimination exists the question should be whether the complainant would have received the same treatment from the defendant but for his or her sex. There are three types of discrimination in employment.

**Direct Discrimination**

This arises when a person of one sex is treated less favourably than a person of another sex and the sex of that person is the reason for the unfavourable treatment. To refuse to employ a woman because "it is a man's job" is direct discrimination. Discrimination against a married person of either sex is also covered by the Act. Thus to automatically terminate a contract of employment on marriage would be unlawful. *North East Midlands Co-operative Society v Allen (1977).*

**Indirect Discrimination**

Indirect discrimination arises

1. when a person applies a condition or requirement to another which is such that the proportion of persons from one sex who can comply with that condition or requirement is considerably smaller than the other sex;
2. it cannot be shown that the condition or requirement is justified irrespective of the sex of the person to whom it is applied; and
3. it is to that person's detriment because he/she cannot comply.

In *Hurley v Mustoe (1981)* the applicant was a married woman with four children and she applied for a job as a waitress. The manager gave her the job on trial but on the first night at work the owner of the restaurant asked her to leave. He said it was against his policy to employ women with young children as he thought they were unreliable. The EAT (Employment Appeals Tribunal) held that the applicant had been directly discriminated against on grounds of sex and indirectly discriminated against on grounds of marital status.

In *Price v Civil Service Commission (1978)* the EAT held that where employers advertised for executive officers, a requirement being that candidates had to be over the age of 17and a half but under the age of 28, there was indirect discrimination because far fewer women than men could comply with this requirement in practice as they were usually bringing up children at the later age.

### Victimisation

Section 4 of the *Sex Discrimination Act 1975* provides that it is unlawful to victimise a person because he/she has

1. brought proceedings under the Act or the *Equal Pay Act 1970*;
2. given evidence or information in connection with proceedings under either Act;
3. done anything in relation to either Act to the discriminator or any other person;
4. has made allegations of a contravention of either Act unless the allegation was false and not made in good faith.

Discrimination may arise in the following areas:

1. the arrangements a person makes for the purpose of determining who shall be employed;
2. the terms on which a person offers employment to another;
3. refusing or deliberately omitting to offer employment because of a person's sex;
4. in the way a person offers access to opportunities for promotion, transfer or training, or to any other benefits, facilities or services or by refusing or deliberately omitting to afford her/him access to them;
5. by dismissing a person or subjecting her/him to any other detriment.

## *Where Discrimination is Possible*

### Health Grounds

It is permissible to discriminate against women in order to protect them against definable health risks, which are specific to women, including risks associated with pregnancy and child birth. In *Page v Freight Hire (Tank Haulage Ltd) (1981)* the court held that it was the duty of an employer under the *Health and Safety at Work Act 1974* to make arrangements for ensuring so far as is reasonably practicable, safety and absence of risk to health in connection with the use, handling, storage and transport of articles and substances.

### Genuine Occupation Qualification

If the sex of the person is a genuine occupational qualification (GOQ) for the job, it follows that an employer does not unlawfully discriminate if he does not employ or if he denies an opportunity for promotion to a person of the other sex. The sex of a person is a genuine occupational qualification in the following circumstances:

1. the essential nature of the job calls for authentic male or female characteristics (excluding physical strength or stamina);

2. the job needs to be held by a person of one sex in order to preserve decency or privacy;
3. the employee is required to live in premises provided by the employer and those which are available are not equipped with separate sleeping accommodation and sanitary facilities;
4. the job has to be done by a person in a hospital, prison or other establishment for people who need special care, supervision or attention and all the in-mates are persons of one sex;
5. the holder of the job provides individuals with personal services promoting their welfare or education which can be most effectively provided by one sex;
6. the job needs to be held by a man because it is likely to involve performance of duties outside the UK in a country whose laws or customs are such that duties could not effectively be performed by someone of the opposite sex;
7. the job is one of two held by a married couple.

## *Enforcement of the Act*

Any person may complain to the industrial tribunal of discrimination on the part of another person. First of all conciliation will be attempted but if this fails and the tribunal finds the complaint well founded then it may:

1. make an order declaring the rights of the complainant;
2. order the respondent to pay compensation;
3. make a recommendation that the respondent takes action to avoid the adverse effect on the complainant of any act of discrimination.

A complaint of discrimination must be laid before the industrial tribunal within three months of the act complained of being done. If the act is a continuing one then the right to bring legal proceedings will continue until three months from the end of the period when the discrimination ceases.

The Equal Opportunities Commission may itself bring proceedings in respect of alleged violations of certain provisions of the Act and obtain an injunction from a County Court to restrain a person from repeating the unlawful act.

There have been attempts to bring discrimination on the grounds of sexual orientation under the provisions of the Act or at least as contrary to *Article 119* of the *Treaty of Rome*. The European Court of Justice ruled against the complainant, however, in *Grant v South-West Trains (1998)*, when she alleged discrimination by her employer. Specifically the train company would not give the same travel concessions to her same-sex partner that it would have given to an employee's partner in a heterosexual relationship.

## *Equal Pay*

This matter is the subject of the *Equal Pay Act 1970* as amended by the *Equal Pay (Amendment) Regulations 1983*. Both of course are subject to the overriding decisions in the European Court of Justice when it applies Article 29 of the Treaty of Rome and the Equal Pay Directive 75/117. Article 119 of the Treaty of Rome 1957 states: "each Member State shall during the first stage ensure and subsequently maintain the application of the principle that men and women should receive equal pay for equal work. For the purposes of this Article, 'pay' means the ordinary basic or minimum wage or salary and any other consideration, whether in cash or in kind, which the worker receives, directly or indirectly, in respect of his employment from his employer."

The effect of the European Law upon the law of this country can be illustrated by reference to *Barber v Guardian Royal Exchange Assurance Group 262/88*. The Guardian Royal Exchange operated a non-contributory pension scheme for men and women and, in the event of redundancy, men who reached the age of 55 and women who were 50 were entitled to an immediate pension. Mr Barker was dismissed by reason of redundancy when he was 52 years old and he complained that he had been unlawfully discriminated against on grounds of sex. A woman who had reached the age of 52 would have received an immediate pension.

His claim was dismissed by the Employment Appeal Tribunal on the ground that occupational pension schemes which take effect on retirement as well as benefits relating to death are excluded from the *Sex Discrimination Act 1975*.

The Court of Appeal referred the complaint to the European Court which held as follows.

1. Benefits paid by an employer to a worker in connection with the latter's redundancy fall within Article 119 of the Treaty of Rome.
2. A pension paid under a contracted-out private occupational pension scheme also falls within Article 119.
3. It is contrary to Article 119 for a man who was made compulsorily redundant to be entitled to claim only a deferred pension when a woman of the same age would receive an immediate pension.
4. Article 119 may be relied on by any person in the national courts.
5. Because of the impact the ruling was likely to have on existing pension schemes it would only apply to those schemes which had been made at the date of the European Court's decision.

## *The Equal Pay Act 1970 as Amended by Equal Pay (Amendment) Regulations 1983*

The Act uses what is known as "the equality clause". This provides that "if the terms of a contract under which a woman is employed at an establishment in Great Britain do not include (directly or by reference to a collective agreement or otherwise) an equality clause they shall be deemed to include one" (Section 1). The effect of this is that if the woman is employed

1. on "like work" with a man in the same employment or
2. the work she is doing is "work rated as equivalent" with that of a man following a job evaluation study or
3. the work the woman is doing is of 'equal value" in terms of the demands upon her to that or a man in the same employment . . .

then if any of these three situations exists and if any term in the woman's contract is less favourable than in a man's contract it must be modified so as to be not less favourable.

**Like Work**

Section 1(4) defines like work in the following terms: "a woman is to be regarded as employed as in like work with men if, but only if, her work and theirs is of the same or a broadly similar nature and the differences (if any) between the things she does and the things they do are not of practical importance in relation to terms and conditions of employment; and accordingly in comparing her work and theirs regard shall be had to the frequency or otherwise with which any such differences occur in practice as well as to the nature and extent of the differences."

In *Capper Pass Ltd v Lawton (1977)* Lawton was a cook in the kitchen which served the directors of the company. She worked a 40 hour week cooking lunches. She sought equal pay with an assistant chef who worked a 45 hour week preparing different meals on a large scale. It was held that she was entitled to an equal hourly rate of pay because any differences were not of practical importance.

In *Dugdale v Kraft Foods Ltd (1976)* it was held that the time which work is performed should be disregarded when considering whether there is "like work". In that case the men worked shifts which was not possible for the women but it was decided that the women should receive equal pay and the fact that the men worked shifts could be compensated by paying a shift premium.

**Work Rated as Being Equivalent**

Section 1(5) states: "a woman is to be regarded as employed on work rated as equivalent with that of any men if, but only if, her job and their job have been given an equal value, in terms of the demand made on a worker under various headings (for instance effort, skill, decision) . . . or would have been given an equal value but for the evaluation being made on a system setting different values for men and women on the same demand under any heading". *Bromley v H and J Quick Ltd (1988).*

**Equal Value**

The leading case under the *Equal Pay (Amendment) Regulations 1983* was *Hayward v Cammell Laird Shipbuilders Ltd (1988).* In that case the applicant was employed as a cook in the shipyard canteen. She claimed she was doing work of equal value to male shipyard workers who were being paid at a higher rate. Her claim for equal pay was based on "work of equal value" and was referred to an independent expert. He evaluated the jobs under the headings of

1. physical demands
2. environmental considerations
3. skill and knowledge
4. planning and decision making
5. responsibility.

He concluded that the work of the applicant was of equal value with the three selected male employees who were used as comparisons and were now earning higher rates.

Eventually the case reached the House of Lords where it was held that the basic salary of the appellant had to be compared with the basic salary in the men's contracts. The House of Lords held that the *Equal Pay Act 1970* required the courts to look at a particular term in a woman's contract which was less favourable and did not require a holding that terms as a whole should not be less favourable.

Finally it should be noted that even though a woman can show that she is employed on like work or work rated as equivalent or work of equal value then the employer may still be able to resist a claim for equal pay on the ground that the variation in pay is "genuinely due to a material factor which is not the difference of sex" (Section 1(3)).

Genuine material differences have been held to be such matters as length of service, academic qualifications, place of employment or indeed the fact that it was necessary to pay a particular rate to men in order to attract them or because their work was more profitable.

## *Remedies*

A complaint by an aggrieved party including a claim for arrears of remuneration or damages may be presented to an industrial tribunal. A claim cannot be referred to an industrial tribunal if the applicant has not been employed in the employment within the six months preceding the date of the reference. (Section (4)). Once a claim for equal pay has been dismissed no further action is possible on those facts.

## *Racial Discrimination*

The *Race Relations Act 1976* follows closely the *Sex Discrimination Act 1975*. Thus there are three ways in which it is unlawful to discriminate against any person on grounds of race: direct discrimination, indirect discrimination and victimisation.

### Direct Racial Discrimination

This arises where a person treats another person less favourably, on racial rounds, than he treats, or would treat, someone else. "Racial grounds" means any of the following grounds: colour, race, nationality, or ethnic or national origins.

### Indirect Racial Discrimination

This will arise where one person applies to another who is seeking some benefit from him, such as a job, a condition or requirement with which he must comply in order to qualify for the benefit or the job, and the condition satisfies all of the following criteria:

1. it is applied, or would be applied, by the discriminator equally to persons of any racial group;
2. it is such that the proportion of persons of the victim's racial group who can comply with it is considerably smaller than the proportion of persons not of that group who can comply with it;
3. it is to the detriment of the victim because he cannot comply with it;
4. it cannot be shown by the discriminator to be justifiable irrespective of the colour, race, nationality or ethnic or national origins of the person to whom it is applied.

### Victimisation

As in the *Sex Discrimination Act 1975* it will be discrimination to victimise any person who has

1. brought proceedings under the Act;
2. given evidence or information connected with proceedings brought by another person;
3. done anything under the Act in relation to the discriminator;
4. made allegations that a person has committed an unlawful act of racial discrimination.

## *Discrimination in Recruitment*

There are three ways in which it is unlawful for an employer to discriminate when recruiting employees.

1. In the arrangements he makes for deciding who shall be offered the job.
2. In relation to any terms offered (for example in relation to pay or holidays).
3. By refusing or deliberately omitting to offer a person employment.

Once a person is in employment it is unlawful to discriminate against him on racial grounds

1. in the terms of employment which are afforded to him;
2. in the way he is afforded access to opportunities for promotion, transfer or training or any other benefit;
3. by dismissing him or subjecting him to any other detriment.

## *Genuine Occupational Qualifications (Section 5)*

It is acceptable to discriminate where being a member of a particular racial group is a genuine occupational qualification for the job. Being of a particular racial group is a genuine occupational qualification (GOQ) for a job:

1. where a job involves participation in a dramatic performance or other entertainment in a capacity for which a person of the racial group in question is required for reasons of authenticity;
2. where the job involves participation as an artist or photographic model in the production of a work of art, picture or film for which a person of the racial group in question is required for reasons of authenticity;
3. where a job involves working in a place where food or drink is provided to and consumed by members of the public in a particular setting for which in that job, a person of the racial group in question is required for reasons of authenticity, such as a Chinese waiter in a Chinese restaurant;
4. where the job holder provides persons of the racial group in question with personal services promoting their welfare and those services can most effectively be provided by a person of the same racial group, for example a social worker belonging to the same racial group.

## *Enforcement*

An individual may submit a claim to an industrial tribunal within three months from the date of the alleged act of discrimination. If there is a continuing act of discrimination, the three months' time limit does not run until the discrimination ceases.

The *Commission for Racial Equality* has power to carry out a formal investigation into any practice carried on by an individual or organisation. If it concludes that a person is committing an unlawful act then it may serve a non-discriminatory notice on him requiring him not to commit any further acts of discrimination. Finally the *Commission for Racial Equality* is the only body which may bring proceedings against any person alleging that he is guilty of:

1. discriminatory practices
2. discriminatory advertisements
3. instructions to discriminate
4. pressure to discriminate.

## *Disability Discrimination*

Since the *Disability Discrimination Act 1995* came into force, it has been unlawful for an employer to treat a disabled person less favourably, without good reason, because of their disability. Some of the Act's provisions, relating to running a service, providing goods or services and letting or selling a property are being phased in over a number of years.

The Act also brought into being the National Disability Council. Its stated purpose is to advise the government on discrimination against disabled people. This function has been taken over by the Disability Rights Commission with effect from April 2000.

In relation to employment issues, the Act only applies to businesses that employ 20 or more people, although those with fewer employees are encouraged to comply with the provisions. Operational employees in the emergency services, on board ships etc. and in the armed forces are not within the scope of the Act either.

Section 6 of the Act compels employers to take reasonable steps to accommodate the needs of disabled people. Examples would include making adjustments to premises such as ramps for those in wheelchairs or altering hours of work or allowing time off to allow for rehabilitation. The emphasis is on "reasonable" so major refurbishment at considerable cost to provide moderate benefit to a disabled employee would not be expected. An employer may treat a disabled person less favourably with good reason, for example, in recruitment, if the disability made it impossible for the employee to complete major parts of the job description.

## *Discrimination Caselaw Developments*

Recent caselaw continues to clarify the coverage of the Act. For example, in *MHC Consulting Services Limited v Tansell (2000)*, the Court of Appeal had to consider whether the Act applied to those who supplied their services through a series of contracts. There was no contract between the applicant and the ultimate employer, Abbey Life, as his consultancy services were supplied through a company, Intelligents

Ltd, and then through an agency. The applicant was dismissed when he began to suffer from diabetes. The Court decided there was an unbroken chain of contracts between the principal and worker and S12(1) of the Act prohibited discrimination by a principal of a disabled worker. A claim for disability discrimination could be made therefore. This is likely to mean that claims under the sex and race discrimination legislation could be made in the same circumstances.

**Questions**

When is victimisation held to arise under the *Sex Discrimination Act 1975*?

When is discrimination possible under the *Sex Discrimination Act 1975*?

When would changes to the workplace to accommodate disabled people not be required under the *Disability Discrimination Act 1995*?

FIFTEEN

# TRADE UNION LAW

*Study Topics*

**Definition of a trade union**
**Collective bargaining**
**Meaning of a trade dispute**

Trade Union law has been consolidated by the *Trade Union and Labour Relations (Consolidation) Act 1992* as amended by the *Trade Union Reform and Employment Rights Act 1993*. The 1992 Act is the main Act and it defines a trade union as an organisation (whether permanent or temporary) which either

1. consists wholly or mainly of workers of one or more descriptions and whose principal purposes include the regulation of relations between workers and employers or employers' associations;
2. consists wholly or mainly of
   i. constituent or affiliated organisations which have those purposes;
   ii. representatives of such constituent or affiliated organisations, and in either case whose principal purposes include the regulation of relations between workers and employers or workers' and employers' associations or include the regulation of relations between the constituent or affiliated organisations.

Section 10 makes it clear that a trade union shall not be a body corporate but nevertheless it will be capable of making contracts, suing and being sued in its own name and may be prosecuted for any offences committed in its name. However any property must be held by its trustees.

## Trade Union Recognition

Recent changes to the law on trade unions can be found in the *Employment Relations Act 1999*. Chiefly this legislation amends the *Trade Union and Labour Relations (Consolidation) Act 1992* and other employment legislation to introduce a new system of trade union recognition. The procedures for recognition are detailed and it is only necessary here to deal with them in outline. In certain circumstances, where there are more than 21 workers employed, it may be possible for a union to apply to the Central Arbitration Committee (discussed further below) to intervene if the employer refuses to recognise it. *Sections 25 and 26* affect the functioning of the Central Arbitration Committee itself, which is a tri-partite panel, to enable it to deal adequately with these applications.

The 1999 Act also deals with related matters such as dismissal connected with strikes and *S10-13* cover the right to be accompanied in disciplinary or grievance proceedings by a union official, someone certified by a union as competent in this role or a co-worker.

## Listing and Certification of Trade Unions (Sections 2 and 6)

The Certification Officer who was created by the *Employment Protection Act* has taken over a list of trade union organisations formerly held by the Registrar of Friendly Societies. Any trade union which is on the list may apply to the Certification Officer for a certificate that it is an independent trade union. This will be so if

1. it is not under the domination or control of an employer or a group of employers or of one or more employers' associations and
2. it is not liable to interference by an employer or any such group or association (arising out of the provision of financial or material support or by any other means whatsoever) tending towards such control (Section 5).

## Advantages of Certification

The 1992 Act gives the following advantages of having a certificate of independence.

1. Representatives of recognised independent trade unions are entitled to receive information for collective bargaining purposes.
2. The rights of employees not to have discriminatory action taken against them (short of dismissal) apply only to members of independent trade unions.
3. Employees who are officials of recognised independent trade unions are entitled to have time off work to carry out their duties as such.
4. Employees who are members of recognised independent trade unions are entitled to have time off work for trade union activities.
5. An employer must consult with representatives of recognised independent trade unions in the event of redundancies arising.

6. An application for interim relief if a dismissal is alleged to be for trade union membership may be made by a member of an independent trade union.
7. It is unfair to dismiss a person because he wishes to join an independent trade union.
8. An independent trade union may obtain public funds for the purpose of holding various ballots.
9. A recognised independent trade union is entitled to be given information and be consulted under the *Transfer of Undertakings (Protection of Employment) Regulations 1981.*
10. A recognised independent trade union is entitled to receive information from an employer concerning occupational pension schemes.
11. An independent trade union may enter into an agreement to exclude statutory rights of unfair dismissal and substitute a dismissal procedure.
12. An independent trade union is entitled to appoint safety representatives.

## *Register of Members*

A trade union shall maintain a register of the names and addresses of its members. Details in this register shall be kept confidential and disclosure will be permitted only when

1. the member consents;
2. when required for the purposes of the discharge of functions by the Certification Officer or of a scrutineer under a ballot; or
3. where required for the purpose of investigating crime or criminal proceedings.

## *Rules of a Trade Union*

At one time, under the common law, any trade union would have been illegal because its rules were in "restraint of trade". This of course was abolished by the *Trade Union Act 1871* and Section 11 of the 1992 Act now provides that the purposes of a trade union or an employers' association shall not, by reason of being in restraint of trade, make any member liable for criminal conspiracy, or make any agreement or trust void or voidable, nor shall the rules be unlawful or unenforceable by virtue of their being in restraint of trade.

The rules constitute a contract between the union and its members and must be strictly observed. If a trade union wishes to take disciplinary action or wishes to expel a member then such powers must be contained in the rules or they cannot be exercised. Membership of a trade union confers certain rights and privileges on its members; they are entitled to damages if these are not forthcoming.

## *Executive Committee*

Section 46 of the 1992 Act provides that every member of the principal executive committee of a trade union shall be elected by a ballot at least every five years. In such a ballot, every member of the union shall be entitled to vote except

1. members who are as a class excluded by the rules from voting
2. members not in employment
3. members in arrears
4. members who are students, trainees, apprentices or new members.

Voting at an election must be on voting papers sent to the voters by post containing a list of candidates. Voting must be in secret and by means of a postal ballot. Before an election is held the trade union must appoint a qualified independent person as a scrutineer.

The Secretary of State is empowered to authorise the Certification Officer to make a payment towards expenditure incurred by the union in respect of ballots. Such payments are only obtainable if the ballots are

1. for obtaining a decision or ascertaining the views of members as to the calling or ending of a strike;
2. carrying out an election for the post of principal executive committee member, president, chairman, secretary or treasurer;
3. electing a worker who is a member of a trade union to be a representative of other members also employed by his employer;
4. amending the rules of the union;
5. voting on a decision to amalgamate with another union;
6. obtaining a decision of members as to the acceptance or rejection of a proposal by an employer relating to the contractual terms and conditions;
7. obtaining a decision on the creation or continuation of the political fund.

Financial assistance towards expenditure on ballots and elections will cease to have effect as from April 1996.

## *Political Funds*

Section 71-74 of the 1992 Act state the necessary requirements before a trade union can have a political fund to pursue political objects. A resolution to establish a political fund must be passed at least every ten years by a ballot of all the union's members. All members of the union are entitled to vote on a ballot concerning the establishment of a political fund. The voting papers must be sent to the members at their homes and they must be given an opportunity to vote by post.

Any member of the union who wishes to contract out of a political fund must be free to do so. If he does contract out he shall not in consequence be excluded from any benefit or disqualified from holding any office or membership.

## *Objects of Political Fund*

The specified political purposes of the fund are:

1. contribution to the funds of, or the payment of any expense incurred by, a political party;
2. the provision of any services or property for the use by or on behalf of a political party;
3. the registration of electors, the candidature of any person, the selection of any candidate, or the holding of a ballot by the union in connection with any election to a political office;
4. the maintenance of any holder of a political office;
5. the holding of any conference or meetings by or on behalf of a political party, or any other meetings the main purpose of which is the transaction of business in connection with a political party;
6. the production, publication or distribution of any literature, document, film, sound recording or advertisement the main purpose of which is to persuade people to vote for a political party or candidate or not to vote for it or him.

Any allegation that a trade union has broken a rule as to the use to which the political fund may be put may be the subject of an investigation by the Certification Officer.

## *Industrial Relations*

It is inevitable that the contract of employment will be affected to a large extent by the rights and duties of trade unions. Indeed it is often the case that a contract of employment will be negotiated by a trade union on behalf of its members.

## *Collective Bargaining*

For the purpose of all stages of collective bargaining it is the duty of the employer, on request, to disclose to a representative of a recognised independent trade union all such information relating to his undertaking as is in his possession, and is information without which the representatives would be to a material extent impeded in carrying on such bargaining, and which it would be in accordance with good industrial relations practice that he should disclose. An employer need not disclose the following information:

1. information the disclosure of which would be contrary to the national interest;

2. any information which he could not disclose without breaking the law;
3. information which he received in confidence;
4. information relating to an individual, unless he has consented to the disclosure;
5. information the disclosure of which would cause substantial injury to the employer's business for reasons other than its effect on collective bargaining;
6. information obtained by the employer for the purpose of bringing or defending any legal proceedings.

The employer is not bound to produce or allow the inspection of any document or to compile information where this would involve an amount of work or expenditure out of all reasonable proportion to its value in the conduct of collective bargaining.

However if an independent trade union wishes to make a complaint that an employer has failed to disclose information then it may report the matter to the Central Arbitration Committee. The matter may then be referred to ACAS which will try to effect a settlement. If the Central Arbitration Committee examines the complaint and finds that it is well founded it will issue a declaration stating

1. the information in respect of which the complaint is well founded;
2. the date on which the employer refused or failed to disclose the information;
3. a period (being more than one week from the date of the declaration) within which the employer ought to disclose the information. If, at the end of that period, the employer still fails to disclose, a further complaint may be made by the trade union.

## *Consultations*

If redundancy arises then the employer must consult with representatives of the union. If the employer proposes to dismiss 100 or more employees within a period of 90 days then he must consult with the union representatives at least 90 days before the first dismissals take effect. If the number to be dismissed is ten or more employees then the employer must consult within 30 days before the first of the dismissals takes effect. In the same way if an undertaking is being transferred then naturally employees of the transferor and the transferee may be affected. *The Transfer of Undertakings (Protection of Employment) Regulations 1981* places a duty upon employers to inform representatives of trade unions about the transfers. The unions must be informed of the legal, economic and social implications of the transfer and the measures (if any) which the employers envisage will be taken in relation to the affected employees.

## *Legal Liabilities and Proceedings*

In pursuing their normal role of combining together to do an unlawful act which would be the procuring of a breach of contract, in other words ordering the employees to withdraw their labour, then unions could fall foul of the law. Indeed this was the case until 1906 when the unions acquired a cloak of statutory protection. Such protection as has been given to trade unions is limited to acts done in furtherance or contemplation of a trade dispute.

## *Trade Dispute*

Section 244 of the *Trade Union and Labour Relations (Consolidation) Act 1992* states that a trade dispute means a dispute between workers and their employers which relates wholly or mainly to one or more of the following:

1. terms and conditions of employment, or the physical conditions in which any workers are required to work;
2. the engagement or non-engagement or termination or suspension of employment or the duties of employment, of one or more workers;
3. the allocation of work or the duties of employment between workers or groups of workers;
4. matters of discipline;
5. membership or non-membership of a trade union on the part of a worker;
6. facilities for officials of trade unions;
7. machinery for negotiations or consultation, and other matters relating to the forgoing including recognition by employers or employers' associations of the right of a trade union to represent workers in any such negotiations or consultations or in the carrying out of such procedures.

The *Employment Act 1982* provides that a dispute must relate "wholly or mainly" to the above matters.

There will be a trade dispute even though it relates to matters occurring outside the United Kingdom provided the persons who are taking action are likely to be affected in respect of one or more of the matters mentioned above. However a strike called for political reasons is not a trade dispute. To be within the statutory definition the Act must "be in contemplation or furtherance of" a trade dispute. In *Bents Brewery v Hogan (1945)* a trade union official obtained from the managers of the brewery information about the firm's salaries, sales, etc. The court held that the union official had induced a breach of the contract between the managers and the company by getting them to disclose confidential information. However it was held that his action was not in contemplation of a trade dispute even though it was preparatory to the dispute.

In order to establish whether or not an act was done "in furtherance of" the trade dispute the test is a subjective one. It depends whether or not the person committing the act in question honestly believed that it assisted in achieving the objectives of the dispute.

## *Immunity of Unions from Legal Action*

Section 219 of the *Trade Union and Labour Relations (Consolidation) Act 1992* provides that an act done by a person in contemplation or furtherance of a trade dispute shall not be actionable in tort on the ground only

1. that it induces another person to break a contract or interferes or induces any other person to interfere with its performance or
2. that it consists of his threatening that a contract (whether one to which he is a party or not) will be broken or its performance interfered with.

Section 219(2) provides that an agreement or combination of two or more persons to do or procure the doing of an act in contemplation or furtherance of a dispute shall not be actionable in tort if the act is one which, if done without such agreement or combination, would not be so actionable. Sometimes an act if done by a number of people in concern and in agreement might amount to a conspiracy and as such be unlawful. However an official strike by a trade union will only have civil immunity provided a secret ballot was taken before the industrial action.

## *Secondary Action*

The immunities contained in Section 219 will only be available when the trade union takes industrial action against an employer with whom there is a trade dispute. There has been a tendency in recent years for what is known as secondary action. This is defined as when a person

1. induces another to break a contract of employment;
2. interferes or induces another to interfere with its performance;
3. threatens that a contract of employment under which he or another is employed will be broken, or its performance interfered with; or
4. threatens that he will induce another to break a contract of employment or to interfere with its performance.

The point here is that the employer under the contract of employment is not the employer who is a party to the dispute. In these cases then Section 219 immunity will not be available for such secondary action which is not lawful picketing.

A trade union may still be made liable for inducing breaches of contract if the balloting provisions of the Act have been ignored. In that case the trade union may be sued in tort and there are limits to the amount of damages which may be awarded. For the union to be made liable the act in question must have been authorised or indorsed by the union and this will be the case if it was done by any person empowered by the rules to authorise or indorse the act or by the principal executive committee, president or general secretary or by any other committee of the union.

## Collective Agreements

A collective agreement is defined as an agreement or arrangement made by or on behalf of a trade union on the one part, and one or more employers or employers' associations on the other part, relating to one or more of the matters contained in the definition of a trade dispute.

A collective agreement will, most importantly, lay down patterns of terms and conditions of employment which will cover the members of the union. Such an agreement shall be enforceable provided it is in writing. Also the parties must expressly state that the collective agreement is to be legally enforceable.

## Peaceful Picketing

Section 220 of the *Trade Union and Labour Relations (Consolidation) Act 1992* provides that it shall be lawful for a person in contemplation or furtherance of a trade dispute to attend:

1. at or near his own place of work; or
2. if he is an official of a trade union, at or near the place of work of a member of that union whom he is accompanying and whom he represents: for the purpose only of peacefully obtaining or communicating information, or peacefully persuading any person to work or to abstain from working. If a person works at more than one place, or at a place where it is impracticable to picket because of its location, his place of work shall be any premises from which he works, or from which his work is administered. A person whose employment has been terminated because of a trade dispute is allowed to picket at his former place of work.

Only in the circumstances set out in Section 220 shall picketing be lawful.

In *Piddington v Bates (1961)* a police officer informed pickets that two were sufficient at a particular place. The defendant disagreed and attempted to push past the constable whereupon he was arrested and charged with obstruction. The court held the defendant was guilty and the court would not say that the constable had no reasonable grounds for anticipating the breach of the peace.

In *Tynan v Balmer (1967)* 40 pickets were walking on the highway with a view to preventing supplies being delivered to a factory. They were requested by the police to disperse but refused and Tynan was arrested and found guilty of obstructing the highway. It was held that pickets do not have power to stop vehicles, for traffic control is a matter for the police. *Broome v DPP (1974).*

The Code of Practice established by the Secretary of State provides that pickets and their organisers should ensure that in general the number of pickets does not exceed six at any entrance to, or exit from, a work place; frequently a smaller number will be appropriate. The point about this is that larger numbers on the picket line are more likely to give rise to fear and resentment and may worsen relations between management and employees and between the pickets and their fellow employees. Thus a mass demonstration is clearly unlawful because it is unlikely that it will be for the purpose of peacefully persuading. Likewise what are known as "flying pickets" are also unlawful because they will not normally be picketing at their own place of work.

## *Ballots*

The *Employment Code of Practice (Industrial Action Ballots and Notice to Employers) Order 2000* is effective from 18 September 2000. This changes the rules on balloting members as to whether they wish to strike over a particular issue. For example, the courts may be able to ignore small accidental failures in the procedures when ballots are organised provided they are not likely to affect the result. The wording on ballot papers is also to be changed to reflect more strongly the protection against unfair dismissal for striking workers. There are numerous other rules which, like most codes, are not legally enforceable but can be used as strong evidence in court proceedings arising out of industrial action.

## *Sit-ins*

A sit-in will occur when the workers remain on the employers' premises and if they refuse to leave after being given reasonable notice to do so they will commit the tort of trespass (now a crime in certain circumstances) and that of interfering with business by unlawful means.

## *The Public Order Act 1986*

This Act created five new statutory offences: riot, violent disorder, affray, causing fear or provocation of violence and causing harassment, alarm or distress. New rules were laid down for marches, processions, demonstrations and public assemblies.

### Questions

What are the advantages of certification?

In collective bargaining when may an employer refuse to disclose information?

What is a trade dispute?

When will picketing be deemed to be lawful?

SIXTEEN

# CONSUMER PROTECTION

# PRODUCT LIABILITY

*Study Topics*

**The law relating to product liability of manufacturers**
**The details of the Consumer Protection Act 1987**

If a person is injured by a defective product then he will wish to sue for damages. The question is whom may he sue and what is his right of action. The situation is well illustrated in the famous case of *Donoghue v Stevenson (1932)*.

In *Donoghue v Stevenson*, Mrs Donoghue's friend purchased for her a bottle of ginger beer which contained the decomposed remains of a snail. The friend gave the ginger beer to Mrs Donoghue who, having drunk some of the poisonous liquid and seen the remains of the snail slither out on to her ice cream, suffered injury. The question was, whom could she sue? As Mrs Donoghue had not herself purchased the ginger beer she was not in contractual relationship with the seller of the ginger beer therefore there was no question of suing that person under the *Sale of Goods Act*. The only possible person who might be liable was the manufacturer of the ginger beer and the importance of *Donoghue v Stevenson* is that it established that a manufacturer, in certain circumstances, may be liable for a defective product if he should have had reasonable foresight of harm occurring to persons whom he should have foreseen were likely to be harmed by his negligence. In the end Mrs Donoghue succeeded in her action against the manufacturer but of course the action was framed in tort because there was no contract between Mrs Donoghue and the manufacturer.

Thus the situation is that the purchaser of defective goods can sue the seller of these goods, and in that case the seller will be strictly liable to the purchaser. This means that the purchaser who has been injured is not required to show any fault on the part of the seller. The seller will be automatically liable merely because he or she has sold defective goods. On the other hand if, as in the case of Mrs Donoghue, the injured party wishes to sue someone other than the seller, then he or she has to prove that the manufacturer is at fault in not taking reasonable care in relation to the goods. This is an action in the tort of negligence.

## *The Tort of Negligence*

Negligence as a tort consists of three basic elements:

1. duty of care owed by the defendant to the plaintiff, or claimant as he would now be called;
2. a breach of that duty by the defendant; and
3. consequent, foreseeable loss to the plaintiff.

To succeed in an action for negligence, the plaintiff must establish the presence of these three elements. He or she must also show that the defendant's breach of duty was the cause (or one of the causes) of his or her loss.

*Donoghue v Stevenson* was in a sense the first case on the modern law of tort in relation to a manufacturer's liability for negligence. Lord Atkin expressed the general principle in that context in the following way.

> A manufacturer of products which he sells in such a form as to show that he intends them to reach the ultimate consumer in the form in which they left him with no reasonable possibility of intermediate examination, and with the knowledge that the absence of reasonable care in the preparation or putting up of the product will result in an injury to the consumer's life or property, owes a duty to the consumer to take reasonable care.

Note that, in the light of subsequent case law, the word "probability" should be substituted for the word "possibility" in the quotation: the effect is to widen the manufacturer's liability.

If products are dangerous in themselves (for example firearms, explosives, poisons), the defendant owes a duty of care to any person who might reasonably be expected to be injured by them. If the goods are not dangerous in themselves but in a dangerous condition (for example a defective motor car), the defendant will be liable if he or she knows that the particular goods are dangerous but does not give a warning. If the goods are not dangerous in themselves but are, in fact, dangerous, as in the *Donoghue* case, the defendant may be liable under the normal head of negligence even if he or she does not know that the goods are dangerous.

The principle in the *Donoghue* case has been extended to cases wherever a person is in control of circumstances which could cause harm if due care is not exercised. Hence an underwear manufacturer has been held liable when he did not exercise care to see that a skin irritant was left out of the fabric during the manufacturing process: see *Grant v Australian Knitting Mills Ltd (1936)*.

The products which may be involved in this context are not of course confined to food and drink; they extend now to all kinds of goods, from underwear to motor cars, from hair-dye to buildings. The manufacturer's liability rule is merely an extension of the "neighbour principle" in the *Donoghue* case. In 1963, the principle was extended to negligent mis-statements causing economic (not only physical) loss: see *Hedley Byrne and Co Ltd v Heller and Partners Ltd (1964)*.

Liability covers the products in question and also their containers and (misleading) labels. Over the years, the categories of possible defendants have also been extended to include not only manufacturers but also erectors, assemblers, repairers, distributors and suppliers. Claimants may be consumers in the strict sense or users of the products concerned, as in the *Grant* case.

If clear instructions provided by a manufacturer as to the use of a product are ignored by the consumer, the manufacturer will not be liable: see *Holmes v Ashford (1950)*, where a hairdresser ignored the manufacturer's warnings on a bottle of hair-dye, as a result of which the customer suffered dermatitis; the customer could not sue the manufacturer for negligence, but could so sue the hairdresser.

This then was the situation before 1 March 1988. On that date the *Consumer Protection Act 1987* came into force. This Act was passed by the United Kingdom Parliament in response to a European Community Product Liability Directive which called upon member states to pass legislation making the producer of defective products liable without any proof of fault.

The second recital of the directive states: "liability without fault on the part of the producer is the sole means of adequately solving the problem, peculiar to our age of increasing technicality, of a fair apportionment of the risks inherent in modern technological production".

Part I of the *Consumer Protection Act* now stands alongside the *Sale of Goods Act* and an action in negligence. A person injured by a defective product may wish to rely on the *Sale of Goods Act* and this he can do if he was the purchaser. If he was not the purchaser, then he may have to prove negligence, but it may be that he will be able to make use of the *Consumer Protection Act*, in which case negligence need not be proved.

## *Consumer Protection Act 1987 - Part I*

### Who May Sue?

Under the *Consumer Protection Act* any person may sue who has been injured by a defect in the product. The claimant will only succeed if he can prove that injury was caused by a defect in the product. Section 3 of the Act states that a product will be regarded as defective when "the safety of the product is not such as persons generally are entitled to expect". The Section goes on to give some guidance as to determining whether or not a product is defective:

"in determining what persons generally are entitled to expect in relation to a product all the circumstances shall be taken into account, including

a. the manner in which, and purposes for which, the product has been marketed, its get-up, the use of any mark in relation to the product and any instructions for, or warnings with respect to, doing or refraining from doing anything with or in relation to the product;
b. what might reasonably be expected to be done with or in relation to the product; and
c. the time when the product was supplied by its producer to another person; and nothing in this Section shall require a defect to be inferred from the fact alone that the safety of a product which is supplied after that time is greater than the safety of the products in question".

The Act has made it imperative for producers to be careful as regards the packaging of their products, and they must not suggest by the packaging that the product can be used in any manner which is unsafe.

### Who is Liable?

Liability will fall upon the following.

1 The producer. Section 1(2) defines the producer as:
   i. the person who manufactured the product;
   ii. in the case of a substance that has not been manufactured but has been won or abstracted, the person who won or abstracted it, which covers mining and quarrying;
   iii. in any case a person who has applied an industrial or any other process affecting the essential characteristics of the product.
2. Any person who puts his own name on the product or uses a trademark or other distinguishing mark in relation to the product. In other words has held himself out as being the producer of the product. This is increasingly occurring in supermarkets that put their own brand on products made by other persons.

3. Any person who imported the goods into a member state of the European Union from a place outside the Union for the purpose of supplying it in the course of a business.
4. Any person to whom Section (3) applies, that is, any supplier who cannot identify the person who produced the product or who supplied it to him. This provision is inserted because on occasions it may be difficult for the injured party to identify the producer or the person who imported the product into the European Union. In this case then the supplier can be made liable provided he supplied the product to someone else, and provided:
   i. he is requested by a person suffering damage to identify any producer, own brander or importer into the European Union;
   ii. the request is made within a reasonable time after the damage occurs;
   iii. at the time of the request it is not reasonably practicable for the injured
   iv. party to identify all of the potential defendants;
   he fails, within a reasonable time, to comply with the request or to identify the person who supplied the product to him.

It can be seen that a number of persons may be made liable for the damage to the plaintiff, and in that case the person who is sued may be entitled to a contribution from any other person who may be liable, under the *Civil Liability (Contribution) Act 1978.*

As has been stated, the basis of liability under the *Consumer Protection Act* is strict. This means that where the injured person can show that there is a causal relationship between the defect and the damage then one or other of the above defendants will be strictly liable.

**Types of Loss**

Section 5 provides that damages are recoverable for death or personal injury. However, there is no liability for loss of or damage to:

1. the product itself;
2. any property in respect of which the amount of the claim would be below £275;
3. any commercial property, that is, property of a type which is not ordinarily intended for private use, occupation or consumption and which is not actually intended by the plaintiff for his or her own private use, occupation or consumption.

If the plaintiff wishes to claim for these excluded losses then he may pursue his claim in contract or negligence.

The *Consumer Protection Act* prohibits absolutely any limitation or exclusion of liability arising under the Act. It will be remembered that exclusion or limitation of liability may be possible in contract or in negligence and subject to the *Unfair Contract Terms Act 1977.*

### Defences Available to the Defendant

Apart from the obvious defences of showing that there was no causal relationship between the defect and the damage or that the product was not in fact defective, the following specific defences are stated in Section 4 of the *Consumer Protection Act*.

1. The defect was attributable to the defendant's compliance with a legal requirement.
2. The defendant did not supply the goods to anyone. In this connection the term "supply" has been widely defined in Section 46, and in a hire purchase case involving a dealer, a hire purchaser and a finance company, the Section provides that the dealer and not the finance company is to be treated as supplying the product to the hire purchaser. Also, where a finished product incorporates component products or raw materials, the supplier of the finished product will not be treated as the supplier of the component products or raw materials merely because he has supplied the finished product.
3. The defendant did not supply the goods in the course of his business and did not own-brand, import into the EU or produce the goods with a view to profit. The effect of this is that homemade goods which cause injury will probably not make the supplier liable.
4. The defect did not exist in the product at the relevant time. The relevant time means the time when the producer supplied it to another person.
5. The state of scientific and technical knowledge at the relevant time was not such that a producer of products of the same description as the product in question might be expected to have discovered the defect if it had existed in his products while they were under his control. It has been argued that this "development risks" defence reduces the effectiveness of the Act. It means that, in effect, any manufacturer will now escape liability provided he can show that he took all reasonable precautions in the light of scientific knowledge at that time. Thus if there were a repetition of the thalidomide tragedy then the victims of that drug would be in no better position now to pursue their claim that they were at the time.
6. The defendant is the producer of a component part of a product, and can show that the defect in the finished product is wholly attributable to its design or to compliance with instructions given by the producer of the finished product.

### Time Limit for Claims

The basic limitation period as far as the injured party is concerned is three years from:

1. the date on which the right to take action arises;or
2. the date on which the claimant is aware:
   i. that he has suffered significant damage;
   ii. that the damage is attributable to a defect in the product;
   ii. the identity of the defendant.

The limitation period is the same whether there is personal injury or property damage. As for the supplier, there is a ten-year cut-off period for each one. This is known as a "period of repose" in the United States, and relates to the particular product and not to the product line.

## *Consumer Protection Act - Part II*

Part II of the Act makes it a criminal offence to supply unsafe goods. The Act provides that: "a person shall be guilty of an offence if he supplied consumer goods which are not reasonably safe having regard to all the circumstances".

As at present, the safety of a range of consumer goods will continue to be controlled by regulations setting out in detail how specific types of goods must be constructed, and what instructions and warnings must accompany them. It is not practical or desirable to make such regulations for every type of consumer product; the general safety requirement therefore closes a gap in the existing safety legislation. As with safety regulations, an offence may have been committed even when nobody has been injured. Contravention of the general safety requirements can result in a fine not exceeding £2,000, up to six months' imprisonment, or both.

Unlike the product liability provisions, the general safety requirements apply to anyone who supplies the goods, although there is an important defence for retailers: that they neither knew nor had reasonable grounds for believing that the goods failed to comply with the general requirements. This part of the Act is restricted to consumer goods. Some consumer goods are, however, not covered by the general requirement, for example growing crops, water, food, aircraft, motor vehicles, controlled drugs, medicinal products and tobacco.

"Safe" is defined in the Act as reducing to a minimum the risk of death or personal injury. The general safety requirements refer to goods being reasonably safe, having regard to all the circumstances. These circumstances include:

1. the manner in which the goods are marketed and any instructions or warnings given with the goods;
2. any published safety standards for those goods; and

3. the means, if any, and the cost of making the goods safer.

A supplier whose goods do not or may not meet the general safety requirements will still not be committing an offence if he can prove one of the following defences:

1. the goods conform in a relevant respect with a European Community obligation;
2. the goods conform to any applicable safety regulations or safety standards approved by the Secretary of State for Trade and Industry for the purpose of the general safety requirement;
3. the goods were for export;
4. the goods were not supplied as new and were not supplied by way of hire (the general safety requirement does not apply to the sale of secondhand goods);
5. if the goods were supplied in the course of retail business, the retailer had no grounds for suspecting that the goods failed to comply with the general safety requirement.

The Act consolidates and improves the regulations, making powers available under previous consumer safety law. It also enables the Secretary of State to make regulations without delay where he considers it necessary on grounds of public protection. The Act retains powers for the Secretary of State to make prohibition notices preventing named suppliers from supplying particular unsafe goods. It also provides power for the Secretary of State to serve notices to warn, requiring named suppliers to publish warnings, at their own expense, about unsafe goods they have supplied.

As with previous safety legislation, enforcement of the safety provisions of the Act is primarily the responsibility of the trading standards officers of local authorities. The Act increases their powers, which include the authority to make test purchases, and limited powers to enter and search premises and obtain information.

Trading standards officers can also issue suspension notices prohibiting suppliers from selling goods which they believe contravene safety legislation. They can apply to a magistrates' court for an order that such goods be forfeited and destroyed.

**Questions**

Who may be liable in an action under the *Consumer Protection Act 1987*?

What defences are available?

Who may bring an action under the Act?

SEVENTEEN

# CONSUMER CREDIT ACT 1974

*Study Topics*

**The scope of the Consumer Credit Act 1974 with regard to regulated agreement**
**The difference between a hire purchase contract, a conditional sale agreement and a credit sale agreement**
**The protection of the debtor as to right of cancellation and the restrictions on the creditor's right to repossess**

Credit, in the sense of payment being deferred for goods or services, has become a feature of our modern life. For many years attempts have been made to control the credit industry and to protect the consumer. This has been done by regulating the supply of credit and by the advertisement of credit by the *Pawnbrokers Act 1872-1960*, the *Moneylenders Acts 1900-1927*, the *Hire Purchase Act 1965* and the *Advertisements (Hire Purchase) Act 1967.*

These Acts gradually became less and less effective and it was evident that some of the legislation was being bypassed. For example, the *Moneylenders Acts* applied only to moneylenders, and to loans made by moneylenders. They did not apply to other forms of credit and certain types of business, such as banking, in the course of which loans of money were made, were exempted from the operation of the Acts.

The *Consumer Credit Act 1974* now regulates many different forms of credit. It is comprehensive in its scope and it controls the business of giving credit by the issue of licenses. It restricts advertising and canvassing and gives wide supervisory powers to the Director General of Fair Trading. It also controls agreements made by individuals by stating the formalities required and it deals with the matters of termination, cancellation and default of agreements.

## *Transactions Affected by the Act*

The two transactions regulated by the Act are consumer credit agreements and consumer hire agreement. The titles given to these agreements bring up a number of concepts which must now be examined in some detail.

Sections 8-20 deal with the various types of credit and hire agreements and linked transactions. Credit is defined as a cash loan and any form of financial accommodation. All types of loan are covered and examples are given in Schedule 2 Part II of the Act:

1. moneylenders' loans
2. bank loans
3. overdrafts
4. pawnbrokers' loans
5. advances on mortgage
6. the sale of goods on instalment credit terms (e.g. credit sales, conditional sales, budget accounts, option accounts, subscription accounts)
7. the supply of services on credit, check and voucher trading
8. credit cards
9. cheque cards.

In all of these cases in return for goods or services payment is deferred whether the payment is to be made in one amount or by instalments.

## *A Consumer Credit Agreement*

A consumer credit agreement is defined as a personal credit agreement by which the creditor provides the debtor with credit not exceeding £15,000. A personal credit agreement is an agreement between an individual called "the debtor" and any other person called "the creditor" by which the creditor provides the debtor with credit. The term "individual" includes a partnership or other unincorporated body of persons not consisting entirely of bodies corporate. Therefore an agreement to provide credit for a company will not be a personal credit agreement and so will not be affected by the Act. An agreement with a partnership can be a personal credit agreement even though the partnership is in business and the loan is for business purposes. Whether or not the Act applies to the transactions will be determined by the status of the debtor and not by the purpose for which the loan has been made and by the amount advanced.

## *A Regulated Consumer Credit Agreement*

This is a consumer credit agreement which is not an exempt agreement.

## *Exempt Agreements*

These are specified in section 16 and include the following.

1. Consumer credit agreements secured by a mortgage over land where the creditor is a local authority or a building society.
2. Agreements secured by mortgage over land where the creditor is one of a number of Insurance Companies, Friendly Societies and Land Improvement Companies specified by the Secretary of State or is a Trade Union of employers or workers.
3. Fixed sum debtor-creditor-supplier agreements (other than hire purchase or conditional sale agreements) when the number of payments to be made by the debtor does not exceed four.
4. A running-account credit agreement where the debtor is required to repay the debt in one single payment. Examples of this type of agreement would be a credit card issued by American Express or Diners Club.
5. Low cost debtor-creditor agreements when the rate of interest does not exceed 13% or 1% above the base rate determined by the Bank of England.
6. Any agreement made in connection with trade in goods or services between the United Kingdom and an overseas country.

The above agreements are exempt agreements and so are not affected by the provisions of the Act. However the fact that an agreement is exempt does not exclude the power of the court to investigate a bargain which it considers to be extortionate in regard to the rates of interest required and other factors (Sections 137-140). Thus the court has power to re-open any agreement regulated or not, whether it is below £15,000 or not.

If the debtor convinces the court that the credit bargain is extortionate then the court may make one of the orders listed in Section 139(2) of the Act, viz.:

1. direct accounts to be taken to between any persons;
2. set aside the whole or part of any obligation imposed on the debtor or a surety by the credit bargain or any related agreement
3. require the creditor to repay the whole or part of any sum paid under the credit bargain or any related agreement by the debtor or a surety whether paid to the creditor or any other person;
4. direct the return to the surety of any property provided for the purposes of the security; or
5. alter the terms of the credit agreement or any security instrument.

Any application to have a credit agreement set aside must be made by the debtor or any surety the High Court or County Court. In England and Wales application in respect of a regulated agreement or any other agreement, not being a regulated agreement under which the creditors provides the debtor with a fixed sum credit or running-account credit, must be made in the County Court.

## *Fixed-Sum and Running-Account Credit*

Section 10 describes the two types of credit. A fixed sum credit is a once and for all credit. The amount of the credit is fixed and agreed between the parties. It may be paid by the creditor to the debtor as a lump sum or by instalments. Examples would be moneylenders' and bank loans, pawnbrokers' loans, hire purchase, a credit sale and conditional sale agreements and check and voucher trading.

In determining whether the amount of credit comes within the £15,000 limit a distinction must be made between credit and the total charge for credit. Thus the important figure is the amount of the loan or the capital sum not including the interest.

A running-account credit is sometimes named as a revolving credit. In this case the debtor does not have to apply for further credit but by his agreement with the creditor he has a right to further credit usually subject to a credit limit. In order to decide whether or not a running-account credit falls within the definition of a consumer credit agreement the credit limit must not exceed £15,000. However this limit may be exceeded merely temporarily (Section 10(2)). Furthermore there are three situations where the agreement will still be subject to the Act even though there is no credit limit or that it exceeds the specified amount (£15,000 at present).

1. If the debtor is not allowed to draw at any time an amount that exceeds £15,000 as credit but excluding any charge for credit. This situation could arise if a bank has allowed a customer overdraft facilities of say £60,000 (or even without limit) but stipulates that he can only draw say £10,000 in any one month.
2. The agreement provides that if the debt exceeds a sum not exceeding £15,000 then the rate of interest will increase.
3 If at the time the agreement was entered into, it is probable that the debit balance will not rise above the specified amount (£15,000).

In each of these cases the agreement would be within the financial limit (£15,000). These exceptions have been made so as to avoid the situation where a creditor might agree to provide credit in excess of the specified amount, knowing that the debtor will not require more than the specified amount (e.g. £15,000) but so as to take the agreement outside the provisions of the Act.

## *Consumer Hire Agreements*

So far we have considered consumer credit agreements. A consumer hire agreement is an agreement made by a person called the owner with an individual (not a company) called the hirer. The agreement must be capable of lasting more than three months and must require the hirer to pay more than £15,000. Also Section 15 makes it clear that a consumer hire agreement is not a hire purchase agreement.

All consumer hire agreements will be regulated agreements if they are not exempt agreements. Such exempt agreements are those exempted by order of the Secretary of State where the owner is a company authorised to supply electricity, gas or water or where the subject of the agreement is a meter or metering equipment owned by the Post Office.

A hire purchase agreement differs from a consumer hire agreement in that in the former case the hirer who has possession of the goods will become the owner of them if the agreement is complied with and he opts to purchase the goods. In a consumer hire agreement there is no question of the hirer becoming the owner of the goods.

## *Small Agreements*

These are regulated consumer credit agreements for credit not exceeding £50 other than a hire purchase or a conditional sale agreement or a regulated consumer hire agreement which does not require the hirer to make payments exceeding £50 provided that in either case the agreement is an agreement which is either unsecured or secured by a guarantee or indemnity only. In the case of a running-account credit the credit limit must not exceed £50.

The provision relating to small agreements is included in the Act so that such small agreements may be excluded by other sections in the Act from certain technical requirements of those sections. Therefore Section 17 makes provision to prevent the splitting up of agreements into two or more agreements below the £50 limit, so as to circumvent the provisions of the Act.

## *Non-Commercial Agreements*

Such an agreement is a consumer credit agreement or a consumer hire agreement not made by the creditor or owner in the course of a business carried on by him. Such private agreements are excluded from some of the provisions of the Act.

## *Mulitple Agreements*

Section 18 provides that an agreement that falls within more than one type of agreement, such as a running-account credit and a fixed-sum credit, shall be called a multiple agreement. Where there is a multiple agreement each part is to be treated as a separate agreement (Section 18(2)).

A credit card agreement will be multiple if the card can be used to obtain goods or services (a debtor-creditor-supplier agreement) or cash (a debtor-creditor agreement).

It should be noted that Section 18(5) provides that in the case of a running-account credit, a term of the agreement that allows the credit limit to be exceeded only temporarily, shall not be treated as a separate agreement or as a separate agreement providing fixed-sum credit in respect of the excess. This will permit a bank to honour cheques drawn on it in the case of a temporary excess of an agreed overdraft.

## *Linked Transactions*

When a person enters into an agreement to obtain goods on credit or to hire goods it is quite usual for an additional agreement to be entered into such as one for installation, insurance or maintenance. Such agreements will be linked to the regulated agreement in the following cases.

1. It is entered into in compliance with a term of the principal agreement.
2. The principal agreement finances the linked transaction. This may occur if the debtor obtains a loan from a finance company to finance his purchase from a dealer. This is known as a debtor-creditor- supplier agreement. The contract between the debtor and the dealer is a linked transaction.
   It will also arise where a debtor uses a credit card or check or voucher in order to obtain goods from a supplier. The contract for the goods or services is a linked transaction.
3. If the creditor, owner, negotiator or credit broker suggests to the debtor or hirer that he should enter into an agreement so as to induce him to enter into a principal agreement, such as when it is suggested by dealer or broker arranging a loan that an insurance policy be entered into with a particular company. That transaction would be linked with the principal agreement.

## *Control of Credit Agreements*

The foregoing is concerned with the various types of credit agreements and the nomenclature used in the *Consumer Credit Act 1974*. The important point to be borne in mind is that certain agreements are regulated by the Act and whether or not an agreement is regulated must be established. The Director General of Fair Trading has been given powers to issue licences to bodies involved with various activities of the credit industry. A person requires a licence if he carries on a business in the course of which regulated agreements are made with customers (debtors or hirers) (Section 21). A licence is not required if the business:

1. provides credit only in excess of £15,000 or which rents goods where the hirer must pay more than £l5,000;
2. provides credit or hire only to companies;
3. provides credit or hire only under exempt agreements.

## *Unlicensed Trading*

Section 39 provides that a person who trades when unlicensed has committed an offence and will be liable to criminal sanctions. Furthermore Section 40 provides that the agreement itself may not be enforced against the debtor or hirer unless the Director General of Fair Trading authorises it. In deciding whether or not to allow the agreement to be enforced the Director must consider to what extent other debtors or hirers have been prejudiced, whether or not he would have been likely to grant a licence and the creditor's degree of culpability in failing to obtain a licence.

## *Seeking Business*

This may be done by advertising, by canvassing or by giving quotations.

### Advertising

The provisions related to advertising and quotations apply not only to persons who are carrying on a consumer credit business or a consumer hire business but also to those who carry on a business in the course of which they provide credit to individuals secured on land and that the advertisement or quotation need not relate to a regulated agreement. The provisions extend to any form of advertising by television, radio, distribution of samples, catalogues, exhibition of models or in any other way.

The Secretary of State is empowered to make regulations concerning the form and content of advertisements. The charge for credit must be expressed as an annual percentage rate (APR).

### Quotation

A quotation is a document in which prospective customers are given information about the terms on which the person who carries out a consumer credit or hire business is prepared to do business. These are all subject to controls.

### Canvassing

This occurs where the canvasser solicits the entry of a consumer into a regulated agreement by making oral representations during a visit not previously arranged. The canvassing is said to be "off trade premises" if it takes place somewhere other than the place of business of the creditor or owner, the supplier, the canvasser or the consumer. Such off-trade-premises canvassing is an offence unless it is in response to a written invitation from the person making the invitation. It is also an offence to send a document to a minor inviting him to borrow money, obtain services, goods or hire on credit. Finally it is an offence to give a person a credit-token if he has not asked for it in writing. Such a credit-token may be given, without request, if it is given under a credit-token agreement already made or in renewal or replacement of a credit-token previously accepted by the debtor.

## *Making a Regulated Agreement*

The agreement between the creditor and the debtor or the owner and the hirer will be made when it has been signed or executed by both parties. Section 61(1)(a). The document must contain all the terms of the agreement and these shall be legible. The form and content of the agreement are laid down by the Secretary of State. In any case the debtor or hirer must be made aware of

1. his rights and duties;
2. the amount and rate for the total charge for credit;
3. the protection available to him.

If the agreement is

1. a non-commercial agreement;
2. a debtor-creditor agreement enabling the debtor to overdraw on a current account; or
3. a debtor-creditor agreement to finance the making of payments, arising on or connected with the death of a person

then, the above provisions will not apply (Section 74).

## *Mortgage of Land*

If the security for the loan or hire is land then Section 58 will apply. This provides that the creditor/owner must give to the debtor/hirer a copy of the unexecuted agreement not less than seven days before the unexecuted agreement is sent for signature. This is called the consideration period and during it no approach must be made by the creditor/owner to the debtor/hirer. This provision will not apply in the following cases.

1. The loan is a restricted-use loan to finance the purchase of mortgaged land. This would apply if a person borrows money from a bank or building society to buy the land which is to be used as security for the loan.
2. The agreement is for a bridging loan in connection with the purchase of the mortgaged land or other land.

## *Restricted-Use and Unrestricted-Use Credit*

Under a credit agreement the credit may be restricted-use or unrestricted- use credit. If the credit is granted by a regulated consumer credit agreement and can only be used in a particular way, for example

1. to finance a transaction between the debtor and the creditor;
2. to finance a transaction between the debtor and a person (the supplier) other than the creditor; or
3. to refinance any existing indebtedness of the debtor whether to a creditor or to another person.

then in these cases the credit is said to be "restricted-use credit".

If it is possible for the credit to be used in any way the debtor chooses even though that might be contrary to an agreement between the creditor and debtor, the credit will be said to be "unrestricted-use credit".

## *Copies of the Agreement*

### Not Signed by Creditor/Owner

If, when the unexecuted agreement is presented personally to the debtor/ hirer for his signature it has not become an executed agreement (because the creditor has not signed), then the debtor/hirer must be given a copy of it. If the unexecuted agreement is sent to the debtor/hirer for his signature then a copy of it must also be sent together with any supporting documents. Later when the creditor/owner signs, a second copy of the agreement must be sent within seven days of the creditor/owner signing unless it is a credit-token agreement.

### Signed by Creditor/Owner

If the unexecuted agreement is presented personally to the debtor/hirer for signature and when he signs it becomes an executed agreement, then a copy of the executed agreement and any supporting documents must be then and there delivered to him, but no further copy is required.

If the unexecuted agreement is sent to the debtor/hirer for him to sign, a copy must be sent at the same time. No further copy is required if the debtor/hirer signs because the creditor/owner has already signed it before sending it.

## *Cancellation*

The normal rule for making a contract requires that a valid offer is made which is accepted unconditionally. So long as the parties really are in agreement, that is there is no mistake or deception, then an agreement has been entered into which cannot be set aside easily. However as regards regulated agreements it may be possible for an individual to change his mind after entering into an agreement provided certain rules are complied with.

Section 67 of the Act provides that a regulated agreement may be cancelled by debtor or hirer if the antecedent negotiations included oral representations made in the presence of the debtor or hirer unless the agreement is signed by the debtor or hirer on trade premises. Also the agreement may not be cancelled if, although signed off trade premises, the debtor has not been subject to face-to-face persuasion.

This provision is intended to protect individuals who are subject to persuasion by door-to-door salesmen and sign the agreement on the doorstep. This would also apply if the negotiations are conducted at a dealer's place of business and if the debtor takes home the agreement to sign. On the other hand if there has been no face-to-face persuasion, such as in a mail order transaction, contracts made in this way cannot be cancelled. Neither can the following agreements be cancelled:

1. a non-commercial agreement;
2. an agreement enabling the debtor to overdraw on a current account if the Director General of Fair Trading so determines;
3. a debtor-creditor agreement to finance the making of payments arising on the death of a person provided the Director General so determines;
4. a small debtor-creditor-supplier agreement for restricted use.

### Cooling-off Period

The period in which the debtor/hirer is permitted to serve notice of cancellation (the cooling-off period) is a period ending on the fifth day following the day on which he received the second copy of the agreement or if no second copy is required the notice informing the debtor of his cancellation rights.

### Effect of Notice of Cancellation

The notice of cancellation is effective at the time of posting whether or not it is actually received. The notice of cancellation must be served on the creditor/owner, the credit-broker or supplier who took part in the antecedent negotiations or any agent of the debtor/hirer or creditor/owner.

The notice of cancellation will cancel the agreement and any linked transaction. Any payments made are recoverable. If however the creditor has advanced a sum of money during the cooling-off period this does not become immediately repayable (Section 71).

## *Connected Lender Liability*

A credit card transaction may be two-party or three-party. If the supplier of the goods issues his own credit card this will be a two-party credit agreement. A three-party transaction is where the issuer of the credit card is not the supplier of the goods. Section 75 of the *Consumer Credit Act 1974* is of importance in this case because that section makes liable the issuer of the credit card jointly and severally with the supplier in respect of any claim of the debtor for misrepresentation or breach of contract in relation to the transaction financed by the agreement.

In the case of a two-party transaction then the supplier and the issuer of the card are one person and of course the supplier will be liable directly to the debtor. This provision whereby the creditor may be made liable together with the supplier is intended to ensure that creditors will take care to associate only with reputable suppliers. Of course Section 75 is of particular value if the supplier himself should become insolvent and then the debtor will still be able to enforce his rights against the creditor. This has occurred quite frequently when tour operators have gone into liquidation and their customers have been able to recover against the credit card company.

Section 75, at present, only applies to a transaction where the cash price exceeds £100 and does not exceed £30,000. Also remember that Section 75 does not apply to American Express or Diners Club credit card agreements.

## *Extortionate Credit Bargains*

An important provision of the *Consumer Credit Act 1974* is contained in Sections 137 to 140. These are concerned with extortionate credit bargains and Section 137 gives the court power to re-open a credit agreement. This power may be exercised by the High Court, the County Court or the Sheriff's Court in Scotland, if the court considers that an agreement is extortionate (caselaw has established that unwise does not necessarily mean extortionate). All credit agreements are subject to this power: not only regulated ones and exempt, small and non-commercial agreements are affected.

Section 138 states the factors to be taken into account in deciding whether or not an agreement is extortionate. In deciding whether a bargain is extortionate the following matters shall be considered:

1. interest rates prevailing at the time the agreement was made;
2. the debtor's age, experience, business capacity and state of health;
3. the degree to which the debtor was under financial pressure when he made the bargain;
4. the degree of risk accepted by the creditor;
5. the creditor's relationship with the debtor;
6. whether or not the cash price was quoted for any goods or services;
7. in relation to a linked transaction factors applicable include how far the transaction was required for the protection of the debtor or the creditor or was in the interest of the creditor;
8. any other relevant consideration.

If the court decides that a credit bargain is extortionate then it may relieve the debtor from any sum in excess of what is fair and reasonable or it may alter the terms of the agreement or even require the creditor to repay any sums already paid.

## *Matters Arising During the Currency of an Agreement*

The creditor has a duty to supply unrequested periodic statements of account in the case of an overdraft or credit card agreement (a running-account credit agreement).

In the case of a fixed-sum credit agreement the creditor, if so requested by the debtor, must give him a copy of the agreement and inform him of the total sum paid, the sum which has become payable and the dates when payment must be made.

If a debtor is liable to make payments to the same creditor in respect of two or more regulated agreements then he has a choice as to which debt any payment he makes may be linked or appropriated. This is the normal rule relating to appropriation.

In the case of credit-tokens which include credit cards the general rule is that the debtor is not liable to the creditor for any loss arising from the use of the credit card by another person who is not the agent of the debtor. In any case Section 66 provides that a debtor shall not be liable under a credit-token agreement unless he has accepted it

1. by signing it;
2. by giving a receipt for it;
3. by using it.

If, after accepting the credit card the debtor permits its use by another person then he will be liable to the creditor.

## *Termination of the Consumer Credit Agreement*

Section 94 provides that a debtor may repay his debt at any time by notice to the creditor and payment of the debt to him. The debtor may then be entitled to a rebate for early settlement (Section 95). He is also entitled to a statement from the creditor of the amount he owes and if the creditor fails to provide this information the agreement cannot be enforced and if the information is not given within one month an offence will have been committed.

**Questions**

What are the two conditions an agreement must comply with in order for it to be a regulated consumer credit agreement?

In what circumstances does a debtor have the right to cancel a regulated agreement?

What is the advantage of using a credit card for the purchase of goods if the seller were to default?

# EIGHTEEN

# THE DATA PROTECTION ACT 1998

*Study Topics*

**Scope and purpose of the Act**

Nowadays computers are commonplace pieces of equipment which are capable of storing, processing and distributing information. It is a possibility that such facilities, in the wrong hands, might pose a threat to individuals and so should be controlled. Furthermore it was decided by the government that the Council of Europe convention for the protection of individuals with regard to automatic processing of personal data must be ratified. Countries who had ratified it might place restrictions on the transfer of personal data to countries which had not done so.

The original *Data Protection Act* was passed in 1984. It applied only to automatically processed information and did not cover information which is held and processed manually, for example in ordinary paper files. *The Data Protection Act 1998* has replaced the 1984 Act as it did not fully comply with EU Directive 95/46/EC. There are some important changes, for example the definition of "processing" is much wider and for the first time paper filing systems are now subject to the Data Protection Principles. There are transitional arrangements which mean that some of the new provisions will not fully take effect until October 2001. Some will not be in force until October 2007. The Act does not cover all computerised information but only that which relates to living individuals. For example it does not cover information which relates only to a company or organisation and not to an individual.

If a person wishes to record and use personal data he will be known as a data user. It does not matter that the data user does not have his own computer but uses a bureau or that the computer he has is only a desk top machine and not a mainframe. In each case he is still a data user and has his responsibilities under the Act. The Act requires that every data user who keeps personal data must make notification to the Data

Protection Registrar, now called Commissioner, and comply with the Act generally. There are important exemptions, for example personal data used in connection with the following may escape some or all of the provisions of the Act:

1. Prevention of crime, apprehending criminals, assessment and collection of taxes
2. Health, education and social work
3. Regulatory activity, for example in the financial services sector
4. Legal professional privilege (client confidentiality)
5. Negotiations, out of court settlements for example
6. Self Incrimination
7. Disclosure ordered by a court or under an enactment
8. Research, history and statistics
9. Journalism, literature or art (special exceptions)
10. Management forecasts and planning
11. Publicly available information such as the electoral roll
12. Examination marks and scripts
13. Confidential references
14. Private domestic purposes, such as a private individual's e-mail address book
15. Corporate finance such as mergers and acquisitions
16. National Security, Armed Forces, Judicial appointments, crown appointments (e.g. ministerial) and hounours list.

In all the above examples where an exemption exists the effect is that the Commissioner cannot take enforcement action and neither can an individual exercise his rights of access under the Act.

The definition of "processing" is wide enough in the 1998 Act to cover almost anything done with the data. For example simply holding the data without altering it in any way would be covered as much as erasing, destroying, organising or consulting it.

## *The Register*

The Act creates a register of data users and every data user who holds personal data must be registered unless the data are exempt. The Data User's Register entry is compiled by the Commissioner from the information give in the application. It contains the data user's name and address together with broad descriptions of the type of data which the data user holds, the purposes for which the data are used, the sources from which the data user intends to obtain the information, the people to whom the data user may wish to disclose the information and any oversea countries to which the data user may wish to transfer the personal data. The register is open to public inspection at the Commissioner's office and an index to the register may be inspected in major public libraries throughout the country.

## *Data Protection Principles*

The Act provides that in addition to registering with the Data Protection Registrar a data user must abide by the eight Data Protection Principles. These state that:

1. personal data must be fairly and lawfully processed
2. personal data must be processed for limited purposes
3. personal data must be adequate, relevant and not excessive
4. personal data must be accurate
5. personal data must not be kept longer than necessary
6. personal data must be processed in accordance with the data subject's rights
7. personal data must be secure
8. personal data must not be transferred to countries without adequate protection.

In order to enforce compliance with the principles the Commissioner can serve the following types of notice.

1. On complaint to the Commissioner that a data subject believes a breach of one of the principles has taken place, the Commissioner can serve an "information notice". This usually requires information in sufficient detail to enable the Commissioner to investigate the matter. Failure to comply constitutes an offence.
2. If the Commissioner believes there has been such a breach he can serve an "enforcement notice". This can require a data controller to, for example, destroy data, correct it or cease processing it. Again failure to comply would render the organisation criminally liable.

In some circumstances breach of the data protection principles can lead to civil liability for damages in addition to the above penalties.

A person on whom a notice is served is entitled to appeal against the Commissioner's decision to the Data Protection Tribunal.

## *Rights of the Individual whose Personal Data Are Held on File*

A person whose data are held on file is called a data subject and he is entitled to seek compensation through the courts if he has suffered damage caused by the loss unauthorised destruction or unauthorised disclosure of his personal data. He may also seek compensation through the courts for damage caused by the use of inaccurate data. If personal data are inaccurate then the data subject may complain to the Commissioner or apply to the courts for correction or deletion of the data.

Every data subject is entitled on written request to be supplied by any data user with a copy of any personal data held about him or her. This right is called "subject access right", although a fee and I.D. may required.

If the data subject considers there has been a breach of one of the principles of data protection then he is entitled to complain to the Data Protection Commissioner. If the complaint is justified and cannot be resolved informally then the Commissioner may use his powers to prosecute or to serve one of the notices already mentioned.

### Disclosure of Personal Data

The Act does not prevent a data user from disclosing information about an individual and such disclosure may be made if either:

1. the person to whom the disclosure is made is described in the disclosure section of the Data User's Register entry; or
2. the disclosure is covered by one of the "non disclosure exemptions". These would include, for example, disclosures required by law or made with the data subject's consent.

## *Data Protection Commissioner*

Formerly known as the Data Protection Registrar, the Commissioner is an independent officer who reports directly to Parliament. His duties include establishing the Register of Data Users, spreading information on the Act, promoting compliance with the Data Protection Principles, encouraging the development of Codes of Practice to help data users comply with the principles and finally considering complaints about breaches of the principles of the Act and where appropriate to prosecute offenders or serve notices on registered data users who are breaking the principles.

If the Commissioner is satisfied that a data user has breached a principle he can serve a notice as discussed above. A data user who receives one of these special notices can appeal to the independent Data Protection Tribunal. The tribunal has the power to substitute its own decision in place of the Commissioner. The Commissioner employs teams of regional investigators who check whether data users are properly registered and investigate complaints of breaches of principle.

### Questions

What are the eight data protection principles?

How may the Commissioner enforce these principles?

What rights does an individual have whose personal data are held on file?

NINETEEN

# THE FINANCIAL SERVICES ACT 1986

*Study Topics*

**The scope and purpose of the Financial Services Act**
**The effects of the Act**

The *Financial Services Act* received the Royal Assent on 7 November 1986 and came fully into force on 29 April 1988. It came about as a result of the appreciation that it was necessary to have the means of regulating investment business and that investors required protection. Prior to the Act there were some methods of protection contained in the *Prevention of Fraud (Investments) Act 1939* which was re-enacted by the *Prevention of Fraud Investments Act 1958*. Professor L. C. B. Gower was appointed in 1981 to head a committee charged with the review of the protection required by investors and the need for some control of dealers in securities, investment consultants and managers.

The *Financial Services Act* itself has effected a complete overhaul of the legal framework for the regulation of investment business. The Act is divided into 10 parts.

Part 1 creates a framework for the regulation of investment business.

Part 2 extends the investment control to Life Assurance when it is used as a form of investment.

Part 3 establishes a framework for the regulation of Friendly Societies.

Part 4 introduces a new regime for the official listing of securities on the Stock Exchange.

Part 5 deals with offers of unlisted securities.

Part 6 provides new rules relating to the take-over offers.

Part 7 makes a number of changes to the law on Insider dealing contained in the *Company Securities (Insider Dealings) Act 1985*.

Parts 8-10 deal with disclosure of information, reciprocity of access for financial business in foreign markets and miscellaneous matters.

It will be apparent that Part 1 is the most important part as far as bankers are concerned and we must now consider that section in some detail.

## *Definition of Investments*

An investment is defined very widely and includes any right, asset or interest which falls within the following categories.

1. Shares and stock in the share capital of a company.
2. Debentures, including debenture stock, loan stock, bonds, certificates of deposit and any other instrument creating or acknowledging indebtedness, cheque or other bill of exchange, a bankers' draft and letter of credit. Bank notes; current, deposit or savings accounts are excluded.
3. Government, local authority or other public authority securities.
4. Warrants or other instruments entitling the holder to subscribe for investments in the above categories.
5. Certificates or other instruments conferring rights to acquire, dispose of, underwrite or convert any investments falling within the above categories.
6. Units in collective investment schemes. This includes units in unit trusts.
7. Options to acquire or dispose of investments as defined.
8. Futures for investment purposes.

A definition of investments excludes, by implication, land and physical commodities such as works of art, antiques and old coins. Similarly gold and silver will not be regarded as investments unless they are expressed in the form of options.

## *Investment Business*

1. Dealing in investments: buying, selling, subscribing for or underwriting investments or offering or agreeing to offer investments, either as principal or as agent.
2. Arranging deals in investments: making, offering, or agreeing to make

arrangements with a view to another person buying, selling, subscribing for or underwriting the particular investment.

3. Managing investments: managing, offering or agreeing to manage assets belonging to another person if these assets consists of or include investments.
4. Advising on investments: giving or offering or agreeing to give advice to investors on the merits of the purchase, sale, subscription for or underwriting of investments or on the exercise of rights conferred by investments to acquire, dispose of, underwrite or convert an investment.

Certain activities which might be considered to constitute investment business are specifically excluded. These include dealing as a principle as where a person buys securities on his own account. Such a person will not be regarded as carrying on an investment business unless he is making a market or is soliciting the public to buy or sell investments. Also it will not be regarded as investment business where a financial package is linked with the sale of goods or supply of services; where a company operates a "share shop" for its employees; a trustee manages investments for his beneficiary or advice is given in the course of a profession, provided the investment dealing is not predominant. Also many daily newspapers contain financial columns which contain investment advice. Even so newspaper proprietors and financial journalists are not required to seek authorisation provided that their primary purpose is not to lead persons to invest in any particular investment.

## *The Framework for Regulation*

The Secretary of State for Trade and Industry is authorised under the Act to regulate the investment industry to protect investors. He may delegate his tasks to a designated agency which is, in the first instance, the Financial Services Authority (FSA). Formerly known as the Securities and Investment Board (SIB), this is a private company limited by guarantee and financed by a levy on certain organisations. It may exercise its power flexibly and quickly but is subject to the control of the Secretary of State. He may remove board members, he may withdraw in whole or in part the powers given to the FSA or he may direct the FSA to alter its rules or practices. In addition the FSA must also submit an annual report to Parliament which will be debated. The FSA will delegate its powers to other bodies, the main categories being Self-Regulating Organisations (SRO) and Recognised Professional Bodies (PRB). In addition the FSA may recognise a Recognised Investment Exchange (RIE) and a Recognised Clearing House (RCH). So the structure is as follows:

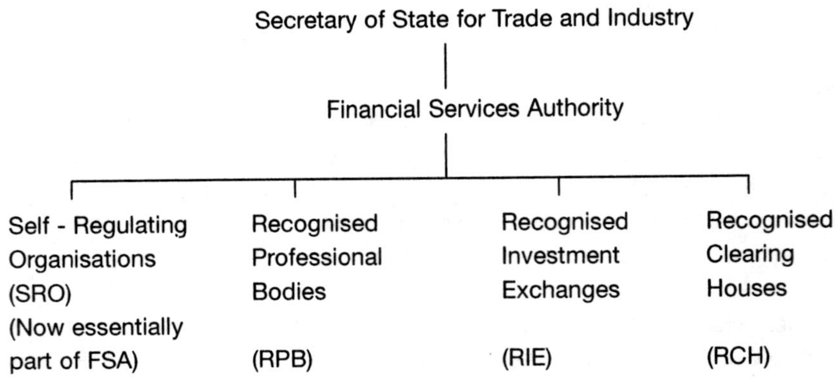


## *Self-Regulating Organisations*

The Financial Services Authority has recognised the following as Self-Regulating Organisations:

1. Investment Management Regulatory Organisation (IMRO): these are investment managers and advisors including managers and trustees of collective investment schemes and in-house pension fund managers.
2. Personal Investment Authority (PIA): this deals with the many high street independent financial advisers who give advice to the general public on mortgages, pensions, insurance and investments generally.
3. The Securities and Futures Authority (SFA): this body deals with those involved in dealing and broking in securities, futures and options, for example, in the City.

## *Recognised Professional Bodies*

In their practice professionals such as accountants, solicitors, etc, provide an important source of investment advice and other investment services such as insurance broking. These professional bodies will only be involved in investment business to an insignificant degree within the main body of their professional activities. However they may be authorised by the FSA provided:

1. the professional body regulates the practice of a profession which is not, wholly or mainly, the carrying on of an investment business;
2. it regulates the practice of a profession recognised for a statutory purpose or in the exercise of statutory powers.

The eight currently recognised professional bodies are:

1. The Association of Chartered Certified Accountants
2. The Institute of Actuaries
3. The Institute of Chartered Accountants in England and Wales
4. The Institute of Chartered Accountants of Scotland
5. The Institute of Chartered Accountants in Ireland
6. The Law Society
7. The Law Society of Northern Ireland
8. The Law Society of Scotland.

Whether or not a body will apply for recognition by the FSA will probably depend upon the amount to which the membership of the profession is involved in public practice. When deciding to recognise a professional body the FSA must be satisfied that the rules of the profession will provide equivalent investor protection to that provided by its own rules. Also the professional body must have adequate arrangements and resources for the effective monitoring and enforcement of compliance to its rules. The enforcement arrangements must provide for the withdrawal or suspension of certification. Also the arrangements must provide a proper balance between the interests of persons certified by the body and the interests of the public. Furthermore arrangements must be made for the investigation of complaints against its members or its regulation of investment business.

## *Recognised Investment Exchanges and Clearing Houses*

Persons running a market or exchange will normally be carrying on investment business and will therefore need to be authorised, unless the market or exchange obtains exemption by becoming recognised by the FSA.

Any body corporate or incorporated association may apply for recognition as a Recognised Investment Exchange. The procedure is the same as for recognition as an SRO. The criteria for recognition include the following.

1. The exchange must have sufficient, financial resources to enable it to perform its functions in a proper manner.
2. Its rules and practices must ensure the orderly conduct of business and afford proper protection to investors.
3. It must limit dealings to investments to which there is a proper market.
4. It must impose information requirements on issues of investments so that people dealing in these can ascertain their current value.
5. It must have arrangements for ensuring the performance of transactions effected on it.
6. It must provide satisfactory arrangements for recording transactions effected on the exchange.
7. It must have adequate arrangements for monitoring and enforcing compliance with its rules.

8. It must have effective arrangements for the investigation of complaints.

The FSA has recognised the following exchanges:

1. London Stock Exchange
2. International Petroleum Exchange of London
3. London International Financial Futures & Options Exchange
4. Tradepoint Stock Exchange
5. London Metal Exchange Ltd
6. OM London Exchange.

The following are Recognised Clearing Houses:

1. The London Clearing House Ltd
2. CRESTCo Ltd.

## *Authorisation*

Anyone who carries on an investment business in the United Kingdom must be authorised subject to certain exemptions.

**Exempt Persons**

1. Bank of England
2. Lloyds
3. Listed Money Market Institutions
4. President of the Family Division of the High Court
5. Accountant General of the Supreme Court
6. The Public Trustee
7. The Central Board of Finance of the Church of England, etc.

In this connection it should be noted that many financial conglomerates will be supervised under other regulatory systems, for example, by the Bank of England in the case of banks and by the Department of Trade and Industry in the case of Insurance Companies.

1. Members of Self-Regulatory Organisations (SROs) are entitled to operate an investment business, that is.:
   i. to deal in investments
   ii. to arrange investment deals for others
   iii. to manage investments
   iv. to advise on investments
   v. to operate a collective investment scheme such as a unit trust.

The SROs will have satisfied the requirements of the Financial Services Authority (FSA).

2. Certain professional bodies will be recognised by the FSA and will be able to authorise persons applying to it to engage in investment business. Authorisation will be granted by means of the issue of an Investment Business Certificate. This may only be granted to persons whose main business is the practice of a profession rather than an investment business.
3. Direct authorisation by the FSA will be granted if the applicant is a fit and proper person to carry on the investment business.
4. Overseas persons will require authorisation if they conduct investment business in the United Kingdom, whether or not they have a place of business in this country. Nationals of other EEC Member States will automatically be authorised provided they lave no permanent place of business in the United Kingdom and are authorised to conduct investment business in their own State.

## *Conduct of Investment Business*

The *Financial Services Act* contains powers to enforce compliance with the statutory rules and other regulations. These powers may be exercised by:

1. Criminal prosecution brought by the Secretary of State or the Director of Public Prosecutions.
2. Civil action by any person who has suffered loss as a result of a transaction. Such a person may bring an action for damages against any person who has broken the rules and regulations (other than the financial resources rules) of the FSA, an SRO or a recognised professional body, as the case may be.
3. Other procedures. In this connection the Act provides for the establishment of a Financial Services Tribunal to serve as a forum to hear appeals against certain decisions made by the Secretary of State or the FSA. The tribunal will consist of three persons nominated from a panel of ten. They must be legally qualified and at least one member must have had recent business experience.

The persons who may refer a matter to the Tribunal will be those who have received from the FSA:

1. notice that the FSA intends to refuse a grant authorisation or to withdraw or suspend authorisation;
2. notice that the FSA intends to terminate or suspend authorisation by virtue of authorisation in another EEC member state;
3. notice of intention to disqualify a person from employment in an investment business;
4. notice of a proposed public statement relating to an authorised person's misconduct;

5. notice of the imposition, rescission or variation of a prohibition or of a refusal to impose, rescind or vary one.

Any person affected has 28 days from the date on which the notice was served to require the FSA to refer the matter to the Tribunal. From the above it will be apparent that the power to bring a criminal prosecution is the most effective sanction.

## *Misleading Statements and Practices*

The Act (Section 47) creates two offences, the first of which is contained in Section 47(1). This Section provides that a person who:

1. makes a statement, promise or forecast which he knows to be misleading, false or deceptive;
2. conceals any material facts; or
3. recklessly makes a statement, promise or forecast which is misleading, false or deceptive shall be guilty of an offence.

The second offence is contained in Section 47(2). This provides that any person who intentionally does any act or engages in any course of conduct which creates a false or misleading impression as to the market in or price or value of any investments shall be guilty of an offence.

For each offence the punishment for a person convicted on indictment is imprisonment for a term not exceeding seven years or to a fine or to both. If convicted before the magistrates the punishment is imprisonment not exceeding six months or a fine or both.

## *Rules for the Conduct of Business*

Section 48 empowers the FSA to make rules relating to the conduct of business. The principles are set out in Schedule 8 of the Act.

1. Investment business should be carried on honestly and fairly.
2. Operators should carry out their responsibilities capably, carefully and to the best of their abilities.
3. They should be fair to their customers, which implies avoiding conflicts of interests.

There are also certain general requirements.

1. Know your customer. This means that the authorised person must take steps to find out about the customer's personal and financial situation so that he may be given the "best advice".
2. Cold calling. Unsolicited calls are forbidden by Section 56 except in relation to life assurance and unit trusts. When a sale results from an unsolicited call in

relation to these two matters the investor must be informed that he has a fourteen day cooling off period in which he can change his mind and cancel the agreement.

3. Customer agreements. The rules relating to customer agreements will apply to all firms except registered life offices and trustees of regulated collective investment schemes.

Two types of investor need not be asked to sign a full customer agreement.

1. Occasional customers who may be offered "occasional customer agreements".
2. Business, experienced or professional customers who may be offered a "terms of business letter".

Apart from these all customer agreements must include the following information.

1. Basic details about the investment business.
2. The type of services offered.
3. If the services include recommending purchases of single premium life policies or units in regulated collective schemes, a warning that the purchases cannot be cancelled, other than by mutual agreement.
4. A statement of whether the customer agrees to the firm making uninvited calls on the customer and if so the circumstances in which such calls may be made.
5. Where non-business and non-professional investors agree to unsolicited calls a warning that the investor will forfeit his right under the cancellation rules to treat any agreement entered into in consequence of such a call as unenforceable.
6. The basic method and frequency of remuneration payable by the customer to the firm and a statement of whether the firm will earn any commissions other than from the customer and whether these will be passed on to the customer.
7. The customers' investment objectives, such as capital growth, income etc.
8. Restrictions or guidelines on what the business should put the investor in to.
9. Statement of particular exchanges or markets which the customer does not want to get involved with.
10. If the type of investment in which the investors funds are to be sunk are not easily realisable, a warning of the risks involved.
11. Arrangements by which a customer can terminate his contract without incurring any penalty charges.
12. Arrangements for receiving instructions and reporting any advice to the customer.
13. The accounting arrangements for the customer and arrangements for holding money or investments for the customer.
14. In the case of a managed portfolio, its initial composition and the periods of accounts for which statements are to be provided.

Where the customer agreement concerns futures, options and contracts for differences, the agreement, in addition to the matters noted above, must also include:

1. a warning of the risky nature of the investment;
2. a statement of the circumstances in which an investor will have to apply a deposit or a margin in support of a transaction or supplement that payment;
3. a statement of the circumstances in which the firm may close out existing contracts without reference to the customer.

A relationship with a customer for which a full agreement is required can be commenced only after the agreement has been received by the customer and he has signed and returned it.

An occasional customer agreement must outline the advice which the firm has given to the customer and any instructions that the customer has given to the firm. The agreement must be received and agreed by the customer before any transactions are conducted under it.

A "terms of business" letter must identify the investments and services for which the customer is to be treated as a business, professional or experienced investor.

## *Financial Services and Markets Act 2000*

This Act only received Royal Assent in June 2000 and is being implemented during the course of 2001. This will enable the FSA to be the single regulator for the industry. The powers of the following organisations will transfer to the FSA:

1. Building Societies Commission
2. Friendly Societies Commission
3. Investment Management Regulatory Organsiation
4. Personal Investment Authority
5. Register of Friendly Societies
6. Securities and Futures Authority.

Furthermore new responsibilities concerned with regulating mortgage lending are to be added. The FSA will be equipped with a fuller range of statutory powers to regulate, investigate and discipline individuals and organisations providing financial services. The Act also creates the Financial Services and Markets Tribunal for the resolution of disputes together with a single ombudsman and compensation schemes for consumers affected by mis-selling and the like.

**Questions**

What is included in the term investment?

Give examples of the contents of a customer agreement.

# TWENTY

# INSURANCE *and* INTERNATIONAL TRADING

*Study Topics*

**Insurable interest**
***Uberrimae fidei***
**Averaging**

The owner of a house or of goods or a ship can never be certain that these things are not going to be damaged or lost. It is of the greatest importance therefore that the owner of any of these things should take out insurance cover.

The nature of an insurance contract is that it is one by which a person (the insurer) agrees, in return for a premium, to pay a sum of money to another person (the insured) on the happening of some future event. The future event may be certain to happen or it may merely be a possibility. Thus the two categories of insurance are:

1. indemnity insurance: this provides an indemnity against loss as in a fire policy on a house, or a marine policy on a ship;
2. contingency insurance: this provides not an indemnity but payment on some contingent event. This is to be found in a life policy or a personal injury policy.

The sum to be paid is not measured by the loss but is stated in the policy. The contracted sum is paid if the life ends or an injury is sustained, irrespective of the value of the life or injury.

Like any other contract, a contract of insurance is an agreement whereby the parties make promises to each other. In this particular contract, one party approaches the insurance company and pays, or promises to pay, a sum of money called a premium; in return the insurer promises to pay out a sum of money if a certain thing occurs in the future.

On the face of it, it appears that a contract of insurance is like a wager, which is also a contract in which one party agrees to pay a sum of money to the other party dependent upon the happening of some uncertain future event. A contract of insurance is enforceable whereas a wager is not. *Gaming Acts 1935-68*.

## Insurable Interest

The difference between a wager and a contract of insurance lies in the fact that in the latter there must be "an insurable interest". *Life Assurance Act 1884.*

An insurable interest has not been defined by Parliament, but in *Halford v Kymer (1830)* it was stated that a person who will suffer pecuniary loss as a consequence of the happening of the risk insured against, as opposed to a chance of winning money, as in the case of a wager, can be said to have an insurable interest. It is up to the courts to decide whether an insurable interest exists, and they have so decided in the following cases.

1 A creditor may insure the life of his or her debtor. *Anderson v Edie (1795)*. Thus according to Paget, *Law of Banking*, a bank may insure the life of its debtor but in practice never does so, preferring to take as security a policy on the life of another person.
2 A guarantor may insure the life of a principal debtor.
3. An employer may insure the life of his or her employee. *Hebdon v West (1863)*. In this connection an employer will frequently insure his or her employees' lives and agree that any benefits be paid to their next of kin.
4. A litigant may insure the life of his or her judge. This has been done in a long, complicated will case where it was apparent that if the judge were to die a retrial would necessitate heavy expense.
5. A husband or wife can insure the life of the other spouse.
6. A father does not have insurable interest in the life of his child unless he can show some, for example a daughter is looking after her father. He can of course take out a policy on his child for his child's benefit.
7. An assignee such as a bank does not need to have an insurable interest. *Ashley v Ashley (1829).*

*The Life Assurance Act 1774* does not apply to insurance on goods. Section 4 of that Act provides "nothing herein contained shall extend or be construed to extend to insurance bona fide made by any person or persons on ships, goods or merchandise". Thus the requirement for an insurable interest in goods is not so stringent as in the case of a life. Even if the insurer has no interest at all, the contract may still not be a wager, as everything will depend on the intention of the parties as expressed in the policy. The three factors which give an insurable interest under a contract for the sale of goods are:

1. property;
2. possession; and
3. risk.

If the goods are still at the seller's risk, or if the property has not yet passed, or if the seller has possession as in the case of an unpaid seller, then the seller can insure the goods without the contract being invalidated as a wager. In the same way the buyer can insure if he or she has acquired property, possession or risk. Even if the buyer has not acquired property, possession or risk, he or she can insure against loss of profit on resale as soon as he or she has agreed to buy the goods.

In marine insurance an insurable interest is also required. A person has an insurable interest if he or she is interested in a marine adventure in consequence of which he or she may benefit by the safe arrival of insurable property or be prejudiced by its loss, damage or detention.

## *Uberrimae Fidei*

Insurance is a contract *uberrimae fidei* ("of the utmost good faith"). All forms of insurance require that there should be the fullest disclosure of all material facts. If a material fact has been omitted to be disclosed then it may render the contract voidable. A circumstance is material if it would influence the judgment of a prudent insurer in fixing the premium or determining whether to take the risk.

> *Mutual Life Insurance Co of New York v Ontario Metal Products Co (1925).* A proposal form asked the name of any physician whom the proposer had consulted in the last five years. The proposer said "none", though in fact, he had consulted a doctor and received tonics, but he had never been away from his work. The insurers' doctor said that if he had known of this he would still have recommended the acceptance of the risk at the ordinary premium. It was held that there was no material concealment and the policy was not avoided.

See also *London Assurance v Mansel (1879).*

## *Indemnity*

As has been stated, insurance may be either an indemnity insurance or a contingency insurance. Contingency insurance covers life policies and personal injury policies. Indemnity insurance provides indemnity against loss, as in a fire policy on a house or a marine policy on a vessel. In an indemnity contract the fundamental rule is that the insured cannot recover or retain for his or her own benefit more than his or her actual loss. An exception to this principle occurs if the parties have agreed at the time of the contract on the value of the subject matter of the insurance. This is known as a valued policy. In this case, where a total loss occurs, a sum representing the agreed value is recoverable by the insured, even though it exceeds his or her actual loss. The most common type of valued policy to be found in non-marine insurance is a policy insuring against loss of profits.

In the event of a total loss, the insurers under an unvalued policy are liable to pay the market value of the property at the time and place of the loss, or the sum insured that is agreed between the parties, whichever is less. This is why a car owner should reduce the cover on his or her car each time he or she pays the annual premium, because almost certainly the value of the car will decrease year by year. If the car is written off, then the insured will only receive the current market value and not the market value at the time when he or she originally entered into the contract of insurance.

The indemnity is based on the market value of the property and not the cost of its purchase or production or reinstatement, unless there has been an agreement to this effect.

If the property has no market value then the insurers are liable to pay the cost of reinstatement or the sum insured, whichever is less. Finally, where the goods are merely damaged then the insurers' liability is based on the cost of repairs or the sum insured, whichever is the less.

## Proposals and Policies

The proposal is a questionnaire issued by the insurer to the proposed insured to enable the risk to be evaluated and premiums and indemnity calculated. The questionnaire acts as the invitation to offer; the completed form, when returned, acts as the offer which, when accepted, makes the contract binding.

The proposal form will request basic information to be disclosed, such as name and address, subject matter, sum insured, a declaration of warranty (utmost good faith), and for commercial insurance contracts a claims history.

The policy is evidence that the contract exists. The policy is always drawn up by the insurers and subsequently the legal dictum of *contra preferentum* will apply; that is, the person who issues the document is responsible for any defects or ambiguities in it and cannot profit from any such clause.

The policy is frequently issued as a two-part document: the schedule, which lists all the relevant facts of contract, and the certificate, which provides evidence that such an insurance contract exists. This is usually the format for marine and cargo insurance, and is compulsory by law for motor vehicle and employer liability insurance.

## *Premiums and Renewals*

The premium is the financial consideration paid to the insurer by the insured. Traditionally premiums have been paid annually in advance, but recently payment by instalments has become more readily acceptable. Premiums are calculated on the information detailed in the proposal form, except for certain marine insurances where calculations are based on the past three years' records, held by the underwriters for the particular risk to be covered.

Renewals are at the discretion of either party; the contract is for a specific period at the end of which neither party is under any obligation to renew. However, if the insured has maintained a good claims history it would generally be in his or her interest to seek renewal and also negotiate a lower premium based on the no-claim or minimal-claim record.

## *Subrogation*

In an indemnity contract, the insurer is entitled to every right of the assured, or, as Brett LJ says:

> As between the underwriter, and the assured, the underwriter is entitled to the advantage of every right of the assured whether such right consist in contract, fulfilled or unfulfilled or in remedy for tort capable or being insisted on or already insisted on, or in any other right, whether by way of condition or otherwise, legal or equitable, which can be, or has been, exercised or has accrued, and whether such right could or could not be enforced by the insurer in the name of the assured by the exercise or acquiring of which right or condition the loss against which the assured is insured can be, or has been, diminished.

This is called the doctrine of subrogation. It entitles the insurer who pays the insured not only to the value of any benefit received by the latter by way of compensation for actual loss, but also to the value of any rights of remedies the insured may have against third parties in respect of the damage. The doctrine applies not only to fire policies but to all indemnity policies. Thus, if A's servant negligently drives A's vehicle and injures B, A's insurers after paying B can sue A's servant for damages for breach of the contract of service.

If the insured renounces or in any way compromises rights to which the insurer would be subrogated, he or she is bound to make up the amount to the insurer. Policies are usually made voidable on such an event. The doctrine does not apply to non-indemnity insurance, such as life assurance and personal accident insurance.

## *Fire Insurance*

Fire insurance is a contract, one party to which undertakes to indemnify the other against the consequences of a fire happening within an agreed period, in return for the payment of money in a lump sum or by instalments. The insured must have an insurable interest in the premises or goods insured at the time of the loss, that is, he must be in such a position that he incurs loss by the burning.

1. A creditor may insure a house over which he or she has a mortgage.
2. A bailee may insure his or her customer's goods for the full value and, if loss occurs, he or she may retain so much of the policy moneys as would cover his or her own interest while being trustee for the owners in respect of the rest. Alternatively a bailee may take out a policy which covers merely his or her own liability as bailee, and it is a matter of construction which type of policy has been taken out.

But a shareholder of an incorporated company, even though he or she may hold all the shares, has no insurable interest in the company's property; nor has an unsecured creditor such an interest. A shareholder may, however, insure against resultant loss in the value of his or her shares.

A contract of fire insurance made by an agent without authority cannot be ratified by the principal after and with knowledge of the loss by fire of the subject matter insured.

The contract being one of indemnity, only the amount of loss actually suffered can be recovered; this Bowen LJ calls "the infallible rule". But the parties may agree beforehand the value of the premises or goods insured. And in the absence of fraud the agreement will be binding.

> *Elcock v Thomson (1949).* Premises were insured in 1940, and it was agreed that £106,850 was the true value and that in the event of loss the property would be assumed to be of such value and would be assessed accordingly. A fire occurred in 1947 and it was found that immediately before the fire the real value of the premises was £18,000 and immediately after the fire it was £12,600. It was held that the estimate was binding on the insurers and, as the real value of the premises had been depreciated by 30% (£18,000 down to £12,600), the insurers were liable to pay 30% of £106,850.

## *Average Clause*

If the insured insures for less than the full value of the property, the insurers are nevertheless liable to indemnify the insured up to the total amount insured, even if there is only partial loss and even though they have only received a small premium. To guard against under-insurance it is very common to insert an average clause in a policy. The words "subject to average" in a Lloyd's policy involve the following standard clause:

> Where ever a sum insured is declared to be subject to average, if the property shall at the breaking out of any fire be collectively of greater value than such sum insured, then the insured shall be considered as being his own insurer for the difference and shall bear a rateable share of the loss accordingly.

Thus if goods worth £50,000 are insured for £25,000 under a policy containing an average clause, and damage is caused totalling £25,000, then the insurers will only be liable to pay half of the damage, that is £12,500. This is the proportion which the sum insured bears to the total value of the property, that is, 50%.

## *Accident and Burglary*

Burglary insurance resembles fire insurance because it is a contract to indemnify the assured against loss from the risk insured against. However, accident insurance is not a contract of indemnity. It is an agreement to pay a specified sum of money upon the happening of certain events. Of course the basic principles of insurance, such as insurable interest, utmost disclosure and subrogation, also apply to these types of insurance.

The deliberate over-valuation of the property insured will avoid a burglary policy. In car insurance the proposer should disclose previous accidents he or she has had in driving.

Accident and burglary policies usually contain a condition that notice of the accident or loss must be given "immediately", "as soon as possible" or "within a fixed number of days".

By the *Third Parties (Rights Against Insurers) Act 1930* an injured person is given rights against the insurance company in the event that the wrongdoer who was insured goes bankrupt.

Every driver of a motor vehicle is, of course, required to be insured against liability in respect of the death or bodily injury to any person, including passengers, caused by the use of the vehicle on the road. A judgment against the insured in respect of such liability can be enforced against the insurer. *Road Traffic Act 1972.* Furthermore a person injured by a road vehicle and unable to receive damages from the driver of the vehicle can, in certain circumstances, receive compensation from the Motor Insurers' Bureau.

## *Marine Insurance*

A contract of marine insurance is one whereby the insurer undertakes to indemnify the assured against marine losses, that is to say the losses incident to a marine adventure.

*Marine Insurance Act 1906* Section 1. There is a marine adventure when:

1. any ship or goods is or are exposed to maritime perils;
2. the earning or acquisition of any freight, passage money, commission, profit, or other pecuniary benefit or the security for any advance is endangered by the exposure of insurable property to maritime perils;
3. liability to a third party may be incurred by the owner of or a person interested in insurable property by reason of maritime perils.

"Maritime perils" means the perils consequent on or incidental to the navigation of the sea, but a marine insurance contract may, by express terms or by usage of a trade, be extended to protect the assured against losses on inland waters. *Marine Insurance Act 1906,* Section 2.

## *Insurable Interest*

A contract of marine insurance where the assured has no insurable interest is a gaming or wagering contract and is void. A person has an insurable interest if he or she is interested in a marine advanture in consequence of which he or she may benefit by the safe arrival of insurable property or be prejudiced by its loss, damage or detention. The following persons have an insurable interest:

1. The lender of money on bottomry or respondentia, to the extent of the loan. Bottomry is a pledge of the ship and freight to secure a loan to enable the ship to continue the voyage. It is named after the bottom or keel of the ship, which is figuratively used to express the whole ship. Respondentia is a pledge of the cargo only and not of the ship.
2. The master and crew to the extent of their wages.
3. A person advancing freight to the extent that the freight is not repayable in case of loss.
4. A mortgagor to the extent of the full value of the property, and a mortgagee for the sum due under the mortgage.
5. The owner to the extent of the full value, notwithstanding that a third party has agreed to indemnify him or her from loss.
6. A reinsurer to the extent of his or her risk.

Defeasible, contingent and partial interests are insurable. The assured must have the insurable interests at the time of the loss, although he or she need not have it when the insurance is effected. If he or she insures property "lost or not lost", the insurance is good although the property may in fact be lost at the date when the insurance is effected, provided the assured did not know that it was lost. If the assured assigns his or her interest in the property insured, he or she does not transfer his or her rights in the insurance to the assignee, unless there is an agreement to that effect.

## Disclosure and Representations

A contract of marine insurance is one in which the utmost good faith (*uberrima fidei*) must be observed, and if it is not, the contract is voidable by the insurer. The assured must disclose to the insurer every material circumstance which is known to him or her, and he or she is deemed to know everything which he or she ought to know in the ordinary course of business. A circumstance is material if it would influence the judgment of a prudent insurer in fixing the premium or determining whether to take the risk (Section 18). The following are examples of the concealment of acts, which have been held to be material:

1. that the ship had grounded and sprung a leak before the insurance was effected;
2. that a merchant, on hearing that a vessel similar to his own was captured, effected an insurance without disclosing this information;
3. that the nationality of the assured was concealed at a time when his nationality was important;
4. in an insurance on a ship, that the goods carried were insured at a value greatly exceeding their real value.

In every case, however, whether a circumstance is material or not depends on the particular facts. The following circumstances need not be disclosed:

1. those diminishing the risk;
2. those known are presumed to be known by the insurer in the ordinary course of his or her business;
3. those which are waived by the insurer.

If the insurance is effected by an agent, the agent must disclose to the insurer every fact which the assured himself ought to disclose and also every material circumstance known to the agent. The agent is deemed to know every fact which he or she ought to know in the ordinary way of business or which ought to have been communicated to him or her (Section 19).

In addition to his or her duty to make a full disclosure, the assured is under a duty to see that every material representation made during the negotiations for the contract is true. If any material representation be untrue the insurer may avoid the contract (Section 20).

## The Policy

The contract of marine insurance is made as soon as the proposal is accepted by the insurer, although the policy may not be issued until later. Before the policy is issued it is usual to issue a document called "the slip" which, when accepted by the underwriter, is a short memorandum of the contract evidencing the date of the commencement of the insurance (Section 21).

The contract is constituted in the following manner. The broker, who acts as agent of the insured, offers the slip to various insurers, such as underwriting syndicates at Lloyd's, and the agent of each of these syndicates writes "a line, that is, accepts to a limited amount (*pro tanto*), until the full amount stated on the slip is covered. The slip thus constitutes an offer and the signature of each of the underwriters, through their agents, is the acceptance *pro tanto*. Consequently, separate binding contracts are concluded by the underwriters when they each accept *pro tanto*, and the validity of these contracts is not conditional on the completion of the slip. This legal position becomes relevant when a loss occurs before the slip is fully underwritten. In this case the insured can hold those underwriters who have already written a line liable *pro tanto*, but, on the other hand, the insured cannot cancel the contracts concluded with them, if such cancellation would be advantageous to him or her for one reason or another.

No action against the insurer can be brought by the insured until the policy is issued; the slip cannot be sued upon but where there is a duly stamped policy, reference may be made to the slip in any legal proceeding (Section 89). The policy must be signed by the insurer, or, if the insurer is a corporation, it may be sealed, and must specify:

1. the name of the assured or of some person who effects the insurance on his or her behalf;
2. the subject matter insured and the risk insured against;
3. the voyage or period of time or both, as the case may be, covered by the insurance;
4. the sum or sums insured;
5. the name or names of the insurers.

The subject matter of the insurance must be described with reasonable certainty, regard being had to any trade usage.

A contract of marine insurance is not admissible in a court of law unless it is embodied in a marine policy in accordance with the *Marine Insurance Act 1906*. This Act contained a Lloyds SG (ship and goods) policy. However, in 1982 modifications were made to the policy, and under the auspices of the Institute of London Underwriters, certain new clauses were introduced. These are Institute Cargo Clauses (A), (B) and (C). They correspond with the:

1. IC Clauses (AR) (All Risks);
2. IC Clauses (WA) (With Average); and
3. IC Clauses (FPA) (Fee of Particular Average).

Thus the policy is the vehicle for the Institute Cargo Clauses. Policies are of the following kinds:

1. voyage
2. time
3. mixed
4. valued
5. unvalued
6. floating.

These are discussed below.

### Voyage Policies

Here the contract is to insure "at and from" or from one place to another. The subject matter is then insured for a particular voyage only.

### Time Policies

Here the contract is to insure for a definite period time.

### Mixed Policies

A contract for both voyage and time may be included in the same policy. This is known as a mixed policy. The underwriter is only liable under it when the loss occurs within the insured period and while the ship is on the described voyage.

### Valued Policies

Here the policy specifies the agreed value of the subject matter insured.

### Unvalued Policies

In these, the value of the subject matter is not specified, but is left to be subsequently ascertained, subject to the limit of the sum insured. The insurable value is ascertained as follows.

1. As to the ship, the value includes its outfit, provisions and stores, money advanced for wages, and disbursement to make the ship fit for the voyage, plus the charges of insurance on the whole. In the case of a steamship, it also includes the machinery, boilers, coals and engine stores.
2. As to the freight, the value is the gross freight at the risk of the assured, plus the charges of insurance.
3. As to the goods and merchandise, the value is the prime cost of the property insured, plus the expenses of and incidental to shipping and the charges of insurance.

### Floating Policies

Here the insurance is described in general terms, leaving the name of the ship and other particulars to be defined by subsequent declaration. The subsequent declarations may be made by endorsement on the policy or in other customary manner, and must be made in order of shipment. They must, in the case of goods, comprise all consignments within the terms of the policy, and the value of the goods must be stated.

Open cover is not a policy, but is an agreement by the underwriter to issue an appropriate policy within the terms of the cover. To this extent it resembles a floating policy.

### Average Payment

"Average" in marine insurance means partial loss - under-insurance in the case of other indemnity policies. In this case the average payment will be exactly the proportion of the under-insurance. For example, if in the policy document the value is stated to be £8,000, whereas its actual value is £10,000, any claim will only receive 80% of its value. This is called the "pro rata condition of average".

## *Carriage by Sea*

There are two types of the contract of carriage by sea, also called the contract of affreightment. They are:

1. contracts contained in a charter party; and
2. contracts evidenced by a bill of lading.

If a cargo owner requires a whole ship, he or she will hire it from the shipowners by way of a charter party. If he requires only shipping space in a ship, the terms of his contract with the carrier are normally stated in a bill of lading, If the carrier does not carry the goods of the cargo owner under a contract, which would be a most unusual occurrence, the carrier would be a common carrier.

## *Charter Parties*

The charter partly is a contract whereby the charter hires a ship from the shipowner. Three types of charter party are in use:

1. the voyage charter party;
2. the time charter party; and
3. the charter party by demise.

By the voyage charter party the parties agree that the charterer hires a specified ship for the carriage of cargo from a named port of shipment to a named port of destination for one voyage or several voyages.

Under a time charter party the charterer is entitled for a period of time within agreed limits to decide how the ship shall be used.

Under a charter party by demise the ship is leased to the charterer in a manner which, for the time being, transfers the control over its working and navigation entirely to the charterer.

Voyage and time charters give the charterer only the use of the ship; the master and the crew are provided by the shipowner, who makes their services available to the charterer, and the shipowner remains in possession of the ship. A charter party by demise is less common than the other two types; the charterer is in possession of the ship and puts in his own master and crew.

## *Bills of Lading*

A bill of lading is a document signed by the shipowner, or by the master or agent on behalf of the shipowner, which states that certain goods have been shipped on a particular ship or have been received for payment. On being signed by or on behalf of the carrier, it is handed to the skipper. A bill of lading may be transferred by endorsement and delivery, and in this way the possession of the goods which it represents may be transferred. If it is the intention of the parties then ownership of the goods may also be transferred. However, a bill of lading is not a negotiable instrument and so a transferee normally gets no better title than that of the transferor.

## *Freight*

This is the consideration paid to the carrier for the carriage of the goods. It is only payable if the carrier has delivered the goods or is ready to deliver them. The person liable to pay freight is the shipper of the goods.

## *The Finance of International Trade*

In the international sale of goods, various methods of paying the purchase price are used. The buyer may pay the seller on open account or the seller may allow the buyer credit. The two most common methods are:

1. payment under a collection agreement; and
2. payment under a letter of credit, also called a documentary credit.

## Collection Arrangements

If the collection of the price at the buyer's place is arranged, the seller hands the shipping documents, including the bill of lading to his or her own bank (the remitting bank), which passes them on to a bank at the buyer's place (the collecting bank). The collecting bank then presents the bill of exchange to the buyer and requests him or her to pay or to accept the bill. When the buyer has done so, the collecting bank releases the shipping document to the buyer. The buyer thus receives the original bill of lading, which enables him or her to obtain the goods from the carrier on arrival of the ship.

The collecting bank must not release the shipping documents to the buyer unless it obtains finance from him or her. If it does so contrary to the instructions of the seller, it renders itself liable to him or her. Sometimes, however, the collecting bank, of which the buyer may be a customer, takes this risk and, notwithstanding the contrary instructions of the seller, releases the bill of lading to the buyer. It will try to protect itself by releasing the bill of lading under a trust receipt. This document provides that the buyer constitutes himself or herself a trustee for the bank in three respects:

1. for the bills of lading;
2. for the goods which he or she receives from the ship; and
3. for the proceeds of sale, when he or she resells the goods.

He will then pay the original purchase price to the collecting bank and retain the profits which he has made on the resale of the goods. If the buyer, in breach of his obligations under the trust receipt, pledges the bill of lading to another bank as a security for a loan and the second bank accepts the bill of lading in good faith, the second bank acquires a good title to the bill and the goods, by virtue of the *Factors Act 1889* Section 2(i), and the first bank loses its title.

## Letters of Credit

Of particular importance are letters of credit. This method of payment applies only if the parties to an export transaction have agreed to it in their contract of sale. The buyer instructs a bank in his country (the issuing bank) to open a credit with a bank in the seller's country (the advising bank) in favour of the seller, specifying the documents which the seller has to deliver to the bank if he or she wishes to receive finance. The instructions also specify the date of expiry of the credit.

If the documents tendered by the seller are correct and tendered before the credit has expired, the advising bank pays the seller the purchase price, or accepts his or her bill of exchange drawn on it, or negotiates his or her bill of exchange which is drawn on the buyer. Whether the credit is a payment, acceptance, negotiation or deferred payment credit depends on the arrangement between the seller and the buyer.

## Types of Letters of Credit

Various types of letters of credit are used according to the agreement of the parties to the contract of sale. Whether the credit is revocable or irrevocable depends on the commitment of the issuing bank. Whether it is confirmed or unconfirmed depends on the commitment of the advising bank. These commitments are undertaken to the seller, who is the beneficiary under the credit. The following are the main types of letters of credit.

1. The revocable and unconfirmed letter of credit. Here neither the issuing nor the advising bank enters into a commitment to the seller. The credit may be revoked at any time. A revocable and unconfirmed credit affords little security to the seller that he or she will receive the purchase price through a bank.
2. The irrevocable and unconfirmed letter of credit. Here the authority which the buyer gives the issuing bank is irrevocable and the issuing bank enters into an obligation to the seller to pay. This obligation is likewise irrevocable; the bank has to honour the credit. This, from the point of view of the seller, is a more valuable method of payment than a revocable and unconfirmed letter of credit. The seller can claim that the issuing bank honour the credit, provided that he or she tenders the correct document before the date of expiry of the credit.
3. The irrevocable and confirmed letter of credit. If the advising bank adds its own confirmation of the credit to the seller, the latter has the certainty that a bank in his or her own locality will provide him or her with finance if he or she delivers the correct shipping documents in the stipulated time.
4. The transferable letter of credit. The parties to the contract of sale may agree that the credit shall be transferable. The seller can use such a credit to finance the supply transaction. The buyer opens the credit in favour of the seller, and the seller (who in the supply transaction is the buyer) transfers the same credit to the supplier (who in the supply transaction is the seller). The credit is transferred on the same terms on which the buyer has opened it, except that the amount payable to the supplier is made smaller because the seller wishes to retain his or her profit from the export transaction.

## The Doctrine of Strict Compliance

The banks which operate the documentary credit act as agents for the buyer, who is the principal. If they exceed his instructions, they have acted without authority and he need not ratify the act; the loss will then fall on the bank in question. This has led to the development of the doctrine of strict compliance, under which the correspondent bank will, on principle, refuse documents tendered by the seller which do not correspond strictly with the instructions. "There is no room for documents which are almost the same or which will do just as well" ( Lord Sumner in *Equitable Trust Co of New York v Dawson Partners Ltd (1926)).*

## *Opening of a Letter of Credit*

The credit must be made available to the seller at the beginning of the shipment period. If the parties have not laid down in their contract a time for opening the credit, it must be a reasonable time before the seller has to make shipment.

**Questions**

What is the difference between indemnity insurance and contingency insurance?

In Marine Insurance what is the difference between a charter party and a bill of lading?

# TWENTY ONE

# INTELLECTUAL PROPERTY

*Study Topics*

**The different types of intellectual property**
**Descrition of patent, trademark and copyright**
**Effect of european law on intellectual property**

All these matters are included in the terms intellectual property or industrial property. Included under this term would be plant breeders' rights, registered designs and the new unregistered design right.

Intellectual property is generally taken to describe all those things which emanate from the exercise of the human brain, such as ideas, inventions, poems, designs, etc. When we look at intellectual property we will consider the rights and the protection of these rights that exist over such things as patents, copyright and trademarks. We will see that these rights in the main give to the owner of the rights a monopoly to enjoy the benefits of the invention or the trademark or the writing for a particular period of time. The law gives rights to the owner of the intellectual property so that he may get the benefit from the time and money that he has expended in producing the item.

It should be remembered that usually there will be an overlap of these intellectual property rights. For example, a person may have invented a particular machine and so therefore he will obtain a patent in respect of that invention; there will probably be drawings of the machine and so he will then own the copyright in those drawings. Finally, very often there will be a trademark which will link the machine with his business so that members of the public, when they purchase the machine, can identify the product.

## *Patents*

Patent is the name given to a bundle of monopoly rights which give the patentee the exclusive right to exploit an invention for a stated period of time and to prevent anyone else from exploiting that invention. Because a patent may well have an international application then there has been a certain amount of international cooperation concerning the filing of an application for a patent.

In 1970 the *Patent Cooperation Treaty (PCT)* was entered into and this came into operation in 1978. By this Treaty about 40 States have agreed that their respective national patent offices will accept and accord a priority date to "international applications" which have been filed at an international receiving office within the previous 20 months. The applicant still has to satisfy local requirement in order to obtain his grant. The scheme is operated under the World Intellectual Property Organisation in Geneva.

The European Patent Convention 1973 (EPC) which came into operation in 1978 creates a common system of law for the grant of patents. The steps leading to a grant, as well as the grant itself, are undertaken by the European Patents Office (EPO) in Munich. The application is searched and examined at the European Patent Office and if the invention satisfies the requirements of the Convention then a separate national patent will be granted for each of the specified countries. Thus a single application may result in what has been termed "a bundle of national patents".

At the moment there is no single patent for the whole of the European Union but the Community Patent Convention 1975 (CPC) is designed to provide a patent which will take effect throughout the European Union.

The three requirements which determine whether or not an invention is capable of being patented are:

1. novelty;
2. an invention step;
3. industrial application.

### Novelty

The *Patents Act 1977* contains the law on patents for the United Kingdom and Section 2 of that Act states that

> an invention shall be taken to be new if it does not form part of the state of the art. The state of the art comprises all matters (whether a product, a process, information about either, or anything else) which has any time before the priority date of that invention been made available to the public (whether in the United Kingdom or elsewhere) by written or oral description, by use or in any other way.

Therefore an applicant for a patent must ensure that his invention is new. However there are three cases of prior disclosure which cannot be used for purposes of objecting to the application. These are:

1. disclosures occurring not earlier than six months before the filing date and made in breach of confidence or resulting from such breach or any unlawful acquisition of information;
2. information disclosed at an international exhibition which does not include a trade exhibition;
3. where the applicant claims a novel use of a known substance "for use in a method of treatment of the human or animal body by surgery or therapy or of diagnosis - provided that the former use was not a medical one."

**An Inventive Step**

It is a matter of some difficulty to decide on occasions whether in fact an invention does involve an inventive step. The test is directed to a man skilled in the art. He has been described as "a skilled technician who is well acquainted with workshop techniques and who has carefully read all the relevant literature." *Technograph Printed Circuits Ltd v Mills and Rockley (Electronics) Ltd (1972)*. Therefore if the invention is not obvious to such a person who is skilled in the art then it probably means that an inventive step has been taken by the inventor.

**Capable of Industrial Application**

The third requirement is that the invention should be capable of industrial application. In other words any method of treatment of the human or animal body by surgery or therapy or diagnosis is excluded. Subject to that, the requirement of "capable of industrial application" will be satisfied by any invention if it can be made or used in any kind of industry, including agriculture.

**Owners of the Patent**

Any person may apply for a patent but if the applicant is not the inventor then he must file a statement identifying that person and showing why he is applying for the patent.

A difficulty may sometimes arise where the inventor is an employee. The question may be whether the employee or the employer is the owner of the invention. It is not enough for the employer to show that the invention was made in the course of his employee's duties. Section 9 of the *Patents Act 1977* must go further and show that the duties were the normal duties of the employee or specifically assigned to him or performed by an employee having a special obligation to further the employer's undertaking. Not only that but there is a further requirement that an invention might reasonably have been expected to result from the employee's carrying out those duties. All other employee inventions belong to the employee.

Where an employer obtained a patent in respect of an employee's invention and it is shown that the patent is of great benefit to the employer then the employee inventor may apply under Section 40 to the court or to the Comptroller of Patents for an award of compensation.

If the owner of the patent does not wish to develop the invention himself then he may licence another person to. do so. A licence may be granted orally and may be non-exclusive or exclusive. In the case of an exclusive licence then the licensee can bring infringement proceedings in his own name.

**Infringement**

There will be direct infringement of a patent if a person not entitled to:

1. makes a patented product;
2. disposes or offers to dispose of or import or keep for disposal a patented product;
3. uses a patented process;
4. offers a patented process for use in the United Kingdom when the infringer knows, or it would be obvious to a reasonable person, that its use in the United Kingdom would be an infringement without the consent of the owner of the patent.

There will also be infringement if a person supplies or offers to supply "means essential for putting an invention into effect" to a person not entitled to work the invention.

**Defences**

A person who is accused of infringing a patent has the following defences in addition of course to the main one which is that he holds a licence to use the patent.

1. Acts done privately for non-commercial purposes.
2. Acts done for experimental purposes relating to the subject matter of the invitation.
3. Extemporaneous preparation by pharmacies of individual prescriptions.
4. Certain uses in respect of foreign ships and aircraft temporarily in United

Kingdom jurisdiction.

5. A right to continue to use the invention which had been commenced before the priority date of the patent.

### Revocation of a Patent

Obviously a person will only be guilty of infringing a patent if in fact the patent has been validly granted in the first place. It follows therefore that if the defendant can show that the patent should never have been granted hen that will be an adequate defence. A patent may be revoked because:

1. the invention is not a patentable invention - the ground most frequently invoked in practice;
2. the patent was granted to a person not entitled to the grant;
3. the specification lacks the clarity and completeness required for the invention to be performed by a person skilled in the art;
4. the matter disclosed in the specification of a patent extends beyond that disclosed in the applications filed;
5. protection has been extended by an amendment which should not have been allowed.

These issues may be related by way of defence or counter-claim to an action for infringement:

1. by applying to the comptroller or court for an order revoking the patent or by applying to the comptroller or court for a declaration that an act or proposed act does not infringe, the applicant having failed to obtain an acknowledgement to like effect from the patentee;
2. by instituting proceedings for groundless threats;
3. at the instance of the Crown in proceedings relating to use for Crown services.

### Remedies for Infringement

Before the trial it may be possible to use an action for discovery as explained in *Norwich Pharmacal v Customs and Excise (1974)*. There is also an Anton Piller Order which compels the defendant to permit entry and search and to deliver into the custody of the plaintiff documents and articles specified in the order. Finally, before action, an interlocutory injunction may be obtained. The principles on which this may be awarded are contained in *American Cyanamid v Ethicon (1975)*. They are that the plaintiff should satisfy the court:

1. that should he succeed at the trial damages would not compensate him for the continuance of the activity complained of until final judgment;
2. that should he lose at the trial (having been granted such relief) the defendant will be adequately compensated by damages payable pursuant to the normal

undertaking required of the plaintiff.

As for final orders which the court may grant, these are as follows.

1. Damages: the award of damages is subject to some limitations and will not be made if the defendant can prove that he was not aware and had no reasonable grounds for supposing that the patent existed.
2. Account of profits: this is an equitable remedy and may be awarded as an alternative to damages. It may be applied for where the provable loss is less that the ill-gotten gains.
3. Order of delivery up or destruction of infringing goods: this is another equitable remedy designed to reinforce an injunction. It is usual for the defendant to be given a choice between the destruction of the goods or delivering them up.

### Final Injunction

In the case of a continuing infringement or where there is a possibility that the infringement may be repeated then an injunction may be asked for.

## *Copyright*

The law relating to copyright may be found in the *Copyright Act 1956* and more recently in the *Copyright Designs and Patents Act 1988.* Copyright is intended to protect the skill, labour and effort which have been expended in producing the work. The author of the work is the only one with a right to copy it in the sense of using it again or publishing it. It follows therefore that no-one else has this right. Copyright arises merely by bringing a work into existence. Unlike a patent there is no need for any registration.

The owner of a copyright, in the same way as the owner of a patent, owns a monopoly. However in the case of copyright the monopoly of its owner is only of a limited variety. The owner of a patent has complete control over the marketability of the invention patented. In the case of copyright the owner can prevent other people from copying his work; but similar works may continue to be produced by competitors.

### Subject Matter of the Copyright

Section 1 of the 1988 Act states that copyright is a property right which subsists in an original literary, dramatic, musical or artistic works; sound recordings, film, broadcast or cable programmes; and typographical arrangements of published editions.

The definition of these terms is quite wide. For example, literary works would include any table or compilation or a computer program. Also artistic works would include a graphic work, a photograph or a sculpture irrespective of any artistic quality. Thus in this way the football association own the copyright in the fixtures list to be played by the football clubs of this country.

### Ownership of Copyright

The first owner of copyright is the author of the work and this means the person who created the work. In the case of employer and employee then if the employee produces any literary, dramatic, musical or artistic work in the course of his employment then the employer will own the copyright. In any other case the author will own the copyright himself.

Under the 1956 Act there were commissioning conditions which meant that when a person commissioned for payment the taking of a photograph or painting or drawing of a portrait then the copyright belongs to the person who commissioned the work. There is no similar provision in the 1988 Act and so the first ownership of the copyright will belong to the author of the work. However, an exception exists in the case of a design right when the design is created following a commission by a person. In that case the commissioner owns the design right. Naturally, this position can be reversed by the making of a contract in writing between the commissioner and the author of the work by which the copyright in the finished work will in fact become the property of the commissioner.

A copyright may be assigned and this must be in writing signed by or on behalf of the assignor. In addition copyright may be transmitted by testamentary disposition or by operation of law as in the case of personal property. An example of this occurred when Agatha Christie left the copyright in her play *The Mousetrap* by will to her nephew who will of course continue to receive royalties in respect of the production of the play.

### Period of Protection

The *Copyright, Designs and Patents Act 1988* provides that a literary, dramatic, musical or artistic work would be protected up to the end of the 50th year from the end of the calendar year of the author's death. However, starting on 1 July 1995, throughout the European Community, copyright protection has been extended from 50 to 70 years after death. Furthermore, this European Directive has retroactive effect. Consequently some work which was out of copyright on 30 May was back in copyright just over a month later.

### Moral Rights

Sections 77-89 of the 1988 Act create new moral rights for English law. These have been introduced to enable the United Kingdom to comply with the Berne Convention. These so-called "moral rights" may be conferred upon the author of a copyright work and these are:

1. the paternity right, that is a right to be identified as the author of a copyright work;
2. the integrity right, that is a right not to suffer derogatory treatment of the work.

The paternity right must be specifically asserted by the author and this is increasingly being done in new editions of books. The right not to suffer derogatory treatment is defined in the Act as "a distortion or mutilation of the work or treatment prejudicial to the honour or reputation of the author".

### Copyright Infringement

Under both the 1956 and the 1988 Acts the copyright owner may ask the court for an injunction to prevent the continuation of the infringement. He may also claim damages for the loss he has suffered or an account of profits gained as a result of the infringement. Exceptions to infringement include dealing for the purposes of research and private study or for the purposes of criticism or review. Reproduction for the purposes of judicial proceedings or for certain educational purposes.

## *Unregistered Design Right*

Prior to the 1988 Act protection of an industrial design could be made by a registration under the *Registered Designs Act 1949* but this would only apply if the design had an aesthetic value. Protection still existed under the *Copyright Act 1956* but this was usually not used to any extent. However the protection under the *Copyright Act* has now, by Section 51 of the 1988 Act, been withdrawn to the extent that the article is not itself an artistic work. In its place a new design right has been created by Sections 213-264 of the 1988 Act. In the same way as copyright, protection of an unregistered design right will arise automatically and no registration is required. However there must exist documentary proof of the industrial design. Section 213(2) states that a design is "any aspect of the shape or configuration (whether internal or external) of the whole or part of an article".

Section 213(3) states what an industrial design is not: it is not (a) a method of principle of construction; (b) features of shape or configuration which enable an article to be connected to, or placed in, around or against, another article so that either article may perform its function (the "must fit" exception); (c) features of shape or configuration dependent upon the appearance of another article of which the article is intended by the designer to former an integral part ("the must match" exception); (d) surface decoration.

The owner of a design right has the right to reproduce the design for commercial purposes.

### Infringement

The owner of a design right may sue for damages, ask for an injunction or an account of profits. The defendant may have a defence as regards damages if he can show that he infringed the design right "innocently".

### Ownership of the Design Right

The designer of the original design is the first owner of the design subject to two exceptions:

1. if the design is created in the course of employment, then the ownership belongs to the employer;
2. designs created under a commission belong to the person who commissioned them.

The period of protection for a design right expires ten years after the first marketing of articles made from the design, subject to an overall limit of 15 years from creation of the design if there has been a delay in marketing the article. In the last five years' licences of right will be available. The terms of these licences will be settled by the Comptroller of Patents in the absence of agreement.

## *Trademarks*

A trademark is any word or symbol or combination of both which is used to indicate a connection in the course of trade between the goods in relation to which the mark is used and the owner of the mark. Such trademarks are protected by the common law of "passing off" and under the *Trademarks Act 1994.*

### Passing Off

This is a common law tort and has been described by the House of Lords: "The principle of law may be very plainly stated, that nobody has the right to represent his goods as the goods of somebody else."

The most recent case which contains the judgment of Lord Diplock in *Warninck v Townend (1980)*. In that case Lord Diplock stated "there are five characteristics which must be present in order to create a valid cause of action for passing off:

1. a misrepresentation;
2. made by the trader in the course of trade;
3. to prospective customers of his or ultimate customers of goods or services supplied by him;
4. which is calculated to injure the business or goodwill of another trader (in the sense that this is a reasonably foreseeable consequence);
5. which causes actual damage to the business or goodwill of the trader by whom the action is brought or will probably do so.

It is the case that the plaintiff in a passing off action may need to show the defendant is engaged in competing business activities. If in fact the defendant is in a totally different line of business then the plaintiff will be in difficulties in convincing the court that there has in fact been confusion in the public mind.

As regards remedies, a plaintiff who is successful will be entitled to an injunction and to damages or an account of profits. He may also obtain an order for obliteration or modification of the mark, name or wording complained of.

**Registered Trademarks**

The present Act is the *Trademarks Act 1994*. This replaces the *Trademarks Act 1938*. It was passed to implement Directive 89/104 E.C. which had as its object the approximation of the rules of the Member States relating to trade marks. It also makes provisions in connection with Regulation 40/94 on the CTM (Community Trademark).

Section 1 provides that a trademark is: "Any sign capable of being represented graphically which is capable of distinguishing goods or services of one undertaking from those of other undertakings". It may consist of words (including personal names), designs, letters, or the shape of goods or their packaging.

Signs which do not satisfy this provision are excluded, including marks with no distinctive character, or solely designating the kind, quality, intended purpose, value, geographical origin, the time of production of goods or of rendering of services, or other characteristics of goods or services, and marks which have become customary: S.3(1). A shape cannot be registered if it results from the nature of the goods themselves, or is necessary to obtain a technical result or to give substantial value to them: S.3(2). Registration is also refused for marks contrary to public policy or accepted principles of morality or likely to deceive the public as to the nature, quality or geographical origin of the goods or services: S.3(3).

Marks cannot be registered if identical to an earlier trademark covering identical goods or services, or where similarity of mark and goods or services is likely to cause confusion to the public. This extends to unregistered marks protected by any rule of law (that is, passing off), or protected in any other form, that is copyright, design right or registered designs: S.5.

**Application for Registration**

Application is to the Registrar and must contain (i) a request for registration; (ii) the name and address of the applicant; (iii) a statement of the goods or services for which registration is sought; and (iv) a representation of the mark. The application must state that the mark is being used by or with the consent of the applicant in relation to those goods or services, or that he has a bona fide intention that it should be so used; and be accompanied by an application fee and the appropriate class fees: S.32. Goods and services are classified according to a prescribed system and questions concerning the class of goods or services is determined by the Registrar: S.34. Trademarks are registered in respect of particular goods or classes of goods, and most countries follow the International Classification of Goods Convention.

A person has priority for registering the trademark for some or all of the same goods or services for six months from filing the first application: S.35(1). If application is made within that period, the relevant date for establishing precedence is the date of filing the first application, and the registrability is not affected by any use of the mark in the UK in the period between that date and the date of the application: S.35(2). Equivalent filing in a Convention country gives rise to the same priority right: S.35(3).

The Registrar carries out a search of earlier trademarks. The applicant must be informed if the requirements for registration are not met and have the opportunity to make representations or to amend the application. The Registrar can accept or reject the applications: S.37. If the registration is accepted, the application is published to give persons the opportunity to oppose the registration within a prescribed time: S.38. The applicant may withdraw his application or restrict the goods or services covered by the application. If the application has been published, notification of withdrawal must also be published. Otherwise an application can only be amended in relation to the name and address of the applicant, errors of wording or of copying, or obvious mistakes and then only where the correction does not substantially affect the identity of the mark or extend the goods or services covered by the application: S.39.

**Validity of a Trade Mark**

Registered marks are valid for ten years and renewable for further periods of ten years under Section 42. If registration is not renewed, the Registrar shall remove the trademarks from the register: S.43. A registered trademark cannot be altered during the period of registration or on renewal, except in respect of alteration of the proprietor's name and address where the mark includes this: S.44. The registered mark is subject to surrender, revocation and invalidity. It may be surrendered in respect of some or all of the goods or services for which it is registered: S.45. The mark may be revoked on the grounds:

1. that within the five years following registration it has not been put to genuine use in the UK by the proprietor or with his consent and there are no proper reasons for the non-use;
2. that such use has been suspended for an uninterrupted period of five years without proper reasons;
3. that, in consequence of acts or inactivity of the proprietor, it has become the common name in the trade for a product or service for which it is registered;
4. that, in consequence of the use made of it by the proprietor or with his consent, it is liable to mislead the public, particularly as to the nature, quality or geographical origin of the goods or services for which it is registered: S.46(1)

The registration can be invalidated on application to the Registrar or the court and, where it is declared invalid, the registration shall be deemed never to have been made.

**Ownership, Assignment and Licensing**

When a trademark is granted to two or more persons, each is entitled to an equal undivided share in the mark, subject to any agreement to the contrary. A registered trademark is transmissible by assignment, testamentary disposition or operation of law in the same way as other personal property and in connection with the goodwill of a business or independently. An assignment or transmission may be partial in that it is for only some of the goods or services for which it is registered, or for use in a particular manner or a particular locality. The assignment must be in writing signed by or on behalf of the assignor or a personal representative or, in the case of a company, by the affixing of a corporate seal. A registered trademark can be charged as security for a loan.

The Act provides for the registration of transactions affecting registered trade marks. Registrable transactions include:

1. assignment of a mark or any right in it;
2. the grant of any licence under a registered trademark;
3. the granting of any security interest (whether fixed or floating) over a registered trade mark or any right in or under it;
4. the making by personal representatives of an assent in relation to a registered trademark or any right in or under it;
5. an order of the court or other competent authority transferring a registered trademark or any right in or under it.

### Licensing

A licence to use a registered trademark may be general or limited and the limited licence may relate to some but not all of the goods or services for which the mark is registered. The licence must be in writing, signed by or on behalf of the grantor, or by the affixing of a corporate seal in the case of a company. The Act allows for a sublicense granted by a licensee. An exclusive licence means a licence, whether general or limited, authorising the licensee to the exclusion of all other persons, including the grantor, to use a registered mark in the manner authorised.

The Act also introduces character licensing which means that rights can be granted for the use of imagery in association with products or services. Manufacturers may thus be permitted to use a character in a variety of products.

### Rights of the Registered Proprietor

The proprietor has exclusive rights in the registered trademark which are infringed by use of the trademark in the UK without his consent. Infringing acts include the use by a person of a registered trademark in the course of a trade which is:

1. identical with the trademark in relation to identical goods or services for which it is registered;
2. identical with the trademark and used in relation to similar goods or services to those for which the trademark is registered; or the sign is similar and is used in relation to identical or similar goods or services for which the mark is registered and there is the likelihood of confusion on the part of the public;
3. identical with or similar to the trademark, and used in relation to non-similar goods or services for which the trademark is registered where the trademark has a reputation in the UK and the use takes unfair advantage of or is detrimental to the distinctive character or the repute of the mark.

A person uses a sign if he:

1. affixes it to goods or the packaging thereof;
2. offers or exposes goods for sale, puts them on the market or stocks them for those purposes under the sign, or offers or supplies services under the sign;
3. imports or exports goods under the sign; and
4. uses the sign on business papers or in advertising.

A person who applies a mark to material to be used for labelling or packaging goods, as a business paper, or for advertising goods or services, is a party to any use of the material which infringes the mark if he knew or had reason to believe that the application was not duly authorised by the proprietor or licensee of the mark.

A registered trademark is not infringed by the use of another registered trademark in relation to goods or services for which the latter is registered but subject to the fact that the registration of a trademark may be declared invalid as being in breach of S.3; in which case it is deemed never to have been registered. There is also no infringement by:

1. the use by a person of his own name or address;
2. the use of indications concerning the kind, quality, quantity, intended purpose, value, geographical origin, the time of production of goods or of rendering of services, or other characteristics of goods or services; or
3. the use of the trademark where it is necessary to indicate the intended purpose of a product or service (in particular as accessories or spare parts), provided the use accords with honest industrial or commercial practices.

**Remedies for Infringement**

Infringement is actionable by the proprietor and all such relief by way of damages, injunctions, accounts or otherwise is available to him as in respect of the infringement of any other property right. There are two specific remedies.

1. Order for erasure of offending sign. The court may order a person who has infringed a trade mark to cause the offending sign to be erased, removed or obliterated from any infringing goods, material or articles in his possession, custody or control, or to secure the destruction of the infringing goods, material or articles in question.
2. Order for delivery up of infringing goods, materials or articles. Infringing goods, material and articles are defined. However an application for an order may not be made after the end of the period of six years from
   i. in the case of infringing goods, the date on which the trademark was applied to the goods or their packaging;
   ii. in the case of infringing material, the date on which the trade mark was applied to the material; or
   iii. in the case of infringing articles, the date on which they were made.

The six-year limit is extended where the proprietor of the registered trademark was under a disability or prevented by fraud or concealment from discovering the facts entitling him to apply for an order.

Where infringing goods, material or articles have been delivered up, an application may be made that they be destroyed or forfeited to such persons as the court thinks fit. If no order is made, the person in whose possession, custody or control they were before being delivered up is entitled to their return. A person threatened with proceedings for groundless infringement proceedings can claim relief including a declaration that the threats are unjustifiable, an injunction against continuance of the threats and damages in respect of any loss sustained. He is entitled to relief if he can show that registration is invalid or liable to be revoked in a relevant respect.

Unauthorised use of a trade mark in relation to goods is a criminal offence unless the person shows that he had reasonable grounds to believe that the use of the sign was not an infringement. The person is liable on summary conviction to imprisonment for a term not exceeding six months or a fine not exceeding the statutory maximum, or both, and on conviction on indictment to a fine or imprisonment for a term not exceeding ten years, or both.

## *Intellectual Property and the European Union*

It is of course a fundamental principle of the European Union that competition for goods or services is the best way of keeping prices down and ensuring that industrial output keeps pace with existing consumer demand.

Articles 30-36 of the Treaty of Rome intend to prohibit any unjustifiable restriction upon the goods that can be imported into or exported from one Member State to another.

Article 85 prohibits the operation of cartels and agreements with the effect of distorting or preventing competition.

Article 85 prohibits the abuse of a position of dominance within the Union by any commercial undertaking.

Thus it is apparent that when one considers that the purpose of intellectual property is to grant to the owners of such property exclusive rights then this is in conflict with the European Union's principle.

The European Court of Justice has attempted to resolve the conflict between the pro-competitive and anti-competitive laws by stating that there is a distinction between the existence of intellectual property rights and the exercise of these rights. The existence of these intellectual property rights is a matter for each Member State. The exercise of them is a matter for Community law.

Thus intellectual property rights may continue to be used provided that by making use of such rights then prohibitions or restrictions are not merely a means of arbitrary discrimination nor are they a disguised restriction on trade.

In *Deutsche Grammophon v Metro-SB Grosstmarkte (1971)* it was held that Article 36 permitted a departure from the provisions of Articles 30 and 34 of the Treaty of Rome but only to the "extent to which they are justified for the purpose of safeguarding rights which constitute the specific subject matter of such property".

In the case of a patent the specific subject matter is the right to exploit an invention by manufacturing and selling a product coupled with the right to prevent an infringement by a third party. This was established in *Centrafarm B V v Stirling Drug Inc (1974).*

*Centrafarm v Winthrop B V (1974)* established that the specific subject matter of a trademark was the grant to the holder of the exclusive right to use the mark and to be the first to market the product under that mark. This principle was extended in *Centrafarm v American Home Products (1979)* and now includes the right of the proprietor to prohibit the repackaging of a product to which the trademark has been affixed by a person without authority.

Article 36 provides

> the provisions of Articles 30-34 shall not preclude prohibitions or restrictions on imports, exports or goods in transit justified on grounds of public morality, public policy or public security; the protection of health and life of humans, animals or plants; the protection of national treasures possessing artistic, historic or archaeological value; or the protection of industrial and commercial property. Such prohibitions or restrictions shall not, however, constitute a means of arbitrary discrimination or disguised restriction on trade between Member States.

*Merck and Co Inc. v Stephar B V (1981)* the European Court held that a patentee may not exercise his rights so as to exclude from one market goods which he has marketed in another member State.

In *Van Zuylen Freres v Hag A G (1974)* the European Court held where trademarks share a common origin, the user of a mark in one Member State may not use his rights to exclude the goods of the user in another Member State. "Common origin" means that the trademark was originally owned by the same undertaking even though ownership had subsequently become split. This might have occurred because of a takeover or a merger.

Apart from Articles 30 and 34 which are concerned with the free movement of goods Articles 85 and 86 may also be affected by intellectual property rights. Article 85 is most likely to apply to an agreement for the exploitation of an intellectual property right. This probably would be a licence granted by the owner of the right to another to manufacture and sell the product which may be restrictive in its terms. Such an agreement would probably come within the terms of the block exemption on patent licensing.

In the same way Article 86 may be considered in connection with intellectual property rights because it is true to say that the owner of any such right has a dominant position in respect of the subject matter of that particular right. However in both these cases the Commission will only be concerned if it can be shown that fair trading has been affected.

As regards the future it is fairly certain that intellectual property law will be harmonised within the European Union. The greatest amount of progress has been made towards a common trademark law. As regards patents the majority of the Member States of the European Union have basically identical laws regarding patentability. A Union Patent Convention which would provide one single patent is quite likely to come into force in the near future.

The least amount of progress has been made in copyright as there appears to be the greatest amount of divergence in copyright law in the various Member States of the Union. There is a proposed directive on software protection which was published in 1988 and so it may be that any advance in harmonisation in copyright law will come through this channel.

**Questions**

What are the requirements for patenting an invention?

What is an unregistered design right?

What may result in the revocation of a trade mark?

TWENTY TWO

# NEGOTIABLE INSTRUMENTS GENERALLY

*Study Topics*

**Definition of a bill of exchange**
**Rules of acceptance**
**Meaning of holder in due course**

Most people's experiences of negotiable instruments in everyday life are in the form of cheques. A cheque is also a "Bill of Exchange" and a "Chose in Action". These terms are explained below and in the next chapter.

Property comprises anything that a person may own and remember that the word "own" means "has a right to". As always the law is concerned with the rights of persons. A person may own either land or anything which is not land called personal property.

The law relating to land is a complex subject on its own so we can ignore that for our present purposes. Let us consider personal property. This is a wide division of property and in itself it may be sub-divided into tangible things and intangible things. Tangible things are designated by the old Norman French phrase "choses in possession". Such things can be seen, touched and counted.

Intangible things are called "choses in action". This is because, as they cannot be seen and touched, then ownership of them can only be evidenced by a piece of paper (an instrument). So oranges can be seen and counted: they are choses in possession. The same applies to coins in my pocket. Instead of the oranges it may be that a cargo of oranges is being transported to this country and before they arrive they may be sold. The buyer can be given a document called a bill of lading which is evidence of his rights to the oranges when they arrive. Instead of the coins in my pocket, I can have a postal order or a cheque entitling me to the amount of the coins. The bill of lading, the postal order and the cheque all entitle the owner of these instruments to something, either the oranges or the money, but of course they are worthless themselves. It is only because of the form of the documents and what they contain that they entitle the owners to something of value. Admittedly, to say that a chose in action is a piece of paper is not entirely accurate because the goodwill of a business or the copyright of an author are choses in action but they are not evidenced by pieces of paper. One other principle of law must be observed here: ownership is a right to something.

When one buys goods one is hoping to acquire a right of ownership in the goods. It follows that if A has stolen something from B and then sells it to C, C will not become the owner, because A did not have the right of ownership and so is not in the position of being able to pass a right of ownership on to C. The principle applies to the transfer of choses in possession, and also to the transfer of choses in action generally.

## *The Transfer of a Chose in Action*

A piece of land may only be transferred by means of a document called "a conveyance" or more correctly the legal ownership of a piece of land is transferred by a conveyance.

A chose in possession in transferred by delivery. Indeed, ownership is usually presumed to reside in the person who has possession of the chose in possession. This is sometimes described by the phrase "possession is nine-tenths of the law".

A chose in action however must usually be transferred in a particular manner laid down by law. Thus to transfer a share certificate it is necessary to use a share transfer form and complete it with the details of the transferee and the company whose shares they are must be notified of the transfer. Finally, the principle regarding the right of ownership also applies; so if a person transfers a chose in action to which he does not have the right of ownership then the transferee will likewise not get a good title

Some choses in action entitle the holder to goods but a number of them entitle the holder to a sum of money. As money is so vitally important in commercial transactions it gradually became desirable to have some rather less formal system of transferring a right to a sum of money. Thus it was that certain choses in action began to be treated differently from others: the need for a formal method of transfer was abolished, it was no longer necessary to notify the person who ultimately would be called upon to make payment, of the transfer. Most importantly of all, the transferee of these special choses in action would get a good title to it, in certain cases, even though the transferor did not have a good title. This last point was of particular importance and in fact is the basis of negotiability. The choses in action which received this special treatment became known as negotiable instruments. They include:

1. bills of exchange including cheques
2. promissory notes

3. divided warrants
4. bearer bonds
5. bearer scrips
6. debentures payable to bearer
7. share warrants
8. treasury bills.

The attributes common to these documents are as follows.

1. They are transferable merely by delivery if payable to bearer, or by endorsement if payable to order.
2. The party who will be called upon to pay on the document need not be notified of the transfer.
3. The transferee who takes in good faith and for value will get a good title notwithstanding any defect in the title of the transferor.

This last point requires some clarification. The transferee is known as the holder of the negotiable instrument. In order to get a good title to it he must have given value for it and the document itself must have been in order. If the document contains a forged indorsement for example, the person to whom it was transferred will not become the owner of it.

Example 1: A draws a cheque payable to bearer and gives it to B. X steals the cheque and gives it to C, to whom he owes money for goods he has purchased. C is the owner of the cheque, provided he took it in good faith.

Example 2: A draws an order cheque payable to B. X steals the cheque and gives it to C to whom he owes money for goods he has purchased. X will of course have to forge B's indorsement and so even though C took the cheque in good faith he will not be the owner of it because of the forgery.

This then is the essence of negotiability. Of the instruments which are negotiable we shall only be concerned with bills of exchange, including cheques. Finally it should be remembered that in this context negotiable does not mean transferable. It refers to the fact that in certain cases a person may become the legal owner of an instrument even though he received it from someone who was not the owner.

Example 3: A cheque marked "not negotiable" may still be transferred. However the person who receives it will get no better title than that of the person from whom he received it.

## *Bill of Exchange*

Let us now consider the operation of a bill of exchange. Say a manufacturer sold goods to a wholesaler for £1,000 and he in turn sold them to the retailer for £1,000. For the sake of simplicity let us ignore any profit margin. So W owes £1,000 to M and R owes £1,000 to W.

Assuming M and W had no more money and also, as is quite likely, W had given R the retailer three months' credit, the situation is that W cannot pay M until he is paid by R and R does not have to pay for three months. Thus all the parties are at a standstill for three months.

£1,000 £1,000

R ——————— W ——————— M

However a bill of exchange would be used to break the impasse. W could draw a bill on R for £1,000 payable in three months' time. He could do this because R owes him the money. Also as W owes M £1,000 it would be convenient if R were ordered to pay M. So the bill is drawn by W (the drawer) on R (the drawee) by which R is ordered to pay M (the payee) £1,000 in three months' time. The bill is then given to M who can do any of three things.

1. M can do nothing and wait for payment from the drawee for three months. Even here he is better off with the bill than without it because if he has difficulty in getting payment at least he has a signed acknowledgement by W (who has signed the bill as drawer) that he owes M £1,000.
2. M can sell the bill or discount it as it is called. If he does this he will receive £1,000 less the interest on that sum for three months, plus handling charges.
3. M can use the bill as cash and transfer it to some person to whom he owes £1,000. In this way the bill may be passed from hand-to-hand until the time when the three months have expired (the bill is said to have matured) when the person who is the holder at that time can obtain his money from the drawee.

**Definition of a Bill (Bills of Exchange Act 1882)**

It must be an unconditional order in writing. Usually the word "Pay" is used. It must not be mere request. However an order may still be unconditional if it is coupled with

1. an indication of the particular fund out of which the drawer is to reimburse himself or a particular account to be debited with the amount;
2. a statement of the transaction which gives rise to the bill.

Where a cheque bears a receipt form on the back the test to determine whether it is a valid bill is whether the direction is addressed to the drawee or the payee. If it is addressed to the drawee the bill is invalid.

The order must be for a sum certain in money. However the money can be paid with interest at a stated rate, by instalments or in foreign currency according to a rate of exchange. There must be a certain or determinable time of payment. Thus the bill may be payable:

1. on demand or at sight or on presentation;
2. at a fixed period after date or sight;
3. on or at a fixed period after a person's death.

The bill must be payable to a payee who can be identified or to the order of that person or to bearer.

At this point one must remember that law is concerned with the rights of people and relating this to bills of exchange it is concerned with the rights of persons to the bill. If a person is the lawful owner of a bill then he can enforce his rights on it against anyone who has signed it. Initially only the drawer's signature will appear on the bill, it is then given to the payee. It is only natural that if it is a time bill (one payable at some future date) then it would be advisable to ask the person who eventually will be called upon to pay up to promise that he will make payment on that future date. This person is the drawee and so usually a bill will be presented to him for acceptance.

### Acceptance of a Bill

When the drawee signifies that he has accepted the bill he must write "accepted" on the bill and sign it. His acceptance may be general or qualified. If it is qualified in any way then the payee may treat the bill as dishonoured by non-acceptance.

### General Acceptance

In this case the drawer agrees to fulfil all the terms of the order of the drawer without qualification.

### Qualified Acceptance

This expressly varies the effect of the bill as drawn. In other words, the drawee states by his acceptance that he does not propose to honour all the terms of the order in the bill. It must be emphasised that a qualified acceptance does not make the order of the bill conditional. It is still unconditional and so the bill remains valid. This is because the drawee is not giving any order. There are five types of qualified acceptance:

1. Conditional: this makes the payment by the acceptor dependent on the fulfilment of a condition stated in the acceptance, for example "Accepted, payable on

giving up a bill of lading for 76 bags of seed."

2. Partial: an acceptance to pay part only of the amount for which the bill is drawn, for example bill drawn for £500 and accepted, as to £300.
3. Local: acceptance to pay only at a particular place, for example "Accepted payable at Barclays Bank, only." If the word "only" is omitted, the acceptance is general.
4. Qualified as to time: for example a bill drawn payable thirty days after date, accepted payable forty days after date.
5. Acceptance by one or more of the drawees but not all: for example where a bill is drawn on X, Y, Z is accepted by X and Y but not Z.

**Effect of a Qualified Acceptance**

1. A holder may refuse to take a qualified acceptance and if he does not obtain an unqualified acceptance he may treat the bill as dishonoured (S.41(1)).
2. If a qualified acceptance is taken and the drawer or indorser has not expressly or impliedly authorised the holder to take a qualified acceptance, or does not subsequently assent to it, such drawer or indorser is discharged from his liability on the bill.
3. In the case of a partial acceptance, the holder may take it and subsequently notify the drawer and indorsers without discharging them from liability.
4. A foreign bill which has been partially accepted must be protested as to the balance (S.44(2)).

**Presentment for Acceptance**

Presentation for acceptance is essential only in three cases (Section 39):

1. Where a bill is payable after sight then presentation for acceptance is necessary in order to fix maturity date of the bill.
2. Where a bill is drawn payable elsewhere than at the residence or place of business of the drawee.
3. Where the bill expressly stipulates that it shall be presented for acceptance.

Apart from Section 39, bills should be presented for the following two reasons:

1. Once the drawee accepts, he becomes liable on it.
2. If he refuses to accept, the holder has an immediate right to sue all prior parties without having to wait until the date of maturity.

Where a drawee accepts a bill payable elsewhere than at this residence or place of business, the bill is said to be "domiciled" at the place of payment. Unless a banker has expressly or impliedly agreed to pay bills domiciled with him, he is under no legal obligation to do so even though the customer has a balance sufficient to cover the bills.

If the banker pays, the relationship between him and the customer then is not debtor and creditor, but principal and agent.

**Presentment for Payment**

By Section 5(1) a general acceptance by the drawee to pay at maturity makes him liable and presentment to him for payment is not necessary. Presentment for payment is necessary where the acceptance is qualified. The rules concerning presentment for payment are similar to those for acceptance but in this case emphasis is placed upon presentment at the proper place. This is defined in Section 45(4) as the place of payment specified in the bill; if no place is specified then at the address of the drawee or acceptor given in the bill or his last known place of business or ordinary residence.

The time for presentment for payment is the last day of the time for payment or if that is not a business day then the succeeding business day. If the bill is payable after a period of time after date, after sight or after the happening of a specified event, the time for payment is determined by excluding the day from which the time is to begin to run and by including the day of payment.

**Dishonour**

A bill may be dishonoured by non-acceptance or by non-payment. If a bill is drawn payable on demand then the drawee must pay when it is presented to him. If he does not, then the payee may treat the bill as dishonoured by non-payment. If the bill is payable at some future time then it may have been accepted but when the holder comes to present the bill for payment it may again be dishonoured by non-payment. If a bill is dishonoured for whatever reason, the holder may enforce his rights against anyone who has signed the bill. In order to do this he must notify the drawer and each indorsee of the fact that the bill has been dishonoured. In practice the holder notifies his previous indorser, who notifies his previous indorser and so on. In this way everyone who is liable on the bill is informed of his liability. By Section 52(3), notice of dishonour is not necessary to render the acceptor/drawee liable.

By Section 48(1) if a bill is dishonoured for non-acceptance and notice of dishonour is not given, the rights of a subsequent holder in due course are not affected by the failure to give notice. For example, A draws on B in favour of C (payee) who indorses it to D, D presents the bill to B who refuses to accept. The bill is dishonoured by non-acceptance (S.43(1)). D, the holder, must give notice of dishonour to A (drawer) and C (indorser) before he can enforce his rights against them. If he fails to do so A and C will be discharged. However, if he subsequently negotiates it to a holder in due course (say E), E can sue A and C and is not prejudiced by D's failure to give notice.

1. To be a holder in due course, E must take the bill without notice that it had been previously dishonoured.
2. If the bill had been dishonoured by non-payment there cannot be a subsequent holder in due course because the bill is then overdue. (See S.29).

The rules as to the giving of notice of dishonour are set out in Section 49. These require that the holder of the bill must give notice of dishonour, verbally or in writing or by the return of the bill, to anyone whom he intends to make liable on the bill. In practice he will merely notify his previous transferor. The notice of dishonour may be given as soon as the bill is dishonoured and must be given within a reasonable time. That means:

1. where the person giving and the person to receive notice reside in the same place the notice must be given or sent off in time to reach the latter on the day after dishonour of the bill;
2. where the person giving and the person to receive notice reside in different places, the notice must be sent off on the day after the dishonour of the bill, and if there be no such post on that day then by the next post thereafter.

Notice is deemed to have been given if it was duly addressed and posted, even if it was lost in the post. The rules as to delay and excuses in giving notice of dishonour are contained in section 50.

**Noting and Protesting**

When a bill is dishonoured a distinction is made between an inland and foreign bills. An inland bill is one which is drawn in the British Isles on a British resident; in any other case the bill is a foreign bill. When a foreign bill is dishonoured then it must be "noted and protested".

1. Noting: where a bill has been dishonoured the holder takes it to a notary public who then represents the bill. If it is again dishonoured, he notes on it:
   i. the date;
   ii. a reference to his register;
   iii. the noting changes; and
   iv. his initials.

He will also attach a ticket stating the answer given when the presentment was made.

2. Protesting: this consists of the obtaining of a certificate from a notary public attesting the dishonour of the bill. The certificate is a formal declaration signed by the notary public. It must contain a copy of the bill. The details of a protest are given in Section 51(7).

Where a bill requires to be protested and a notary public is not available, any householder or substantial resident of the place may, in the presence of two witnesses, give a certificate signed by them attesting the dishonour of the bill. A specimen form of "house-holder's protest" is given in the First Schedule to the Act.

A protest must be made by the day following the day of dishonour. In order to extend this period of time the dishonour of the bill may be noted and then a protest may be made at any time after the noting.

Noting and protesting are essential in the case of a foreign bill because the procedure provides evidence of the dishonour which will be acceptable to foreign courts. In addition an inland bill must be protested if payment from a referee in case of need is requested. A referee in case of need is a person whose name is inserted on the bill by the drawer to whom the holder may turn for acceptance or payment should the drawee refuse to accept it or pay upon it. In the same way a person may intervene if a bill is dishonoured, and accept the bill or pay it for the honour of a person who is liable. Legal proof of payment for honour should always be obtained, this is "a notarial act of honour".

**Transfer of a Bill**

Once issued a bill may then be transferred from one person to another and of course what is actually being transferred is the right to the sum of money that the bill will entitle the holder to receive. If the bill is made payable to bearer then it may be transferred by simple delivery and the holder of such a bill will be the person who has possession of it.

If the bill is made payable to a named payee or order, then it is an order bill. It may be transferred by the payee indorsing the bill, designating the indorsee and giving delivery to him. The indorsee will then become the holder.

**Holder in Due Course**

As was mentioned earlier, a feature of bills of exchange is that a person can be the legal owner of a bill even though he received it from a person who was not the legal owner of it. Thus a thief may steal a bearer bill and pass it to X and X will become the legal owner of it, provided of course that X did not know he was receiving the bill from a thief and also provided X had given something of value for the bill.

However if the thief has stolen an order bill and, because an order bill requires indorsing before it can be transferred, the thief had forged the indorsement of the person from whom he had stolen the bill and then passed it to X, X will now not become the legal owner of the bill because of the forged indorsement. Now this is rather hard on X who may have given something of value for the bill and may have received it not knowing he was taking it from a thief. The forged indorsement makes all the difference.

To summarise the position: the holder in due course, as he is called, is a holder who has a right to enforce payment on the bill against all parties who are liable on it. He will get a good title (become the legal owner) to the bill notwithstanding the fact that he takes it from a person who had no title to it. However, in order to establish himself as a holder in due course he must have taken the bill in good faith not knowing of the lack of title of the person from whom he received it, and he must have given value for it. The bill itself must be complete and regular and especially must not contain a forged indorsement if it is an order bill. S.29(1).

### Discharge of a Bill

A bill is said to have been discharged, which means all rights of action on it are extinguished, in the following ways.

1. By payment by the drawee/acceptor to the holder. Payment to any other person such as one claiming under a forged indorsement will not discharge the drawee's liabilities.
2. By express waiver.
3. By cancellation.
4. By material alteration.

### Questions

What are the requirements of a bill of exchange?

What are the ways in which a bill of exchange can be transferred?

What advantages does a holder in due course have?

TWENTY THREE

# CHEQUES – IN PARTICULAR

*Study Topics*

**The legal definition of a cheque**
**The relationship between a banker and his customer and their rights and duties**
**Crossings and their significance**
**The statutory protection of the paying banker and the collecting banker**
**A banker is a holder in due course when he gives value for a cheque**

A cheque is defined as a bill of exchange drawn on a bank and payable on demand. Thus the drawee of a cheque is always a banker. A cheque does not need to be accepted and the drawer is never discharged by the holder's failure to present the cheque for payment within a reasonable time.

The relationship between the drawer and the drawee, in the case of a cheque, is important because it is the relationship between a bank and its customer. This relationship is a contractual one that creates a debtor-creditor relationship. By reason of the contract between bank and customer there are duties placed on each party. The main duty of the bank is to pay its customers' cheque up to the amount of the credit balance of their accounts provided the following conditions are complied with.

1. The cheque must be in writing, it must demand payment and be signed by the drawer (or customer).
2. The cheque must be drawn on the branch which holds a credit balance and the request for payment must be made during banking hours.
3. The cheque must be in unambiguous form. This means that as a cheque is a mandate from the customer to the banker then "the banker has a right to insist on having his mandate in a form which does not leave room for misgiving as to

what he is called upon to do." Lord Haldane *in London Joint Stock Bank Ltd v Macmillan and Arthur (1918).*

4. If any modifications to the contract between bank and customer are to be made then they must be communicated expressly to the customer and it probably would not be sufficient for the banker to place a notice in the cheque book especially if there had been a course of dealing between the customer and the banker before the charges were made. *Burnett v Westminster Bank Ltd (1965).*
5. There must be sufficient funds in the account on which the cheque is drawn. In this connection one should remember a banker may be able to consolidate two accounts of a customer even if these accounts are at different branches. *Garnett v McKewon (1872).* This facility applies to a bank but not to a customer. He has no right to insist on payment of a cheque at one branch where he has no funds merely because he has funds at another branch. In England, a cheque is not an assignment of funds and so the holder of the cheque has no claim against the banker if he refuses, for whatever reason, to pay on the cheque. In Scotland, a cheque operates as an assignment to the payee of the amount for which it was drawn out of the credit balance of the customer's account. If therefore in Scotland a customer draw a cheque for an amount in excess of the credit balance on his account the practice is for the banker to transfer the balance to a separate account to be held for the holder of the cheque. In England a banker is not bound to pay part of a cheque if he has insufficient funds to pay the whole amount.
6. It is the custom of bankers not to pay cheques which are out of date or "stale", that is if six months or sometimes 12 months have elapsed after their issue.
7. Postdated cheques are not invalid but should not be paid by a banker because the customer may countermand payment before the due date of the cheque. If a banker pays a postdated cheque he may have to dishonour other cheques which he would otherwise have been able to pay.

## *Crossings*

A particular feature of cheques is the crossing. This consists of two parallel transverse lines drawn across the face of the cheque. The effect of this is to ensure that the cheque cannot be cashed across the counter of the paying (drawer's) bank but must instead be paid into another bank and that bank will collect the proceeds for its customer. The purpose of crossing a cheque is obviously to make it more difficult for the wrong person obtain the proceeds. In addition to the general crossing just referred to there is also special crossing where the name of a banker is written across the face of the cheque and the cheque is only payable to that named bank.

### Account Payee

This is an instruction to the collecting banker to collect the proceeds for the account of the person named on the face of the cheque as payee. Before 16 June 1992, the words "account payee" did not prevent the cheque being transferred, and so if a cheque bearing these words was indorsed in blank and then stolen, a holder in due course would get a good title.

This situation began to cause some anxiety in financial circles. The advice then given was to always add on the words "not negotiable" after the "account payee" crossing. Another aspect was that a banker who credited the account of a person other than the payee would forfeit his right to protection under Section 80 of the *Bills of Exchange Act 1882* and also under Section 4 of the *Cheques Act 1957*, on the grounds that he was negligent in crediting someone other than the payee.

However on 16 June 1992, the *Cheques Act 1992* came into force and it states that a cheque crossed and bearing across its face the words "account payee" or "a/c payee" either with or without the word "only", shall not be transferable, but shall only be valid as between the parties thereto.

Furthermore if a banker credits an account other than that of the payee he shall not be treated for the purpose of Section 80 nor Section 4 as having been negligent by reason only of his failure to concern himself with any purported indorsement of a cheque which is not transferable. The purpose of this change in the law is to ensure that the drawer of a cheque, by crossing it "account payee", can be certain that only the payee named will have a right to the proceeds of it.

The change caused a problem for the banks: whether or not to print the crossing "account payee" on their cheques. The effect of this is to destroy one feature of a cheque by withdrawing its transferability. This is inconvenient to a person without a bank account who receives an "account payee" cheque. However larger numbers of people than ever before have bank accounts and in any case the place of cheques is being taken over, to some extent, by credit and debit cards.

To summarise the situation: if a person steals an "account payee" cheque no person to whom he fraudulently indorses it can ever become the owner of it. If a bank does credit the wrong person with the proceeds then the bank will not be liable.

### Not Negotiable

These words may be added to a general or a special crossing and they have the effect of destroying the cheque's negotiability. This means that although it may still be transferred, the person who receives it will get no better title than that of the person from whom he received it. *Universal Guarantee Property Ltd v National Bank of Australasia (1965)*.

In the case of a bill of exchange other than a cheque the words "not negotiable" prevent the bill being transferred. *Hibernian Bank v Gysin and Hanson (1939).*

## *Revocation of a Banker's Authority*

Section 75 of the *Bills of Exchange Act 1882* provides that "The duty and authority of a banker to pay a cheque drawn to him by his customer are determined by (1) countermand of payment, (2) notice of the customer's death".

1 A banker will require the written and signed authority of his customer, accompanied by the date, number, amount and name of the payee of the cheque. If a verbal request to stop payment is received the bank may merely suspend payment pending the receipt of written confirmation. If the account is joint and the bank's mandate does not require all parties to draw a cheque then a countermand of a cheque drawn by one party may be lodged by another party. *Gaunt v Taylor (1843).* The conditions for a countermand to be effective are:

   i. The countermand must actually come to the notice of the banker. In *Curtice v London City and Midland Bank Ltd (1908)* a customer sent a telegram to his bank countermanding payment of a cheque but the telegram was left in the bank's letter box until 2 November. On I November a cheque had been paid and so the customer claimed against the bank. The Court of Appeal held that the claim must fail as the cheque had not been effectively countermanded.
   ii. The stop notice must be sent to the branch of the bank where the account is held. *London Provincial and South-Western Bank Ltd v Buszard (1918).*
   iii. If the customer fails to adequately identify the cheque he wishes to be stopped he cannot blame the bank if it pays on that cheque. *Westminster Bank Ltd v Hilton (1926).*
   iv. The countermand must be given to the bank before payment of the cheque and the question may arise as to what moment of time payment takes place.

   The customer must not have agreed not to countermand payment, which would be the case if a cheque card were used. Also it is only the drawer who can stop a cheque, not the payee. If the payee notifies the bank that he has lost the cheque then the bank should get in touch with the customer.

2. In the event of a customer's death or insanity it is the notice of death or insanity and not the event itself that terminates a banker's authority to pay cheques. In general any credit balance of a customer must be held by a banker and only paid to an executor, administrator or Committee in Lunacy after the appropriate legal formalities have been complied with.

## *Other Events that Determine a Banker's Authority*

1. Insolvency of the customer.
2. Garnishee proceedings. This is an order of the court which a judgment creditor may obtain to restrain a bank from paying funds it owes to a judgment debtor, the service of a garnishee order on a bank will suspend its duty to honour its customer's cheques. So if A has obtained judgment against B for a sum of money but B has omitted to pay up, A can get a garnishee order from the court directed at any person who owes money to B, such as his bank. This person is called the garnishee.
3. An injunction restraining a bank from paying out money from a customer's account (for example a Mareva injunction).
4. Outbreak of war between the country where the bank is situated and the country of which the customer is a national.

### Breach of Contract

If a bank fails to pay its customer's cheque when there are adequate funds in his account then the bank would be in breach of contract, and would be liable to the customer. If the customer is a trader he may claim substantial damages without proof of actual loss. If he is not a trader he can only claim nominal damages unless he can establish actual loss.

### Defamation

In addition the banker runs the risk of a libel action on the grounds that by not honouring his customer's cheques (incorrectly) he has given the payee and others the impression that the customer is the sort of person who issues "dud" cheques. A bank therefore should make every effort to avoid a libel action if possible, by taking care as to the comments it makes on the cheque. Answers such as "Requires confirmation", "Words and figures differ", or "Indorsement irregular" would not be libellous. If such phrases cannot be used then "Refer to drawer" would be in order.

In *Evans v London and Provincial Bank (1917)* the wife of a naval officer, who sued for the dishonour of a cheque, received only one shilling in damages.

In *Cox v Cox and Co (1921)* when a cheque had been returned marked "N.S. Present again in a few days" the plaintiff sued for dishonour of the cheque and for libel. The bank paid £50 into court in respect of the breach of contract which the plaintiff accepted and continued the action for alleged libel. The jury found in favour of the defendants and Darling J stated that he considered the plaintiff would not have recovered the amount of £50 if it had not been paid in.

The customer for his part owes the bank a duty to take care in drawing his cheques and a duty to disclose to the bank any forgeries of which he is aware.

In order for an instrument to be a valid cheque it must be made payable to a specified person or his order or to bearer.

## *Bearer Cheques*

These do not require indorsement and so a person who receives a bearer cheque from a thief who has stolen it from the rightful owner will nevertheless become the rightful owner of it provided he took it without the knowledge that he was receiving it from a thief. An order cheque will be treated as a bearer cheque in the following circumstances.

1 If it is indorsed in blank, in other words if the rightful owner of the cheque indorses it merely by signing his name without naming the indorsee. In that case the order cheque will require no further indorsement.

2 Section 7(3) of the *Bills of Exchange Act 1882* provides: "Where the payee is a fictitious or non existing person the bill may be treated as payable to bearer." If therefore a clerk issues a cheque of his employer payable to a fictitious person and then the clerk indorses the cheque to an innocent person for value, the innocent person will get a good title to the proceeds of the cheque because of Section 7. The person who receives the cheque will be able to enforce it against the drawer and the fact that it is not a genuine indorsement will be irrelevant because the cheque/bill has become a bearer cheque/bill by virtue of Section 7(3).

   The question that remains is what is a fictitious person? The courts have decided that depends on whether the drawer intended the payee to receive the money. This is a good reason for making the bill not negotiable.

*Bank of England v Vagliano Brothers* (1891). Glyka, an employee ofVagliano Brothers, forged a signature of a person named Vucina as drawer of a bill in favour of Petridi and Co, with whom Vagliano did business. Vagliano accepted the bill which had been drawn on him, and Glyka then forged Petridi's indorsement before presenting it to Vagliano's bank for payment. The bank, having paid Glyka, then debited Vagliano's account but Vagliano, on learning of the fraud, claimed that his account should not have been charged by the bank. Held, although Petridi was an actual person, the drawer of the bill (i.e. Glyka) never intended that he should receive payment under the bill. Petridi, as payee, was therefore in effect a fictitious person so far as the bill was concerned; consequently the bill was payable to bearer. As the bank had paid the bearer of the bill (namely, Glyka), Vagliano's claim failed, and the bank was in order in charging his account with the amount of the bill.

*Vinden v Hughes (1905)*. X, an employee of Vinden, persuaded V to draw cheques in favour of certain persons who were actual customers of V, by telling V untruthfully that the amounts of the cheques were owing to the persons concerned. X then forged the indorsements of the payees and obtained payment of the cheques by purporting to negotiate them to Hughes. As the payees were existing persons, and the drawer of the cheques (Vinden) intended payment to be made to those payees, the forgeries by X prevented Hughes from obtaining a good title. Vinden was therefore able to recover from Hughes the amount paid to Hughes by Vinden's banker.

In *North and South Wales Bank v Macbeth (1908)*, Macbeth was induced by the fraud of White to draw a cheque in favour of Kerr who was an existing person. Macbeth intended him to receive the money. White obtained the cheque, forged Kerr's indorsement and paid the proceeds into his account with the appellant bank. Macbeth sued the bank, claiming it had converted his money. The bank replied that the cheque was drawn in favour of a fictitious person and so it became a bearer cheque. The House of Lords decided the section did not apply as the drawer intended the payer to receive the money. The bank was therefore liable.

## Order Cheques

**Cheques are usually payable to the payee or to his order. Thus the payee may receive the proceeds of the cheque. Sometimes a cheque is made payable to "wages or order" or to "cash". Such an instrument is not a cheque but is a mandate to pay money. The collecting banker has the same statutory protection as he has in relation to cheques.**

*Orbit Mining and Trading Co Ltd v Westminster Bank Ltd (1962)*. Mr Epstein had an account at the Westminster Bank. Some years after opening it he became a director of the plaintiff company, Orbit. Cheques in Orbit's account required the signatures of two directors. Before leaving for a business trip abroad, one director, Mr Woolf, signed a number of crossed blank cheque forms and left them with Epstein who took one, made it out to "Cash or order", added his own signature and the words "For and on behalf of Orbit Mining and Trading Co Ltd", and paid it into his private account. He did this on two other occasions. Epstein was authorised to sign cheques only for company business and so these three documents were fraudulent. The company claimed the money back and the bank claimed its statutory protection as collecting for a customer under Section 4(2). The Court of Appeal found for the bank. "It cannot be the duty of the bank to keep itself up to date as to the identity of a customer's employer" (Harman, LJ). Epstein's signature as drawer of the cheques was illegible and the bank could not be expected recognise the name signed as being the same as that of the holder of the account into which the mandate for payment (it was technically not a cheque as it was payable "To cash") was being paid.

## *Liability of Paying Bank*

The main duty of a bank, as was stated above, is to pay its customers' cheques quickly. In doing so it runs the risk of paying one to the wrong person. How may this occur? Say, A draws a cheque payable to B. X, a thief, steals the cheque and now wants to get the money. If it is an uncrossed cheque then X can go to A's bank and if the cheque is for a reasonable amount, he will probably be paid over the counter.

If it is a crossed cheque then the proceeds of the cheque can only be paid into a bank account. So X, the thief, must either forge B's indorsement and then pay the cheque into his own or another person's account; or X may open an account in the name of B and pay the cheque into that. The second method is obviously more difficult because it requires X to obtain references who will state that he (X) is in fact B.

These then are the two methods by which a thief may obtain the proceeds of a stolen cheque. Note that in either of these two situations A's bank (the paying banker) will pay the proceeds of the cheque to the wrong person. On the face of it that bank will then be liable to A (for paying A's money to someone other than A had designated) also to B the rightful owner of the money (for wrongfully interfering with B's goods).

The bank on which the customer has drawn his cheque is called the paying bank because that bank will be paying the money to the bank into which the cheque has been paid for collection called the collecting bank. The paying bank then will be liable to its customer and to the rightful owner of the money and the collecting bank will be liable only to the rightful owner of the money.

If this state of affairs had been allowed to continue then banks would have found it very difficult to operate. Consequently Parliament stepped in and provided the following protection for banks.

## *Banker's Protection*

### Paying Banker

A banker is under a duty to pay his customers' cheques quickly and in doing so it may be that he pays the wrong person. Section 59 of the *Bills of Exchange Act 1882* provides protection for a bank which pays the holder of a bearer bill and that holder was not entitled to the money. The section reads

> A bill is discharged by payment in due course by or on behalf of the drawee or acceptor. "Payment in due course" means payment made at or after maturity of the bill to the holder thereof in good faith and without notice that his title to the bill is defective.

It will be noticed that reference is made to a bill and not merely a cheque, so this Section covers all bills of exchange; also payment must be to the "holder". The only person who can be a holder of a cheque to which he is not entitled is the bearer of a bearer cheque. If it is an order cheque then the indorsement must have been forged by the thief and so consequently the person to whom he negotiates the cheque cannot be "a holder" because of the forged indorsement. Therefore Section 59 is not of great importance to bankers because it only applies to bearer cheques which are not particularly common

Section 60 of the *Bills of Exchange Act 1882* provides protection if the bank pays out on a cheque bearing a forged indorsement. The section reads:

> Where a bill payable to order on demand is drawn on a banker, and the banker on whom it is drawn pays the bill in good faith and in the ordinary course of business, it is not incumbent on the banker to show that the indorsement of the payee or any subsequent indorsement was made by, or under the authority of the person whose indorsement it purports to be, and the banker is deemed to have paid the bill in due course, although such indorsement has been forged or made without authority.

It will be seen that Section 60 covers the situation where there is a forged indorsement, also the protection only applies to cheques. In addition, in order to get the protection, the banker must have acted in good faith and in the ordinary course of business.

Probably the good faith of a banker would not be doubted but the requirement that payment must be made "in the ordinary course of business" was examined in the following case.

> In *Baines v National Provincial Bank (1927)* the bank cashed a cheque payable to Mr Wood at five minutes past three o'clock, which was five minutes outside normal banking hours. In the ordinary course of business the bank ceased trading for that day at 3 p.m. The next day Mr Baines cancelled payment on the cheque but the cheque had already been paid the day previously. Mr Baines then claimed the bank had not acted in the ordinary course of business. The court held that normally paying a cheque outside the banking hours would not be in the ordinary course of business but five minutes leeway was permitted so far as people already on the bank's premises were concerned. The meaning of payment in due course was further considered in *Auchteroni and Co v Midland Bank Ltd (1928)*.

*Auchteroni and Co v Midland Bank Ltd (1928).* In this case a fraudulent person presented a bill to the paying bank and was paid cash over the counter. The court held this was unusual but did not deprive the bank of its protection under S.59. Examples of payments not in the ordinary course of business would be

1. payment to a tramp, postman or office boy;
2. payment after hours, but a few minutes could make no difference particularly if the payees were in the building.

Section 80 of the *Bills of Exchange Act 1882* provides

> Protection to banker and drawer where cheque is crossed. Where the banker, on whom a crossed cheque (including a cheque which under section 81A below or otherwise is not transferable) is drawn, in good faith and without negligence pays it, if crossed generally, to a banker, and if crossed specially, to the banker to whom it is crossed, or his agent for collection being a banker, the banker paying the cheque, and, if the cheque has come into the hands of the payee, the drawer, shall respectively be entitled to the same rights and be placed in the same position as if payment of the cheque had been made to the true owner thereof.

In other words if a banker pays out on a cheque according to the crossing and if he does so in good faith and without negligence then he is protected if he pays to the wrong person.

Section 59 applies to bills of exchange, generally where payment is to a holder of the bill. Section 60 covers the case of a forged indorsement on a cheque and Section 80 deals with crossed cheques.

## *Analogous Instruments*

The above protection is extended to instruments other than bills of exchange and cheques by the following provisions.

### Section 1 of the Cheques Act 1957

This provides protection to bankers paying unindorsed or irregularly indorsed cheques in the following ways

1. Where a banker in good faith and in the ordinary course of business pays a cheque drawn on him which is not indorsed or is irregularly indorsed, he does

not, in doing so, incur any liability by reason only of the absence of, or irregularity in, indorsement, and he is deemed to have paid it in due course.

2. Where a banker in good faith and in the ordinary course of business pays any such instrument as the following, namely:
   i. a document issued by a customer of which, though not a bill of exchange, is intended to enable a person to obtain payment from him of the sum mentioned in the document;
   ii. a draft payable on demand drawn by him upon himself, whether payable at the head office or some other office of the bank; he does not, in doing so, incur any liability by reason only of the absence of, or irregularity in, indorsement, and the payment discharges the instrument.

Section 1 of the *Cheques Act 1957* gives to a paying banker the same protection that he will get in the case of unindorsed or irregularly indorsed cheques to banker's drafts and conditional orders, crossed or uncrossed. Section 1 extends the protection given to a paying banker if he pays to the wrong person

1. a banker's draft;
2. a mandate for payment. This is not a cheque but is intended to enable a person to obtain payment from the banker.

The bank must of course be acting in good faith and in the ordinary course of business.

A banker's draft is drawn by a banker upon himself and it is not "addressed by one person to another". A conditional order lacks an essential requirement of a cheque which is that it must be an unconditional order.

Section 1 of the *Cheques Act 1957* does away with need for an indorsement on cheques except for the purpose of negotiation. However on 23 September 1957 the Committee of London Clearing Banks issued a memorandum to their members. This requires a paying bank to obtain indorsement of a cheque if it is either: a cheque marked "R" (by this the drawer signifies that he requires a receipt for payment of the cheque); or an open cheque presented at the counter for payment in cash. In addition promissory notes, travellers cheques and ordinary bills of exchange will also require indorsements.

**Section 5 of the Cheques Act 1957**

This applies certain provisions of *Bills of Exchange Act 1882*, to instruments not being bills of exchange. The provisions of the *Bills of Exchange 1882* relating to crossed cheques shall, so far as applicable, have effect in relation to instruments (other than cheques) to which the last foregoing section applies as they have effect in relation to cheques.

Section 5 of the *Cheques Act 1957* gives to a paying banker the same protection he will get under Section 80 of the *Bills of Exchange Act*. Section 5 applies to instruments other than cheques ( instruments that do the work of cheques but do not comply with the definition of a cheque), for example, banker's drafts, conditional orders, drafts drawn upon the Paymaster General or the Queen's and Lord Treasureris Remembrancer. Therefore Section 80 gives similar protection to a paying banker in respect of these instruments if they are crossed, as he gets for crossed cheques. Section 19 of the *Stamp Act* covers crossed or uncrossed banker's drafts.

**Collecting Banker**

If a banker collects the proceeds of a cheque for his customer he will incur liability in conversion if the cheque did not belong to his customer. The rogue may have opened an account in the name of the payee named on the cheque or he may have forged the payee's indorsement and paid the cheque into his own account. In either case the banker who collected the proceeds of the cheque will have done so (albeit innocently) for the wrong person. He will therefore, prima facie, be liable to the rightful owner of the money. The collecting banker may be protected by Section 4(1) of the *Cheques Act 1957*, in the following cases

1. Where a banker, in good faith and without negligence receives payment for a customer of a cheque or other instrument specified in Section 4(2). The instruments referred to in Section 4(2) are:
   i. cheques (including cheques which under section 81A (i) of the *Bills of Exchange Act 1882* or otherwise are not transferable.)
   ii. any document issued by a customer of a banker which, though not a bill of exchange, is intended to enable a person to obtain payment from that banker of the sum mentioned in the document.
   iii. any document issued by a public officer which is intended to enable a person to obtain payment from the Paymaster General or the Queen's and Lord Treasurer's Remembrancer of the sum mentioned in the document but is not a bill of exchange.
   iv. any draft payable on demand drawn by a banker upon himself, whether payable at the head office or some other office of the bank.
2. Where a banker having credited a customer's account with the amount of the cheque, etc, receives payment thereof for himself, and the customer had no title (for example because the indorsement was forged), or a defective title (for example he obtained the cheque by fraud).
3. The banker does not incur liability to the true owner of the instrument by reason only of having received payment thereof.

Before the banker can claim the benefit of the protection, however, he must satisfy the following conditions.

1. He must have acted in good faith. This means that what he does when collecting the cheque must be done honestly.
2. Section 4(1) confers protection only where the person for whom payment is collected is a customer. A customer is a person who has a banking account with a banker even if the cheque with which he opened the account is the subject-matter of the action in respect of which the banker claims the protection of Section 4(1).

*Ladbroke & Co v Todd (1914).* On one occasion thieves intercepted letters which Ladbroke the bookmakers had sent to clients containing their winnings cheques. The thieves took out the cheques and substituted forgeries. One such cheque was for £75 11s 3d payable to a Mr Jobson and crossed "A/c payee only". One of the thieves took this cheque to the John Bull Bank, which was owned by Mr Todd, and opened an account in Jobson's name using the stolen cheque as an initial deposit and asked for that cheque to be specially presented. This was done and the cheque was paid. The next day "Mr Jobson" withdrew the money from his account and disappeared. Mr Todd said that he had not made any enquiries at all about "Mr Jobson" because he was obviously a university man and told a plausible story about not wishing his usual banker to see a cheque drawn by a bookmaker. The court held that "Mr Jobson" was a customer of the bank from the moment his account was opened but that the banker had been negligent in not making enquiries, for example, at the college he claimed to attend, which would have revealed him as an impostor.

The account may be a deposit or a current account. *Great Western Railway Co v London and County Banking Co Ltd (1901).* Section 4(1) applies to all cheques, whether crossed or uncrossed. It also applies to bankers' drafts, conditional orders and Paymaster-General's warrants (see Section 4(2) of the *Cheques Act 1957).*

3. The banker must have collected without negligence. The meaning of negligence must be ascertained from the cases, but Section 43(3) of the Act provides that he is not to be treated as having been negligent by reason only of his failure to concern himself with the absence of, or irregularity in, indorsement of an instrument. Whether the banker has been negligent or not will be decided by reference to the practice of reasonable men carrying on the business of banking and endeavouring to do so in a manner calculated to protect themselves and others against fraud.

Through the cases it has been established that a bank may be negligent in the following areas.

1. Failure of the bank to obtain or follow up references when an account is being opened for a prospective customer may be negligence. If the banker acts on the reply from only one referee, he is not necessarily negligent, though where the prospective customer is a foreigner it may be desirable for the bank to confirm the reply by an examination of the customer's passport.

*Marfani and Co v Midland Bank Ltd (1967).* Marfani and Co's office manager, calling himself Mr Eliaszade (with whom the company did business) cultivated the acquaintance of a restaurant proprietor called Akkadas Ali. Shortly before Mr Marfani left to visit Pakistan, the office manager opened an account in the name of Eliaszade at the Midland Bank giving Ali's name as a reference. Ali was well known as a substantial customer of the bank, and he had previously introduced good new customers. The office manager then got Mr Marfani to sign a cheque for £3,000 payable to Eliaszade, pretending that money was owed to him in the normal course of business. He paid this cheque into his account, withdrew the money and disappeared. The bank claimed statutory protection as collecting for a customer but Marfani & Co claimed the bank had been negligent. The court found for the bank but said, "If the defendant bank here exercised sufficient care, it was in my view only just sufficient." The bank had not enquired about the employment of "Eliaszade" and had presented the cheque before receiving Ali's reference.

*Lumsden and Co v London Trustee Savings Bank (1971).* In this case a collecting banker was found guilty of conversion without the protection of Section 4, *Cheques Act 1957* in that he failed to obtain a satisfactory introductory reference relating to a new customer. The latter was a stranger who offered the name of "Dr Blake" as a referee who replied favourably to the bank but did not supply the name of his own bankers. The bank was informed that Dr Blake had recently arrived in the UK from Australia. Cheques drawn by Lumsden and Co were misappropriated and passed through the defendant bank, the proceeds being quickly withdrawn. The whole story of the thief turned out to be a lie which would have been revealed, said the court, if the defendant bank had been more diligent, demanding at least the sight of the "Dr Blake" with his passport. The case is notable, however, for the fact that the damages awarded to the plaintiffs, were reduced by 10% because they had been contributory negligent in not drawing the cheques correctly.

2. In collecting for a customer who is an employee a cheque drawn by or in favour of the employer. When opening an account, the banker is under a duty to inquire as to the name of his new customer's employer if the banker knows that the

customer occupies a position which involves the handling and opportunity of stealing his employer's cheques. If the customer is a married woman, the banker must inquire as to the name of her husband's employer.

*Savory and Co v Lloyds Bank (1932).* E.B. Savory and Co were London stockbrokers and two of their clerks, Perkins and Smith, from time to time misappropriated bearer cheques drawn by their employers payable to stock jobbers and paid them into London branches of Lloyds Bank for the credit of, in the case of Perkins, his account at the Wallington branch of that bank and in Smith's case for his wife's account at the Redhill and, later, the Weybridge branches of that bank. The branches of Lloyds Bank that conducted these accounts had not, on opening the accounts: in the case of Perkins, ascertained the name of his employers and in the case of Mrs Smith, ascertained the name of her husband's employers. The bank failed to obtain statutory protection from its common law liability for conversion since it was considered to be guilty of negligence in two respects, viz

i. the branches which maintained the accounts were not possessed of information to enable the bank to keep watch on what was paid into the account so to detect any misappropriation of the employers' cheques;
ii. the London branches failed to pass on to the "home" branch details of the cheques paid in by Perkins and Smith and cleared by the London branches on behalf of the "home" branches.

However in 1968 (the *Marfani* case) Diplock LJ said of the *Savory* case that it depended on its own facts and there were matters to arouse suspicions in the social conditions of the 1920s. The case is merely an illustration of the principle that a banker must exercise reasonable care in all the circumstances of the case. *Savory* was decided in the light of banking practice as it was at that time.

3. In not enquiring further into circumstances which should have aroused suspicion. Where there is evidence on the face of the cheque of possible misappropriation the banker who fails to inquire further may be negligent. In the following cases further inquiry will be needed before a banker:
   i. collects for a private account a cheque payable to a public official. *Ross v London County, Westminster and Parr's Bank Ltd (1919).*
   ii. collects for an employee's private account or his wife's account cheques drawn by or in favour of his employer. *Savory (E B) and Co v Lloyds Bank Ltd (1932).*

iii. collects for a customerís private account cheques payable to the customer as "agent for the Marquis of Bute". *Bute v Barclays Bank Ltd (1954).*
iv. collects for a director's private account a cheque payable to his company. *AL Underwood Ltd v Bank of Liverpool and Martins Ltd (1924).*
v. collects a cheque marked "account payee" or "account, payee only" for some other account. *Ladbroke v Todd (1914).*
vi. collects an amount inconsistent with the status of the customer: *Nu-Stilo Footwear Ltd v Lloyds Bank Ltd (1956).*

McGaw had been the manager of three sheep farms owned by the Marquis of Bute. After the termination of his employment he received three warrants totalling £546, being subsidies, payable to McGaw "for the Marquis of Bute". They were collected and credited to McGaw's private account without enquiry by Barclays Bank, Barnsley. In defence, Barclays Bank stated that: as the warrants were payable to McGaw he was the true owner notwithstanding that he was accountable for the proceeds to the Marquis; the Marquis was estopped against the bank since he knew that the warrants would be issued payable to McGaw; the bank was entitled to statutory protection if its defence in failed. The court held that although the warrants were payable to McGaw, the intention of the drawer was that the Marquis should receive the money and not McGaw; the latter was merely accountable to the Marquis. Consequently conversion of the warrants had taken place and the bank was guilty of conversion. The statutory protection it claimed was lost because the court declared that it was clear that McGraw was to receive the money only as an agent and so such documents should not have been credited to the agent's private account without enquiry.

*Nu-Stilo Footwear Ltd v Lloyds Bank Ltd (1956).* Nu-Stilo Footwear employed M as its Secretary. M opened an account at Lloyds Bank in the false name of B saying he, B, was a freelance agent just commencing business. For references he gave his real name and address and later, when Lloyds Bank followed up the reference he, not surprisingly, said that "B" was a, suitable person to be given banking facilities. Subsequently nine cheques drawn by Nu-Stilo, most of them payable to B were collected by Lloyds Bank for "B's" account. Since the total of these cheques was £4,855 the court ruled that the amount was inconsistent with B's commencing business as a freelance agent. Consequently negligence was attributed to the bank which therefore failed to get the statutory protection it claimed.

## *Banker Acting Both as Collecting and Paying Banker*

Where a banker acts in the dual capacities of collecting and paying banker, he must, to escape liability to the true owner of the cheques he has dealt with (in an action for conversion), bring himself within the scope of the statutory protection afforded to both the paying and collecting banker. In other words, he cannot, for example, say "I concede I was negligent when I was acting as collecting banker but in my separate capacity as the paying banker I am entitled to the protection of Section I of the *Cheques Act 1957.*"

> In *Carpenters' Co v British Mutual Banking Co (1937)* a clerk of the Carpenters' company procured cheques from the company dishonestly and paid them into his private account at the defendant bank, which also acted as the company's bankers. The bankers claimed to be protected either by Section 60 or Section 82 (now Section 4 of the *Cheques Act 1957*). It was held that, although the bankers were protected by Section 60, they had been negligent in the collection of the cheque and were therefore liable to the company.

## *Collecting Banker as Holder for Value*

It should be remembered that a banker may collect the proceeds of a cheque in one of two capacities.

1. He may collect as agent of his customer and then Section 4 of the *Cheques Act 1957* may protect him.
2. He may collect the proceeds of the cheque for himself. In order for that situation to arise he must have given value for the cheque. In that case he will come within the definition of a holder for value or in due course and so will be able to sue the drawer of the cheque. The fact that the cheque, paid in by the customer, will probably not be indorsed will not affect the situation. Section 2 of the *Cheques Act 1957* provides that a banker who gives value for, or has a lien on, a cheque payable to order which the holder delivers to him for collection without indorsing it has such (if any) rights as he would have had if; upon delivery, the holder had indorsed it in blank. In other words the unindorsed cheque will be treated as a bearer cheque. A banker will be deemed to have given value for a cheque if
   - i. he lends further sums to the holder on the strength of the cheque;
   - ii. he pays over the amount of the cheque or part of it in cash or on account before it is cleared;
   - iii. he agrees either then or earlier, or as a course of business, that the customer may draw against the cheque immediately, before it is cleared;
   - iv. the cheque is paid in specifically to reduce an existing overdraft;

v. he gives cash over the counter for the cheque at the time it is paid in for collection;

vi. he has a lien on the cheque.

Section 2 of the *Cheques Act 1957* covers only cheques and it will not apply if the cheque bears a forged indorsement.

*Westminster Bank v Zang (1965).* The application of Section 2 of the *Cheques Act* is illustrated by the above case. Zang lost money gambling. He asked Tilley who was then watching if he could let him have £1,000 in return for a cheque. Tilley gave Zang the money in return for the cheque. Tilley had taken the £1,000 from a company, Tilley Autos Ltd. He was the company's managing director and controlling shareholder. Consequently he paid it in for the company's account but as the cheque had been made payable to himself he should have indorsed it before paying it in. This he did not do and this omission was not noticed by the collecting branch cashier. On presentation the cheque was dishonoured and Tilley borrowed it to sue Zang on it but abandoned his action. The bank later sued Zang themselves because Tilley Autos' account was overdrawn. To do so successfully they had to establish that they were holders for value. The bank lost the action because even though Section 2 of the Cheques Act could be satisfied, the bank was held not to have given value for the cheque. The bank's argument, that by crediting the cheque to the account of Tilley Autos Ltd, and reducing the company's overdraft by £1,000 they had given value, was dismissed on the ground that the bank's paying-in slip had a note to the effect that the bank reserved the right to refuse to pay against uncleared effects. This prevented an implied agreement from arising in the circumstances. The bank lost its lien when it lent the cheque to Tilley. It was further held that the words "for collection", which appear in Section 2 of the *Cheques Act 1957*, are not to be confined to cases where the bank is to collect for a customer's account. It applies if the cheque is being collected for any account.

## *Electronic Transfer of Funds*

The physical movement of paper used in the transfer of funds is a very expensive process. Consequently in recent years a number of electronic systems have been developed using computers and designed to reduce the amount of paper used.

### BACS (Bankers' Automated Clearing Service)

BACS Ltd is the company which operates the service. It deals with standing orders, direct debits, salary credits and other credits, such as trade settling amounts due. The BACS system is used by the banks and by customers. The user prepare details of the transactions, such as sort code number, account number, account name, amount and reference number.

The details are sent to the BACS computer centre at Edgware, Middlesex. They are contained on a tape or disc and are then read by computer at the centre. The entries are then sorted electronically, placed on magnetic tapes which are then passed to the appropriate bank. The advantages are reduced clerical costs, lower bank charges, cash flow benefits, interest saved and increased security.

### CHAPS (Clearing House Automated Payment System)

This is a high value clearing system which is operated electronically. At present the system is available for payments of £5,000 or more. The settlement bank transmits the payment to the computer systems of the other settlement banks. When a payment has been fed into the system it cannot be stopped and so the funds are guaranteed as having been cleared. The CHAPS system has taken over from Town Clearing which only applies to the City of London. This new system operates throughout the UK and is used when a guaranteed and speedy method of payment is required. Apart from that, the payee's bank account is credited immediately the payer orders his settlement bank to make the transfer.

### EFTPOS (Electronic Funds Transfer at Point of Sale)

This is the technical name for the system which makes use of plastic cards, either debit cards issued by banks or buildings societies, or credit cards. This method of transfer of funds sometimes goes under the names of "Connect" "Switch", "P.D.Q." or "Accept".

When the customer presents his card, the retailer "swipes" it through the electronic reader. Details of the transaction are transmitted to a central computer, the cost of the goods is checked against the cardholder's balance in his bank or building society. The customer's account is then debited and the retailer's account is credited.

If it is an "off-line" EFTPOS system then all the transactions for a day are collected together and then sent to the central computer by disc or tape or the bank's own computer system is used.

The advantage to the customer is convenience and there is no need to write a cheque. To the retailer it means greater efficiency, less cash to handle and a guaranteed payment once acceptance has been made.

### ATMS (Automated Teller Machines)

Most banks now have an ATM outside their premises. The user operates the ATM by inserting his card into the machine and keying in his PIN (Personal identity number). The machine looks up the account in the bank's computer and then carries out the orders of the user. These may be cash withdrawal; statement request; cheque book request. Some machines will also accept deposits and carry out payment of bills.

The advantages to a customer are that these machines allow him to pay bills and withdraw cash without drawing a cheque. Over the years the banks have co-operated and created shared ATM networks; for example HSBC, National Westminster, LloydsTSB and Clydesdale Barclays; Royal Bank of Scotland and the Bank of Scotland; Link Co-op Bank, Girobank and some building societies.

The European Commission is critical of many of the existing transfer procedures as they are often slow, expensive and labour intensive. The European consumer organisation has calculated that simply exchanging £100 through each of the EC countries will lose £50 in charges. This risk has been reduced by the success of ERM (Exchange Rate Mechanism) in bringing about greater exchange rate stability. In the final stages of EMU (European Monetary Union) the risk would disappear but, pending a single currency, one option would be for national bank notes to carry an indication of their Euro value printed on them. Banks would then exchange them at par value for notes of other Member States.

These disadvantages are not faced by business in the USA. A New York-based business man investing in Texas has no such problems because the value of the dollar is always the same anywhere in the USA. A similar arrangement was followed in the UK after the merger of Scotland and England. For 10 years after the union in 1707 bank notes in Scotland showed values both in pounds sterling and Scottish pounds.

The Commission considers the ACHs (Automated Clearing Houses) should be expanded and standard practices be adopted in order to provide efficient cross-border services. This will require wider banking co operation including central bank involvements. Priority is likely to focus on improvements in electronic payments via Eurocheques. However, if machine readable code lines for electronic processing can be standardised in the EU, ordinary cheque usage could increase.

Since 1987 progress has been made with the acceptance of payment cards at ATMs in all Member States. The UK leads with nearly 16,000 but surprisingly Germany had fewer than 6,000 in June 1989.

### Questions

How does the definition of a cheque differ from that of a bill of exchange?

A banker pays without authority in three cases. What are they?

TWENTY FOUR

# INSOLVENCY

*Study Topics*

**The ways in which a company can be placed in compulsory liquidation by the court**
**The liability of the directors of companies in insolvent liquidation to contribute to the assets of the company and the possibilities of disqualification**
**The procedure leading to a bankruptcy order and the powers of the trustee in bankruptcy over the bankrupt's property**
**The priority of the creditors**

Often the words insolvency, bankruptcy and winding up or liquidation become intermixed in a person's mind. However one should be aware of the differences implied by these terms. Insolvency simply means inability to pay one's debts. Assuming B owes A £1,000 then A may have to establish his right to that sum of money by going to a court of law. If A wins then he can say he has obtained judgment against B and so B becomes a judgment debtor and A is the judgment creditor. But A still has not received his money. If that is the case A must consider enforcing his judgment against B and will have to seek the help of the court. This may consist of the court ordering the bailiffs to "distrain on B's goods", in other words the goods are seized, sold and the money raised used to pay off the debt. In practice this method rarely raises enough money to satisfy the whole sum. The use of bailiffs therefore tends to be more of a "scare" tactic, at least in the first instance. Another method would be, if B is employed, to get an attachment of earnings order by which B's employer is ordered to deduct a certain sum each week or month from B's wages and to pay the money deducted to A. However these methods are only used in order to assist A to recover his money. If B owes money not only to A but also to C, D, E and F, etc. it might mean by concentrating on one creditor the other creditors could be unfairly treated and may not be able to recover any part of their debt. In that case it may be advisable from the point of view of all creditors that a united front is maintained against B and that he is made bankrupt.

The main purpose of bankruptcy proceedings is to ensure that each creditor is dealt with fairly. When one considers the assets of B a personal action against him would only succeed in gaining control of assets he owns at that time. A feature of bankruptcy, however, is that it may be possible in certain cases to follow assets which formerly belonged to the debtor and to recover them so that they can be distributed amongst the creditors.

In the case of companies, the procedure for collecting in their assets and distributing them amongst the creditors is called winding-up or liquidation. One point to be observed is that a human person is made bankrupt because he cannot pay his debts; a company may be wound up for other reasons although the insolvency of a company is probably the main reason.

Thus insolvency means inability to pay debts and from that there may follow the formal procedures of winding-up or liquidation in the case of a company or bankruptcy in the case of an individual. However if these formal procedures are adopted it may result in there being less for distribution amongst the creditors because the expenses of these formal procedures will have to be paid before there is any distribution. Consequently it may be preferable for the creditors to come to some arrangements with the debtor company or the individual debtor. These voluntary arrangements are a feature of the new legislation contained in the *Insolvency Act 1986* which facilitates the making of such arrangements.

The various methods of dealing with an insolvent company other than having it wound up are as follows.

1. Bank rescues. Sometimes, instead of winding up a company it is advisable to lend it more money, in the hope that it will become profitable and eventually the creditors will recover the full amount of their debts. In such a case if a bank lends money then it will take a fixed debenture as security.
2. Receivership. An ordinary receiver is one appointed by the creditors under power contained in the debenture certificate. An administrative receiver is a receiver or manager of the whole of the company's property. He is appointed by the holders of any debentures secured by a floating charge.
3. Administration order. The *Insolvency Acts* have introduced a new procedure whereby the court may make an "administration order" in regard to a company. The effect of this is to place the management of the company in the hands of an administrator and while the administration order is in force no resolution may be passed nor any order made for the winding up of the company, nor may an administrative receiver be appointed. The appointment of an administrator may

be blocked by the holder of a floating charge but not by the holder of a fixed charge. The administrator is given specific powers in particular to carry on the business of the company, to take possession of the company's property and to raise or borrow money and in that connection to grant security over the property.

## *Voluntary Arrangements*

These may be arrangements, assignments or compositions. An arrangement may include a reorganisation of the company's share capital so the creditors can convert some debts into ordinary shares. A composition is an agreement of creditors not to take action against the company in return for payment by the company of part of their debts. An assignment involves a transfer of the company's property to the creditors or to a nominee of them all. Section 425, *Companies Act 1985.*

In addition the *Insolvency Act 1986* has created a new scheme of voluntary arrangements. This requires supervision by a nominee, who must be an insolvency practitioner. If these voluntary arrangements are unsuccessful it may be necessary to have the company wound up.

## *Winding Up*

The procedures for the winding up of a company are contained in the *Insolvency Act 1986* which consolidates parts of the *Companies Act 1985* and the *Insolvency Act 1985.* A company is usually wound up because it is unable to pay its debts but it may be wound up also on technical grounds such as the company did not commence business within a year after it was incorporated, or the number of its members has been reduced below two. A company may be wound up merely because the shareholders wish it to be wound up. A company may be wound up compulsorily by the court or voluntarily by its members or creditors.

## *Winding Up by the Court*

The court may order the winding up of a company only if one or several of the following grounds for winding up are present. Application to the court is made by petition called a winding-up petition which if successful will result in the court making a winding-up order. Under Section 122 of the *Insolvency Act 1986*, a company may be wound up by the court if:

1. the company has by special resolution resolved that the company be wound up by the court;
2. the company does not commence its business within a year from its incorporation or suspends its business for a whole year;

3. the number of members is reduced below two;
4. the company is unable to pay its debts;
5. the court is of opinion that it is just and equitable that the company should be wound up.

## *Company Unable to Pay its Debts*

Section 123 of the *Insolvency Act 1986* provides that a company may be deemed unable to pay its debts in the following cases.

1. If a creditor to whom the company is indebted in a sum exceeding £750 has served on the company (at its registered office) a written demand for the payment of the debt and the company has for three weeks thereafter neglected to pay the sum or to make some other arrangement satisfactory to the creditor about its payment.
2. If in England and Wales, execution or other process issued on a judgment of any court in favour of a creditor of the company is returned unsatisfied in whole or in part. Execution is where a judgment creditor is seeking to enforce his judgment against the debtor company.
3. If it is proved in any other way to the satisfaction of the court that the company is unable to pay its debts. In this case, the court has a discretion and the amount owed need not exceed £750. Usually, the fact that the petitioner has made repeated demands for payment, and that the company has neglected to pay affords cogent evidence that the company is unable to pay its debts. Unless the company bona fide disputes the claim, a winding-up order will be made.
4. Asset test: if it is proved to the satisfaction of the court that the liabilities of the company exceed its assets. S.123.

## *Just and Equitable*

The power of the court to wind up a company on "just and equitable grounds" is discretionary. What is "just and equitable" will depend upon the allegations made by the petitioner. In the following situations the courts have made winding-up orders.

1. Where the main object of the company can no longer be realised.
2. If the company is a "bubble", that is it never had any business or assets.
3. If the company was formed for purposes of fraud or to conduct illegal business.
4. That the articles of association provided for a winding up in the event which has happened.
5. That, in a small private company, the company was in substance a partnership and the facts would justify the dissolution of a partnership. This happens usually

where the relationship between the persons owning its share capital is analogous to a partnership relationship. *Re Yenidje Tobacco Company Ltd (1916).*

## Petition for Winding Up?

A petition may be presented by the following:

1. the company or its directors
2. a creditor
3. a contributory
4. the Official Receiver
5. Department of Trade and Industry or Bank of England (in special cases).

A petition by the company would be very unusual because it only needs to pass an appropriate special resolution to be wound up. Contributories are not very common because they only exist in the case of shares which are not fully paid.

The liquidator must prepare a list of persons who are liable to contribute to the assets of the company in the event of its being wound up. "A" list contains the names of present members of the company and "B" list the names of past members who ceased to be members within a year preceding the winding up. In the event of a person on "A" list being unable to contribute the unpaid amount of his share, a person on "B" list may be asked to contribute, but only in respect of debts incurred before he ceased to be a member. The more likely petitioner will of course be a creditor.

The Official Receiver may petition if the company is in voluntary liquidation and he feels that the interests of creditors or contributories are in danger. The Secretary of State for the Department of Trade and Industry may petition under Section 440 of the *Companies Act 1985* if it appears that it is expedient in the public interest that the company should be wound up on the basis of information he has been given from his inspectors.

## Consequences of a Winding Up Order

If a winding-up petition is successful, the court will make an order for winding up. The order relates back to the date of the commencement of the winding up. Under Section 129 *Insolvency Act 1986* the winding up commences either:

1. at the time of the presentation of the winding-up petition, or
2. where, before a petition was presented, the company was in voluntary liquidation, on the passing of the resolution for voluntary winding up.

The effect of a winding-up order is as follows.

1. To make void all dispositions of the company's property; any transfer of shares made after the commencement of the winding up is void unless sanctioned by the court. S.127.
2. Any attachment, sequestration, distress or execution against the estate of the company after the commencement of the winding up is void. S.128.
3. After a winding-up order has been made or a provisional liquidator has been appointed, no action can be proceeded with or commenced against the company except by leave of the court. S.130(2).
4. The Official Receiver becomes provisional liquidator until he or another person is made a liquidator. S.136(2)(3).
5. The employment of employees and other agents of the company is terminated. Further, the directors are dismissed and their powers to act on behalf of the company cease.
6. All invoices, orders for goods or business letters of the company must state that the company is in liquidation. S.188.

## *Proceedings After a Winding Up Order Has Been Made*

The court may require a statement of affairs to be produced by the official receiver. He must also carry out two investigations:

1. if the company has failed, into the reason for the failure;
2. in any case, into the promotion, formation, business dealings, and affairs of the company.

In order to assist him in his investigation, he may apply to the court for the public examination of:

1. anyone who has been an officer of the company;
2. anyone who has acted as liquidator, administrator, receiver or manager of its property; or
3. anyone else who has been concerned in the promotion, formation or management of the company.

The official receiver must apply for a public examination if so requested by one-half of the creditors or three-quarters of the contributories. S. 133(2).

## *Appointment of a Liquidator*

The Official Receiver becomes the first liquidator until another person is appointed. Within 12 weeks of the winding-up order the Official Receiver must decide whether or not to summon separate meetings of the company's creditors and contributories in order to choose a liquidator. If he decides not to call a meeting he must notify the creditors and then he may be obliged to call a meeting if requested by one-quarter in value of the creditors. The Official Receiver may apply to the Secretary of State for the appointment of a liquidator.

## *Duties and Powers of the Liquidator*

The liquidator is not a trustee for the individual creditors but is the agent of the company. However he will be liable in damages to any creditor for breach of any of his statutory duties. He must

1. assist the official receiver;
2. take into his custody the property of the company;
3. settle the list of contributories;
4. summon meetings of creditors;
5. summon a final meeting in accordance with S.146.

He may

1. bring and defend actions in the name of the company;
2. carry on the business of the company so far as is necessary for the winding up;
3. pay any classes of creditors;
4. compromise or make arrangements with creditors;
5. disclaim any onerous property such as unprofitable contracts or any property which is unsaleable.

## *Voluntary Winding Up*

The main attraction of voluntary winding up from the members' point of view is that there are not a great many formalities to be complied with. A voluntary winding up may be either

1 a members' voluntary winding up; or
2 a creditors' voluntary winding up. S.90.

Whether the winding up is a members' or creditors' voluntary winding up, it is initiated by the members of the company passing an appropriate resolution to that effect and not, as in the case of a compulsory winding up, by a petition to the court.

### Voluntary Winding-up Resolutions

Under Section 94 of the *Insolvency Act 1986*, a company may be wound up voluntarily in the following circumstances.

1. When the period, if any, fixed for its duration by the articles expires, or the event, if any, occurs, on the occurrence of which the articles provide that the company is to be dissolved, and the company in general meeting passes a resolution requiring the company to be wound up (in this case an ordinary resolution will suffice).
2. If the company resolves by special resolution that the company be wound up voluntarily.
3. If the company resolves by extraordinary resolution to the effect that it cannot by reason of its liabilities continue its business, and that it is advisable to wind up.

The reason for allowing the extraordinary, instead of the special, resolution in the last case is to dispense with the requirement of 21 days' notice when the company is insolvent and the winding up is urgent.

What determines the type of voluntary winding up is whether or not a declaration of solvency can be made by the directors. This is a statement by the majority of them that they have inquired into the company's affairs and have formed the opinion that the company will be able to pay its debts in full together with interest within a specified period not exceeding 12 months from the commencement of the winding up.

The declaration must be made within the five weeks immediately preceding the date of the passing of the winding-up resolution. The declaration must be filed with the Registrar within 15 days of the passing of the resolution. It must embody an up-to-date statement of assets and liabilities of the company.

If the declaration is made, the winding up proceeds as a members' voluntary winding up. If the declaration is made by the director without reasonable grounds, the makers are liable to a fine or imprisonment or both. The fact that after the declaration the company's debts are not paid in full within the stipulated time raises a presumption that it was made by the directors without reasonable grounds. S.89(5)

### Members Voluntary Winding Up

This is entirely managed by the members and the liquidator is appointed by them. No meeting of creditors is held. Until the liquidator has been appointed the directors cannot exercise their powers without the sanction of the court; except those which relate to the disposal of perishable goods.

If the liquidator is of the opinion that the company will in fact be unable to pay its debts in full in accordance with the declaration of solvency then he must call a creditors' meeting within 28 days, giving them seven days' notice by post and advertising it in the *Gazette.*

The liquidator must lay before the meeting a statement of the affairs of the company. The effect of holding this meeting is that the winding up proceeds as if a declaration of solvency had not been made, that is as a creditors' voluntary winding up. S.96.

### Creditors Voluntary Winding Up

The company must call a meeting of the creditors for a date not later than 14 days after the passing of the resolution for voluntary winding up. This meeting must also be advertised in the *Gazette*. The notice must name the insolvency practitioner who will act. The business of the meeting is for the creditors:

1. to receive the directors' statement of the company's affairs together with a list of the creditors and the estimated amount of the claims. S.99;
2. to appoint a liquidator. S.100;
3. to appoint a liquidation committee. S.101.

### The Effect of a Voluntary Winding Up

1. As from the date of the passing of the resolution to wind up, the company must cease to carry on business except so far as is required for beneficial winding up.
2. No transfer of shares can be made without the sanction of the liquidator.
3. On the appointment of the liquidator the powers of the directors cease except so far as the company in general meeting, the liquidator (in a members' voluntary winding up) or the creditors or committee of inspection (in a creditors' voluntary winding up) may sanction their continuance. S.103.

## *Powers and Duties of the Liquidator in a Voluntary Winding Up*

1. He can without sanction, commence or defend legal proceedings on behalf of the company.
2. He can carry on the business of the company, so far as it is beneficial for the winding up.
3. He can exercise all the powers of a liquidator in a compulsory winding up.
4. He may apply to the court to determine any question arising in the winding up or to exercise any of the powers which the court could exercise if the company were being wound up by the court.

In the case of a compulsory winding up, when the affairs of the company have been completely wound up the liquidator may give notice to the Registrar that the final meeting has been held and that the winding up is complete. Three months after the registration of the notice the company will be automatically dissolved. In a voluntary winding up the three months' period begins with the registration of the liquidator's final account and returns. When a company has been dissolved the court may within 12 years make an order declaring the dissolution void.

## *Individual Insolvency: Voluntary Arrangements*

### Deeds of Arrangements

A debtor is sometimes able to make a private arrangement with his creditors known as a deed of arrangement (or assignment) as prescribed by the *Deeds of Arrangement Act 1914*. By such a deed a debtor assigns his property to a trustee as a representative of the creditors, and his deed must be distinguished from a scheme or arrangement.

A deed of arrangement is any instrument, whether under seal or not, made for the benefit of creditors generally or made by an insolvent debtor for the benefit of three or more creditors. It may be

1. an assignment of property;
2. a deed or agreement for a composition, and in cases where the creditors obtain control over the debtor's property;
3. a letter of licence;
4. an agreement for the carrying on or winding up of the debtor's business.

A deed of arrangement will be void unless it is registered at the Department of Trade within seven days after first execution and is properly stamped. A deed for the benefit of creditors generally is void unless assented to by a majority in number and value of the creditors before or within 21 days of registration, and within 28 days of registration a statutory declaration must be filed confirming that the assents have been obtained. Within a further seven days the trustee under the deed must give security unless the creditors dispense with it, and in default the court may declare the deed void or appoint a new trustee.

The problem with a deed of arrangement is that it does not prevent a dissenting creditor from petitioning for a bankruptcy order. A deed of arrangement is outside the bankruptcy provisions. In addition, voluntary arrangements may be made under the *Insolvency Act 1986*.

### Composition and Scheme of Arrangement

The debtor may submit a composition or a scheme of arrangement to a meeting of his creditors. The distinction between a scheme and a composition is that where a debtor makes over his assets to be administered by a trustee, that is a scheme; but where a debtor keeps his assets and undertakes to pay over to the creditors a certain sum, that is a composition. *Re Griffith (1986)*. Any composition or scheme of arrangement must normally offer at least 25p in the £, and must be approved by a majority in number and three-quarters in value of the creditors. Where this is done, the composition or scheme will be considered by the court and if it provides for the payment of the preferential creditors and is one which the court considers reasonable, and calculated to benefit the general body of creditors, the court will sanction it. However, if the debtor fails to pay any instalment due under the scheme, or the scheme cannot, in consequence of legal difficulties or for any sufficient cause, proceed, or where approval of it was obtained by fraud, the scheme may be annulled and the court retains the right to adjudicate without starting bankruptcy proceedings again.

## *Interim Order*

When an individual intends to make a proposal to his creditors on the above lines then an application may be made to the court for an "interim order". The application may be made by the debtor or, if he is an undischarged bankrupt, by him, the trustee of his estate or the official receiver. An "interim order" lasts for 14 days in the first instance and its effect is to stay any actions against the debtor and no bankruptcy petition may be presented against him.

An "interim order" will only be made if the court is convinced that the debtor is serious in attempting to reach agreement with his creditors. A nominee, who must be an insolvency practitioner, is appointed and the debtor must give him details of the arrangements he is trying to make.

## *Petition for Bankruptcy*

The petition for a bankruptcy order to be made against the debtor may be filed by:

1. the debtor himself;
2. the supervisor of a voluntary arrangement;
3. the Official Petitioner where a criminal bankruptcy order has been made;
4. more usually by a creditor who must show:
   i. that he is owed at least £750;
   ii. it is a liquidated sum:
   iii. it is unsecured;
   iv. the debtor is unable to pay the debt.

Inability to pay his debts is proved by the creditor showing

1. that he has served a statutory demand on the debtor and it has been ignored for three weeks; or
2. enforcement proceedings in relation to a judgment against the debtor have not been satisfied.

The three weeks may be dispensed with and the petition may be filed earlier if it can be shown that the assets of the debt may be reduced during that petition.

## *After the Presentation of the Petition*

Any disposition of property or payment of money made after petition has been presented is void if the debtor is eventually adjudged bankrupt, unless the court approves the transaction. If a person has dealings with the debtor after the presentation of the petition and before the granting of the bankruptcy order then that person may be protected if he acted in good faith for value and without notice of the presentation of the petition.

The court can stay any action, execution or legal process against the property or person of the debtor. The court may consider it necessary, for the protection of the debtor's estate, to appoint an interim receiver.

This will usually be the Official Receiver. He will have all the powers of a receiver and manager appointed by the High Court. He will have power to sell perishable goods and any goods which are likely to diminish in value if not sold.

## *Bankruptcy Order*

It is within the discretion of the court whether or not to make a bankruptcy order. If it does so then it will terminate any interim receivership and the debtor becomes an undischarged bankrupt and loses ownership of his assets. The Official Receiver becomes the manager of the bankrupt's estate pending the appointment of a trustee in bankruptcy. He can sell perishable goods and goods which will diminish in value if not sold. The bankrupt must prepare a statement of affairs within 21 days and if he refused or neglects to do so can he can be punished for contempt of court. The Official Receiver can at any time apply to the court for a public examination of the bankrupt.

## *The Trustee in Bankruptcy*

The trustee may be appointed by creditors, the court or the Secretary of State. Usually the creditors will appoint. They will do so when the Official Receiver, who commences to act when the bankruptcy order is made, calls a meeting to consider the appointment.

The meeting must be called within 12 weeks of his taking office. If the Official Receiver decides not to call a meeting then he will become the trustee in bankruptcy.

The court may appoint as trustee the insolvency practitioner who reported on the debtor's affairs or if the bankruptcy order follows upon a scheme or composition it can appoint the supervisor of the scheme. If the creditors fail to appoint a trustee then the Secretary of State may do so.

The trustee must collect, realise and then distribute the assets of the bankrupt. He has all the powers of a receiver appointed by the High Court. He has power to carry on the business of the bankrupt and to mortgage assets to raise money. He also has power to disclaim onerous contracts which are unprofitable and property which is unsaleable.

The trustee is subject to the general control of the court. The creditors may also appoint a committee to exercise certain functions. The trustee is of course liable for misapplication of the estate, misfeasance or breach of duty and the court has full discretionary powers to order a remedy.

## *Assets in the Bankruptcy*

The bankrupt's estate "comprises all property belonging to or vested in the bankrupt at the commencement of the bankruptcy". The bankruptcy commences on the date when the bankruptcy order is made. The bankrupt's tools, books, vehicles and other items used by him in his employment and provisions necessary for the domestic needs of the bankrupt and his family are exempt.

If an income payments order is made then a proportion of the income of the bankrupt will automatically pass to the trustee as in the case of profits of the business. The trustee succeeds to the bankrupt's property on the "commencement of the bankruptcy".

Any disposition of property by the bankrupt between the date of presentation of the petition and the date when the bankrupt's estate vests in the trustee is void. However persons who took property or money from the bankrupt before the date of the bankruptcy order in good faith, for value and without notice of the presentation of the petition may be allowed to keep these transfers. Persons who took property from the bankrupt after the bankruptcy order are given no protection and will have to appeal to the court.

### Family Homes

The *Matrimonial Homes Act 1983* gives a right to a spouse who is not the legal owner of the matrimonial home to register a charge on the home which cannot be upset except by an order of the court. This situation is accepted by the *Insolvency Act* and application must be made to the court if it is desired to realise the bankrupt's interest in the home.

## *Duration of Bankruptcy*

In the majority of cases bankruptcy will end automatically after three years have elapsed since the bankruptcy order was made. The Official Receiver can inform the court that the bankrupt has failed to comply with his obligations and the court may order that the time under the three year period shall stop running.

Where the bankrupt has been an undischarged bankrupt within 15 years before his current bankruptcy, he will not be discharged automatically but must apply to the court for discharge after five years have elapsed.

## *Principles Common to Corporate and Individual Insolvency*

It is a well-founded principle of insolvency law that all creditors must be treated equally or *pari passu*. Exceptions to this rule are

1. preferential creditors are paid out in preference to ordinary creditors;
2. secured creditors also get priority.

Any contractual arrangement for a creditor, for example a bank, to receive priority would be unacceptable but non-contractual rights such as a right of combination or lien will be unaffected. *British Eagle International Airlines Ltd v Compagnie Nationale Air France (1975).*

It is important to consider the effect upon a bank account of the presentation of a petition to make an individual bankrupt or for a company to be wound up. In this connection Sections 127 and 284 are of importance.

Section 127 provides that: "In a winding-up by the court any disposition of the company's property and any transfer of shares, or alteration in the status of the company's members made after the commencement of the winding-up is, unless the Court otherwise orders, void".

The effect of this section is that cheques paid out of an account in credit may have to be refunded to the liquidator and cheques paid into an overdrawn account may have to be returned to the liquidator. Debts in an overdrawn account arising after the date of the petition would cause an increase in the debt owned to the bank which the bank could not prove.

Thus, once a winding up petition has been presented against a company the bank must stop the account. *Re Grays Inn Construction Co Ltd (1980).* More recent cases include *Re Tramway Buildings and Construction Co Ltd (1988) and Re Pressdee Ltd (1985).*

In the cases of an individual insolvency Section 284 will apply. The effect of this section is similar to that of Section 127. It provides that any payment to a bank, after the presentation of the petition, shall be held by the bank for the trustee unless it can show that it acted in good faith, a transaction took place for value, and had no notice that the petition had been presented.

Once the bank becomes aware of a bankruptcy petition, it should stop the account and allow no further payments to be made from it. Sometimes it may be possible for the liquidator or trustee in bankruptcy to recover money or property transferred to third parties. This situation may arise because the bankrupt or company has been involved in a transaction at an undervalue, a fraudulent transaction or a preference.

### Transaction at an Undervalue

This will arise where the debtor has transferred property and has either received no consideration for it or the consideration was less than the market value of the property. It also arises where the debtor has entered into a transaction in consideration of marriage. Liability will arise from the fact of the transaction and the state of the debtor's mind will be irrelevant. The period during which transactions at an undervalue may be avoided by the trustee in bankruptcy is five years before the presentation of the petition for a bankruptcy order.

If the trustee can "avoid" a transaction it means that the trustee can recover the property from the person who acquired it. The bankrupt must have been insolvent at the time of the transaction. Transactions within two years of the petition are affected irrespective of the bankrupt's insolvency. Also, if an "associate" is involved, insolvency is presumed. If any property is transferred at an undervalue during the relevant periods, it may be recovered by the trustee. An associate includes spouses and other relatives, partners, etc.

The same principles apply in the case of companies and transactions at an undervalue may be avoided by the liquidator. However, where a company is concerned the basic period is two years and not five years before the relevant time and in the case of a company this is the date of the presentation of the petition (compulsory winding up) or the date of the resolution (voluntary winding up).

### Preferences

These arise if the debtor does anything which results in the creditor being in a better position, in the event of a bankruptcy of the debtor, than he would have been in if that thing had not been done. The periods during which the preference transactions must have occurred are:

1. if the transaction is not at an undervalue and is entered into with an associate of the debtor - two years before the presentation of the petition. (An associate is the bankrupt's spouse or former or reputed spouse and any brother, sister, uncle, aunt, nephew or niece of them);

2. if the person preferred is not an associate and the transaction is not at an undervalue - six months before the presentation of the petition.

The same periods apply in the case of a company.

For a transaction to amount to a preference there must have been the intention on the part of the debtor to improve the position of the recipient of the preference. The debtor must have been insolvent at the time of the transaction.

Insolvency is defined as "where the debtor was unable to pay his debts as they fell due; or where the value of the debtor's assets was less than his liabilities, including contingent and prospective liabilities."

The recipient of the preference may not always be a creditor who receives payment but may sometimes be a bank to which the debtor makes payment, not to favour the bank, but to favour the guarantor of his debt. However the bank may be protected so long as it received the benefit in good faith, for value and without notice of the relevant circumstances. Where a bank is involved in a possible preference transaction it will be protected

1. if it received payment in good faith and for value and without notice of bankruptcy proceedings;
2. if the bank has to repay a credit received, the court may permit it to retain the security;
3. in practice a bank will include a clause in its security forms allowing it to retain the security until the danger of preference has disappeared. *Re K M Kushler (1943).*

In practice banks will usually include a clause in their security documents by which they will be allowed to keep the security until the danger of preference has disappeared. The periods which apply are six months in the case of an ordinary guarantee but 24 months if the guarantee was given by a spouse, partner or company with which the customer was connected.

In the case of preferences as in undervalues the court may make an order, the effect of which will be to put the parties back to their original positions which they occupied before the transaction. Preferences are not prohibited unless the individual is insolvent at the time of the transaction or becomes insolvent because of it.

**Fraudulent Transactions**

Sometimes a transaction may be at an undervalue and made with the intention of putting the assets beyond the reach of actual or potential claimants. Undervalue has the normal meaning of the word mentioned above. However a fraudulent undervalue has no restriction as to when it is made and so the periods which are relevant to an ordinary undervalue transaction do not apply to a fraudulent undervalue. *Insolvency Act 1986*; Sections 423-425.

## *Realisation and Distribution of Assets*

When it is desired to realise any security of an individual or of a company it may become necessary for a person to be appointed to deal with the business of realising the assets and distributing the proceeds amongst the debenture holders or creditors. Under the Act, there are a number of "office holders" who may act in connection with an insolvent company. These include an administrator appointed under an administration order, a liquidator whether under a compulsory or voluntary winding-up and an administrative receiver under a floating charge. The *Insolvency Act 1986* allows the court to order anyone who holds information or has records concerning the company to produce these to the "office holder". Clearly, this could affect the bank. Similar powers may also be obtained by the trustee in a personal bankruptcy.

Where individuals are concerned a receiver will only be appointed if it is desired to realise land. The power to appoint a receiver will arise and become exercisable in the same way as the power of sale. In practice an individual will probably only consider appointing a receiver if the land has been leased and it is considered that the proper course is to defer selling the land, and to continue to receive the rents. Such rents collected by the receiver must be applied by him in:

1. discharge of expenses in connection with the property such as taxes and rates;
2. payment of interest on prior encumbrances;
3. payment of insurance premiums;
4. payment of repairs and his own commission;
5. payment of interest under the mortgage;
6. discharge of the principal debt.

More commonly a receiver will be appointed by a bank when it is owed money by a company or by an individual. The bank will have such power conferred in its debenture form. The receiver may realise the security whether or not a liquidation or bankruptcy has occurred.

## *Administrative Receiver*

The receiver appointed under a floating charge is called an administrative receiver if the charge covers the whole of the company's property. He must be an insolvency practitioner.

If an application is made for the appointment by the court of an administrator under the *Insolvency Act 1986* S.9 then the court will give notice of this application to any holder of a floating charge. If the court is satisfied that an administrative receiver is in office it shall dismiss the application to appoint an administrator. If the creditor has not appointed an administrative receiver then he will have five days in which to do so. If he does not do so within that period the court will make an administration order.

The effect of the administration order is that the creditor may be prevented from realising his security. The creditor will not be deprived of his security rights but may only receive the proceeds when the security has been realised. Once an administrator is appointed no debenture holder can realise his security except with the court's consent. An administrator must consider the interests of the company and of the general creditors. For this reason a creditor will in future usually take a floating charge so that it will be in a position to appoint an administrative receiver. The creditor will then be able to realise its security if he wishes. Within three months of appointment the administrator must produce proposals for the creditors and if he fails to do so the administration order will lapse.

A receiver may be appointed by the creditor under the power conferred by the debenture form. He must be appointed in writing not necessarily under seal. The appointment takes effect when it is received by the receiver who must accept by the end of the following business day and the acceptance must be confirmed within seven days.

After appointment the receiver must notify the company and the creditor within 28 days. The debenture holder must notify the Registrar of companies within seven days and a note is made in the register of charges.

As stated earlier, a receiver appointed under a floating charge is an administrative receiver and is merely a receiver under a fixed charge. A receiver is the agent of the company and so can bind the company by his transactions. However, he is also personally liable on contracts he makes. He must have regard for the interests of the company and when selling the assets he must take reasonable care to get the best price available. *Cuckmere Brick Co Ltd v Mutual Finance Ltd (1971)*. The powers of an administrative receiver are contained in the *Insolvency Act 1986* (Part III) and include the making of reports and the calling of creditors' meetings.

The order in which the disposition of assets is to take place follows that used by a liquidator.

1. the rightful owners of the property;
2. costs and expenses;
3. holders of fixed charges;
4. preferential creditors;
5. holders of floating charges;
6. unsecured creditors;
7. any surplus for the members of the company.

It very often happens that soon after a receiver has been appointed a liquidator is appointed to wind up the company. When that occurs the receiver's powers cease. He ceases to be the agent of the company but he does not automatically become agent of the debenture holder.

## *Distribution of the Assets*

To prove a debt means to claim for it in a bankruptcy or winding up proceedings. Debts which may be claimed are said to be provable and they are

1. debts which existed before the date of the bankruptcy order/ winding up order;
2. debts for which the debtor may become liable because of an obligation incurred before the commencement of the bankruptcy/ winding up;
3. the interest on a debt but that does not apply to interest payable after commencement of the bankruptcy/winding up;
4. amounts specified in a criminal bankruptcy order.

The first three of these apply to companies and individuals alike, the last one only to individuals.

### Order of Application of Assets in Payment of Debts

Once the liquidator/trustee has "collected" in all the property of the bankrupt or company he must proceed to pay those creditors who are entitled to be paid.

### Secured Creditors

The respective rights of secured and unsecured creditors must be maintained. A secured creditor is one who has some mortgage, charge or lien on the debtor's property. In order that the respective rights of secured and unsecured creditors may be maintained secured creditors are allowed to rely primarily on their security for payment. In this respect they have four clear choices:

1. they may rest entirely on their security and not prove in the bankruptcy or winding up at all;
2. they may realise their security and prove only for the deficiency;
3. they may value it and prove for the deficiency, after deduction of the assessed value, in which case the liquidator/trustee may redeem the security at such assessed value;
4. they may surrender the security to the liquidator/trustee and prove for the whole debt in the winding up or bankruptcy.

Once a secured creditor has exhausted his rights against his security, any balance of the debt owed to him is owed to him as an ordinary unsecured creditor. As soon as the above considerations are disposed of, the liquidator/ trustee can proceed to make actual payments to unsecured creditors in the following order.

1. Costs, charges and expenses properly incurred in the winding up/ bankruptcy, including the remuneration of the liquidator/trustee.
2. Preferential debts:
   i. deductions from wages which should have been made under the PAYE scheme in the 12 months before the relevant date or the date of the making of the winding up/bankruptcy order;
   ii. value added tax payable in the months before the relevant date;
   iii. social security contributions for 12 months before the relevant date;
   iv. state and occupational pension scheme contributions which the debtor should have made;
   v. employees' arrears of wages for months before the relevant date up to a maximum of £800 per employee. Loans made for the payment of wages would be included here, consequently a bank which lends money for this purpose would be treated as a preferential creditor.

   The "relevant date" in a compulsory winding up is, when the provisional liquidator was appointed, the date of his appointment; otherwise it means the date of the winding-up order. In the case of a voluntary winding up the date of the passing of the resolution for winding up. Schedule 19 *Companies Act 1985*.
3. Holders of floating charges rank behind the preferential creditors even though the floating charge crystallises before liquidation. This provision only applies to companies.
4. If after payment of the preferential creditors in full, there are still funds left, the next class of creditors to be paid is the ordinary unsecured creditors. They also rank equally amongst themselves and abate *pari passu* if the company's/individual's assets are insufficient.
5. Interest on debts since the bankruptcy/winding up commenced.
6. In the unlikely event that the liquidator is able to pay all the above creditors in full, and if there are still assets available, he must then pay the debts which are normally not provable in winding up, such as unliquidated damages in tort. This is because, in such a case, the company is solvent and by Section 611, *Companies Act 1985*, all debts may be proved.
7. If after paying the above, there is still some money left, it goes to the members of the company according to their rights in a winding up. Sometimes preference shareholders take the capital in preference to ordinary shareholders.

The order of priority in the case of an individual is the same, except that "floating charges" do not apply and any assets remaining after "interest on debts" has been paid goes to pay any debts owed to the bankrupt's spouse. Finally any surplus is returned to the bankrupt.

### Wages Account

In 2(v) above we have seen that arrears of wages rank as a preferential debt. By subrogation this privilege applies also to persons who have made advances for the purposes of paying the wages. The person who lent the money shall rank as a preferential creditor to the extent that the employee would rank as a preferential creditor, that is £800 per employee.

A person (company, partnership or sole trader) which is borrowing from a bank for the payment of wages is often requested to open a special wages account to which all cheques for salaries and wages may be debited. It becomes essential therefore for bankers and the borrowers to know precisely what payments may be debited to the wages account with a view to obtaining preferential treatment. It is not legally necessary to open a separate wages account to establish a preferential claim (*Re Rampgill Mill Ltd (1967)* however the advantages of doing so are:

1. it avoids disputes as to the reason for borrowing money;
2. it avoids the operation of the rule in Clayton's case.

If a bank has a preferential and a non-preferential debt then any money it receives it would obviously wish to appropriate to the non-preferential debt so as to keep the preferential debt as large as possible to be proved in the winding up. In Re *Unit 2 Windows Ltd (1985)* the court held that the correct solution was to apply the money received proportionately between the preferential debt and the non-preferential debt. All preferential payments rank equally among themselves and must be paid in full in priority to all other debts. If there are insufficient funds to pay them in full they abate proportionately.

### Questions

Distinguish between an administrative receiver and other receivers.

What distinguishes a member's voluntary winding up from a creditor's voluntary winding up?

What options are open to a secured creditor of a bankrupt?

Give some examples of preferential debts. Where do they come in the order of discharge?

# TWENTY FIVE

# THE CONCEPT *of a* EUROPEAN UNION

*Study Topics*

**The original treaties leading to the Treaty of Rome 1958**
**The Maastricht Agreement**

After two devastating conflicts in Europe within a period of 20 years there was a general desire in 1945 for some type of organisation that might prevent any repetition of the horrors of war. Although the idea of a united Europe had been discussed on a number of occasions before 1945, it is generally agreed that in his speech on 19 September 1946 at Zurich University, Winston Churchill proposed what he referred to as "a sovereign remedy". This was intended "to recreate the European family, or as much of it as we can, and provide it with a structure under which it can dwell in peace, in safety and in freedom. We must build a kind of United States of Europe." At the end of the Second World War, the states of Europe were more amenable to some kind of integration than at any time in their history.

The first tangible implementation of this idea is contained in the *Treaty of Paris 1951*. That Treaty created the *European Coal and Steel Community* (ECSC). Robert Schuman, the French Foreign Minister, in 1950, declared that a United Europe was essential for world peace and that a gathering of the European nations required the elimination of the century-old opposition between France and Germany. In order to take the first steps towards this goal he proposed "to place the whole Franco-German coal and steel production under one joint high authority, in an organisation open to the participation of the other countries of Europe". The Treaty was signed by France, Germany, the Netherlands, Belgium, Luxembourg and Italy.

The next stage in the integration of Europe occurred in 1957. On 25 March 1957, in Rome, the European Atomic Energy Community Treaty (EURATOM) and the European Economic Community Treaty (EEC) were signed. These Treaties became effective on 1 January 1958 and the signatories to both of them were the same as to the initial *European Coal and Steel Community Treaty of 1951*, that is France, Germany, the Netherlands, Belgium, Luxembourg and Italy.

Thus after 1957 there were three European Communities. The European Coal and Steel Community (ECSC), the European Atomic Energy Community (EURATOM) and the European Economic Community (EEC). Each of these Communities had its own interests but obviously the EEC had wider interests than the other two. Each Community had its own institutions until 1965 when the *Merger Treaty* was passed. From that date there was one Council and one Commission for all three Communities. Prior to 1965 only the Assembly and the Court of Justice were common to all Communities.

In 1973 the United Kingdom, Denmark and Eire joined the Community. In the United Kingdom this was achieved by Parliament passing the *European Communities Act 1972*. In 1981 Greece joined, in 1986 Spain and Portugal and in 1995 Austria, Sweden and Finland.

The need for some type of cooperation to prevent future conflicts was expressed in the preamble to the ECSC Treaty where it was stated that it was necessary "to substitute for age-old rivalries a merging of essential interests; to create, by establishing an economic Community, the basis for a broader and deeper Community among people long divided by bloody conflicts; and to lay the foundations for institutions which will give direction to a destiny hence-forward shared". These aims eventually became wider and involved other forms of economic activity.

Since the entry into force of the *Treaties of Rome* on I January 1958 three separate Communities have existed, each based on its own instruments of foundation. From a legal point of view this situation has remained unchanged to the present day, since no formal merger of the three Communities has ever taken place. There are, however, good reasons for regarding these three Communities, different as they are in the fields they cover, as one unit so far as their political and legal structure is concerned. They have been set up by the same Member States and are based on the same fundamental objectives, as expressed in the preambles to the three Treaties: to create "an organised and vital Europe", "to lay the foundations of an ever closer union among the peoples of Europe", and to combine their efforts to "contribute . . . to the prosperity of their peoples". This approach was also adopted in the resolution of the European Parliament of 16 February 1978, which proposed that the three Communities should be designated "the European Community". Common usage too, both in the media and in every day life, has long since come to regard the three Communities as one.

The legal order created by the European Community has already become an established component of our political life. Each year, on the basis of the Community Treaties, thousands of decisions are taken that crucially affect the lives of the Community

Member States and of their citizens. The individual has long since ceased to be merely a citizen of his town, district or state; he is also a Community citizen.

## *Single European Act 1986*

Although originally the concept was for various forms of economic cooperation, gradually these aims were widened until in 1986 the *Single European Act* was signed by the 12 participating States.

This Act added further goals, for example those of economic and monetary cooperation, health and safety of workers, research and technological development, environmental and consumer protection and co operation in the field of foreign policy. In addition, by late 1985, it had become apparent that the Community's seven-year timetable for abolition of barriers to movement and trade within the Community was running late. There were 300 detailed decisions which the Council had agreed must be made before 1992. The reason for the delay was the requirement that every agreement in the Council of Ministers must be unanimous. Eventually, therefore, it was decided that the *Treaty of Rome* should be amended by substituting majority voting for unanimity in certain areas. The whole question of majority voting versus unanimity is a serious stumbling block to any further progress in the Community because if majority voting were to be allowed in all areas then certain States would not be able to get their own way. In this connection what is known as the Luxembourg Compromise was adopted and in effect this gives any Member State a right of veto if its "vital national interests" are at stake.

## *The Treaty on European Union and Economic and Monetary Union and Associated Protocols*

The agreement known as the *Maastricht Agreement* extends Community action into areas not previously covered by EC Treaties, especially economic and monetary union and defence. It was intended to maintain the momentum already commenced by the *Single European Act from 1987* and the creation of the Single Market.

The text itself says: "This Treaty marks a new stage in the process of creating an ever closer Union among the peoples of Europe, where decisions are taken as closely as possible to the citizens."

The *Treaty on European Union* is wider in scope than any previous EC treaties. It expands many of the existing responsibilities of the European Union and brings in new policy areas, both within the *Treaty of Rome* and outside it. The Treaty introduces the concept of Union citizenship and increases the decision making powers and right of inquiry of the European Parliament.

A common foreign and security policy and a common policy on judicial affairs will form separate pillars standing beside the EC Treaties. Each will have its own ways of working, but the Treaty says that the Union shall have a single-institutional framework.

The European Council will bring together EU leaders at least twice a year in order to give the Union its impetus and political guidelines. The Council of Ministers and the Commission must see that there is no conflict between external relations, security, economic and development policies.

The European Community is the main part of the European Union. Technically, foreign policy and interior policy are not part of the Community; they are part of the Union. The Community will act within the limit of the powers conferred upon it by the Treaty and of the objectives assigned to it. In areas which do not fall within its exclusive competence, the Union shall take action, in accordance with the principle of subsidiary, only if and in so far as the objectives of the proposed action cannot be sufficiently achieved by the Member States and can therefore, by reason of the scale or effects of the proposed action, be better achieved by the Union. Any action by the Union must not go beyond what is necessary to achieve the objectives of the Treaty.

The tasks entrusted to the Union will be carried out by the European Parliament, the European Council, the Commission, the Court of Justice and the Court of Auditors. Each will keep within the limits of the powers conferred upon it by the Treaty. The Council and the Commission will be assisted by an economic and social committee (ECOSOC) and a Committee of the regions, both acting in an advisory capacity. A European System of Central Banks (ESCB) and a European Central Bank (ECB) will be established in accordance with the procedures laid down in the Treaty. They will act within the limits of the powers conferred upon them by the Treaty and by their statutes and a European Investment Bank will also be established.

## *Union Citizenship*

The Treaty creates citizenship of the European Union. Everybody holding the nationality of a Member State will be a citizen of the Union with rights and duties conferred by the Treaty. Every citizen of the Union shall have the right to move and reside freely within the territory of the Member States, subject to the limitations and conditions laid down in the Treaty.

Every citizen of the Union living in a Member State of which he is not a national will have the right to vote and to stand as a candidate at municipal elections in that country under the same conditions as nationals of that State.

Every citizen of the Union living in a Member State of which he is not a national will have the right to vote and stand as a candidate in elections to the European Parliament in that country, under the same conditions as nationals.

Every citizen of the Union will be entitled to protection by the diplomatic or consular authorities of any other Member State on the same conditions as the nationals of that State, where his or her own country does not have diplomatic representation. Every citizen of the Union will have the right to petition the European Parliament, and to apply to the European ombudsman.

## *The Treaty of Amsterdam 1997*

This Treaty amended the Treaty on European Union and the other Treaties. It moves forward the work of the European Union as regards:-

freedom, security and justice.

policies for the benefit of citizens of the Union.

An effective and coherent external policy.

It also made some changes in the Union's Institutions and in particular extended the areas where qualified majority voting is used to adopt acts by the Council.

## *Subsidiarity*

This word has probably been used more than any other in discussions concerning the European Community. It has been defined by F. Mount in his book *The British Constitution Now: Recovery or Decline?* as the principle that "functions should be exercised at the lowest practicable level of government". The principle of subsidarity says that no policy issue should be settled at a higher level than necessary. The proper place for action is as close to the citizen as possible.

There is no doubt that, to many people, the Brussels Commission is viewed as a remote centralised body immune from control and continuously issuing bureaucratic rules on Europe's citizens. Therefore in an attempt to curb its powers ideas are being sought as to how to take some of the centralised power away from Brussels and to give it to the Member States. This is, in fact, the crux of the problem concerning the European Community. How much power is each Member State willing to give up to be subject to the centralised power of Brussels?

This has always been a problem which has occupied the minds of the members of the European Community and in fact the principle of subsidiarity assumed importance when the Luxembourg compromise was created. This recognises a Member State's right to insist on unanimous, rather than majority, voting in cases of vital national interest. The difference is that the principle of subsidiarity which sets the limits of Community action is now enshrined in the Treaty.

**Questions**

What do you understand by subsidiarity?

Who is a citizen of the European Union?

# TWENTY SIX

# THE INSTITUTIONS *of the* EUROPEAN COMMUNITY

*Study Topics*

**How laws are made in the European Community?**
**The Commission**
**The European Courts**

Every organisation is run according to rules or law. In each organisation there must be a body which proposes new laws or changes to existing law, a body to pass the laws, a legislature, a body to apply the laws and finally a body to act in the event of disputes arising.

In the United Kingdom the proposing body is the Cabinet. The body which passes laws is called Parliament consisting of the House of Commons, the House of Lords and the Queen. The body which applies the laws is the Civil Service and in the event of disputes arising, these will be resolved by the courts of law.

Some countries have a written constitution and in the case the written constitution is supreme and must be interpreted by the supreme court of the particular state.

As far as the EC is concerned there are similar institutions to those mentioned above but their functions are not entirely identical with them.

## *The European Parliament*

The European Parliament can trace its history back to the Common Assembly of the European Steel and Coal Community set up by the *Treaty of Paris* in 1951. In the course of time the EC Treaty and the EURATOM Treaty created other assemblies, councils, commissions and courts of justice. However a convention to each of these Treaties provided for a single assembly and a single Court of Justice for the three communities.

Later, by the *Merger Treaty of 1965*, a single Council and Commission of the European Communities were established to replace the then existing Councils, Commission of the Coal and Steel Community and EURATOM.

The Assembly changed its name in 1962 and became known as The European Parliament. This change was given legal recognition by the *Single European Act in 1987*.

## *Membership*

Members of the European Parliament (MEPs) are now elected by direct universal suffrage and elections must be held "in accordance with a uniform procedure in all Member States". This has, so far, not been achieved and in fact MEPs are elected in accordance with the national method of voting. Although the UK still uses the "First Past the Post" system for General Elections to the National Parliament, proportional representation was used for the first time in the June 1999 elections to the European Parliament. This means that all the Member States elect their MEPs by some form of proportional representation.

The first direct elections for Parliament took place in June 1979. In the year before MEPs were elected to Parliament, they were designated by their respective national Parliaments from amongst their members. Now, although they do not have to be members of their national Parliament, they may in fact have a double mandate although few are in that category.

MEPs are elected for a term of five years and anybody can stand including, in the United Kingdom, peers of the realm and ministers of religion who of course cannot be members of the United Kingdom House of Commons.

## *Administration of Parliament*

The European Parliament is administered by the Bureau. This consists of a president and 14 vice presidents. It also includes five additional members elected by Parliament called quaestors, but they have no voting rights.

The President of the European Parliament chairs the proceedings of Parliament and acts in fact like the Speaker of the House of Commons. He also exercises administrative functions and represents Parliament on ceremonial occasions.

The Bureau can be enlarged by accepting the leaders of various political groups. The Bureau then takes decisions on Parliament's internal organisation and on relations with non-community institutions and organisations.

The European Parliament sits for one week every month except the month of August. The site of the sittings is usually Strasbourg, in France. There has been, for some time, a running discussion as to whether Parliament should sit at Strasbourg in France or Brussels in Belgium. At present committee meetings are held in Brussels spread over two weeks in each month. Luxembourg is the third place of work of the European Parliament but at present only members of the Secretariat act from that site.

It is obviously extremely inefficient for MEPs and other officials to travel between three sites but so far the three States concerned have been unable to agree on one permanent site for the European Parliament.

## *Organisation and Operation*

The new European Parliament, after the accession of Austria, Finland and Sweden, contains 626 MEPs. The new membership will be as follows; Belgium 25, Denmark 16, Germany 99, Greece 25, Spain 64, France 87, Ireland 15, Italy 87, Luxembourg 6, the Netherlands 31, Portugal 25, the United Kingdom 87, Sweden 22, Austria 21 and Finland 16.

At the elections in 1999 members have been elected by a very low voter turn-out which is estimated to be on average 49%. In the UK the turnout was 24%. According to the European Parliament's own figures this is the lowest in any Member State since 1979.

MEPs do not sit in national groupings but in political groups. A minimum number of 23 members is required to form a political group if all members come from a single Member State. The corresponding number is 18 if the members come from two Member States and 12 if they come from three or more Member States. All groups now include members from several different countries which enables them to see beyond purely national concerns.

## *Powers and Functions of Parliament*

Historically Parliament has never been a legislative body as it is in the United Kingdom. According to the Treaty, Parliament exercises only "advisory and supervisory" powers. Since being elected by universal suffrage, Parliament has seen a marked increase in its authority, both *de facto* and *de jure*.

The tasks of Parliament were defined in the EEC Treaty as follows:

1. to participate in the legislative procedure;
2. to put questions to the Council and the Commission;
3. to adopt a motion of censure where it disapproves of the activities of the

Commission;

4. to discuss the annual general reports submitted to it by the Commission;
5. to participate in the budgetary procedure;
6. to initiate procedures in the Court of Justice against the Council or the Commission in case they fail to act, or to protect its own rights and to intervene in other cases;
7. to participate in other activities of the communities.

## *Other Powers of the European Parliament*

Outside the legislative and budgetary areas of the European Community the European Parliament has a veto over the accession to the Community of new Member States. Also the *Maastricht Treaty* has given Parliament the power to assent to certain Community legislation other than the accession of new Member States. The proposals which require the assent of Parliament include provisions facilitating the exercise of the rights of citizens of the European Union to move and reside freely within the territory of the Member States; in stage 3 of Economic Monetary Union, provisions preferring upon the European Central bank specific tasks concerning policies relating to the prudential supervision of credit institutions and other financial institutions with the exception of insurance undertakings. These are some of the areas in which Parliament has the power of veto.

It has always been possible for any citizen of a Member State to petition Parliament on any matter. This attempt to open up the affairs of the Community was further extended at Maastricht because there it was agreed that the European Parliament will appoint an ombudsman after each election of the Parliament for the five-year lifetime of the Parliament. The ombudsman will be in full-time employment and will of course be completely independent in the performance of the duties of his office. He is likely to have at least 20 senior administrative officials to assist him.

## *The Council*

Until July 1967 (the *Merger Treaty*) the three Communities had separate Councils and Executive Commissions (known as the High Authority in the ECSC). Since then there has been a single Commission and a single Council, which exercise all the powers and responsibilities which had been given to their respective predecessors by the three Community Treaties.

The Council is the Union's decision-making body. The membership of the Council fluctuates according to the matters with which the Council is dealing. Thus the Council of Ministers may consist of Ministers of Agriculture, Finance, Social Affairs and so on. It is therefore not unusual to have various Council meetings in session at the same moment dealing with different matters. In addition to these specialised Council meetings which deal with specific subjects there are "general" Councils which are composed of the Ministers of Foreign Affairs.

Each Member State of the Community has a seat on the Council and each Member State holds the Presidency for a period of six months in rotation.

## *COREPER*

COREPER is the French acronym for Committee of Permanent Representatives. As the Council of Ministers is not a permanent body much of the work of the Council has been taken over by COREPER. This is an administrative arm of the Council and is in two parts, one composed of the permanent representatives who are high level civil servants with Ambassador ranks and the other are Ambassadors to the Union. If an agreement on Union policy is reached at COREPER level it will be formally ratified by Ministers in the Council without discussion by them. Whenever possible less contentious issues are resolved at the level of COREPER and are then passed on to the Council of Ministers as an "A" point for formal agreement without discussion. The Committee of Permanent Representatives is either COREPER 1 in the case of deputies or COREPER 2 in the case of ambassadors.

COREPER is assisted in its work by a series of working groups. When a Commission proposal is sent to the Council, it is examined in the first place by COREPER which decides either to examine it further or ask one of the working groups to examine it and report to the Committee. Once a proposal is lodged, a dialogue begins between the Ministers and then Council who put their national points of view and the Commission which seeks to uphold the interest of the Community as a whole and to find European solutions to common problems.

### *Voting*

The most important aspect of procedure in the Council is the voting procedure to be adopted. Although Article 148(1) of the *Treaty of Rome* states "save as otherwise provided in this Treaty, the Council shall act by a majority of its members", in practice the Treaty does provide for a different system of voting in most cases and only in a few instances is simple majority voting sufficient. The Council's rules of procedure can be adopted by a simple majority, the adoption of the agenda, the adoption of the minutes of the meetings and authorising the production of a copy or an extract of the Council minutes for use in legal proceedings.

Apart from the simple majority voting procedure the qualified majority voting procedure is now commonly used. This is a system of weighted voting.

## The European Council

When a matter under discussion concerns high-level policy then the Council may consist of heads of state. In that case the Council is renamed the European Council. Such a meeting can sometimes be called a summit meeting of the heads of government and it was at such a meeting of heads of state and of government in 1974 that the participants recognised the need for an overall approach to the internal problems involved in achieving European unity and the external problems facing Europe - considered essential to ensure progress and overall consistency in the activities of the communities and on the work on political co-operation - and have therefore decided to meet, accompanied by the Ministers of Foreign Affairs, three times a year and whenever necessary, in the Council of the Communities and in the context of political co-operation.

Since that time the heads of state have met three times a year as the European Council.

The *Single European Act* recognised the existence of the European Council and stated "the European Council shall bring together the Heads of State and of Government of the Member States and the President of the Commission of the European Communities. They shall be assisted by the Ministers for Foreign Affairs and by a member of the Commission. The European Council shall meet at least twice a year."

In its early years the European Council mainly confined itself to issuing general guidelines which were then acted upon by the Council and the Commission. It would no doubt have been possible for the European Council to have participated in law-making but it refrained from doing so and merely confined itself to dealing with policy issues.

However, the *Treaty of Maastricht* has stated that certain Council decisions should be taken at the level of heads of state and of government. The extent of the new functions of the European Council remain to the observed but nevertheless it can be said that the European Council fulfils an extremely important role in determining policies, both within the Community and towards third countries.

## The Commission

The Commission is an unusual organisation to British eyes. It appears to be the civil service of the European Community but has much more power than our civil service. On the other hand the Commission has no power to legislate; that remains with the Council of Ministers. The Commission can only formulate policy in the main but can sometimes make legislation under powers delegated to it by the Council. This arises in competition matters.

In the Commission there are 20 commissioners and they act as a College. All 20 must agree upon any proposal before it can be sent to the Council. The commissioners are appointed by agreement amongst the governments of the Member States for four years and the appointment is renewable.

The president is designated for six months before he takes office. Since Maastricht the Commission has a discretion to appoint one or two vice presidents from amongst the commissioners. All are appointed for a period of two years; these appointments are renewable.

The new procedure, agreed at Maastricht, was used for the first time in respect of the president and the other members of the Commission whose terms of office began on the 7 January 1995. The present President of the Commission is Romano Prodi.

Individual members of the Commission including the president can be dismissed during their term of office by the Court of Justice on an application by the Council or the Commission. This will only be done if the commissioner no longer fulfils the conditions required for the performance of his or her duties or has been found guilty of a serious misconduct. As was mentioned earlier the whole Commission can be dismissed by the European Parliament if a motion of censure were to be carried by a two-thirds majority of the votes cast, provided it constituted a majority of the members of the European Parliament.

Each commissioner is responsible for one or more portfolios and each of these portfolios is administered by a Directorate General at the head of which is a Director General. The Directorate General (DGs) include DGI External Relations, DG2 Economic and Financial Affairs, DG4 Competition, DG6 Agriculture and so on.

A former President, Monsieur Jacques Delors has said that a Commission official has six functions:

1. to innovate as the needs to the Community change;
2. to be a law maker, preparing the legal texts needed for Community decisions;
3. to manage the growing number of Community policies;
4. to control respectable Community decisions at all levels;
5. to negotiate constantly with all the different actors in the Community process;
6. to be a diplomat in order to be successful in the five other functions.

From this, it can be seen that the Commission has the responsibility of acting as the power house for the Community. It prepares action programmes in consultation with all other interested parties. Any one commissioner must of course consult with his fellow commissioners in preparing any proposals. Apart from acting as the power house of Community work, the Commission must ensure that the rules promulgated by the Community are adhered to. In order to do this, the Commission has powers of its own. In the case of the day-to-day operation of major policies such as the Common Market, the Common Agricultural Policy, and the rules of Fair Trade and Competition, the Commission has a direct rule.

In this connection the word comitology describes the type of committee procedure used to implement European Commission decisions and the day-to-day running of certain EU policies such as Agriculture, where management committees meet fortnightly to assess the market for produce from cereals to beef.

There are various types of committee, usually composed of representatives of the EU Member States' governments. The weight of their decisions varies according to the policy area and, as if to complicate it still further, the Article of the Treaty on which the legislation is based. The European Parliament has taken the Commission to court for failing to use the right comitology procedure.

The Commission is a very important part of the institutions of the European Community. Its main functions are as follows.

1. To act as the motive power behind Community policy. It is the starting point for every Community action, as it is the Commission that has to present proposals and drafts for Community legislation to the Council (this is termed the Commission's right of initiative). The Commission is not free to choose its own activities. It is obliged to act if the Community interests so require. The Council may also ask the Commission to draw up a proposal. Under the ECSC Treaty, however, the Commission also has law-making powers. In certain circumstances, these are subject to the assent of the Council, which enables it to overrule Commission measures.
2. To act as the guardian of the Community Treaties. It ensures that the Treaty provisions or the measures adopted by the Community institutions are properly implemented. Whenever they are infringed the Commission must intervene as an impartial body and, if necessary, refer the matter to the Court of Justice.
3. To defend the Community's interests. It must constantly endeavour to make the Community's interests prevail and to seek compromise solutions that take account of that interest. In so doing, it also plays the role of mediator between the States, a role for which, in view of its neutrality, it is particularly suited and qualified.
4. The Commission is an executive body. Examples of this are the implementation of the Community budget, competition law and the administration of the protective clauses contained in the Treaties and the secondary legislation. Much more extensive than the "primary" executive powers are the "derived" powers devolved on the Commission by the Council. These essentially involve adopting the requisite detailed rules for implementing Council decisions. As a rule, however, it is the Member States themselves that have to ensure that Community rules are applied in individual cases. This solution chosen by the Treaties has the advantage that citizens are brought closer to what is still to them the "foreign" reality of the European system through the workings and in familiar form of their national system.

## *The European Court of Justice*

The European Court of Justice sits in Luxembourg and its function is to ensure that in the interpretation and application of the *Treaty of Rome* the law is observed. The Court of Justice consists of 16 judges and when all sit together they sit in plenary session. However, they may form chambers each consisting of three or five judges either to undertake preparatory enquiries or to adjudicate on particular categories of cases. The Court of Justice shall sit in plenary session when a Member State or a Community institution that is a party to the proceedings so requests.

Each Member State nominates one judge and there is an additional one. The President of the Court is elected from among their number by the judges themselves.

## *Advocates General*

In addition to the judges there are advocates general for whom there is no real equivalent in English Law. Their job is to sum up in public the case before the Court and to give an expert legal opinion before the judges make their ruling.

The advocates general have the same qualifications as the judges and they represent neither party. Their duty is to act with complete impartiality and independence. They must make, in open court, reasoned submissions on cases brought before the Court of Justice, in order to assist the Court in the performance of the task assigned to it in Article 164, that is to interpret and apply the Treaty. The advocates general deliver their opinions to the Court and in the majority of cases the Court accepts their conclusions. The Court is not, of course, bound by their opinions and gives a "collegiate decision". If that differs from that of the advocate general then that would be a dissenting opinion.

The judges and advocates general shall be chosen from persons whose independence is beyond doubt and who possess the qualifications required for appointment to the highest judicial offices in their respective countries or who are juris-consults of recognised competence; they shall be appointed by common accord of the governments of the Member States for a term of six years.

Every three years there shall be a partial replacement of the judges. Seven and six judges shall be replaced alternately. Every three years there shall be a partial replacement of the advocates general. Three advocates general shall be replaced on each occasion. Retiring judges and advocates general shall be eligible for re-appointment. The judges shall elect the president of the Court of Justice from among their number for a term of three years. He may be re-elected.

Thus it can be seen that the practices and procedures used in the Court of Justice are taken from continental models. However in developing a substantive role, the Court draws on principles and decisions from all Member States.

Lord Diplock stated in *R v Henn (1981)* that the European Court, in contrast to English courts, applies teleological rather than historical methods to the interpretation of the Treaties and other Community legislations. It seeks to give effect to what it conceives to be the spirit rather than the letter of the Treaties; sometimes, indeed, to an English judge, it may seem to the exclusion of the letter. This is sometimes referred to as "purposive interpretation". In other words the purpose of the legislation and not so much the literal meaning of the words is important in trying to interpret the intentions of those who enacted the law. The European Court views the Communities as living and expanding organisms and the interpretation of the provisions of the Treaties as changing to match their growth.

It should be noted that the European Court does not consider itself bound by precedent as is the case in the English legal system. However it seeks to achieve consistency in its judgments but remains free to depart from previous decisions in the light of new facts.

The European Court of Justice in Luxembourg should not be confused with the International Court at the Hague which is concerned with disputes arising between States. Neither should it be confused with the European Court of Human Rights. This was established by the *European Convention on Human Rights* (ECHR). The convention, although signed by all the Member States, is a source of law with a separate court and administration. At present under EC law it is treated as no more than a guideline to be followed and cannot be relied on as of right. However there is a strong movement for the Convention to be integrated with EC law. A difficulty that might arise would be a possible source of conflict between the Court of Justice and the Court of Human Rights on the application and the interpretation of the Convention. Another suggestion to avoid this is to empower the Court of Justice to refer automatically all questions of interpretation to the Court of Human Rights.

## *Court of First Instance*

Under the *Single European Act 1987* the Council was empowered to set up, by unanimous decision, a Court of First Instance to be responsible for dealing with certain classes of action. On 24 October 1988 the Council availed itself of this possibility and adopted a decision setting up such a Court.

The Court of First Instance has its seat in Luxembourg together with the European Court and consists of 12 members. There are no advocates general attached to the Court of First Instance but any of its members may perform the task of advocate general. The Court of First Instance usually hears cases in chambers of three or five judges and it operates with five chambers.

### Jurisdiction

The Court of First Instance may deal with:

1. disputes between the institutions and their servants;
2. actions brought against the Commission by undertakings concerning ECSC levies and production, prices;
3. actions brought against an institution by natural or legal persons relating to the implementation of EC competition rules applicable to undertakings;
4. actions for compensation for damage caused by an institution for an act or failure to act which is the object of an action in which the Court of Instance has jurisdiction; and
5. actions brought against an institution concerning dumping and subsidies.

As far as procedure is concerned in the Court of First Instance this follows that of the European Court of Justice except that the Court of First Instance may dispense with the written procedure.

## *Appeals*

Any party to an action in the Court of First Instance has a right of appeal to the European Court on a point of law. Such an appeal must be lodged within two months of the decision being made and Member States or Community institutions can bring an appeal even though they were not parties to the case before the Court of First Instance.

If the appeal is allowed by the European Court then that Court shall quash the decision of the Court of First Instance, may itself give final judgment in the matter or it can refer the case back to the Court of First Instance for judgment.

The *Treaty on European Union* passed at Maastricht gave power to the Council to transfer any area of the European Court's jurisdiction to the Court of First Instance, except for preliminary rulings under Article 177 of the *Treaty of Rome*. It may be therefore that in the course of time the Court of First Instance will hear all direct actions and the European Court of Justice becomes an appellate Court and the only Court dealing with requests from national courts for preliminary rulings under Article 177.

### Questions

What are the powers and functions of the European Parliament?

What are the functions of the Commission?

What is the jurisdiction of the European Courts?

# TWENTY SEVEN

# SOURCES AND APPLICATION *of* COMMUNITY LAW

*Study Topics*

**Types of legislation**
**Directly applicable and of direct effect**

## *Primary Source of Community Law*

The first source of Community Law is provided by the three Treaties: the Treaty of the *European Coal and Steel Community* (ECSC) 1951 in Paris; the *Treaty of Rome* 1957 which created the European Atomic Energy Community (EUROTOM); and the *Treaty of Rome* 1957 which created the European Economic Community (EEC).

These Treaties have various annexes and protocols attached to them and they have been amended by later Treaties, in particular the *Merger Treaty* of 1967 which came into effect with the purpose of rationalising the administration of the three European Communities, the *Single European Act* of 1986 which made a number of important amendments to the structure of the European Community by expanding its formal competencies and adjusting its institutional structure, and the *Treaty on European Union* (Treaty of Maastricht) of 1991. This Treaty founded the European Union, changed the name of the European Economic Community to that of the European Community, created the status of a citizen of the Union, amended the EC's legislative procedures and established a timetable for progress towards economic and monetary union.

Because the law contained in these treaties was created directly by the Member States themselves, it is known as the Primary Community Legislation. These founding charters are mainly confined to setting out the objectives of the Community, establishing its mechanism, and laying down a timetable in which the objectives are to be achieved. It sets up institutions with the task of filling out the constitutional skeleton, in the interest of the Community as a whole, and confers on them legislative and administrative powers to do so.

## *Secondary Source of Community Law*

Law made by the Community institutions in the exercise of the powers conferred on them by the Treaties is referred to as Secondary Legislation, a second great source of Community Law. Article 189 of the *Treaty of Rome* as amended by the *Treaty of European Union* states "in order to carry out their task and in accordance with the provisions of this Treaty, the European Parliament acting jointly with the Council, the Council and the Commission shall make regulations and issue directives, take decisions, make recommendations or deliver opinions."

Article 191 provides:

1. Regulations, directives and decisions adopted in accordance with the procedure referred to in Article 1 9b shall be signed by the President of the European Parliament and by the President of the Council and published in the Official Journal of the Community. They shall enter into force on the date specified in them or, in the absence thereof, on the 20th day following that of their publication.
2. Regulations of the Council and of the Commission, as well as directives of those institutions which are addressed to all Member States, shall be published in the Official Journal of the Community. They shall enter into force on the date specified in them or, in the absence thereof, on the 20th day following that of their publication.
3. Other directives, and decisions, shall be notified to those to whom they are addressed and shall take effect upon such notification.

## *Types of Legislation*

### Regulations

The *Treaty of Rome* states: "A regulation shall have general application. It shall be binding in its entirety and directly applicable in all Member States". Thus a regulation does not require further implementation by a Member State in order for it to take effect. It gives rise to rights and obligations for states and individuals as it stands.

In other words, regulations replace national rules with Community rules. They are the legal acts that enable the Community institutions to encroach furthest on the domestic legal systems. This makes them by far the most important legal acts in the Community. Two features, very unusual in international law, mark them out: their Community character which means that they lay down the same law throughout the Community, regardless of State borders, and apply in full in all Member States; and their direct applicability, which means that they do not have to be transformed into domestic law, but confer rights or impose duties directly on the citizens of the Community in the same way as domestic law. The Member States and their governing institutions and courts are bound directly by Community law and have to comply with it as they have to comply with domestic law. But in spite of all their similarities with the statute law passed in individual Member States they cannot, strictly speaking, be described as the equivalent at European level as they are not enacted by the European Parliament and thus, from a formal point of view at least, they lack the essential characteristics of legislation of this kind.

It may be that the direct effect of a regulation is not automatic. It could be that a provision in a regulation is conditional or not sufficiently precise or it may require further implementation before it can take full legal effect.

### Directives

The Treaty provides (Article 189) that: "A directive shall be binding, as to the result to be achieved, upon each Member State to which it is addressed but shall leave to the national authorities the choice of form and methods". Directives are addressed to Member States, sometimes to all and sometimes to specified ones.

A directive does not become binding on the citizen until his government or parliament has transformed it into national law. Thus the *European Product Liability Directive* of 15 July 1985 became immediately effective when it was published in the Official Journal. It was left to the individual Member States to enact a similar piece of legislation and this occurred in the United Kingdom in the *Consumer Protection Act 1987*. The reasoning behind this form of legislation is that it allows intervention in domestic, legal and economic structures to take a milder form, and in particular enables Member States implementing the Community rules to take account of special domestic circumstances. The draftsmen of the Treaties have proceeded on the assumption that the far reaching changes in national arrangements needed to implement the Treaties often make it advisable to leave it to each State, which is naturally in the best position to know its own circumstances and to judge how its own requirements can best be reconciled with the needs of the Community.

A second guiding principle is also reflected here, namely the desire to achieve the necessary measure of unity while preserving the multiplicity of national characteristics.

When they implement a directive the Member States have to introduce new domestic law, or recast or repeal their existing domestic, statutory and administrative rules to being them in line with the objectives set out in a directive.

This form of Community legislation therefore provides the chief method used for the "harmonisation process", in which inconsistencies between the various national legal or administrative rules are removed or differences gradually ironed out, and for aligning the economic policies of the Member States.

Article 100, as amended, on the subject of approximation of laws states

> the Council shall, acting unanimously on a proposal from the Commission and after consulting the European Parliament and the Economic and Social Committee, issue directives for the approximation of such laws, regulations or administrative provisions of the Member States as directly affect the establishment or functioning of the Common Market.

Directives do not confer direct rights and duties on Community citizens as they are addressed solely to the Member States. Citizens acquire the relevant rights and duties only when the directive or recommendation is incorporated into domestic law by the responsible authorities in the Member State. This point is of no importance to the citizen as long as the Member State complies with its obligations. But there would be disadvantages for the citizen where a Member State does not take the necessary implementing measures to achieve an objective set out in a directive that would benefit him, or where the measures taken are inadequate. The Court of Justice has refused to accept these disadvantages, and has ruled that in such cases Community citizens can invoke the directive directly. This is possible only after the time the directive allows for incorporation into national law has expired.

In *Grad v Finanzant Traunstein (9/70)* the court stated that "both directives and decisions are directly effective provided they are clear and precise, unconditional and leave no room for discretion in implementation".

Before a person can rely upon Community legislation it must have "direct effect". In other words it must create directly effective rights which individuals can enforce against a Member State or against other individuals. Such Community rights must be enforced by the national courts and override any existing or subsequent national laws to the contrary. The test of direct effect is that it must impose on the Member state the following provisions.

1. A clear and precise obligation.
2. It must be unconditional, that is not accompanied by any reservations.
3. The application of the Community rule must not be conditional on any subsequent legislation whether of the Community institutions or of the Member States; and must not lead to the latter having an effective power of discretionary judgment as to the application of the rule in question (the provision must be "directly applicable" in the sense of not needing implementing legislation).

These tests would be satisfied for example where a directive required a Member State to abolish a particular tax, and the Member State failed to comply with its obligation within the time allowed. A citizen who would benefit from the abolition of the tax could invoke the directive and refuse to pay, once the time allowed for implementation had expired.

In *Pubblico Ministero v Ratti (148/78)* the Court of Justice held that as the time limit for the implementation of one of the directives on which Mr Ratti had sought to rely had not expired it was not directly effective. He could however rely on the other directive for which the implementation date had passed.

## Directly Applicable and of Direct Effect

A regulation is directly applicable in all the Member States and is binding in its entirety. The regulation will be binding upon the citizens of each Member State even though that State has taken no action to make it so. Indeed the regulation takes precedence over national law. A regulation will also have direct effect because it is capable of creating individual rights which must be protected by the national court of each Member State.

Directives are not directly applicable because they require implementing measures to be taken by each Member State. Nevertheless their provisions can have direct effect according to the circumstances. These must be ascertained in each individual case.

## Vertical and Horizontal Effects

If a State has not implemented a directive it should be answerable to the litigants: this is known as the vertical effect. The question may arise whether an individual may invoke against another individual a directive which has not been implemented: this is known as the horizontal effect.

In *Marshall v Southampton and South West Hampshire Area Health Authority (Teaching) (152/84)* the question of horizontal and vertical effects was discussed. In Marshall's case she was challenging the Health Authority's compulsory age for retirement of 65 for men and 60 for women as discriminatory, in breach of the *Equal Treatment Directive 76/207*. The difference in age was permissible under the *Sex Discrimination Act 1975*, but may also have been in breach of directive 76/207. Could directive 76/207 be relied on by Mrs Marshall?

The European Court of Justice held that the different compulsory retirement age was in breach of directive 76/207 and could be invoked against the Area Health Authority. On the other hand since a directive is binding only on each Member State to which it is addressed then it follows that a directive may not of itself impose obligations on an individual and that a provision of a directive may not be relied upon as such against such a person. The Court went on to say that if this distinction was arbitrary and unfair then it could easily be avoided if the Member State concerned has correctly implemented the directive in national law. It does seem therefore that Marshall's case has put an end to the dispute concerning vertical and horizontal effects and has decided that a directive which has not been implemented will only have a vertical effect and cannot therefore be used by one individual against another (horizontal effect).

Problems still remained after the *Marshall* case, in particular as to the interpretation of "public body" or "agency of the State". It would appear that where a Member State has neglected to implement a directive or has inadequately done so then an individual will be unable to invoke the directive in the context of a private claim. In two cases which were decided before the *Marshall* case, *Von Colson* and *Kamann v Land Nordrhein Wesfalen (14/83)* and *Harz v Deutsche Tradax GmbH (78/83)*, there were claims by the litigants that they had been unfairly treated contrary to the Equal Treatment Directive 76/207.

## *The Von Colson Principle*

In the *Von Colson* case the decision of the court did not focus on the vertical or horizontal effects of the directive but turned to Article 5 of the EEC Treaty. Article 5 requires States to "take all appropriate measures" to ensure fulfilment of their Community obligations. The ECJ stated that this applied to all authorities of the Member States including the courts. Thus it expected the courts to interpret national law so as to ensure that the objectives of the directive could be achieved. The result of this approach is that although Community law may not apply directly, in other words it is not directly effective  it may still be applied indirectly as domestic law by means of interpretation. This principle is known as the *Von Colson* Principle.

This principle has been discussed in the courts of the United Kingdom in several cases. The House of Lords gave its view in *Litster v Forth Dry Docks Engineering Company Limited (1989)*. This concerned a private claim against an employer based on Directive 77/187 which safeguards employee's rights in the event of a transfer of undertakings. The House of Lords in that case was prepared to interpret a domestic regulation in such a way as to comply with a directive as interpreted by the Court of Justice. It did this because the domestic regulation had been introduced for the purpose of complying with the directive. Thus the situation seems to be that where domestic legislation has been introduced for the purpose of complying with the Community directive the courts of the United Kingdom have a duty following *Litster* to apply the *Von Colson* principle and to construe domestic law so as to comply with EC law.

A limit to the *Von Colson* principle occurs where criminal proceedings are involved. In *Officier van Justitie v Kolpinghuis Nijmegen (80/86)* the Court of Justice stated that where an interpretation of domestic law would run counter to the legitimate expectations of individuals then the Von Colson principle will not apply.

The Von Colson principle was extended to some extent in *Marleasing SA v La Comercial Intemational de Alimenticion SA (106/89)*. In that case the European court confirmed the *Von Colson* principle and extended it by stating that "the obligation applied whether the national provisions in question were adopted before or after the directive." Whether or not the national courts will go along with this extension of the *Von Colson* principle remains to be seen.

A new aspect in this matter concerning the importance of directives is contained in *Francovich v Italian State (9/90) (1992 and 1993)*. In that case the court held "it should be stated that the full effectiveness of Community provisions would be affected and the protection of the rights they recognised undermined if individuals were not able to recover damages when their rights were infringed by breach of Community law attributed to a Member State".

The court held that an individual could proceed against the State for non-implementation of a directive where

1. the directive involved rights conferred on individuals;
2. the contents of those rights could be identified on the basis of the provisions of the directive; and
3. there was causal link between the State's failure and the damage suffered by the persons affected.

Thus if the decision in *Francovich* is established then it will mean that a remedy is obtainable against the State and it will not be necessary to rely on the *Von Colson* principle. However there are problems in applying the *Francovich* decision and so only time will tell whether or not it can be relied upon.

Regulations and directives are of course the main secondary source of Community law. But Section 189 of the Treaty also makes provision for decisions, recommendations and opinions.

A decision is binding in its entirety upon those to whom it is addressed. It may be addressed to a Member State or a legal or natural person. Decisions are normally of an administrative nature and can be taken by the Council and by the Commission.

Recommendations and opinions have no binding force. However that is not to say that they have no legal effect whatsoever because, although they cannot create rights which can be invoked in the courts, national judges must take recommendations into consideration when dealing with cases before them. It can be said that recommendations aim at obtaining a given action or behaviour from the person to whom they are addressed whereas an opinion merely expresses a point of view which has been requested by a third party. Having no binding effect, the legality of recommendations and opinions cannot be reviewed by the court.

**Questions**

How does a regulation differ from a directive?

What is the test of direct effect?

TWENTY EIGHT

# THE FOUNDATIONS *of the* EUROPEAN COMMUNITY

*Study Topics*

**The aims of the European Community**
**The "four freedoms"**

Article 2 of the *Treaty of Rome* sets out the aims of the European Economic Community as being to promote "throughout the Community a harmonious development of economic activities, a continuous and balanced expansion, an increase in stability, an accelerated raising of the standard of living and closer relations between the States belonging to it". These aims are to be achieved by establishing "a Common Market and progressively approximating the economic development of Member States".

In greater detail Article 3 enumerates the activities of the Community which will bring about not only a considerable uniformity of the economic systems of the Member States, but will also establish the community as a unit in the world market. These activities include:

1. the elimination, between Member States, of customs duties and of quantitative restrictions on the import and export of goods, and of all other measures having equivalent effect;
2. the establishment of a common customs tariff and of a common commercial policy towards third countries;

3. the abolition, between Member States, of obstacles to freedom of movement for persons, services and capital;
4. the adoption of common policy in the sphere of agriculture;
5. the adoption of a common policy in the sphere of transport;
6. the institution of a system ensuring that competition in the Common Market is not distorted;
7. the application of procedures by which the economic policies of Member States can be co ordinated and disequilibria in their balance of payments remedied;
8. the approximation of the laws of Member States to the extent required for the proper functioning of the Common Market;
9. the creation of a European Social Fund in order to improve employment opportunities for workers and to contribute to the raising of their standard of living;
10. the establishment of a European Investment Bank to facilitate the economic expansion of the Community by opening up fresh resources;
11. the association of the overseas countries and territories in order to increase trade and to promote jointly economic and social development.

Thus it can be seen that the foundations of the Economic Community laid down in the Treaty include

1. free movement of goods;
2. free movement of persons;
3. freedom of establishment and provision of services;
4. free movement of capital.

These are known as the "four freedoms". In addition there is the Common Agricultural Policy and the Common Transport Policy which are specialist areas and are not dealt with here.

## *Free Movement of Goods*

The idea of a Common Market was the underlying philosophy of the American Constitution of 1787. It implies a geographical area in which, unhampered by restrictions, the market forces of supply and demand are brought face to face. This means in practical terms the elimination of economic frontiers between the Member States of the Community and the creation of a customs union in which the market will operate on the basis of free movement of goods, persons, services and capital.

However the mere removal of customs barriers and obstacles to the interplay of supply and demand would be insufficient to create a single economic area. Economic policies themselves must be harmonised. The abolition alone of customs duties and similar charges will not be sufficient to guarantee the free movement of goods within the

Common Market. Therefore other protectionist practices which hinder the free flow of goods from one State to another must also be abolished.

**Quantitative Restrictions**

Article 30 prohibits quantitative restrictions on imports. Articles 31-33 provide for the gradual abolition of import restrictions during the transitional period. Article 34 prohibits quantitative restrictions on exports. Quantitative restrictions have been interpreted as any measures amounting to total or partial restraint on imports, exports or goods in transit.

The above Articles 30-34 are addressed to Member States and in addition they are binding upon Community institutions and individuals. However Community institutions may depart from these provisions where they are authorised to do so.

Article 36 provides the provisions of Articles 30-34 shall not preclude prohibitions or restrictions on imports, exports or goods in transit justified on grounds of public morality, public policy or public security; the protection of health and life of humans, animals or plants; the protection of national treasures possessing artistic, historic or archaeological value; or the protection of industrial and commercial property. Such prohibitions or restrictions shall not, however, constitute a means of arbitrary discrimination or disguised restriction on trade between Member States.

Article 36 has been restrictively interpreted by the European Court of Justice. The Court has held that the purpose of Article 36 is not to reserve certain matters to the exclusive jurisdiction of the Member States. In an important case known as *Cassis de Dijon (1979)* the European court has made it clear that:

1. only requirements strictly necessary for such protection can be justified;
2. there should be a mutual recognition of other States' safety standards.

This judgment has been used as the basis for the Commission's "new approach" to harmonisation directives in the Single Market Campaign. In other words the Commission did not expect that the relevant laws of the Member States should be harmonised to a single European standard (except in certain areas like telecommunications). But, instead, a mutual recognition of national standards should be ensured by providing that standards meet the essential protection laid down in the directives. This approach has been applied in relation to services, capital, workers' qualifications and rights of establishment, for example for banks.

Apart from departing from Articles 30 and 34, as provided in Article 36, derogation is also permitted in the interests of national security and in regard to measures to meet short-term economic difficulties, balance of payment difficulties and measures to meet deflections of trade which might obstruct the application of community commercial policy or economic difficulties in any Member State resulting from the implementation of commercial policy.

Article 37 is complementary to Articles 30 and 34 and this requires a Member State "to adjust any State monopolies of a commercial character so as to ensure that when the transitional period had ended no discrimination regarding the conditions under which goods are procured and marketed exists between nationals of Member States". Article 37 is not intended to abolish monopolies but to ensure that they do not operate in a discriminatory manner thus obstructing the free movement of goods and distorting competition within the Community.

**Equivalent Measures**

In addition to quantitative restrictions on imports and exports there are also other measures which have an equivalent effect. In *Procureur du Roi v Dassonville (1974)* the European Court of Justice held that "all trading rules enacted by Member States which are capable of hindering, directly or indirectly, actually or potentially, intra-Community trade are to be considered as measures having an effect equivalent to quantitative restrictions". Measures which have been prohibited include:

1. import and export licences and similar requirements, even where they are purely a formality;
2. customs formalities;
3. "buy national" campaigns even where they are non-binding. *Commission v Ireland (1982).*
4. excessive road worthiness tests on vehicles imported from other Member States. *Schloh v Auto Controle Technique Sprl 50/84.*

**The Rule of Reason and Proportionality**

In the Cassis de Dijon case, also known as *Rewe-Zentral AG v Bundesmonopolverwaltung fur Branntwein (1979)*, the above two principles were stated. This case was concerned with a German law which required certain alcoholic drinks to have a minimum alcohol level. This had the effect of excluding cassis from the German market. The ECJ held in this case that if a Member State takes measures to prevent unfair practice in regard to the import of products, then such restrictions are subject to the condition that they should not act as a hindrance to trade between Member States and should be available to all Community nationals.

The Rule of Reason is qualified by the statement that such measures must not constitute an arbitrary discrimination or a disguised restriction on trade between Member States. The Rule of Reason has been upheld on the grounds that it:

1. maintains fair competition;
2. permits fiscal supervision;
3. it protects consumers;
4. it protects the environment and biological resources and promotes Community-wide cultural interests.

The other principle is the proportionality test and this has been described as meaning that the measures taken to prevent unfair practices in regard to the import of goods must be no more than is necessary to achieve the desired objective. The measures must be proportionate to the end to be achieved and so barriers to trade will only be permitted to go as far as is necessary for the achievement for the reasonable purpose for which they were introduced. Thus, in the *Cassis de Dijon* case the ECJ held that the German laws on alcoholic content went beyond what was required for consumer protection.

## Free Movement of Persons

The Treaty makes a distinction between

1. wage earners (workers), that is anyone who pursues an activity as an employed person and,
2. non-wage earners, that is professional people, tradesmen, etc. These persons include not only human persons but companies.

## Free Movement of Workers

Article 48 provides for freedom of movement for workers within the Community, and for the abolition of any discrimination based on nationality as regards employment, remuneration and other conditions of work. Freedom of movement of workers may be interfered with by:

1. imposing restrictions on the ground of nationality;
2. treating family and dependants less favourably than the nationals of the host state;
3. depriving the worker of social security rights.

All these impediments have been discarded by Community Law and the provisions of the Treaty in regard to these are directly enforceable in the courts of the Member States.

The latest cases on these points are *Cowan v Le Tresor Public (186/87)*. In this case the courts gave judgment in 1989 and found against the Member State, France, because Cowan had been refused compensation for assault because the victim, Cowan, was not domiciled in France.

*Delbar v Caisse d'Allocations Familiales (114/88).* In this case also decided in 1989 it was decided that family allowances should be payable even when the dependants do not live in the same Member State.

It is the intention of the European Union to allow nationals of Member States to enter another Member State in order to accept an offer of employment and to look for employment provided that they can produce a passport or identity card. Member States are obliged to issue entry documents and to allow the worker to leave his home country. All these rights apply to EU nationals, the spouse, and descendants who are under the age of 21 or who are dependants. The nationality of a member of the family is irrelevant provided that the worker is an EU national and he has exercised his right to move to a different Member State.

The Treaty in Article 48(3) does permit Member States to limit the free movement of workers on "grounds of public policy, public security or public health". For these reasons Member States may refuse entry into or residence within their territory or expel workers who are nationals of another Member State. Furthermore the principle of non-discrimination on the ground of nationality does not apply to employment in the public service.

## *Freedom of Movement of Non-wage Earners*

This topic may be considered under the headings of "Right of Establishment" and "Services".

### Right of Establishment

This includes the right to take up and pursue activities as self-employed persons and to take up and manage undertakings, agencies, branches or subsidiaries "under the conditions laid down for its own nationals by the law of the country where such establishment is effected". Article 52(2).

The difference between freedom of establishment and freedom of services is that the former implies the setting up in the host State of a base from which services or other activities are provided inside the State. Services on the other hand are normally provided directly from the home country and might require only occasional, or temporary entry into the other Member State.

In regard to both these freedoms the principle of non-discrimination applies as it does in the case of freedom of movement of wage-earners. Again, the principle of non-discrimination does not apply to activities which are connected, even occasionally, in the Member State with the exercise of official authority.

### Freedom to Provide Services

Article 52 of the Treaty provides that the freedom to provide services concerns, in particular, activities of an industrial or commercial character and activities of craftsmen and the professions. Again the principle of non-discrimination on the basis of nationality will apply. However a Member State may impose specific requirements upon a person providing services because of the particular nature of the service to be provided. It may be that there are some professional rules which are for the general good; or particular rules relating to the organisation, qualification, professional ethics, supervision and liability which are binding upon a person providing that kind of service.

To facilitate the exercise of the freedom to provide services and also freedom of establishment there are provisions for the mutual recognition of diplomas, certificates and other qualifications.

An exception to the freedom to provide services is the same as those provided for the freedom of establishment, that is activities which are connected, even occasionally, with the exercise of official authority and limitations resulting from provisions laid down by law, regulation or administrative action providing special treatment for foreign nationals on grounds of public policy, public security or public health. Article 56.

## *Movement of Capital*

Articles 67-73 of the Treaty provide that restrictions on the movement of capital belonging to persons resident in Member States and any discrimination based on the nationality or place of residence of the parties or on the place where such capital is invested shall be progressively abolished. This elimination is, however, only required "to the extent necessary to ensure the proper functioning of the common market".

It has of course been established that persons must be allowed to finance their needs in the exercise of one of the freedoms already mentioned such as freedom to work in a different member State and to set up a new home.

Again Article 106 provides for the free movement of payments. This means that Member States must authorise payment from a debtor in one Member State to a creditor residing in another Member State, but only in so far as they are connected with the free movement of goods, services and capital.

If the free movement of payments were interfered with then the other freedoms could not be used because the financial results of their application could not then be brought back to the Member State of the person involved.

### Questions

Name some activities which will bring about uniformity of the economic system.

What is the difference between "right of establishment" and services?

TWENTY NINE

# THE EUROPEAN RULES *relating to* COMPETITION

*Study Topics*

**Article 85**
**Article 86**
**Dumping**

It is a fundamental principle of the Common Market that competition is not distorted (Article 3). The Treaty seeks to establish a system of sound competition based on three sets of rules:

1. rules applying to undertakings;
2. rules against dumping;
3. rules governing State aids.

## Rules Applying to Undertakings

Articles 85 and 86 are concerned with the main rules relating to undertakings in general. An undertaking is not defined in the *Treaty of Rome* but is accepted as being any person or organisation that carries on some economic or commercial activity. It includes limited companies, partnerships, sole traders, individuals, state corporations and trade associations. It may also include Sovereign States and local authorities carrying out commercial activities.

In a recent case, decided on 10 June 1991 in the Queens Bench division, it was held "Regulatory bodies performing the function of a public authority with the power to levy charges are not thereby a commercial organisation and not therefore subject to the provisions against anti-competitive practices of Article 86 of the EEC Treaty". *Irish Aerospace (Belgium) NV v European Organisation of the Safety of Air Navigation.*

Thus it is necessary to ensure that each party to an agreement comes within the definition of an "undertaking". Not only that, but the agreement in question must have some actual or potential effect on inter-State trade. It does not follow that merely because an agreement is made between two UK companies that in fact such an agreement would escape the EC competition rules. For example an agreement could be made between two companies in this country and one term of the agreement might be that the activities of one of the parties could be restricted and so inter-State trade might be affected.

The competition rules of the EC are basically contained in Articles 85 and 86. Article 85 prohibits anti-competitive agreements and Article 86 prohibits abuses of a dominant position.

## *Article 85*

This Article relates to anti-competitive behaviour by two or more undertakings or decisions by their associations that it prohibits agreements or other practices which distort competition and which are liable to affect trade between Member States.

1. The following shall be prohibited as incompatible with the common market: all agreements between undertakings, decisions by associations of undertakings and concerted practices which may affect trade between Member States and which have as their object or effect the prevention, restriction or distortion of competition within the common market, and in particular those which:
   i. directly or indirectly fix purchase or selling prices or any other trading conditions;
   ii. limit or control production, markets, technical development, or investment;
   iii. limit share markets or sources of supply;
   iv. apply dissimilar condition to equivalent transactions with other trading parties, thereby placing them at a competitive disadvantage;
   v. make the conclusion of contracts subject to acceptance by the other parties of supplementary obligations which, by their nature or according to commercial usage, have no connection with the subject of such contracts.
2. Any agreements or decisions prohibited pursuant to this Article shall be automatically void.

The provisions of paragraph 1 may, however, be declared inapplicable in the case of:

i. any agreement or category of agreements between undertakings;
ii. any decision or category of decisions by associations of undertakings;
iii. any concerted practice or category of concerted practices;

which contributes to improving the production or distribution of goods or to promoting technical or economic progress while allowing consumers a fair share of the resulting benefit, and which does not:

a. impose on the undertakings concerned restrictions which are not indispensable to the attainment of these objectives;
b. afford such undertakings the possibility of eliminating competition in respect of a substantial part of the products in question.

Thus it can be seen that the following activities will be prohibited by Article 85.

1. Price fixing either directly or indirectly. This includes an agreement whereby an undertaking will restrict itself as to the trading conditions applied in business dealings such as on what basis discounts are granted, credit terms, etc.
2. Market or production sharing. Arrangements to control production itself such as limitations imposed by quotas as well as long-term plans regarding production will normally not be allowed.
3. Agreements to discriminate. This may arise where A and B agree to apply more advantageous conditions to buyer C than to buyer D.
4. Collective boycotts. This would arise where there is an agreement between undertakings with the objective of forcing a potential competitor out of the market or preventing market entry by others.
5. Tie-ins. These are agreements which impose tie-in arrangements which oblige a buyer of one product or service also to buy another product or service. Such agreements are not allowed.

The above agreements are known as horizontal agreements. These are agreements between competitors or potential competitors. They should be contrasted with vertical agreements which are agreements between undertakings in different stages of the process through which a product or service passes from the manufacturer to the final consumer. Further horizontal agreements which may pose problems are:

1. joint purchasing agreements between competitors and even between non-competing firms which may lead to a restriction on competition;
2. joint selling agreements which limits the freedom of the parties to fix their selling prices';
3. sales promotion, for example trade fairs, joint advertising and the use of a common quality control label;
4. exchange of information through a central agency on quantities, prices, discounts and other terms of business;

5. trade associations or market for closure: usually undertakings may validly pursue common interests by creating a trade association, but problems may arise if the activities of the trade association tend to deprive members of their freedom to determine their own business policies;
6. non-competition clauses in connection with the sale of an undertaking.

All these situations are not invalid automatically but they may in fact violate Article 85.

The other type of agreement is called a vertical agreement. These agreements are concerned with the distribution of the product of an undertaking unlike a horizontal agreement which is concerned with arrangements by competitors restricting their independent business behaviour.

Whether or not a vertical agreement concerned with distribution will contravene Article 85 will depend on the extent in which the parties, the supplier and his distributor, agree to restrict their commercial freedom. A simple distribution agreement where neither the supplier nor the distributor is bound by any restrictive obligations will not fall within Article 85. However an exclusive distribution agreement by which the supplier agrees to supply only one distributor in a determined territory may be affected by Article 85. Such an exclusive distribution agreement may be beneficial by contributing to market unification. For this reason an exclusive distribution agreement may be given a block exemption, provided certain specific provisions are complied with. These are:

1. the agreement must involve two parties only;
2. the products must be supplied for resale;
3. the sales area must be either a defined part of the common market or the entire territory of the common market;
4. the only permitted restriction on the supplier is the obligation not to sell to other re-sellers in the sales area allocated to the exclusive distributor;
5. the supplier may not be required to guarantee absolute territorial protection for the distributor;
6. the supplier may agree not to make direct sales himself to customers within the distributor's territory;
7. The distributor may agree to purchase all his requirements from the supplier;
8. the agreement must not involve competing manufacturers since this could lead to horizontal market sharing;
9. there must be no effort by the parties to create absolute territorial protection for the distributor.

Any agreement which satisfies these conditions will be automatically exempted and the parties do not need to notify the agreement to the Commission.

In the same way there may be an exclusive purchasing agreement. This is an agreement by which a re-seller is obliged to buy his supplies exclusively from a stated manufacturer or other supplier without being allotted an exclusive sales territory.

An exclusive purchase obligation is permitted as part of an exclusive distribution agreement. Otherwise it is only allowed within the terms of the exclusive purchase block exemption. The maximum duration of the exclusive purchasing obligation must be limited to five years (renewable) and the range of products covered by the obligation must be limited to products which either by their nature or by commercial usage are connected to each other. There are special provisions in the new group exemptions for exclusive purchasing agreements relating to beer (and other drinks) and petrol.

## *Selected Distribution Agreements*

Certain manufacturers may want their products to be sold only by approved dealers. This is true in the case of technically sophisticated products such as electronic equipment, watches or automobiles. This gives the manufacturer control of the way in which his product is sold. However it is also a way of maintaining retail prices and of isolating dealers from competition. It is therefore regarded with suspicion by the Commission and the only block exemption for selective distribution is for motor vehicle distribution.

Outside the motor vehicle sector, manufacturers or importers wishing to sell through dealer networks must either ensure that the agreements fall outside Article 85 or they must seek an individual exemption. Agreements will only fall outside Article 85 if:

1. the products concerned require specialist retailers, that is they are technically complex
2. the dealers are selected on the basis of their ability to do the job or the suitability of their premises, but nothing else;
3. there are no anti-competitive clauses in the dealer agreements which might influence retail prices or restrict classes of customers or ban exports.

## *Franchising*

A franchising agreement enables the franchiser to establish a uniform distribution network without the need for major investment. It will also allow the independent trader to set up an outlet more rapidly and with a greater chance of success than if he had to do so without the experience and assistance of the franchiser.

In 1988 the Commission enacted a Block Exemption Regulation in the field of franchising agreements. The Commission treats franchise networks differently from selective distribution networks.

## *Industrial Property*

Industrial property rights include patents, copyrights, trademarks, performing rights, registered designs and models. These rights can be obtained and used by each Member State according to the national laws of each State. The owner of an industrial property right has a legal monopoly in his protected product process or name because he can prevent others from infringing his rights. Furthermore he has the sole right to permit others to do what otherwise would be an infringement. Thus the owner of an industrial property right has the opportunity to restrict competition and divide up the common market and place restrictions on licensees.

European Community competition law recognises and respects the existence of monopolies created by industrial property rights. However, although the mere existence of an industrial property right cannot infringe Articles 85 or 86, an improper or abusive exercise of these rights can.

In *Consten SA and Grundig v EC Commission* the German firm Grundig entered into an agreement with Consten, a French firm, whereby Consten became the sole representative of Grundig for France, and Corsica. Consten undertook to buy Grundig products, carry out publicity, and set up repair workshops and also undertook not to sell similar products or to compete with Grundig. On the other hand Grundig undertook to supply only Consten in France and not to deliver either directly or indirectly to other persons within the area covered by the agreement. Furthermore Grundig authorised Consten to use the name and emblem of Grundig as registered in Germany and Consten registered in France, in its own name, the trademark of Grundig GINT. In April 1961 Consten found that another Company, UNEF was buying Grundig products from German traders and reselling these in France at more favourable prices than those charged by Consten. So Consten brought actions against UNEF for unfair competition and for infringement of the GINT trademark. Eventually the matter came before the Court of Justice which considered the effect of the arrangement of inter-State trade notwithstanding the fact that the volume of trade between the States had been increased. The court decided that the agreement was capable of endangering freedom of trade between member States which could harm the attainment of the object of a single market between States.

## *Patent Licensing*

Patent licensing agreements may present problems in view of the territorial restriction they impose which may result in the isolation of national markets. They also confer on the licensee an exclusive right to manufacture and/or sell the product covered by the patent.

However patent licensing confers a number of benefits. The agreements allow firms to obtain access to newly developed technologies and they also encourage the innovative activities of smaller firms which lack the financial resources to exploit their inventions themselves throughout the whole community.

In recognition of the beneficial effects the Commission has adopted a group exemption in the area of patient licensing which is characterised by three main principles.

1. It recognises a need for certain degree of protection for the holder of the patent (licensor) and his licensees.
2. It aims to assure effective competition and subject to certain limitations, a freedom of intra-community trade for the patented products.
3. It provides security for the parties to the contract.

In patent licenses the following are prohibited.

1. The charging of royalties or the imposing of restrictions after the patent has expired.
2. An obligation on the licensee to assign to the patentee any rights in improvement in the patented product or process.
3. No-challenge clauses, which mean that the licensee is not allowed to challenge the validity of the patents.
4. Non-compete clauses which means that the licensee is not allowed to manufacture or sell competing products.
5. Charging royalties on the manufacture of non-patented products.

## *Know-How Licensing*

Know-how licensing agreements are also covered by a block exemption dated 30 November 1988. A know-how agreement is not actually an industrial property right but it is sometimes treated in a similar manner. The duration of clauses granting the licensee exclusive rights and restricting exports in a know-how licence is limited to ten years. In copyright and trademark licences the same principles apply. Know-how, for this purpose, is defined as "a body of technical information that is secret, substantial, and identified in any appropriate form".

## *Activities Outside the Scope of Article 85(1)*

### Notifications of Negative Clearance and Exemption

If the parties to an agreement consider that it may violate Article 85 and want to be informed on this particular point they may apply to the Commission for a decision. This procedure is known as "notification". One type of notification is known as "an application for negative clearance". This means that the parties want the Commission to confirm that their agreement falls outside Article 85(1) altogether. Another type of notification is called "a notification for exemption". In this case the parties may consider that their agreement falls within Article 85(3) but are now asking the Commission for an exemption. If of course an agreement falls under one of the group exemptions then notification is not necessary.

The procedure for notification requires that it must be made in writing or an official form A/B issued by the Commission. The applicants must give detailed information on the form relating to the parties to the agreement, the essential features and aims of the agreement. The form together with a copy of the agreement must be sent to the Commission.

The procedure for granting a formal exemption or negative clearance is an expensive one and sometimes the parties may decide that a less expensive method will be acceptable. In this case the Commission will be asked to issue a formal or an informal "comfort letter". Such a document falls short of a formal exemption but for practical purposes serves the same purpose and is much quicker to obtain. If the Commission issues a formal "comfort letter" it will first publish brief details of the agreement in the official journal and invite comments from third parties. It will subsequently publish details in its annual report on competition policy. If it issues an informal "comfort letter" it will merely agree to close its file and take no action.

**The De Minimis Rule (Agreements of Minor Importance)**

Small or medium-sized firms should be aware that many of the agreements they conclude will not be considered as violating the competition rules because the economic effect involved is not significant enough. This can be measured by market share and turn-over. As a guideline the Commission has stated that normally agreements will not be caught by Article 85(1) if two conditions are met.

1. Market share: the goods or services which are the subject of the agreement an other goods or services of the participating undertakings, considered by consumers to be similar by reason of their characteristics, price or use, must not represent more than 5% of the total market in the area of the Union where the agreement has effect.
2. Turn-over: the aggregate turn-over of the participating undertakings must not exceed 200 million Euros.

## *Relations Between Undertakings to which the Competition Rules Do Not Apply*

### Commercial Agents

The Commission has stated in 1962 that a contract with a commercial agent transacting business on behalf of a principal does not fall under Article 35(1). The agent must not assume financial risks as part of his duties, for example buying and selling goods, providing marketing support or providing an after-sales service. Also he must not act for more than one principal.

### Parent Companies/Subsidiaries

Article 85(1) can only apply where the competition which exists between undertakings is capable of being restricted. Agreements between a parent company and its subsidiaries or between subsidiaries themselves, in other words undertakings forming one economic unit, will not be caught by Article 85(1) where the subsidiary does not have any real freedom to determine its course of action on the market and the agreement relates merely to the allocation of tasks within the concern.

### Activities which by Nature are not Anti-Competitive

The Commission has stated that certain forms of co operation between undertakings of certain types of subcontracting agreements do not conflict with the competition rules. The size of the undertakings involved is generally not relevant in this context.

### Cooperation Agreements

The Commission has indicated that the following 18 types of agreement are considered not to restrict competition where their object is one of the following forms of cooperation:

1. an exchange of opinion or experience
2. joint comparative studies of enterprise or industries
3. joint preparation of statistics and calculation models
4. joint market research
5. co-operation in accounting matters
6. joint provision of credit guarantees
7. joint debt collecting association
8. joint business or tax consultant agencies
9. joint implementation of research and development contracts

10. joint implementation of research and development projects
11. joint placing of research and development contracts
12. sharing out of research and development projects among participating enterprises
13. joint use of production, storage and transport equipment
14. joint execution of orders (but only when the participants do not compete with each other as regards the work to be done)
15. joint selling arrangements by non-competing firms
16. joint after-sales and repairs services when the participants are non-competing firms, or even if they are competitors, when these services are provided by an undertaking independent of them
17. joint advertising (but no restriction is allowed on the participants also to advertise independently)
18. joint quality marks (but only where the label is available to all competitors on the same conditions).

**Sub-Contracting**

A sub-contracting agreement is a form of work distribution whereby one firm, the sub-contractor, supplies goods, work or services for another firm, the contractor, in accordance with the latter's specification. This distinguishes it from an ordinary sale of goods or supply of services.

## *Exemptions - Article 85(3)*

As has been stated, the general rule is that restrictive practices which affect inter-state trade are not allowed; those engaged in such activities will be ordered to stop doing so and run the risk of incurring a fine. However there is an important exception to this rule. The prohibition of Article 85 can be declared inapplicable by the Commission (not by the national courts) if the harmful effects of a restrictive agreement or practice are sufficiently counter-balanced by a number of beneficial elements. The following are four conditions which must be met before an exemption can be granted by the Commission.

1. The agreement must contribute to an improvement in production or distribution or economic progress.
2. A fair share of the resulting benefits must be allowed to consumers in the form of lower prices or an improvement in the quality of the goods or services.
3. Only restrictions of competition which are indispensable in order to achieve the beneficial results will be allowed.
4. Competition in respect of a substantial part of the goods or services in question must not be eliminated.

If the above four requirements are met then an exemption may be granted either on an individual basis or by way of a group or block exemption. For the Commission to grant an exemption in an individual case the parties must first have notified their agreement to the Commission as mentioned earlier.

Agreements need not be notified but will nevertheless benefit from an exemption if they fulfil the requirements contained in the so-called group exemption regulations which exist with respect to certain categories of agreements. At present, block exemptions are in force with respect to the following types of agreements:

1. Specialisation agreements;
2. Exclusive distribution agreements;
3. Exclusive purchasing agreements;
4. Patent licensing agreements;
5. Research and development agreements;
6. Distribution agreements in the automobile sector;
7. Franchising agreements;
8. Know-how licensing agreements.

**Consequences - Article 85(2)**

If an agreement falls within the prohibition of Article 85(1) the following consequences apply.

1. It is null and void from the outset. An agreement can be declared void and thus unenforceable by a national court, if the parties are involved in a law suit about the agreement. The Commission can also order parties to put an end to such a prohibited agreement.
2. The Commission has the power to order the parties to terminate the illegal conduct and it may impose fines of up to 1 million Euros, or a larger sum up to 10% of the annual turnover of the undertakings concerned. Fines are paid to the Commission, not to any parties injured by the anti-competitive behaviour. The latter, however, may seek damages in the national courts.

## *Article 86 - Abuse of a Dominant Position*

Whilst Article 85 prohibits certain arrangements which may affect inter-State trade and are likely to distort free competition within the Commission, Article 86 prohibits abuse of a "dominant position" which has a similar effect. Article 85 will involve more than one party whereas Article 86 may be infringed unilaterally by one party itself. Article 86 provides that any abuse by one or more undertakings of a dominant position within the Common Market or in a substantial part of shall be prohibited as incompatible with the Common Market in so far as it may affect trade between Member States. Such abuse may, in particular, consist in:

1. directly or indirectly imposing unfair purchase or selling prices or other unfair

trading conditions;
2. limiting production, markets or technical development to the prejudice of consumers;
3. applying dissimilar conditions to equivalent transactions with other trading parties, thereby placing them at a competitive disadvantage;
4. making the conclusion of contracts subject to acceptance by the other parties of supplementary obligations which, by their nature or according to commercial usage, have no connection with the subject of such contracts.

The elements necessary for Article 86 to apply are as follows.

1. The undertaking must be in a dominant position. Although market share is the major element in assessing dominance (as a rule a share below 40% precludes a finding that the undertaking is dominant) it is by no means the only factor. An undertaking can be deemed to be dominant if, because of various factors, such as ready access to raw materials or capital, it has the power to act independently without seriously to take into account its competitors, purchasers, or suppliers.
2. The dominant position must be in the Common Market or a substantial part of it.
3. There must be an abuse of the dominant position in the sense that advantage is taken of the dominant position which causes injury to third parties. Examples of abusive conduct are:
   i. charging unfair purchase or selling prices;
   ii. discriminatory prices, for example charging customer A more than customer B for exactly the same transactions, thereby placing customer A at a competitive disadvantage;
   iii. refusal to sell to a customer without valid, objective reasons;
   iv. attempts to hold on to customers for example by granting fidelity rebates;
   v. acquisitions of competing undertakings, thereby affecting the competitive structure within the Common Market.

It will be seen that Article 86 will usually apply to the major market leaders or to state or privatised monopolies. It would not normally be a problem for small or medium-sized businesses. However it can apply to smaller businesses which produce very specialised products or services for which there can be no substitute, especially if protected by patents, designs or copyright. It is more likely that it will be small businesses who will find themselves the victims of breaches of Article 86 and these may consist of refusals to supply or discriminatory treatment.

If it is found that an infringement has occurred then the Commission may be notified of this or may become aware of such an infringement in any other way. In that case the Commission must give the parties concerned notice of its objections to their behaviour in the form of a written communication known as "the statement of objections". The parties concerned may examine the Commission's document supporting their allegation and they must prepare their response. They must also respond in writing to the Commission's objections.

After the written response has been filed then the parties can also request an opportunity to argue their case orally. This oral hearing is organised by the Directorate General for Competition and is conducted by the "Hearing Officer" of that department. Following the oral hearing the Commission must consult the advisory committee on restrictive practices and dominant positions and after these procedural steps have been taken the Commission can come to a final decision.

If the Commission decides that an infringement does in fact exist then it will order the undertakings involved to put an end to it forthwith. This order is known as a "cease and desist" order. If the parties have already terminated the infringements then the decision may simply consist of a declaration that the behaviour in question did in fact constitute an infringement.

The Commission also has power to impose fines of up to one million Euros or 10% of the world annual turnover of the undertaking concerned in the previous business year whichever of the two is greater. Such a fine may be imposed where it is found that an undertaking has infringed Articles 85(1) or 86 intentionally or through negligence.

If it is found that owing to the complexity of any case it may take the Commission a substantial period of time to reach a final decision then it is possible for the Commission to take immediate action in the form of so-called "interim measures" to stop the objectionable behaviour.

Many cases that can come before the Commission are concluded by way of an informal settlement. This will occur where the undertaking concerned voluntarily eliminates any objectionable practices. In the case of an informal settlement this would take place by way of "administrative letters" in which the Commission informs the party that there is no reason to take any action under the competition rules and that the relevant file will therefore be closed. These letters do not have the legal binding effect of decisions but may be useful as guidance.

## *Control Over the Commission by the European Court of Justice*

The European Court of Justice has the following powers of review over decisions taken by the Commission.

1. The court has the power to confirm, reduce, cancel or increase fines and penalty payments imposed by Commission decisions.
2. All formal decisions by the Commission such as negative clearances, decisions granting or refusing exemption, orders to terminate infringement, decisions requesting information, orders to submit to an investigation and provisional decisions relating to the immunity from fines can be reviewed and, if necessary, annulled or varied by the court.

In addition appeals can be brought before the Court where the Commission has failed to act for example, failure to examine a formal complaint that has been submitted to it or to inform the complainant of its reasons for not pursuing the matter after preliminary examination.

## *UK Competition Legislation*

The *Restrictive Trade Practices Acts 1976* and *1977* have gone the way of the preceding legislation and been repealed. The *Competition Act 1998* has replaced these legislative provisions and has given effect to the principles of Articles 85 and 86 but in relation to UK agreements. Chapter 1 of the 1998 Act concerns itself with agreements which affect fair competition. In particular, S2 contains the prohibition on agreements preventing, restricting or distorting competition unless they fall within an exemption. Sections 4 to 11 detail such available exemptions.

Chapter 2 of the *Competition Act 1998* deals with abuse of a dominant market position within the UK similar to the provisions in Article 86. Specifically S18 contains the prohibition against such activities.

## *State Aids*

In this connection Articles 92 and 93 of the *Treaty of Rome* set out the control that may be exercised by the Commission.

### Article 92

This Article provides that as a general rule all government aid to business is forbidden: "Save as otherwise provided in this Treaty, any aid granted by a member State or through State resources in any form whatsoever which distorts or threatens to distort competition by favouring certain undertakings or the production of certain goods shall, in so far as it affects trade between member States, be incompatible with the Common Market."

Aid in this connection covers not only government grants, cheap loans and interest subsidies but also tax concessions, public guarantees of corporate borrowing from banks or the capital market, provision of goods and services on preferential terms and in some circumstances, the acquisition of public share holdings in public businesses.

However the Article goes on to provide that certain types of aid are compatible with the Common Market, namely aid having a social character which is granted to individual consumers or aid to make good damage caused by natural disasters. The following categories of aid may be considered compatible with the Common Market.

1. Aid to promote the economic development of areas where the standard of living is abnormally low or where there is serious under-employment.
2. Aid to promote the execution of an important project of common European interest or to remedy a serious disturbance in the economy of a Member State.
3. Aid to facilitate the development of certain economic activities or of certain economic areas, where such aid does not adversely affect trading conditions to an extent contrary to the common interest.
4. Such other categories of aid as may be specified by a decision of the Council acting by a qualified majority or a proposal from the Commission.

**Article 93**

Under this Article, Member States are required to notify the Commission in advance of any plans to introduce new aid schemes or to alter existing ones. The Member State may not implement the aid scheme until the Commission has taken a final decision. The Commission has two months in which to state its position on a notified scheme. If the Commission does not think it will be able to authorise the scheme then a special procedure is followed by which the Commission must give the Member State a certain period, usually one month, in which to defend its scheme against objections raised by the Commission. At the end of the procedure, the Commission takes a final decision in which it takes into account the arguments of the Member State concerned and the reactions of the other Member States and interested parties who have been notified of the scheme in the Official Journal of the European Communities. The Commission then reaches a decision and if the Member State disagrees with this it has two months in which to demand a judicial review by the European Court of Justice.

## *Dumping*

Dumping has no place in the internal market, governed, as it is, by the free movement of goods. However anti-dumping rules exist to protect the EU from having its trade affected by goods being dumped in the EU by third countries. Dumping occurs when the export price of the goods is less than the normal value of a like product. If a Member State considers that dumping is taking place, it may complain to the Commission which will hold an investigation. It may then impose an anti-dumping duty.

**Questions**

What types of activity will be prevented by Article 85?

What exemptions are there to Article 85?

What elements are required for Article 86 to apply?

THIRTY

# CONFLICT *of* LAWS

*Study Topics*

**Purpose of conflict of laws**
**Proper law of contract**
**Incoterms**

This subject is sometimes called private international law. It has been defined by one writer as "that part of law which comes into play when the issue before the court affects some fact, event or transaction that is so closely connected with the foreign system of law as to necessitate recourse to that system."

Each state in the world has it own system of law which is used in connection with that state and to decide disputes that arise within the state. Within a country there may be more than one state. This arises of course in the United States of America but also arises in the United Kingdom where Scottish law is different from the law used in England and Wales.

Conflict of laws or private international law must be distinguished from public international law. This is a set of rules which determines the relations between countries in the world. Thus there can be international agreement between one country and another and public international law includes the laws relating to armed conflict, to salvage of ships and international air travel.

Private international law must not be confused with European Community law. The intention is to make the European Union a single state eventually. It will then have its own system of law which will apply to each of the Member States. At present this political fusion has not occurred but nevertheless where there are transactions between the Member States then European community law may apply and in some cases will be superimposed upon the national law of the Member States.

The body of rules known as conflict of laws will be used to determine any dispute which may arise in a number of situations. It can arise where property has been purchased which is situated abroad. It may arise where a couple have been married in a foreign country. It can arise where there is a question of legitimacy or adoption or very frequently where there is a negotiable instrument. From a commercial law point of view the most obvious example would be where there is a contract with a foreign element. This could arise where A is an Englishman who is visiting France and enters into a contract with B who is a German. The purpose of the contract is to perform some service in Spain. It will be apparent that a number of systems of law may be called upon to solve any dispute that may arise.

If a dispute does arise and the matter is brought before an English court then this court must first of all decide whether it has jurisdiction to hear the case in the first place. If it does so decide that it has jurisdiction then it must secondly decide which system of law must be applied in resolving the dispute.

It should be noted that as a rule any person can sue and be sued before an English court. The main exceptions are if the defendant has diplomatic immunity and secondly if the plaintiff is an alien enemy. In all other cases the action may be heard by an English court but whether or not it is so heard will of course depend upon the circumstances. It may be that the parties when entering into the contract agree at that time that in the event of any dispute arising it should be resolved by reference to an English court of law.

In deciding whether or not to bring an action before an English court the obvious consideration must be that, in the event of succeeding in his action, the plaintiff will be able to enforce any judgment. If the defendant is domiciled abroad then it may be impossible, or at least very difficult, for a successful plaintiff to proceed against any assets of the defendant in the foreign country. Of course if the defendant is a company in this country with large assets then the problem will have disappeared.

If the problem is brought before a court of this country it must decide whether or not it has jurisdiction to hear the case. If the court does decide that it has jurisdiction it must then consider what system of law is to be applied to the problem.

This process is known as classification. This means that the English judge, because of course this is a matter for English law, makes his own analysis of the question before him and assigns it to a particular legal category. The legal categories may be wider than the categories of the internal law of the state. Nevertheless in practice the classification process will place the problem into the following categories.

1. Law of property divided into the law of immovables and the law of movables.
2. Family law, that is the relationship between husband and wife, marriage and divorce.

3 Legitimacy, legitimation and Adoption.
4. Torts.
5. Contracts.

## *Lex Causae*

Having classified the problem into one of the categories then the court must decide which body of law to apply to the problem in order to resolve it. The law to be applied to the case is known as the *lex causae*; this means the law applicable to the case. If the *lex causae* is a foreign system of law then this law must be proved before an English court in the same way as any other evidence. The evidence as to what is the foreign law must be brought into court by an expert witness. This does not mean that the witness must be a lawyer but he must have practical experience.

In one case a Roman Catholic bishop was allowed to testify as to the matrimonial law of Rome. A secretary to the Persian Embassy was allowed to depose to the law of Persia and the evidence of a London bank director with experience of banking in South America was preferred to that of a young man who had been at the Chilean bar for a number of years when the problem concerned the meaning of a bill of exchange given in Chile.

## Contracts

As far as commercial law is concerned, of course, contract is its basis and we must now consider the actions of the courts of this country where there is a contract with a foreign element.

Where a contract is concerned then there may be a dispute between the parties in regard to any of the essentials of the contract. Capacity is one of the essentials leading to the formation of the contract. This includes offer and acceptance, consideration and intention to create legal relations. Other aspects are the essential validity of the agreement and such matters as mistake, the effect of mistake, misrepresentation, duress and illegality. Finally there is the interpretation and effect of the contract and the manner of performance as well as the method of discharge. In all these cases a dispute may arise between the parties and the question that remains, if there is a foreign element, will be which body of law must be used in order to solve the particular dispute.

## The Proper Law of the Contract

In English law where there is a contract with a foreign element then it is the proper law which is used in order to solve any dispute. Dicey's view is that "the term proper law of contract means the law or laws by which the parties intended, or may fairly be presumed to have intended, the contract to be governed". This is known as the subjective view and the emphasis of course is placed upon the intention of the parties.

The other view is the objective view which Lord Denning favoured. He stated that "the proper law of the contract depends not so much on the place where it is made, nor even on the intention of the parties or on the places where it is to be performed but on the place with which it has the most substantial connection". *Boissevain v Weil (1949).*

It should always be remembered that the parties, when they enter into their agreement, may state the body of law which they wish to make use of in the event of any dispute arising. Again Lord Denning said: "It is clear that if there is an express clause in a contract providing what the proper law is to be, that is conclusive in the absence of some public policy to the contrary." *Tzortzis v Monark Line A/B (1968).*

In cases where the parties have not themselves stated which body of law is to be used in the event of a dispute then a case called *The Assunzione (1954)* provides a good example of how the courts determine which is the proper law of a contract. In that case there was a charter party entered into between the plaintiffs who were French and the owners of the ship, the *Assunzione*, who were Italian. The ship was to carry grain from Dunkirk to an Italian port and the question was whether French or Italian law governed the situation. Neither party contended that English law applied although the case was heard before the courts of this country. There were points of contact with French law.

1. The charter party was headed Paris 7 October 1949 and was therefore concluded in France.
2. The charter party itself was written in English but was followed by a supplement written in French.
3. The bills of lading were written in French and in the French standard form.
4. The charterers were French brokers and were acting on behalf of the French government.

On the other hand there were the following points of contact with Italian law.

1. The ship flew the Italian flag and was owned by two Italian brothers carrying on business at Genoa and Naples.
2. Italy was the place of performance in the sense that delivery was due at Venice.
3. Freight and demurrage were payable at Naples in Italian currency.
4. The bills of lading had been indorsed with the consignees in Italy.

Thus it appeared that both the French and Italian elements of the contract were in equipoise. There was obviously no outstanding fact which was decisively significant and so the question was what would a reasonable man decide: should the contract be regarded as Italian or French? Eventually the Court of Appeal decided that the contract must be decided according to Italian law. The Court of Appeal did make the point that the crucial factors were that the charterers had to pay freight and demurrage at Naples in Italian currency.

Since these cases, the matter of the proper law of the contract has been considered by the European Community and in 1990, in Rome, a Convention was made which had the aim of providing a uniform method for deciding the law governing international contracts. The Convention is world-wide in effect and applies to all international contracts. The law contained in the convention has been ratified by the United Kingdom Parliament and now appears in the form of a statute named *Contracts (Applicable Law) Act 1990.*

Section 2 of the Act provides that the Rome Convention, signed by the United Kingdom on 7 December 1981, shall have the force of law in the United Kingdom. This Convention provides uniform rules which apply where there is a conflict of laws in relation to contractual obligations. It is worldwide in effect and applies to all international contracts which come within the scope of the convention and which come before the United Kingdom courts. The Act came into force on 1 April 1991.

## *The Rome Convention*

Article 3 provides that the parties are free to choose any law whatever to be applied to their contract. An exception is where all the other elements relevant to the situation are concerned with one country only. Then the rules of that country, called "mandatory rules", shall be applied.

Article 4 provides that in the event of the parties not choosing a particular law to govern the contract then the contracts shall be governed by the law of the country with which it is mostly connected. The Convention would appear to be complying with the rules used in English law to decide which is the proper law of the contract. In English law, before the Convention, the court determined all the elements of the contract and decided which body of law should govern it and made use of no presumptions. However, in the Convention, Article 4(2) provides "in the absence of choice by the parties then the law governing the contract shall be the law of the country where the party who is to effect the performance of the contract shall have his residence or, in the case of a company, its central administration."

In the case of a contract of sale the question is where the characteristic performance of the contract takes place. It has been held that in a contract of sale the characteristic performance of the contract takes place in the country where the seller has his residence. The law governing other types of contracts will of course be determined in other ways. In the case of an individual employment contract, then the law governing that contract will be the law of the country in which the employee habitually carries out his work in performing the contract or, if the employee does not habitually carry out his work in any one country, then it will be governed by the law of the country in which the place of business through which he was engaged is situated.

The validity of a contract shall be determined by satisfying the formal requirements of the law which governs it according to the Convention of the law of any one of the countries. When determined then this will govern such matters as .

1. interpretation;
2. performance;
3. the consequences of breach including the assessment of damages;
4. the ways of extinguishing obligations and limitation of actions;
5. the consequences of nullity of a contract.

All these matters therefore are to be determined by the applicable law. Article 10(2) does provide that in relation to the manner of performance then regard shall be had to the law of the country in which performance takes place.

From the above it is apparent that determining the applicable law of the contract may sometimes be quite a difficult task. To avoid any difficulties it is obvious that the parties to any contract which has a foreign element in it should at the outset determine and agree which body of law shall govern that contract in the event of a dispute.

## *International Sale of Goods*

In international trading it is customary to incorporate special trade terms in the contracts. These terms sometimes differ between countries and so the International Chamber of Commerce has published a set of incoterms so as to prevent any misunderstanding. Those terms will apply to all contracts of international sale of goods if the parties have incorporated them into their contract.

The terms are changed from time to time to take into account different methods of payment, transport and documentation. A new term is DDU (delivery duty unpaid). This has been introduced to apply to exports within the EU when duties between Member States have been abolished. In this case the seller must deliver the goods to a named place in the country to which they are being exported. The seller must bear the costs of transport but not duties, taxes or import charges. The alternative term is DDP which is the same as DDU except that the seller must bear the payment of duties, taxes and import charges.

The latest version of the incoterms is identical in both English and French. These terms state the duties and responsibilities of the seller of the goods. Some examples are as follows.

FCA: free carrier. Here the seller is not liable once he has handed the goods to a carrier at a named place.
FAS : free alongside ship, and FOB, free on board, have obvious meanings.
CFR: cost and freight. The buyer assumes risk of damage or loss when the goods have passed the ship's rail.
CIF: cost, insurance and freight. This is similar to CFR but the exporter must pay for the insurance.

CPT: carriage paid to a named place, and CIP, carriage and insurance, are similar and are used when the goods are being carried in containers.
DAF: delivered at frontier, DES, delivered ex ship, and DEQ, delivered ex quay a named port of destination, have obvious meanings.

## Uniform Laws on International Sale of Goods Contracts

When parties in different States enter into a contract it will sometimes result in difficulties because of the variation in the rules applying in each of the States. In order to achieve some sort of uniformity in the laws which in different States apply to contracts for the international sale of goods some conventions were entered into at the Hague. The first was the *Uniform Law on the International Sale of Goods*. The second was the *Uniform Law on the formation of Contracts for the International Sale of Goods*. These are contained in schedules 1 and 2 of the *Uniform Laws on International Sales Act 1967*. However on 11 April 1980, the UN convention on contracts for the international sale of goods was signed in Vienna. This Convention was based on the two Hague conventions and supersedes them.

This Convention has now been brought into operation. It applies to business (non-consumer) sales between parties who have places of business in different States provided the States concerned have accepted the Vienna Convention and the proper law of the contract is that of the acceding State. The Vienna Convention becomes part of the law of the State but it does not apply to issues of liability for death or personal injury caused by the goods supplied and the parties to the contract may exclude or vary any of its provisions by express agreement or by usage.

The Vienna Convention has incorporated a number of concepts which are strange to English lawyers such as the avoidance of a contract in part, the buyer's right to demand specific performance, repair or replacement of defective goods and the seller's right to remedy his deficiency. Whether or not business men will incorporate the terms of the convention into their contracts will remain to be seen.

## Questions

What is the *lex causae*?

What is the uniform law on international sales?

What is the effect of the *Contracts (Applicable Law) Act 1990*?

# INDEX


agency Ch 3 *passim*
  termination of 28

agent 20 *et seq*
  duties of 25-7
  liability of 21
  rights of 27
  signature of 21-3

arbitration Ch 2 *passim*
  agreement 15-6
  alternative dispute resolution (ADR) 18
  awards 16-7
  exclusion agreement 15
  judicial review 14-5
  structured settlement procedure 18

attorney, power of 24-5

bankruptcy - *see* insolvency

banks, banking 301 *et seq*
  collecting/paying banks 314-15
  electronic transfer of funds 315 *et seq*

barristers 7

case law 10

cheques Ch 24 *passim*
  analogous instruments 307 *et seq*
  banker's authority 301-05
  banker's liability 305
  banker's protection 305-7
  bearer cheques 303-04
  crossings 299-301
  order cheques 304-5

common law 3
company borrowing Ch 6 *passim*
  bank charges 56-7, 60-2
  debenture forms 56-7, 63-8

company law Ch 5 *passim*
  articles of association 43-4
  bank account 50-2
  capital 48-50
  directors 44 *et seq*
  meetings 47-8
  memorandum of association 39-40
  name of 42
  objects of 41-2

conflict of laws Ch 31 *passim*
consumer credit Ch 18 *passim*
  agreements 227 *et seq*
  cancellation 235 *et seq*
  canvassing 233
  control 231-2
  cooling-off period 235
  extortionate bargains 236-7
  fixed-sum credit 229
  linked transactions 231
  mortgage of land 233-4
  running account 229
  seeking business 232 *et seq*
  termination 227-8
  unlicensed trading 222

consumer protection Ch 17 *passim*
  defences 223
  liability 221-2
  loss 222-3
  time limit 224
  tort of negligence 219-20

Consumer Protection Act 1987 221 *et seq*

contracts Ch 7, 8, 9, 10 *passim*
  assignment of rights 136-8
  Battle of Forms 84
  breach of 126 *et seq*
  capacity to contract 116 *et seq*
    corporations 118-9
    mentally disordered persons 118-9
    minors 116-8
    trade unions 120
    unincorporated associations 119-20
  compensation 130-1
  consideration 75 *et seq*
  Consumer Contracts
  Regulations 1994 95 *et seq*
  damages 131-2
  discharge of contract Ch10 *passim*
  agreement 124-5
  frustration 125-6
  performance 123-4
  doctrine of fundamental breach 87 *et seq*
  essentials of contract 67 *et seq*
  exclusion clauses 82 *et seq*, 94-5
  formation of contract 77
  illegality 111 *et seq*

# INDEX


contracts (cont'd)
- injunctions 134-6
- invalidation Ch 9 *passim* 78
  - disclosure of material facts 106-7
  - duress 109
  - misrepresentation 104 *et seq*
  - mistake 101 *et seq*
  - recession 107-8
  - undue influence 109-10
- offer 69 *et seq*
  - acceptance 72 *et seq*
  - counter offer 72
  - death of offeror/offeree 72
  - lapse of 71
  - notification of 70
  - rejection 72
  - revocation 71
- reasonableness 93-5
- sale of goods 92-3
- severance 115-6
- standard form contract 83 *et seq*
- terms of contract Ch 8 *passim*
  - complex 82
  - express 81
  - implied 80-1
- Unfair Contract Terms Act 1977 90 *et seq*

copyright 275 *et seq*
- infringement 277
- moral rights 277
- ownership 276
- period of protection 276
- subject matter 275-6
- unregistered design right 277-8

Courts, the Ch 1 *passim*

Data Protection Act 1984 Ch 19 *passim*
- data subject's rights 242-3
- data user's register 241
- disclosure of personal data 242-3
- principles 241-2
- registrar 243

discrimination Ch 15 *passim*
- equal pay 197 *et seq*
- racial discrimination 204 *et seq*
- recruitment 205
- sex discrimination 194 et seq

employment law Ch 13 *passim*
- collective agreements 179-80
- contract of employment 176 *et seq*
  - duties and rights of parties 180-2
  - formation of contract 178-9
- implied terms 180
  - multiple test 178
  - organisational test 177-8
  - termination of contract 182-3
- health and safety 190 *et seq*
- statutory intervention Ch 14 *passim*
  - dismissal 187-8
  - lay off 189-90
  - maternity pay 185
  - pay statements 186
  - sick pay 185
  - time off 185
  - wages 186

European Community, foundations Ch 29 *passim*
- free movement of goods 367-70
- free movement of persons 370-2
- movement of capital 372
- Treaty of Rome 366

European Community Institutions Ch 27 *passim*
- Commission, the 351-2
- COREPER 350-1
- Council, the 349
- Court of Justice, the 353 *et seq*
  - Advocates General 354-5
  - Court of the First Instance 355-6
- European Parliament 347 *et seq*

European Community Law Ch 28 *passim*
- directives 360 *et seq*
- regulations 360 *et seq*
- sources of 358-9
- Von Colson principle 363-5

European Union Ch 26 *passim*
- citizenship 343-4
- history of 340 *et seq*
- Maastricht Agreement 342-3
- Single European Act 1986 342
- subsidiarity 344

European Union, competition Ch 30 *passim*
- Article 85 375 *et seq*
- Article 86 384 *et seq*
- Article 92 387
- Article 93 387-8
- dumping 388
- franchising 378
- industrial property 379
- patents 379-80

# INDEX


Financial Services Act Ch 20 *passim*, 6-7, 166, 167

health and safety at work 186 *et seq*

insolvency Ch 25 *passim*
- administrative receiver 334
- assets 330 *et seq*
- corporate insolvency 331 *et seq*
- individual insolvency 327 *et seq*
- liquidator 323 *et seq*
- preferences 332
- secured creditors 336
- transactional undervalue
- voluntary arrangements 320 et seq
- wages accounts 338
- winding up 320 et seq

insurance 254 *et seq*
- accident, burglary 260
- average clause 260
- fire insurance 259
- indemnity 257
- insurable interest 255-6
- marine insurance 261 *et seq*
- policies/proposals 257-8
- premiums/renewals 258
- subrogation 258-9
- *uberrimae fidei* 256

intellectual property Ch 22 *passim*
- and EU, 284 *et seq*
- *see also* patents, copyright, trademarks

international law (private) *see* private international law

international trade 267 *et seq*
- collection arrangements 267
- doctrine of strict confidence 269
- letters of credit 268-9
- investments 245 *et seq*

law, definition 1-2
- application of 9
- legal executives 7
- sources of law 3-6
- statutory law 11

marine insurance 261 *et seq*
- bills of lading 266
- carriage by sea 265-6
- charter parties 266
- disclosure 262
- freight 266-7
- insurable interest 261-2
- international trade 267 *et seq*
- types of policy 263 *et seq*

negotiable instruments Ch 23 *passim*
- bills of exchange 290 *et seq*
  - acceptance 292-3
  - discharge 297
  - dishonour 294-5
  - holder in due course 296-7
  - noting and protesting 295-6
  - payment 294
  - transfer 296
- choses in action 289 *et seq*

partnership Ch 4 *passim*
- bankruptcy 36-7
- dissolution 35 *et seq*
- firm name 32
- partners 33-4

patents 271 *et seq*
- industrial application 272
- infringement 273-4
- inventive step 272
- novelty 271-2
- owners of 272-6
- revocation 274

principal, duties of 28
- liability of 23-4
- rights of 27

private international law (conflict of laws) Ch 31 *passim*
- contracts 392-4
- international sale of goods 395-6
- *lex causae* 392
- Rome Convention 394-5

property, transfer of Ch 12 *passim*

*ratio decidendi* 4, 10

Romalpa clause 158 *et seq*

sale of goods Ch 11, Ch 12 *passim*
- acceptance of goods 168 *et seq*
- contract 144 *et seq*
  - conditions 144
  - implied conditions 145 *et seq*
  - performance 164
  - warranties 144-5

# INDEX


delivery 164 *et seq*
disposal 157-8
goods 142
illustrative cases 150-1, 156-7, 166, 167
lien 172-3
market overt 164
motor vehicles (hire purchase) 163-4
ownership/possession 141, 171 *et seq*
property in goods 142, Ch 12 *passim*
purchaser, protection of 143
remedies for breach of contract 149, 169 *et seq*
Romalpa clause 158 *et seq*
sale by sample 148
Sale of Goods (Amendment) Act 1995 155-6
specific goods 153-5
Supply of Goods and Services Act 1982 142-3
time 149, 153
transfer of title 161 *et seq*
unascertained goods 155

Securities and Investment Board 246 *et seq*
Self-Regulating Organisations 247 *et seq*

title, transfer of 161 *et seq*

trademarks 278 *et seq*
infringement 283-4
ownership/licensing 281-2
passing off 278-9
registration 279-80

trade unions Ch 16 *passim*
executive committee 210-11
industrial relations 212 *et seq*
collective agreements 215
collective bargaining 212-13
consultations 213
listing and certification 209
political funds 211-12
register of members 210
rules of membership 210
trade disputes 213 *et seq*
immunity 214-15
picketing 216
Public Order Act 1986 217
secondary action 215

Turquand's Case rule in 45-6

ultra vires, doctrine of 40-1
Unfair Terms in Consumer Contracts Regulations 1994 95-97

Printed in the United Kingdom
by Lightning Source UK Ltd.
100841UKS00001B/3-20